SHURLEY ENGLISH

HOMESCHOOL MADE EASY

LEVEL 2

Teacher's Edition

By
Brenda Shurley

Shurley Instructional Materials, Inc., Cabot, Arkansas

In Loving Memory of
Gilbert Edwin Strackbein
(Gil)

Dedication

This book is gratefully dedicated to my husband, Billy Shurley, for his love, support, and encouragement during this momentous undertaking.

Acknowledgements

We gratefully thank the following people for their help and support in the preparation of this book:

Ardean Coffman	Stacey See	Rachel Speer
Keith Covington	Billy Ray Shurley, Jr.	Andrea Turkia
Jamie Geneva	Kim Shurley	Jani-Petri Rainer Turkia
Janice Graham	Shurley Method Staff	Bob Wilson, Ph.D.

11-05
Homeschool Edition
ISBN 1-58561-044-5 (Level 2 Teacher's Manual)

Copyright ©2001 by Shurley Instructional Materials, Inc., 366 SIM Drive, Cabot, AR 72023. All rights reserved. Printed in the United States of America.

No part of this book may be reproduced or transmitted in any form or by any means, electronic or mechanical, including photocopying, recording, or by any information storage or retrieval system, without written permission from the Publisher.
♦ For additional information or to place an order, write to Shurley Instructional Materials, Inc., 366 SIM Drive, Cabot, AR 72023.

1 2 3   05 03 02

Level 2—Shurley English—Homeschool Edition

TABLE OF CONTENTS

Chapter 1	Pages 1-10
Lesson 1	**How to get started**, **Long-Term Goals** and **Short-Term Goals**, **ACTIVITY**
Lesson 2	**Beginning Setup Plan for Homeschool**, **WRITING** (journal), **ACTIVITY**
Lesson 3	**SKILL** (Introduce Alphabetizing), **PRACTICE EXERCISE**, **ACTIVITY**
Lesson 4	**STUDY**, **TEST**, **CHECK**, **WRITING** (journal)
Lesson 5	**STATE ACTIVITY**

Chapter 2	Pages 11-24
Lesson 1	**Jingle Guidelines**, **JINGLE** (Sentence), **SKILLS** (Synonyms, Antonyms), **Four-Step Vocabulary Plan**, **VOCABULARY #1**
Lesson 2	**JINGLES** (Noun, Verb), **GRAMMAR** (Noun, Verb), **ACTIVITY**, **VOCABULARY #2**
Lesson 3	**JINGLES**, **GRAMMAR** (Introductory Sentences, Question and Answer Flow, classifying, labeling, subject noun, verb), **ACTIVITY**
Lesson 4	**JINGLES**, **GRAMMAR** (Practice Sentences), **SKILL** (Five Parts of a Complete Sentence), **PRACTICE EXERCISE**, **ACTIVITY**
Lesson 5	**JINGLES**, **STUDY**, **TEST**, **CHECK**, **WRITING** (journal), **STATE ACTIVITY**, **SENTENCE TIME**

Chapter 3	Pages 25-40
Lesson 1	**JINGLE** (Adverb), **GRAMMAR** (Introductory Sentences, Adverb), **VOCABULARY #1**
Lesson 2	**JINGLES**, **GRAMMAR** (Practice Sentences), **SKILL** (A/An choices), **PRACTICE EXERCISE**, **VOCABULARY #2**
Lesson 3	**JINGLE** (Adjective), **GRAMMAR** (Introductory Sentences, Adjective), **PRACTICE EXERCISE**, **ACTIVITY**
Lesson 4	**JINGLES**, **GRAMMAR** (Practice Sentences), **SKILL** (Parts of Speech), **PRACTICE EXERCISE**
Lesson 5	**JINGLES**, **STUDY**, **TEST**, **CHECK**, **WRITING** (journal), **STATE ACTIVITY**, **SENTENCE TIME**

Chapter 4	Pages 41-56
Lesson 1	**JINGLE** (Article Adjective), **GRAMMAR** (Introductory Sentences, Article Adjective), **VOCABULARY #1**
Lesson 2	**JINGLES**, **GRAMMAR** (Practice Sentences), **SKILL** (Three Kinds of Sentences), **PRACTICE EXERCISE**, **VOCABULARY #2**
Lesson 3	**JINGLES**, **GRAMMAR** (Practice Sentences), **SKILLS** (Skill Builder Checks, Noun Checks), **PRACTICE EXERCISE**
Lesson 4	**JINGLES**, **STUDY**, **TEST**, **CHECK**, **WRITING** (journal), **STATE ACTIVITY**, **SENTENCE TIME**
Lesson 5	**WRITING** (Practice and Improved Sentence), **ACTIVITY**

Chapter 5	Pages 57-73
Lesson 1	**JINGLES**, **GRAMMAR** (Practice Sentences), **SKILLS** (Reviewing Noun Check, Singular and Plural Nouns), **PRACTICE EXERCISE**, **VOCABULARY #1**, **ACITIVITY**
Lesson 2	**JINGLES**, **GRAMMAR** (Practice Sentences), **SKILLS** (Skill Builder Check, Common and Proper Nouns), **PRACTICE EXERCISE**, **VOCABULARY #2**, **ACTIVITY**
Lesson 3	**JINGLES**, **GRAMMAR** (Practice Sentences), **SKILL** (Practice and Improved Sentence)
Lesson 4	**JINGLES**, **STUDY**, **TEST**, **CHECK**, **WRITING** (journal), **STATE ACTIVITY**, **SENTENCE TIME**
Lesson 5	**WRITING** (Finding a Topic, Supporting and Non-Supporting Ideas and Sentences), **PRACTICE EXERCISE**, **ACTIVITY**

Chapter 6	Pages 74-89
Lesson 1	**JINGLES**, **GRAMMAR** (Practice Sentences), **SKILLS** (Skill Builder Check, Simple Subject, Simple Predicate, Complete Subject, Complete Predicate), **PRACTICE EXERCISE**, **VOCABULARY #1**
Lesson 2	**JINGLES**, **GRAMMAR** (Practice Sentences), **SKILL** (Noun Job Chart), **PRACTICE EXERCISE**, **VOCABULARY #2**
Lesson 3	**JINGLES**, **GRAMMAR** (Practice Sentences), **SKILL** (Practice and Improved Sentence)
Lesson 4	**JINGLES**, **STUDY**, **TEST**, **CHECK**, **WRITING** (journal), **STATE ACTIVITY**, **SENTENCE TIME**
Lesson 5	**WRITING** (Reviewing Topics, Supporting and Non-Supporting Ideas and Sentences), **PRACTICE EXERCISE**, **ACTIVITY**

Level 2—Shurley English—Homeschool Edition

TABLE OF CONTENTS

Chapter 7	Pages 90-113
Lesson 1	**JINGLES, GRAMMAR** (Introductory Sentences, Pattern 1, End Punctuation, Skill Builder Check), **PRACTICE EXERCISE, VOCABULARY #1**
Lesson 2	**JINGLES, GRAMMAR** (Introductory Sentences, Complete Subject, Complete Predicate), **SKILL** (Add Vocabulary Check to Skill Builder Time), **VOCABULARY #2**
Lesson 3	**JINGLES, GRAMMAR** (Practice Sentences, Practice and Improved Sentence)
Lesson 4	**JINGLES, STUDY, TEST, CHECK, WRITING** (journal), **STATE ACTIVITY, SENTENCE TIME**
Lesson 5	**WRITING** (Expository, Writing Definitions, Two-Point Paragraph), **WRITING ASSIGNMENT #1**

Chapter 8	Pages 114-128
Lesson 1	**JINGLES** (Preposition, Object of the Preposition), **GRAMMAR** (Practice Sentences), **SKILLS** (Skill Builder Check, Practice and Improved Sentence), **VOCABULARY #1, ACTIVITY**
Lesson 2	**JINGLES, GRAMMAR** (Introductory Sentences, Preposition, Object of the Preposition, Prepositional Phrase, Add the Preposition to the Parts of Speech), **VOCABULARY #2**
Lesson 3	**JINGLES, GRAMMAR** (Practice Sentences), **SKILLS** (Add Object of the Preposition to the Noun Check, Skill Builder Check)
Lesson 4	**JINGLES, STUDY, TEST, CHECK, WRITING** (journal), **STATE ACTIVITY**
Lesson 5	**WRITING ASSIGNMENT #2, SENTENCE TIME**

Chapter 9	Pages 129-142
Lesson 1	**JINGLES, GRAMMAR** (Practice Sentences), **SKILLS** (Skill Builder Check, Homonyms), **PRACTICE EXERCISE, VOCABULARY #1, ACTIVITY**
Lesson 2	**JINGLES, GRAMMAR** (Practice Sentences), **SKILL** (Practice and Improved Sentence), **PRACTICE EXERCISE, VOCABULARY #2**
Lesson 3	**JINGLES, GRAMMAR** (Practice Sentences), **PRACTICE EXERCISE, ACTIVITY**
Lesson 4	**JINGLES, STUDY, TEST, CHECK, WRITING** (journal), **STATE ACTIVITY**
Lesson 5	**WRITING ASSIGNMENT #3, SENTENCE TIME**

Chapter 10	Pages 143-159
Lesson 1	**JINGLES, GRAMMAR** (Practice Sentences), **SKILLS** (Skill Builder Check, Subject/Verb Agreement), **PRACTICE EXERCISE, VOCABULARY #1**
Lesson 2	**JINGLES, GRAMMAR** (Practice Sentences, Practice and Improved Sentence), **PRACTICE EXERCISE, VOCABULARY #2**
Lesson 3	**JINGLES, GRAMMAR** (Practice Sentences), **PRACTICE EXERCISE, ACTIVITY**
Lesson 4	**JINGLES, STUDY, TEST, CHECK, WRITING** (journal), **STATE ACTIVITY**
Lesson 5	**WRITING ASSIGNMENT #4, SENTENCE TIME**

Chapter 11	Pages 160-175
Lesson 1	**JINGLES, GRAMMAR** (Practice Sentences), **SKILL** (Skill Builder Check), **PRACTICE EXERCISE, VOCABULARY #1**
Lesson 2	**JINGLES, GRAMMAR** (Practice Sentences, Practice and Improved Sentence), **PRACTICE EXERCISE, VOCABULARY #2, ACTIVITY**
Lesson 3	**JINGLES, GRAMMAR** (Practice Sentences), **PRACTICE EXERCISE, ACTIVITY**
Lesson 4	**JINGLES, STUDY, TEST, CHECK, WRITING** (journal), **STATE ACTIVITY, SENTENCE TIME**
Lesson 5	**WRITING** (Changing Plural Categories to Singular Points), **WRITING ASSIGNMENT #5**

© SHURLEY INSTRUCTIONAL MATERIALS, INC.

TABLE OF CONTENTS

Chapter 12	Pages 176-190
Lesson 1	**JINGLES** (Pronoun, Subject Pronoun), **GRAMMAR** (Introductory Sentences, Noun Check with Pronouns, Add Pronouns to the Parts of Speech, Skill Builder Check), **VOCABULARY #1**
Lesson 2	**JINGLES**, **GRAMMAR** (Practice Sentences), **SKILL** (Capitalization Rules), **PRACTICE EXERCISE**, **VOCABULARY #2**
Lesson 3	**JINGLES**, **GRAMMAR** (Practice Sentences, Practice and Improved Sentence), **PRACTICE EXERCISE**
Lesson 4	**JINGLES**, **STUDY**, **TEST**, **CHECK**, **WRITING** (journal), **STATE ACTIVITY**
Lesson 5	**WRITING ASSIGNMENT #6**, **SENTENCE TIME**

Chapter 13	Pages 191-205
Lesson 1	**JINGLE** (Possessive Pronoun), **GRAMMAR** (Introductory Sentences, Skill Builder Check, Reviewing the Six Parts of Speech), **VOCABULARY #1**
Lesson 2	**JINGLES**, **GRAMMAR** (Practice Sentences), **SKILL** (Punctuation Rules), **PRACTICE EXERCISE**, **VOCABULARY #2**
Lesson 3	**JINGLES**, **GRAMMAR** (Practice Sentences, Practice and Improved Sentence), **PRACTICE EXERCISE**, **ACTIVITY**
Lesson 4	**JINGLES**, **STUDY**, **TEST**, **CHECK**, **WRITING** (journal), **STATE ACTIVITY**
Lesson 5	**WRITING ASSIGNMENT #7**, **SENTENCE TIME**

Chapter 14	Pages 206-219
Lesson 1	**JINGLES**, **GRAMMAR** (Practice Sentences, Skill Builder Check, Reviewing the Six Parts of Speech), **PRACTICE EXERCISE**, **VOCABULARY #1**
Lesson 2	**JINGLES**, **GRAMMAR** (Practice Sentences), **PRACTICE EXERCISE**, **VOCABULARY #2**
Lesson 3	**JINGLES**, **GRAMMAR** (Practice Sentences, Practice and Improved Sentence), **PRACTICE EXERCISE**
Lesson 4	**JINGLES**, **STUDY**, **TEST**, **CHECK**, **WRITING** (journal), **STATE ACTIVITY**
Lesson 5	**WRITING ASSIGNMENT #8**, **SENTENCE TIME**

Chapter 15	Pages 220-236
Lesson 1	**JINGLES**, **GRAMMAR** (Introductory Sentences, Possessive Noun, Noun Check with Possessive Nouns, Skill Builder Check), **PRACTICE EXERCISE**, **VOCABULARY #1**
Lesson 2	**JINGLES**, **GRAMMAR** (Practice Sentences), **SKILL** (Making Nouns Possessive), **PRACTICE EXERCISE**, **VOCABULARY #2**
Lesson 3	**JINGLES**, **GRAMMAR** (Practice Sentences, Practice and Improved Sentence), **PRACTICE EXERCISE**
Lesson 4	**JINGLES**, **STUDY**, **TEST**, **CHECK**, **WRITING** (journal), **STATE ACTIVITY**
Lesson 5	**WRITING** (Three Point Expository Paragraph), **WRITING ASSIGNMENT #9**, **SENTENCE TIME**

Chapter 16	Pages 237-251
Lesson 1	**JINGLES**, **GRAMMAR** (Practice Sentences, Skill Builder Check), **PRACTICE EXERCISE**, **VOCABULARY #1**
Lesson 2	**JINGLES**, **GRAMMAR** (Practice Sentences), **SKILL** (Introduce Contractions), **PRACTICE EXERCISE**, **VOCABULARY #2**
Lesson 3	**JINGLES**, **GRAMMAR** (Practice Sentences, Practice and Improved Sentence), **SKILL** (More Contractions), **PRACTICE EXERCISE**
Lesson 4	**JINGLES**, **STUDY**, **TEST**, **CHECK**, **WRITING** (journal), **STATE ACTIVITY**, **ORAL CONTRACTION REVIEW**
Lesson 5	**WRITING ASSIGNMENT #10**, **SENTENCE TIME**

Level 2—Shurley English—Homeschool Edition

TABLE OF CONTENTS

Chapter 17	Pages 252-266
Lesson 1	**JINGLES**, **GRAMMAR** (Practice Sentences, Skill Builder Check), **SKILL** (More Contractions), **PRACTICE EXERCISE**, **VOCABULARY #1**
Lesson 2	**JINGLES**, **GRAMMAR** (Practice Sentences), **SKILLS** (Contractions, Oral Contraction Review), **PRACTICE EXERCISE**, **VOCABULARY #2**, **ACTIVITY**
Lesson 3	**JINGLES**, **GRAMMAR** (Practice Sentences, Practice and Improved Sentence), **PRACTICE EXERCISE**
Lesson 4	**JINGLES**, **STUDY**, **TEST**, **CHECK**, **WRITING** (journal), **STATE ACTIVITY**, **ORAL CONTRACTION REVIEW**
Lesson 5	**WRITING ASSIGNMENT #11**, **SENTENCE TIME**

Chapter 18	Pages 267-284
Lesson 1	**JINGLES**, **GRAMMAR** (Practice Sentences, Skill Builder Check, Review Six Parts of Speech), **SKILLS** (Complete Sentence, Sentence Fragments, Matching Subject Parts and Predicate Parts, Correcting Sentence Fragments), **PRACTICE EXERCISE**, **VOCABULARY #1**, **ACTIVITY**
Lesson 2	**JINGLES**, **GRAMMAR** (Practice Sentences), **PRACTICE EXERCISE**, **VOCABULARY #2**
Lesson 3	**JINGLES**, **GRAMMAR** (Practice Sentences, Practice and Improved Sentence), **PRACTICE EXERCISE**
Lesson 4	**JINGLES**, **STUDY**, **TEST**, **CHECK**, **WRITING** (journal), **STATE ACTIVITY**
Lesson 5	**WRITING** (Introduce Descriptive Writing), **Writing ASSIGNMENT #12**, **SENTENCE TIME**

Chapter 19	Pages 285-299
Lesson 1	**JINGLES**, **GRAMMAR** (Practice Sentences, Skill Builder Check, Review the Six Parts of Speech), **PRACTICE EXERCISE**, **VOCABULARY #1**
Lesson 2	**JINGLES**, **GRAMMAR** (Practice Sentences), **PRACTICE EXERCISE**, **VOCABULARY #2**
Lesson 3	**JINGLES**, **GRAMMAR** (Practice Sentences, Practice and Improved Sentence), **PRACTICE EXERCISE**, **ACTIVITY**
Lesson 4	**JINGLES**, **STUDY**, **TEST**, **CHECK**, **WRITING** (journal), **STATE ACTIVITY**
Lesson 5	**WRITING ASSIGNMENT #13**, **SENTENCE TIME**

Chapter 20	Pages 300-315
Lesson 1	**JINGLES**, **GRAMMAR** (Practice Sentences, Skill Builder Check, Review Six Parts of Speech), **SKILL** (Identify Verb Tenses), **PRACTICE EXERCISE**, **VOCABULARY #1**, **ACTIVITY**
Lesson 2	**JINGLES**, **GRAMMAR** (Practice Sentences), **SKILL** (Identify Regular and Irregular Verbs), **VOCABULARY #2**
Lesson 3	**JINGLES**, **GRAMMAR** (Practice Sentences, Practice and Improved Sentence), **PRACTICE EXERCISE**
Lesson 4	**JINGLES**, **STUDY**, **TEST**, **CHECK**, **WRITING** (journal), **STATE ACTIVITY**
Lesson 5	**WRITING ASSIGNMENT #14** , **SENTENCE TIME**

Chapter 21	Pages 316-327
Lesson 1	**JINGLES**, **GRAMMAR** (Practice Sentences, Skill Builder Check, Review the six parts of speech), **PRACTICE EXERCISE**, **VOCABULARY #1**
Lesson 2	**JINGLES**, **GRAMMAR** (Practice Sentences), **PRACTICE EXERCISE**, **VOCABULARY #2**
Lesson 3	**JINGLES**, **GRAMMAR** (Practice Sentences), **PRACTICE EXERCISE**
Lesson 4	**JINGLES**, **STUDY**, **TEST**, **CHECK**, **WRITING** (journal), **STATE ACTIVITY**
Lesson 5	**WRITING** (Introduce Narrative Writing), **WRITING ASSIGNMENT #15**, **SENTENCE TIME**

Level 2—Shurley English—Homeschool Edition

TABLE OF CONTENTS

Chapter 22	Pages 328-342
Lesson 1	**JINGLES, GRAMMAR** (Practice Sentences), **SKILL** (Writing a Friendly Letter), **VOCABULARY #1, ACTIVITY**
Lesson 2	**JINGLES, GRAMMAR** (Practice Sentences), **SKILL** (Friendly Letter), **PRACTICE EXERCISE, VOCABULARY #2**
Lesson 3	**JINGLES, GRAMMAR** (Practice Sentences), **SKILL** (Friendly Letter), **PRACTICE EXERCISE**
Lesson 4	**JINGLES, STUDY, TEST, CHECK, WRITING** (journal), **STATE ACTIVITY**
Lesson 5	**WRITING ASSIGNMENT #16, SENTENCE TIME**

Chapter 23	Pages 343-355
Lesson 1	**JINGLES, GRAMMAR** (Practice Sentences), **SKILL** (Parts of an Envelope), **VOCABULARY #1, ACTIVITY**
Lesson 2	**JINGLES, GRAMMAR** (Practice Sentences), **SKILL** (Parts of an Envelope), **PRACTICE EXERCISE, VOCABULARY#2**
Lesson 3	**JINGLES, GRAMMAR** (Practice Sentences), **PRACTICE EXERCISE**
Lesson 4	**JINGLES, STUDY, TEST, CHECK, WRITING** (journal), **STATE ACTIVITY**
Lesson 5	**WRITING ASSIGNMENT #17, SENTENCE TIME**

Chapter 24	Pages 356-367
Lesson 1	**JINGLES, GRAMMAR** (Practice Sentences, Skill Builder Check, Review the Six Parts of Speech), **SKILL** (Thank-You Notes), **PRACTICE EXERCISE, VOCABULARY #1**
Lesson 2	**JINGLES, GRAMMAR** (Practice Sentences), **PRACTICE EXERCISE, VOCABULARY #2**
Lesson 3	**JINGLES, GRAMMAR** (Practice Sentences), **ACTIVITY**
Lesson 4	**JINGLES, STUDY, TEST, CHECK, WRITING** (journal), **STATE ACTIVITY**
Lesson 5	**WRITING ASSIGNMENT #18, SENTENCE TIME**

Chapter 25	Pages 368-378
Lesson 1	**JINGLES, GRAMMAR** (Practice Sentences, Skill Builder Check), **SKILL** (The Three Main Parts of the Library), **ACTIVITY**
Lesson 2	**JINGLES, GRAMMAR** (Practice Sentences), **ACTIVITY**
Lesson 3	**JINGLES, GRAMMAR** (Practice Sentences), **PRACTICE EXERCISE**
Lesson 4	**JINGLES, STUDY, TEST, CHECK, WRITING** (journal), **STATE ACTIVITY**
Lesson 5	**WRITING ASSIGNMENT #19, SENTENCE TIME**

Chapter 26	Pages 379-390
Lesson 1	**JINGLES, GRAMMAR** (Practice Sentences), **SKILL** (Introduce the Front Parts of a Book), **PRACTICE EXERCISE**
Lesson 2	**JINGLES, GRAMMAR** (Practice Sentences), **SKILL** (Introduce the Back Parts of a Book), **PRACTICE EXERCISE**
Lesson 3	**JINGLES, GRAMMAR** (Practice Sentences), **PRACTICE EXERCISE**
Lesson 4	**JINGLES, STUDY, TEST, CHECK, WRITING** (journal), **STATE ACTIVITY**
Lesson 5	**WRITING ASSIGNMENT #20, SENTENCE TIME**

Chapter 27	Pages 391-400
Lesson 1	**JINGLES, GRAMMAR** (Practice Sentences), **STATE ACTIVITY**
Lesson 2	**JINGLES, GRAMMAR** (Practice Sentences), **STATE ACTIVITY**
Lesson 3	**JINGLES, GRAMMAR** (Practice Sentences), **STATE ACTIVITY**
Lesson 4	**JINGLES, STUDY, TEST, CHECK, WRITING** (journal)
Lesson 5	**WRITING ASSIGNMENT #21, SENTENCE TIME**

Chapter 28	Pages 401-403
Lesson 1	**WRITING ASSIGNMENT #22**
Lesson 2	**STATE ACTIVITY**
Lesson 3	**STATE ACTIVITY**
Lesson 4	**ACTIVITY**
Lesson 5	**ACTIVITY** (continued)

Level 2 Homeschool Teacher's Manual

SHURLEY ENGLISH ABBREVIATIONS FOR LEVEL 2

Abbreviation	Description
N	Noun
SN	Subject Noun
Pro	Pronoun
SP	Subject Pronoun
V	Verb
Adv	Adverb
Adj	Adjective
A	Article Adjective
P	Preposition
OP	Object of the Preposition
PP	Possessive Pronoun
PN	Possessive Noun

Level 2 Pattern	
SN V P1	Subject Noun Verb Pattern 1
Sentences	
D	Declarative Sentence
E	Exclamatory Sentence
Int	Interrogative Sentence

CHAPTER 1   LESSON 1

Objectives: How to Get Started, Long-term Goals and Short-term Goals, and Activity.

HOW TO GET STARTED

1. The word *students* will be used throughout the text in reference to the child/children you are teaching. The adult teaching this program will be referred to as *teacher*.

2. Stay one lesson ahead of your students. Study the entire lesson thoroughly before you present it. Then, read each lesson like you read a storybook: word-for-word. Your teacher's manual will give you teaching scripts to read out loud to your students. It will give you teacher's notes, and it will tell you when your students are to participate with you. Do not skip anything, and do not jump ahead. In just a few days, you will be in a comfortable routine that will help your students develop a love of learning.

3. All jingles and references are found in the **Jingle and Reference Sections** in the front of the student book. *Note: The sample exercises in the Reference Section of the student's book are keyed to serve as a study guide for the student.* A **Practice Section** is located after the Jingle and Reference Sections to give students practice on the skills they are learning. A **Test Section** is located after the Practice Section to test students on the skills taught. Last, a **Sentence Section** fine-tunes sentence skills by giving students scrambled sentence parts to unscramble according to a specific sequence of sentence labels.

4. The lessons in this book are divided into chapters. Each lesson takes approximately twenty to fifty minutes to complete. For best results, you should do one lesson every day.

5. Your Shurley kit contains a teacher's manual, a student workbook, and an audio CD which demonstrates the Jingles and the Question and Answer Flows for the Introductory Sentences.

STUDY SKILLS TIME

TEACHING SCRIPT FOR SETTING GOALS

Good study skills do not just happen. Getting organized is the foundation for good study skills. It takes time, determination, and the practice of certain guidelines to get organized. The study skills chapter will concentrate on the guidelines you need for success in developing good study habits. Follow them carefully until they become habits that will help you for a lifetime.

Everyone has the same 24 hours, but everyone does not use his/her 24 hours in the same way. In order to get the most for your time, it is important to set goals. Goals will keep you pointed in the direction you want to go, will focus your time, and will keep you on track. With a list of goals, you can check your progress. Long-term goals are what you want to accomplish in life, usually concentrating on your education and your career. Short-term goals will help you plan things to do a week or a month at a time. You will be given guidelines that will help you know specific things to do each day to help you achieve your goals.

CHAPTER 1 LESSON 1 CONTINUED

Listen to the examples of long-term and short-term goals as I read them. (*Read the examples below or write them on the board.*)

Examples of goals for a person interested in becoming a writer:

Long-term Goals	**Short-term Goals**
1. Get a scholarship for college.	1. Make a daily schedule to plan my time.
2. Earn a degree in English.	2. Earn good grades this school year.
3. Become a well-known speech writer or write for a local newspaper.	3. Set aside 20 minutes every night for study time.
	4. Earn spending money by helping with extra chores.
	5. Spend 15 minutes every day doing some kind of writing, which includes making entries in my personal journal.

Examples of goals for a person interested in art:

Long-term Goals	**Short-term Goals**
1. Get an art scholarship for college.	1. Make a daily schedule to plan my time.
2. Earn a degree in art.	2. Earn good grades this school year.
3. Become a famous artist.	3. Set aside 20 minutes every night for study time.
	4. Earn spending money by helping with family chores.
	5. Spend 30 minutes every day doing some kind of art.

Notice that getting organized and setting aside study time are always important short-term goals because they help you achieve your long-term goals. You will now write down your own long-term and short-term goals. Write two or three long-term goals and three or four short-term goals. You can add more as you think of them. (*Give students time to write down their long-term and short-term goals. You may want to discuss what kind of goals were written. Have students make English folders and put their goals in the folders.*)

ACTIVITY / ASSIGNMENT TIME

Have students map out their goals. Their starting point on the map should be marked with today's date. Each goal should be indicated by a dot anywhere on the page. Have students label each dot with the corresponding goal and draw a line connecting the goals in order. As a goal is accomplished, students should mark the goal with the completion date. Students may also decorate their maps.

(End of lesson.)

Level 2—Shurley English—Homeschool Edition

CHAPTER 1   LESSON 2
Objectives: Beginning Setup Plan for Homeschool, Writing (Journal), and Activity.

STUDY SKILLS TIME

TEACHING SCRIPT FOR STUDY PLANS

We have learned that goals are important because they are a constant reminder of what you want to happen in your future. To make the most of your goals, you should take time to evaluate your goals at the end of every month to see if there are any adjustments you wish to make. Goals change as your needs change and as your abilities increase.

Remember, goals are your destination. A schedule is your road map. You may take a few detours, but you still know the direction in which you are headed and how to get there. (*Have discussion time with your students at the beginning of each month to evaluate goals and schedules. Help students make any necessary adjustments. This is a worthwhile learning activity that is done nine times for the whole school year. It should be a meaningful experience for your students.*)

The first step in good organization is to make and follow a daily schedule. Turn to page 9 and look at Reference 1. Follow along as I read the guidelines that will help you establish a daily schedule to follow during study time and school time. These guidelines will help you get organized with the least amount of wasted effort. (*Read and discuss with your students the plan reproduced below.*)

Reference 1: Beginning Setup Plan for Homeschool

You should use this plan to keep things in order!

1. Have separate color-coded pocket folders for each subject.
2. Put unfinished work in the right-hand side and finished work in the left-hand side of each subject folder.
3. Put notes to study, graded tests, and study guides in the brads so you will have them to study for scheduled tests.
4. Have a paper folder to store extra clean sheets of paper. Keep it full at all times.
5. Have an assignment folder to be reviewed every day.

Things to keep in your assignment folder:

A. Keep a monthly calendar of assignments, test dates, report-due dates, project-due dates, extra activities, dates and times, review dates, etc.

B. Keep a grade sheet to record the grades received in each subject. (*You might also consider keeping your grades on the inside cover of each subject folder. However you keep your grades, just remember to record them accurately. Your grades are your business, so keep up with them! Grades help you know which areas need attention.*)

C. Make a list every day of the things you want to do so you can keep track of what you finish and what you have not finished. Move the unfinished items to your new list the next day. (*Making this list takes time, but it's your road map to success. You will always know at a glance what you set out to accomplish and what still needs to be done.*)

6. Keep all necessary school supplies in a handy, heavy-duty Ziploc bag or a pencil bag.

Level 2—Shurley English—Homeschool Edition

CHAPTER 1 LESSON 2 CONTINUED

 **WRITING TIME**

TEACHING SCRIPT FOR JOURNAL WRITING

Now, turn to your Reference Section and look at Reference 2 on page 10. You will begin journal writing today, but, before you begin, I want to share some important information about this type of writing. (*Read the information in the reference box below.*)

Reference 2: What is Journal Writing?

Journal Writing is a written record of your personal thoughts and feelings about things or people that are important to you. Recording your thoughts in a journal is a good way to remember how you felt about what was happening in your life at a particular time. You can record your dreams, memories, feelings, and experiences. You can ask questions and answer some of them. It is fun to go back later and read what you have written because it shows how you have changed in different areas of your life. A journal can also be an excellent place to look for future writing topics, creative stories, poems, etc. Writing in a journal is an easy and enjoyable way to practice your writing skills without worrying about a writing grade.

What do I write about?

Journals are personal, but sometimes it helps to have ideas to get you started. Remember, in a journal, you do not have to stick to one topic. Write about someone or something you like. Write about what you did last weekend or on vacation. Write about what you hope to do this week or on your next vacation. Write about home, school, friends, hobbies, special talents (yours or someone else's), or the hopes and fears you have about things now and in the future. Write about what is wrong in your world and what you would do to "fix" it. Write about the good things and the bad things in your world.

If you think about a past event and want to write an opinion about it now, put it in your journal. If you want to give your opinion about a present or future event that could have an impact on your life or the way that you see things, put it in your journal. If something bothers you, record it in your journal. If something interests you, record it. If you just want to record something that doesn't seem important at all, write it in your journal. After all, it is your journal!

How do I get started writing in my personal journal?

You need to put the day's date on the title line of your paper: **Month, Day, Year.** Skip the next line and begin your entry. You might write one or two sentences, a paragraph, a whole page, or several pages. Except for the journal date, no particular organizational style is required for journal writing. You decide how best to organize and express your thoughts. Feel free to include sketches, diagrams, lists, etc., if they will help you remember your thoughts about a topic or an event. You will also need a spiral notebook, a pen, a quiet place, and at least 5-10 minutes of uninterrupted writing time.

Note: Use a pen if possible. Pencils have erasers and lead points that break, both of which slow down your thoughts. Any drawings you might include do not have to be masterpieces—stick figures will do nicely.

Level 2—Shurley English—Homeschool Edition

CHAPTER 1 LESSON 2 CONTINUED

TEACHER INSTRUCTIONS

Have students write the title *My Personal Journal for the Year* ____, indicating the current year on the front covers of their journal notebooks or folders. Students should use their journal notebooks for their journal-writing assignments.

Writing Assignment: Have students make the first entry in their journals at this time.

Teacher's Notes: Journal writing helps students express themselves in written form, helps students feel comfortable with writing, and gives students an opportunity to practice what they are learning. Check to make sure students are making their entries. Make it a writing routine to have a five-to-ten minute journal-writing time whenever journal writing is assigned. If students finish early, have them go back and read earlier entries. Keeping a journal should develop into a life-long habit.

 ACTIVITY / ASSIGNMENT TIME

Put the scrambled words and the word bank below on the board or on notebook paper. All the words in the first list have scrambled spellings. Have students use References 1 and 2 on pages 9 and 10 and the word bank to help them unscramble the reference words below. Tell students that not all words in the word bank will be used. Then, have students scramble their own list of English words. They can give their scrambled words to friends or family to unscramble. Students need to make a key and word bank for their scrambled words.

Scrambled Words	Word Bank	
1. scholohoem 2. assigmnten 3. darcalen 4. suplpies 5. tones 6. jonrual 7. ercord 8. pesrolan 9. tirew 10. atde	calendar notes record memories write topic plan	date homeschool personal supplies journal folder assignment
Key for Scrambled Words: (1) homeschool, (2) assignment, (3) calendar, (4) supplies, (5) notes, (6) journal, (7) record, (8) personal, (9) write, (10) date		

(End of lesson.)

Level 2—Shurley English—Homeschool Edition

CHAPTER 1   LESSON 3
Objectives: Skill (Introduce Alphabetizing), Practice Exercise, and Activity.

SKILL TIME

TEACHING SCRIPT FOR INTRODUCING ALPHABETIZING

Today, we are going to review the alphabet by repeating all the letters in order. (*Repeat the letters of the alphabet with your students.*) When we talk about alphabetical order, we are talking about putting words in the same sequence as the alphabet. This is called alphabetizing, or putting things in ABC order.

There are several reasons for learning to alphabetize words. Alphabetical order is often used to arrange words or facts so that they can be easily found. How are words in a dictionary arranged? (*in alphabetical order*) How are names in a phone book listed? (*in alphabetical order*) How are the names of students enrolled in a school listed? (*in alphabetical order*) How are the names of students in a Sunday school class listed? (*in alphabetical order*) As you can see, learning about alphabetical order is very important because it makes things in our lives so much easier.

First, we will learn to put letters in alphabetical order. I will write a group of letters on the board, and I want you to tell me how the letters should be arranged in alphabetical order. (*Write the following letters on the board and discuss the correct alphabetical order.*)

1. i r h v   (**h, i, r, v**)

2. s d n y g k   (**d, g, k, n, s, y**)

3. e q a u l z f b   (**a, b, e, f, l, q, u, z**)

You have just practiced alphabetizing letters of the alphabet. Next, you will practice alphabetizing words. Sometimes studying involves looking <u>words</u> up in a dictionary. You may need to see if you have spelled a word correctly, or you may want to check a word's meaning. A dictionary gives you the correct spelling, pronunciation, meanings, and usage of words. We learn to alphabetize words because words are arranged in alphabetical order in a dictionary. The best way to learn alphabetizing is to alphabetize letters and words for practice. Look at Reference 3 on page 11 in your Reference section.

Reference 3: Alphabetical Order									
Directions: Put each group of words in alphabetical order. Use numbers to show the order in each column.									
Math Words		**"M" Words**		**Farm Words**		**Language Words**		**"J" Words**	
_1_	1. add	_2_	3. melon	_2_	5. tractor	_1_	7. noun	_1_	9. juice
_2_	2. subtract	_1_	4. meadow	_1_	6. barn	_2_	8. verb	_2_	10. jump

Level 2—Shurley English—Homeschool Edition

CHAPTER 1 LESSON 3 CONTINUED

There is a simple way to put words in alphabetical order. When the first letters of the words to be alphabetized are different, you only have to look at the first letter to put words in alphabetical order. Let's read the directions for the sample. (*Read the directions*.) Look at the two words under the title "Math Words." In the words *add* and *subtract*, the first letters, *a* and *s*, are different. Since *a* comes before *s* in the alphabet, *add* comes before *subtract*. A number *1* has been written in the blank in front of *add* and a number *2* has been written in the blank in front of *subtract*, as demonstrated in the sample.

When the first letters of words to be alphabetized are the same, you should look at the second or third letters to put them in alphabetical order. Now, look at the two words *melon* and *meadow* under "M Words." In the words *melon* and *meadow*, the first two letters are the same. Go to the third letter in each word. Since *a* comes before *l* in the alphabet, *meadow* comes before *melon*. A number *1* has been written in the blank in front of *meadow* and a number *2* has been written in the blank in front of *melon*, as demonstrated in the example. (*Call on students to demonstrate this process orally with the rest of the sample words*.)

 PRACTICE TIME

Have students turn to page 35 in the Practice Section of their book and find Chapter 1, Lesson 3, Practice. Go over the directions to make sure they understand what to do. If students need a review, have them study the information and examples in the Reference Section of their books. Check and discuss the Practice after students have finished. (*Chapter 1, Lesson 3, Practice key is given below*.)

Chapter 1, Lesson 3, Practice: Put each group of words in alphabetical order. Write numbers in the blanks to show the order in each column.

Travel Words	Picnic Words	"D" Words	Family Words
_1_ 1. airport	_4_ 5. sandwich	_3_ 9. dolphin	_3_ 13. mother
_3_ 2. luggage	_3_ 6. blanket	_2_ 10. dog	_2_ 14. father
_4_ 3. ticket	_2_ 7. basket	_1_ 11. daisy	_1_ 15. brother
_2_ 4. hotel	_1_ 8. ants	_4_ 12. dragon	_4_ 16. sister

 ACTIVITY / ASSIGNMENT TIME

Have students make up different lists in which all words are alphabetized correctly. These lists might include the following: toys, sports, animals, colors, food, etc. Students could recruit family members to help them make the lists. Family members could also alphabetize students' lists. Students should make a key to check each list.

(End of lesson.)

Level 2—Shurley English—Homeschool Edition

CHAPTER 1 LESSON 4
Objectives: Study, Test, Check, and Writing (Journal).

 STUDY TIME

Have students look in the Reference Section of their workbooks to review alphabetizing letters and words. As a reminder, the sample exercises in the Reference Section of the student's book are keyed to serve as a study guide for students.

 TEST TIME

Have students turn to page 80 in the Test Section of their book and find Chapter 1 Test *(Exercises 1–5)*. Tell them that grammar is not tested yet. Go over the directions to make sure they understand what to do. *(For total points, count each required answer as a point.)* *(Chapter 1 Test key is given on the next page.)*

 **CHECK TIME**

After students have finished, check and discuss their test papers. Make sure they understand why their answers are right or wrong. *(For total points, count each required answer as a point.)*

Teacher's Notes: Grading Ideas
1. **One Grade:** You can take one grade on the whole test.
2. **Two Grades:** You can take one grade on the grammar sentences and another grade on the skill exercises.
3. **Possible Points:** For total points, count each required answer as a point.

(End of lesson.)

Level 2—Shurley English—Homeschool Edition

Chapter 1 Test
(Student Page 80)

31 pts

Exercise 1: Write the letters in each group below in alphabetical order.

1. n z f c (c, f, n, z)

2. p d v h (d, h, p, v)

3. c x k o u r (c, k, o, r, u, x)

4. w g l t e z b m (b, e, g, l, m, t, w, z)

Exercise 2: Put each group of words in alphabetical order. Use numbers to show the order in each column.

Space Words		Color Words		"G" Words	
1	1. astronaut	1	3. black	2	5. grape
2	2. moon	2	4. brown	1	6. glaze

Exercise 3: Put each group of words in alphabetical order. Use numbers to show the order in each column.

Hospital Words		"O" Words		Fruit Words	
3	1. patient	3	4. ostrich	1	7. mango
1	2. doctor	2	5. omelet	2	8. peach
2	3. nurse	1	6. olive	3	9. pear

Exercise 4: Put each group of words in alphabetical order. Use numbers to show the order in each column.

Movie Words		"L" Words		"V" Words	
2	1. popcorn	2	5. laugh	3	9. velvet
3	2. previews	4	6. light	1	10. value
1	3. candy	3	7. leopard	4	11. view
4	4. soda	1	8. language	2	12. vanish

Exercise 5: In your journal, write a paragraph summarizing what you have learned this week.

Level 2 Homeschool Teacher's Manual

Level 2—Shurley English—Homeschool Edition

CHAPTER 1   LESSON 5
Objectives: State Activity.

 STATE ACTIVITY TIME

(Have a recipe box and a package of lined index cards ready for your children to use for the state activity in each chapter. Find a map of the United States that your students can use to draw or trace each state.)

General Directions: Starting with Chapter 1, you will have a state activity in each chapter until you have covered all 50 states. You will make an index card for each state. First, on the blank side of the index card, you will draw (or trace) and color the state assigned. Then, on the lined side of the index card, you will write some information about the state. The information you will use is listed on page 8 in the Reference Section of your book. Turn to page 8, and I will show you how this information is arranged. Look at number 1. The C1 means you have a state assignment in Chapter 1. The state is Alabama. The capital of Alabama is Montgomery, and the postal abbreviation is AL.

State Information for the 50 States			
Chapter	State	Capital	Postal Abbreviation
1. C 1	Alabama	Montgomery	AL

Now, I will show you how to put the State Information for Alabama on an index card. You will use the Card Sample on page 9 in the Reference Section of your book. *(Have students turn to page 9 and look at the Card Sample with you.)*

You will use the questions that are in this sample for all 50 states, changing the name of the state and other information each time. Remember, the first thing you must do is draw and color the state of Alabama on the blank side of the index card. The first question will verify the state that you are recording on the index card. The rest of the questions are answered from the information prepared for you on the State Information page. *(Read and discuss the questions and answers on the Card Sample below. Tell students that they will use this sample and the information provided on the State Information page 8 to complete each assignment.)*

You may use your state cards to quiz family members, friends, and relatives.

Card Sample for State Information
1. What is the state on the front of this card? **Alabama**
2. What is the capital of Alabama? **Montgomery**
3. What is the postal abbreviation of Alabama? **AL**

(End of lesson.)

CHAPTER 2   LESSON 1

Objectives: Jingle Guidelines, Jingle (Sentence), Skills (Synonyms, Antonyms), Four-Step Vocabulary Plan, and Vocabulary #1.

 **JINGLE TIME**

Read the five *Jingle Guidelines* below before you teach jingles to your students. These guidelines will give you ideas and help you establish procedures for the recitation of jingles.

Jingle Guidelines

1. **Jingles are used** to learn English definitions. Knowing English definitions makes learning English concepts easier because children can use the definitions to remember how to classify words used in sentences.

2. **Approach Jingle Time** as a learning time. Most of the jingles are presented as choral chants with enough rhythm to make them easy to remember, but you can also sing, rap, or just read them. Learning definitions in jingle form makes this necessary practice more fun. *(Listen to the CD for an example.)*

3. **Jingles are more fun** if you make up motions for each jingle. Motions use the kinesthetic learning style of students and help them learn faster. Motions should be incorporated for several of the jingles. Relax and have fun. Have your children help make up motions they enjoy.

4. **You only need** to spend a short time on jingles (*five to ten minutes daily*) because you will be working with the jingles every day. Jingle Time should be fun as well as educational.

5. **Demonstrate each new jingle** for your students; then, lead them in reciting the jingles. Let your students lead the jingles as soon as they are ready.

Have students turn to page 2 in the Jingle Section of their books. The teacher will lead the students in reciting the Sentence Jingle below. Practice the new jingle several times until students can recite it smoothly. Emphasize reciting with a rhythm. Students and teacher should be together! (*Do not try to explain the jingle at this time. Just have fun reciting it. Add motions for more fun and laughter.*)

Jingle 1: Sentence Jingle

A sentence, sentence, sentence　　Add a capital letter, letter
Is complete, complete, complete　　And an end mark, mark.
When 5 simple rules　　　　　　　　Now, we're finished, and aren't we smart!
It meets, meets, meets.　　　　　　Now, our sentence has all its parts!

It has a subject, subject, subject　　REMEMBER
And a verb, verb, verb.　　　　　　　Subject, Verb, Com-plete sense,
It makes sense, sense, sense　　　　Capital letter, and an end mark, too.
With every word, word, word.　　　　That's what a sentence is all about!

CHAPTER 2 LESSON 1 CONTINUED

SKILL TIME

TEACHING SCRIPT FOR SYNONYMS AND ANTONYMS

Words are important to your future. Knowing different vocabulary words can help you express exactly what is on your mind, and it will also help others to fully understand your thoughts and ideas. The ability to communicate is more effective when you do not use the same words over and over again. That is why it is necessary to learn a wide variety of vocabulary words.

Today, we will learn about synonyms and antonyms and how to mark them. Turn to page 11 in the Reference Section of your book and look at Reference 4. (*Reference 4 is reproduced below.*) Listen carefully as I read the definitions for synonyms and antonyms. (*Read the definitions for synonyms and antonyms in the reference box below.*) Now, I will read the directions for identifying synonyms and antonyms. (*Read the directions for identifying synonyms and antonyms in the reference box below.*)

Reference 4: Synonyms and Antonyms
Definitions: Synonyms are words that have similar, or almost the same, meanings. Antonyms are words that have opposite meanings.
Directions: Identify each pair of words as synonyms or antonyms by putting parentheses ( ) around **syn** or **ant**.
1. small, tiny **(syn)** ant   2. gentle, kind **(syn)** ant   3. wild, tame syn **(ant)**

Look at the words **small** and **tiny** beside number 1. What are the meanings of the words **small** and **tiny**? (*Discuss the meanings of the words small and tiny.*) Do the words **small** and **tiny** have almost the same meanings, or do they have opposite meanings? (*almost the same meanings*) Since they have almost the same meanings, are they synonyms or antonyms? (*synonyms*) How do we indicate that they are synonyms? (*By putting parentheses around the syn*) (*For number 1, have students note the parentheses around the syn in their practice box.*)

Look at number 2. Let's discuss the meanings of the words **gentle** and **kind**. (*Discuss the meanings of the words gentle and kind.*) Do these words have almost the same meanings, or do they have opposite meanings? (*almost the same meanings*) Since they have almost the same meanings, are they synonyms or antonyms? (*synonyms*) How do we indicate that they are synonyms? (*By putting parentheses around the syn*) (*For number 2, have students note the parentheses around the syn in their practice box.*) Remember, synonyms may not have the same meanings, but their meanings will be similar. That is why they are called synonyms.

Look at number 3. Let's discuss the meanings of the words **wild** and **tame**. (*Discuss the meanings of the words wild and tame.*) Do these words have almost the same meanings, or do they have opposite meanings? (*opposite meanings*) Since they have opposite meanings, are they synonyms or antonyms? (*antonyms*) How do we indicate that they are antonyms? (*By putting parentheses around the ant*) (*For number 3, have students note the parentheses around the ant in their practice box.*) Remember, antonyms have different meanings because they are opposite words. They do not mean the same thing. That is why they are called antonyms.

Level 2—Shurley English—Homeschool Edition

CHAPTER 2 LESSON 1 CONTINUED

If the thought of learning new words is overwhelming, think about the resources you have available. You have two valuable tools to help you in this task: the dictionary and the thesaurus. The nice thing about these tools is that you alone, at any time, can use the dictionary or thesaurus (*for free*) to learn more words with which to express yourself. (*Discuss the dictionary and the thesaurus at this time if your students are not familiar with these reference books.*)

Today, you will begin expanding your knowledge of words. You will advance your vocabulary by learning synonyms and antonyms. Remember that synonyms are words that have almost the same meanings, and antonyms are words that have opposite meanings. Now that we have discussed several synonym and antonym words, I want you to name two pairs of words and identify one pair as synonyms and one pair as antonyms. (*Allow students to use a dictionary or a thesaurus to look up each pair of words if needed. Check students' identification of the words for accuracy.*)

Since we will be learning or reviewing synonyms and antonyms in almost every chapter, we will call this time **Vocabulary Time**. The purpose of Vocabulary Time is to learn new words; so, you will keep a Vocabulary notebook. During Vocabulary Time, you will always follow the Four-Step Vocabulary Plan. You will find this plan in Reference 5 on page 11 in your book. You will use this plan every time you enter vocabulary words in your notebook. (*Have students follow along as you read and discuss the vocabulary plan with them.*)

Reference 5: A Four-Step Vocabulary Plan
(1) Write a title for the vocabulary words in each chapter.   Example: **Chapter 1, Vocabulary Words**
(2) Write each vocabulary word in your vocabulary notebook.
(3) Look up each vocabulary word in a dictionary or thesaurus.
(4) Write the meaning beside each vocabulary word.

You will have a list of synonyms and antonyms to define in each chapter. These words are listed on pages 6 and 7 in the Reference Section of your workbook. (*Have students turn to page 6 and look at the eight words listed for Chapter 2.*) I will tell you the words you will define during Vocabulary Time. Any of the words you learn during Vocabulary Time could appear in the Vocabulary portion of your test. You may also use your vocabulary notebook to record any vocabulary word you wish to define for future reference.

 VOCABULARY TIME

Assign Chapter 2, Vocabulary Words **#1** on page 6 in the Reference Section for students to define in their Vocabulary notebooks. Tell students they are to use a dictionary or thesaurus to look up the meanings of the vocabulary words. (*Show students how to use the dictionary and/or thesaurus to look up words if they are not familiar with these reference books.*)

Chapter 2, Vocabulary Words #1
(enthusiastic, eager, gallop, crawl)

(End of lesson.)

CHAPTER 2   LESSON 2

Objectives: Jingles (Noun, Verb), Grammar (Noun, Verb), Activity, and Vocabulary #2.

 **JINGLE TIME**

Have students turn to the Jingle Section in their books and recite the previously-taught jingle. Then, lead students in reciting the new jingles (*Noun and Verb*) below. Practice the new jingles several times until students can recite them smoothly. Emphasize reciting with a rhythm. Students and teacher should be together! (*Do not try to explain the new jingles at this time. Just have fun reciting them. Remember, add motions for more fun and laughter.*)

Jingle 2: Noun Jingle

This little noun
Floating around
Names a person, place, or thing.
With a knick knack, paddy wack,
These are English rules.
Isn't language fun and cool?

Jingle 3: Verb Jingle

A verb shows action,	Action verbs are fun to do.	Wiggle, jiggle, turn around;
There's no doubt!	Now, it's time to name a few.	Raise your arms
It tells what the subject does,	So, clap your hands	And stomp the ground.
Like sing and shout.	And join our rhyme;	Shake your finger and wink your eye;
	Say those verbs in record time!	Wave those action verbs good-bye.

 GRAMMAR TIME

<u>TEACHING SCRIPT FOR THE NOUN AND VERB</u>

The purpose of studying English is to learn the vocabulary and English skills that will help you speak and write well. We will begin our study of English with nouns and verbs.

The noun jingle that you learned today says a **noun** names a person, place, or thing. The noun is also known as a naming word. Words like **teacher** and **Jacob** name people. Can you tell me two more nouns that name people? (*Give students time to respond.*) Words like **frogs** and **bears** name animals. Can you tell me two more nouns that name animals? (*Give students time to respond.*)

CHAPTER 2 LESSON 2 CONTINUED

Words like **hospital** and **desert** name places. Can you tell me two more nouns that name places? (*Give students time to respond.*) Words like **lamp** and **truck** name things. Can you tell me two more nouns that name things? (*Give students time to respond.*) (*Have students identify several nouns in the room.*) We use the abbreviation **N** for the word **noun** when we do not spell it out.

You have already learned several things about the verb from the verb jingle. A word that shows action is a verb. The **verb** tells what a person or thing does. Words like **write** and **play** tell what children do. Children **write**, and children **play**. Can you tell me two more verbs that tell what children do? (*Give students time to respond. Have students repeat the noun <u>children</u> with each verb.*) Can you tell me two verbs that tell what birds do? (*Give students time to respond. Have students repeat the noun <u>birds</u> with each verb.*) Can you tell me two verbs that tell what monkeys do? (*Give students time to respond. Have students repeat the noun <u>monkeys</u> with each verb.*) We use the abbreviation **V** for the word **verb** when we do not spell it out.

ACTIVITY / ASSIGNMENT TIME

To help illustrate the concept of nouns, fill a large bucket or bowl with water. Have ready small plastic toys and other items that will float. As you and your students sing the noun jingle, have each child drop a "noun" in the water and stir it around. Substitute the name of the toy for the word "noun" in the noun jingle. (*Advanced Option: You can vary this activity by having students first spell a noun word with plastic letters and then drop the letters in the water.*)

VOCABULARY TIME

Assign Chapter 2, Vocabulary Words **#2** on page 6 in the Reference Section for students to define in their Vocabulary notebooks. Tell students they are to use a dictionary or thesaurus to look up the meanings of the vocabulary words.

Chapter 2, Vocabulary Words #2
(impolite, respectful, salute, tribute)

(End of lesson.)

Level 2—Shurley English—Homeschool Edition

CHAPTER 2   LESSON 3
Objectives: Jingles, Grammar (Introductory Sentences, Question & Answer Flow, Classifying, Labeling, Subject Noun, Verb), and Activity.

 **JINGLE TIME**

Have students turn to the Jingle Section of their books. The teacher will lead the students in reciting the previously-taught jingles.

 GRAMMAR TIME

Put the introductory sentences from the box below on the board. Use these sentences as you go through the new concepts covered in your teaching scripts. For the greatest benefit, students must participate orally with the teacher. (*You might put the introductory sentences on notebook paper if you are doing one-on-one instruction with your students.*)

Chapter 2, Introductory Sentences for Lesson 3
1. Children clapped.
2. Pony galloped.
3. Flags flew.

TEACHING SCRIPT FOR THE QUESTION & ANSWER FLOW

Understanding how all the parts of a sentence work together makes writing sentences easier and more interesting. Learning how to ask the right questions to get answers will help you identify the parts of a sentence. The questions you ask and the answers you get are called a **Question and Answer Flow**. Let's repeat the definition of the Question and Answer Flow together: <u>The questions you ask and the answers you get are called a</u> **Question and Answer Flow**.

As you use the Question and Answer Flow to find what each word in a sentence is called, you are classifying the sentence. As you classify a sentence, you write an abbreviation label above each word to identify what that word is called. Now, we will practice using the Question and Answer Flow as we learn to classify sentences.

TEACHING SCRIPT FOR SUBJECT NOUN AND VERB IN A SENTENCE

I am going to show you how to use the noun and verb definitions and the Question and Answer Flow to find the subject noun and verb in a sentence. The subject of a sentence tells who or what a sentence is about. Since a noun names a person, place, or thing, a subject noun tells who or what a sentence is about. **The abbreviation *SN* is used for the words *subject noun* when we do not spell them out.**

Level 2—Shurley English—Homeschool Edition

CHAPTER 2 LESSON 3 CONTINUED

We ask a subject question to find the noun that works as the subject of the sentence. The subject questions are **who** or **what**. We ask *who* if the sentence is **about people**. We ask *what* if the sentence is **not about people,** but about an animal, a place, or a thing.

Look at Sentence 1: Children clapped.
Who clapped? children - subject noun (*Write SN above children.*)
Since the word *children* refers to people, we ask the subject question *who*.
The subject noun *children* tells *who* the sentence is about.

Now, let's learn the Question and Answer Flow to find the verb. The verb definition says the verb shows action. The verb tells what the subject is doing. To find the verb, ask **what is being said about** the subject. Let's say **what is being said about** five times. Go. (*Have your students recite "what is being said about" with you at least five times. This will help them remember this important verb question.*) Now, we will ask the verb question.
What is being said about children? children clapped - verb (*Write V above clapped.*)

Remember, the questions you ask and the answers you get are called a Question and Answer Flow. I will classify Sentence 1 again, but this time you will classify the sentence with me. After we finish Sentence 1, you will classify Sentences 2 and 3 with me.

Teacher's Note: Make sure students say the Question and Answer Flows correctly.

Question and Answer Flow for Sentence 1: Children clapped.

1. Who clapped? children - subject noun (Trace over the SN above *children.*)
   (Since *children* are people, we use the subject question *who*.
   The subject noun *children* tells *who* the sentence is about.)
2. What is being said about children? children clapped - verb (Trace over the V above *clapped.*)

Classified Sentence: SN   V
                              Children clapped.

Question and Answer Flow for Sentence 2: Pony galloped.

1. What galloped? pony - subject noun (Write SN above *pony.*)
   (Since *the word pony is an animal*, we use the subject question *what*.
   The subject noun *pony* tells *what* the sentence is about.)
2. What is being said about pony? pony galloped - verb (Write V above *galloped.*)

Classified Sentence: SN   V
                              Pony galloped.

Question and Answer Flow for Sentence 3: Flags flew.

1. What flew? flags - subject noun (Write SN above *flags.*)
   (Since *flags* are things, we use the subject question *what*.
   The subject noun *flags* tells *what* the sentence is about.)
2. What is being said about flags? flags flew - verb (Write V above *flew.*)

Classified Sentence: SN   V
                              Flags flew.

Level 2—Shurley English—Homeschool Edition

CHAPTER 2 LESSON 3 CONTINUED

TEACHER INSTRUCTIONS

Have students recite the Question and Answer Flows for the first two sentences with you again, but this time they are to trace the labels on their desks with the first three fingers of their writing hand as they classify. This is excellent practice to develop dexterity and to learn at a faster pace.

Have students write the third sentence on a piece of paper. Then, students should go through the Question and Answer Flow with you again, but this time they are to write the labels above the words they classify. This will give them practice writing the labels before they are tested on them.

The key to success is to keep students constantly saying the Question and Answer Flows until they know them automatically. Follow the suggestions below for your students to get the greatest benefits from the grammar lessons.

1. Be sure to have the students read each sentence with you, in unison, before classifying it.
2. Make sure students are saying the **questions** and the **answers** with you as each Question and Answer Flow is recited.

ACTIVITY / ASSIGNMENT TIME

(For this activity, you will need 10 sheets of white typing paper and 2 sheets of colored construction paper for each student. Students will use the typing paper to prepare the inside pages of their book. They will use the construction sheets for the cover.) Students will make synonym and antonym books. Give students a copy of the synonyms and antonyms listed in the boxes below. After students have finished all the inside pages of their books, have them put the books together. They should follow the directions listed below.

1. Make a page for each pair of synonyms. (5 inside pages) Print the title "**Synonyms**" at the top of each page, and glue or print one synonym word pair under the "Synonyms" title.
2. For each synonym word pair, find as many examples as possible from newspapers, magazines, catalogs, coloring books, etc. Cut the synonym examples out and glue them in a pleasing arrangement on each corresponding synonym page.
3. Follow the same directions as you work with the antonym word pairs.
4. Arrange the inside pages together in the order that you want them. Then, put the inside pages between the two sheets of construction paper and staple the pages together down the left side to make a book. Number the inside pages. Put the title "My Synonym and Antonym Book" on the front cover and illustrate the cover page. Share your book with family, friends, and relatives.

Synonyms	
1. hats	caps
2. coats	jackets
3. airplanes	jets
4. boats	ships
5. houses	buildings

Antonyms	
1. land	water
2. big	small
3. dogs	cats
4. boys	girls
5. fruits	vegetables

(End of lesson.)

CHAPTER 2   LESSON 4
Objectives: Jingles, Grammar (Practice Sentences), Skill (Five Parts of a Complete Sentence), Practice Exercise, and Activity.

 **JINGLE TIME**

Have students turn to the Jingle Section of their books. The teacher will lead the students in reciting the previously-taught jingles.

 GRAMMAR TIME

Put the Practice Sentences from the box below on the board or on notebook paper. Use these sentences as you practice the concepts that have been taught. For the greatest benefit, students must participate orally with the teacher.

Chapter 2, Practice Sentences for Lesson 4
1. _____ Jimmy shouted.
2. _____ Puppies barked.
3. _____ Crayon broke.

TEACHING SCRIPT FOR PRACTICE SENTENCES

We will classify three different sentences to practice the Question and Answer Flows. We will classify the sentences together. Begin. (*You might have students write the labels above the sentences at this time.*)

Question and Answer Flow for Sentence 1: Jimmy shouted.
1. Who shouted? Jimmy - subject noun (Write SN above *Jimmy*.)   (Since *Jimmy* is a person, we use the subject question *who*.   The subject noun *Jimmy* tells *who* the sentence is about.)
2. What is being said about Jimmy? Jimmy shouted - verb (Write V above *shouted*.)
Classified Sentence: SN   V   Jimmy shouted.

Question and Answer Flow for Sentence 2: Puppies barked.
1. What barked? puppies - subject noun (Write SN above *puppies*.)   (Since *puppies* are animals, we use the subject question *what*.   The subject noun *puppies* tells *what* the sentence is about.)
2. What is being said about puppies? puppies barked - verb (Write V above *barked*.)
Classified Sentence: SN   V   Puppies barked.

CHAPTER 2 LESSON 4 CONTINUED

> **Question and Answer Flow for Sentence 3: Crayon broke.**
>
> 1. What broke? crayon - subject noun (Write SN above *crayon*.)
>   (Since *crayon* is a thing, we use the subject question *what*.
>   The subject noun *crayon* tells *what* the sentence is about.)
> 2. What is being said about crayon? crayon broke - verb (Write V above *broke*.)
>
> **Classified Sentence:** SN   V
>   Crayon broke.

SKILL TIME

<u>*TEACHING SCRIPT FOR THE 5 PARTS OF THE COMPLETE SENTENCE*</u>

Let's recite just the Sentence Jingle again. As you recite the Sentence Jingle, listen for the five parts that make a complete sentence. (*Recite the Sentence Jingle.*) Did you hear the five parts that make a complete sentence when we recited the Sentence Jingle? Of course, you did. Listen carefully as I go over the definition and the crucial parts of a complete sentence.

A **complete sentence** is a group of words that has a subject, a verb, and expresses a complete thought. A complete sentence should also begin with a capital letter and end with an end mark. Since you will be required to know the five parts of a sentence on a definition test later, you will learn the five parts of a sentence the easy way: by reciting the Sentence Jingle during Jingle Time.

Now, listen for the five parts of a sentence as you recite the Sentence Jingle one more time. (*Recite the Sentence Jingle again.*) Now, I want you to recite only the five parts of a sentence. (*Have students recite the section under REMEMBER several times.*)

> **REMEMBER**
> Subject, Verb, Com-plete sense,
> Capital letter, and an end mark, too.
> That's what a sentence is all about!

CHAPTER 2 LESSON 4 CONTINUED

PRACTICE TIME

Have students turn to page 35 in the Practice Section of their book and find Chapter 2, Lesson 4, Practice (1-3). Go over the directions to make sure they understand what to do. Check and discuss the Practices after students have finished. (*Chapter 2, Lesson 4, Practice keys are given below.*)

Chapter 2, Lesson 4, Practice 1: Put each group of words in alphabetical order. Use numbers 1-4 in the blanks to show the order in each column.

Restaurant Words		"A" Words	
2	1. menu	4	5. apple
1	2. chef	3	6. alligator
3	3. table	1	7. afternoon
4	4. waiter	2	8. album

Chapter 2, Lesson 4, Practice 2: Put the letters below in alphabetical order.
   o s i b j p z d   **Key: b, d, i, j, o, p, s, z**

Chapter 2, Lesson 4, Practice 3: Match the definitions. Write the correct letter beside each numbered concept.

H	1. verb question	A.	what
A	2. subject-noun question (thing)	B.	a capital letter
F	3. parts of a complete sentence	C.	verb
D	4. noun	D.	person, place, or thing
G	5. subject-noun question (person)	E.	sentence
B	6. sentences should begin with	F.	subject, verb, complete sense
C	7. tells what the subject does	G.	who
E	8. ends with an end mark	H.	what is being said about

ACTIVITY / ASSIGNMENT TIME

Make a list of nouns that can be found in the house or in the yard around your house. Write the list on paper so that your students can carry this list with them during this activity. (*Make sure the objects are small enough and clean enough for students to pick them up.*) Tell your students that they are going on a scavenger hunt. They are to search the house and yard for these objects and collect them in a paper sack as they find them. At the end, you will discuss how these objects are nouns as you go through your students' treasure bags.

Sample list: rubber band, spoon, leaf, bar of soap, sock, twig, candle, plastic bowl, comb, piece of paper, small rock, pencil, empty bottle, shoe, etc.

(End of lesson.)

Level 2—Shurley English—Homeschool Edition

CHAPTER 2   LESSON 5
Objectives: Jingles, Study, Test, Check, Writing (Journal), State Activity, and Sentence Time.

 **JINGLE TIME**

Have students turn to the Jingle Section of their books. The teacher will lead the students in reciting the previously-taught jingles.

 STUDY TIME

Have students look in the Reference Section of their notebooks to review alphabetizing letters and words.

 TEST TIME

Have students turn to page 81 in the Test Section of their book and find Chapter 2 Test. Go over the directions to make sure they understand what to do. (*Chapter 2 Test keys are given on the next page.*)

 CHECK TIME

After students have finished, check and discuss their test papers. Make sure they understand why their answers are right or wrong. (*For total points, count each required answer as a point.*)

 STATE ACTIVITY TIME

(*Have a recipe box and a package of lined index cards ready for your children to use for this activity.*) Find a map of the United States. Draw or trace the state of Alaska on the blank side of an index card. On the lined side of the card, write the following questions and answers.

1. What is the state on the front of this card? **Alaska**
2. What is the capital of Alaska? **Juneau**
3. What is the postal abbreviation of Alaska? **AK**

Color this state. Use the card to quiz family members, friends, and relatives. You may want to time the responses to your questions.

(End of lesson.)

Level 2—Shurley English—Homeschool Edition

Chapter 2 Test
(Student Page 81)

36 pts

Exercise 1: Classify each sentence.

1. SN   V
   Carpenters worked.

2. SN   V
   Horse trotted.

Exercise 2: Put the letters below in alphabetical order.

1. t d n o z a w p   **Key: (a, d, n, o, p, t, w, z)**

Exercise 3: Put each group of words in alphabetical order. Use numbers 1-4 in the blanks to show the order in each column.

	Winter Words		Plant Words		"R" Words
1	1. coat	2	5. leaf	1	9. rabbit
4	2. snow	4	6. stem	4	10. roll
3	3. mittens	1	7. flower	3	11. right
2	4. ice	3	8. root	2	12. ready

Exercise 4: Identify each pair of words as synonyms or antonyms by putting parentheses ( ) around **syn** or **ant**.

| 1. eager, enthusiastic | **(syn)** ant | 3. impolite, respectful | syn **(ant)** |
| 2. crawl, gallop | syn **(ant)** | 4. tribute, salute | **(syn)** ant |

Exercise 5: Match the definitions. Write the correct letter beside each numbered concept.

G	1. verb question	A.	person, place, or thing
E	2. subject-noun question (thing)	B.	who
D	3. parts of a complete sentence	C.	a capital letter
A	4. noun	D.	subject, verb, complete sense
B	5. subject-noun question (person)	E.	what
C	6. sentences should begin with	F.	sentence
H	7. tells what the subject does	G.	what is being said about
F	8. ends with an end mark	H.	verb

Exercise 6: In your journal, write a paragraph summarizing what you have learned this week.

Level 2 Homeschool Teacher's Manual

Level 2—Shurley English—Homeschool Edition

CHAPTER 2 LESSON 5 CONTINUED

TEACHER INSTRUCTIONS

Use the Question and Answer Flows below for the sentences on the Chapter 2 Test.

Question and Answer Flow for Sentence 1: Carpenters worked.

1. Who worked? carpenters - SN (subject noun)
2. What is being said about carpenters? carpenters worked - V (verb)

Classified Sentence: SN   V
                       Carpenters worked.

Question and Answer Flow for Sentence 2: Horse trotted.

1. What trotted? horse - SN (subject noun)
2. What is being said about horse? horse trotted - V (verb)

Classified Sentence: SN   V
                       Horse trotted.

SENTENCE TIME

Chapter 2, Lesson 5, Sentence: Use colored markers to match each label with the correct sentence part by drawing a line from one to the other. Then, use the labels to arrange the sentence parts into a sentence that you will write on the sentence line below. *(The order of the words in your sentence should be in the same sequence as the vertical list of sentence labels.)* Create other labels and scrambled sentence parts on notebook paper for family members to solve. You may color code the sentence parts. *(See page 109 in the student book.)*

Labels for Order of Sentence	Scrambled Sentence Parts
SN	howled
V	coyotes

Sentence: Coyotes howled.

(End of lesson.)

CHAPTER 3   LESSON 1

Objectives: Jingle (Adverb), Grammar (Introductory Sentences, Adverb), and Vocabulary #1.

 **JINGLE TIME**

Have students turn to the Jingle Section in their books and recite the previously-taught jingles. Then, lead students in reciting the Adverb Jingle below. Practice the new jingle several times until students can recite it smoothly. Emphasize reciting with a rhythm. (*Do not try to explain the new jingle at this time. Just have fun reciting it. Remember, add motions for more fun and laughter.*)

Teacher's Notes: Again, do not spend a large amount of time practicing the new jingles. Students learn the jingles best by spending a small amount of time consistently, **every** day.

Jingle 4: Adverb Jingle
An adverb modifies a verb, adjective, or another adverb.
An adverb asks *How? When? Where?*
To find an adverb: **Go, Ask, Get**.
Where do I **go**? To a verb, adjective, or another adverb.
What do I **ask**? How? When? Where?
What do I **get**? An ADVERB! (Clap) (Clap) That's what!

 GRAMMAR TIME

Put the introductory sentences from the box below on the board. Use these sentences as you go through the new concepts covered in your teaching scripts. For the greatest benefit, students must participate orally with the teacher. (*You might put the introductory sentences on notebook paper if you are doing one-on-one instruction with your students.*)

Chapter 3, Introductory Sentences for Lesson 1
1. Children clapped enthusiastically today.
2. Pony galloped wildly.
3. Flags flew proudly.

TEACHING SCRIPT FOR THE ADVERB

You are learning that jingles give you a lot of information quickly and easily. I will review several things that the Adverb Jingle tells us about the adverb. Listen carefully. **The Adverb Definition:** An adverb modifies a verb, adjective, or another adverb. **The Adverb Questions:** How? When? Where?

CHAPTER 3 LESSON 1 CONTINUED

The adverb definition uses the word *modifies*. The word **modify** means to describe. When the adverb definition says that an adverb modifies a verb, it means that an adverb describes a verb. The abbreviation you will use for an adverb is **Adv**.

You will now learn how to use the adverb definition and the Question and Answer Flow to find the adverbs in sentences. But, first, we will classify the main parts of a sentence, the subject and verb, before we find the adverbs.

Classify Sentence 1: Children clapped enthusiastically today.
Who clapped enthusiastically today? children - subject noun (*Write SN above children.*)
What is being said about children? children clapped - verb (*Write V above clapped.*)

The adverb jingle tells you the adverb definition and the adverb questions. Look at the Adverb Jingle in the Jingle Section on page 3 and repeat the Adverb Jingle with me. (*Repeat the Adverb Jingle with your students again.*) I am going to ask you some questions that will show you how to use the Adverb Jingle to find adverbs. You may look at the Adverb Jingle in your book so you can answer my questions about adverbs.

1. Where do you go to find an adverb? (*to the verb, adjective, or another adverb*)
2. Where do you go **first** to find an adverb? (*to the verb*)
3. What is the verb in Sentence 1? (*clapped*)
4. What do you ask after you go to the verb *clapped*?

    (*one of the adverb questions: how? when? where?*)
5. How do you know which adverb question to ask?

    (*Look at the words around the verb: enthusiastically, today. These words will guide you.*)
6. Which adverb question would you use to find the first adverb in this sentence? (*how?*)

This is how you would ask an adverb question and give an adverb answer in the Question and Answer Flow: **Clapped how? enthusiastically - adverb** (*Write Adv above the word enthusiastically.*)

Look at the sentence again. As you can see, there is another word that needs to be classified. In order to classify this word, you must again ask the questions that you have learned. You will continue this question and answer procedure until all words in the sentence have been identified. That is why we call it the Question and Answer Flow.

Let's go back to the verb and do the Question and Answer Flow for another adverb:
Clapped when? today - adverb (*Write Adv above the word today.*)

I will classify Sentence 1 again, but this time you will classify it with me. I will lead you as we follow the series of questions and answers that I have just demonstrated. Then, we will classify Sentences 2-3.

CHAPTER 3 LESSON 1 CONTINUED

Question and Answer Flow for Sentence 1: Children clapped enthusiastically today.

1. Who clapped enthusiastically today? children - subject noun (Trace over the SN above *children*.)
2. What is being said about children? children clapped - verb (Trace over the V above *clapped*.)
3. Clapped how? enthusiastically - adverb (Trace over the Adv above *enthusiastically*.)
4. Clapped when? today - adverb (Trace over the Adv above *today*.)

Classified Sentence: SN   V   Adv   Adv
                   Children clapped enthusiastically today.

Question and Answer Flow for Sentence 2: Pony galloped wildly.

1. What galloped wildly? pony - subject noun (Write SN above *pony*.)
2. What is being said about pony? pony galloped - verb (Write V above *galloped*.)
3. Galloped how? wildly - adverb (Write Adv above *wildly*.)

Classified Sentence: SN   V   Adv
                   Pony galloped wildly.

Question and Answer Flow for Sentence 3: Flags flew proudly.

1. What flew proudly? flags - subject noun (Write the SN above *flags*.)
2. What is being said about flags? flags flew - verb (Write V above *flew*.)
3. Flew how? proudly - adverb (Write Adv above *proudly*.)

Classified Sentence: SN   V   Adv
                   Flags flew proudly.

TEACHER INSTRUCTIONS

If this is the first year for Shurley English, have students recite the Question and Answer Flows for the <u>first</u> and <u>second</u> sentences with you again, but this time they are to trace the labels on their desks with the first three fingers of their writing hand as they classify. This is excellent practice to develop dexterity and to learn at a faster pace. Next, have students classify the <u>third</u> sentence on a piece of paper. This will give them practice writing the labels before they are tested on them.

VOCABULARY TIME

Assign Chapter 3, Vocabulary Words #1 on page 6 in the Reference Section for students to define in their Vocabulary notebooks. Tell students they are to use a dictionary or thesaurus to look up the meanings of the vocabulary words.

Chapter 3, Vocabulary Words #1
(magnificent, splendid, brisk, sluggish)

(End of lesson.)

Level 2—Shurley English—Homeschool Edition

CHAPTER 3   LESSON 2
Objectives: Jingles, Grammar (Practice Sentences), Skill (A/An Choices), Practice Exercise, and Vocabulary #2.

 **JINGLE TIME**

Have students turn to the Jingle Section of their books. The teacher will lead the students in reciting the previously-taught jingles.

 GRAMMAR TIME

Put the Practice Sentences from the box below on the board or on notebook paper. Use these sentences as you practice the concepts that have been taught. For the greatest benefit, students must participate orally with the teacher.

Chapter 3, Practice Sentences for Lesson 2
1. _____ Soldiers saluted respectfully.
2. _____ Frogs jumped away hastily.
3. _____ Girls giggled nervously.

TEACHING SCRIPT FOR PRACTICE SENTENCES

We will classify three different sentences to practice adverbs as we add them to the Question and Answer Flows. We will classify the sentences together. Begin. (*You might have students write the labels above the sentences at this time.*)

Question and Answer Flow for Sentence 1: Soldiers saluted respectfully.
1. Who saluted respectfully? soldiers - subject noun (Write SN above *soldiers*.)
2. What is being said about soldiers? soldiers saluted - verb (Write V above *saluted*.)
3. Saluted how? respectfully - adverb (Write Adv above *respectfully*.)
Classified Sentence: SN   V   Adv
Soldiers saluted respectfully.

CHAPTER 3 LESSON 2 CONTINUED

Question and Answer Flow for Sentence 2: Frogs jumped away hastily.

1. What jumped away hastily? frogs - subject noun (Write SN above *frogs*.)
2. What is being said about frogs? frogs jumped - verb (Write V above *jumped*.)
3. Jumped where? away - adverb (Write Adv above *away*.)
4. Jumped how? hastily - adverb (Write Adv above *hastily*.)

Classified Sentence: SN   V   Adv   Adv
                              Frogs jumped away hastily.

Question and Answer Flow for Sentence 3: Girls giggled nervously.

1. Who giggled nervously? girls - subject noun (Write SN above *girls*.)
2. What is being said about girls? girls giggled - verb (Write V above *giggled*.)
3. Giggled how? nervously - adverb (Write Adv above *nervously*.)

Classified Sentence: SN   V   Adv
                              Girls giggled nervously.

 SKILL TIME

<u>TEACHING SCRIPT FOR A / AN CHOICES</u>

I am going to introduce how to use the words *a* and *an* correctly. This is an easy concept, but you need to practice in order to know it well. Look at Reference 6 on page 11 in your Reference Section. There are two rules at the top of the reference box. Follow along as I read these rules for choosing *a* or *an*. (*Read the information in the reference box below.*)

Reference 6: A and An Choices
Rule 1: Use the word **a** when the next word begins with a consonant sound. (*Example: a delicious orange.*)
Rule 2: Use the word **an** when the next word begins with a vowel sound. (*Example: an orange.*)
Sample Sentences: Write **a** or **an** in the blanks.
1. Mary was __**an**__ artist.   3. Thomas sang __**a**__ beautiful song.
2. Mary was __**a**__ talented artist.   4. Thomas sang __**an**__ amazing song.

Now, we will discuss the sample sentences in the reference box. First, we should always read the directions very carefully before we start the exercise. The directions say to write ***a*** or ***an*** in the blanks.

Level 2—Shurley English—Homeschool Edition

CHAPTER 3 LESSON 2 CONTINUED

Look at number 1. Before we can choose *a* or *an* to put in the blank, we have to look at the word that comes next. Does *artist* start with a consonant or vowel sound? (*vowel sound*) The rule says to use the word *an* before words that begin with a vowel sound. We will write the word *an* in the blank before the word *artist*.

Look at number 2. Does the word *talented* start with a consonant or vowel sound? (*consonant sound*) The rule says to use the word *a* before words that begin with a consonant sound. We will write the word *a* in the blank before the word *talented*.

Look at number 3. Does the word *beautiful* start with a consonant or a vowel sound? (*consonant sound*) The rule says to use the word *a* before words that begin with a consonant sound. We will write the word *a* in the blank before the word *beautiful*.

Look at number 4. Does the word *amazing* start with a consonant or a vowel sound? (*vowel sound*) The rule says to use the word *an* before words that begin with a vowel sound. We will write the word *an* in the blank before the word *amazing*.

 PRACTICE TIME

Have students turn to page 36 in the Practice Section of their book and find Chapter 3, Lesson 2, Practice. Go over the directions to make sure they understand what to do. Check and discuss the Practice after students have finished. (*Chapter 3, Lesson 2, Practice key is given below.*)

Chapter 3, Lesson 2, Practice: Write *a* or *an* in the blanks.

1. The car had **an** alarm.
2. The ship dodged **an** iceberg.
3. Stacy baked **a** pecan pie.
4. Joe caught **a** cricket.
5. My truck has **an** oil leak.
6. Amanda chased **a** rabbit.
7. **an** owner
8. **a** guitar
9. **an** injury
10. **a** whisker
11. **an** author
12. **a** balloon

 VOCABULARY TIME

Assign Chapter 3, Vocabulary Words **#2** on page 6 in the Reference Section for students to define in their Vocabulary notebooks. Tell students they are to use a dictionary or thesaurus to look up the meanings of the vocabulary words.

Chapter 3, Vocabulary Words #2
(cautious, hasty, fly, soar)

(End of lesson.)

Level 2—Shurley English—Homeschool Edition

CHAPTER 3   LESSON 3
Objectives: Jingle (Adjective), Grammar (Introductory Sentences, Adjective), Practice Exercise, and Activity.

 **JINGLE TIME**

Have students turn to the Jingle Section in their books and recite the previously-taught jingles. Then, lead students in reciting the Adjective Jingle below. Practice the new jingle several times until students can recite it smoothly. Emphasize reciting with a rhythm. Students and teacher should be together! (*Do not try to explain the new jingles at this time. Just have fun reciting the jingles. Remember, add motions for more fun and laughter.*)

Jingle 5: Adjective Jingle
An adjective modifies a noun or pronoun.
An adjective asks *What kind? Which one? How many?*
To find an adjective: **Go, Ask, Get**.
Where do I **go**? To a noun or pronoun.
What do I **ask**? What kind? Which one? How many?
What do I **get**? An ADJECTIVE! (Clap) (Clap) That's what!

 GRAMMAR TIME

Put the introductory sentences from the box below on the board. Use these sentences as you go through the new concepts covered in your teaching scripts. For the greatest benefit, students must participate orally with the teacher. (*You might put the introductory sentences on notebook paper if you are doing one-on-one instruction with your students.*)

Chapter 3, Introductory Sentences for Lesson 3
1. Eight young soldiers saluted respectfully.
2. Three frightened frogs jumped away hastily.
3. Silly young girls giggled nervously.

<u>TEACHING SCRIPT FOR THE ADJECTIVE</u>

Remember, jingles give you a lot of information quickly and easily. I will review several things that the Adjective Jingle tells us about the adjective. **The Adjective Definition:** An adjective modifies a noun or pronoun. **The Adjective Questions:** What kind? Which one? How many?

Level 2—Shurley English—Homeschool Edition

CHAPTER 3 LESSON 3 CONTINUED

The adjective definition also uses the word *modifies*. The word **modify** means to describe. When the adjective definition says that an adjective modifies a noun, it means that an adjective describes a noun. The abbreviation you will use for an adjective is **Adj**.

You will now learn how to use the adjective definition and the Question and Answer Flow to find the adjectives in sentences. But first, we will classify the subject, verb, and adverb before we find the adjectives.

Classify Sentence 1: Eight young soldiers saluted respectfully.
Who saluted respectfully? soldiers - subject noun (*Write SN above* **soldiers**.)
What is being said about soldiers? soldiers saluted - verb (*Write V above* **saluted**.)
Saluted how? respectfully - adverb (*Write Adv above the word* **respectfully**.)

We will use the same procedure to find the adjectives. The Adjective Jingle tells you the adjective definition and the adjective questions. Look at the Adjective Jingle in the Jingle Section and repeat the Adjective Jingle with me. (*Repeat the Adjective Jingle with your students again.*)

I am going to ask you some questions that will show you how to use the Adjective Jingle to find adjectives. You may look at the Adjective Jingle in your book so you can answer my questions about adjectives.

1. Where do you go to find an adjective? (*to a noun or pronoun*)
2. Where do you go **first** to find an adjective? (*to the subject noun*)
3. What is the subject noun in Sentence 1? (*soldiers*)
4. What do you ask after you go to the subject noun *soldiers*?
   (*one of the adjective questions: what kind? which one? how many?*)
5. How do you know which adjective question to ask?
   (*Look at the word or words around the noun: eight, young. These words will guide you.*)
6. Which adjective questions would you use to find an adjective in this sentence?
   (*What kind? How many?*)

This is how you would ask an adjective question and give the adjective answer in the Adjective Question and Answer Flow: **What kind of soldiers? young - adjective** (*Write Adj above the word* **young**.)

Look at the sentence again. As you can see, there is another word that needs to be classified. In order to classify this word, you must again ask the questions that you have learned. You will continue this question and answer procedure until all words in the sentence have been identified. That is why we call it the Question and Answer Flow.

Let's go back to the noun and do the Question and Answer Flow for another adjective:
How many soldiers? eight - adjective (*Write Adj above the word* **eight**.)

CHAPTER 3 LESSON 3 CONTINUED

I will classify Sentence 1 again, but this time you will classify it with me. I will lead you as we follow the series of questions and answers that I have just demonstrated. Then, we will classify Sentences 2-3.

Question and Answer Flow for Sentence 1: Eight young soldiers saluted respectfully.

1. Who saluted respectfully? soldiers - subject noun (Trace over the SN above *soldiers*.)
2. What is being said about soldiers? soldiers saluted - verb (Trace over the V above *saluted*.)
3. Saluted how? respectfully - adverb (Trace over the Adv above *respectfully*.)
4. What kind of soldiers? young - adjective (Trace over the Adj above *young*.)
5. How many soldiers? eight - adjective (Trace over the Adj above *eight*.)

Classified Sentence: Adj Adj SN V Adv
Eight young soldiers saluted respectfully.

Question and Answer Flow for Sentence 2: Three frightened frogs jumped away hastily.

1. What jumped away hastily? frogs - subject noun (Write SN above *frogs*.)
2. What is being said about frogs? frogs jumped - verb (Write V above *jumped*.)
3. Jumped where? away - adverb (Write Adv above *away*.)
4. Jumped how? hastily - adverb (Write Adv above *hastily*.)
5. What kind of frogs? frightened - adjective (Write Adj above *frightened*.)
6. How many frogs? three - adjective (Write Adj above *three*.)

Classified Sentence: Adj Adj SN V Adv Adv
Three frightened frogs jumped away hastily.

Question and Answer Flow for Sentence 3: Silly young girls giggled nervously.

1. Who giggled nervously? girls - subject noun (Write SN above *girls*.)
2. What is being said about girls? girls giggled - verb (Write V above *giggled*.)
3. Giggled how? nervously - adverb (Write Adv above *nervously*.)
4. What kind of girls? young - adjective (Write Adj above *young*.)
5. What kind of girls? silly - adjective (Write Adj above *silly*.)

Classified Sentence: Adj Adj SN V Adv
Silly young girls giggled nervously.

Level 2—Shurley English—Homeschool Edition

CHAPTER 3 LESSON 3 CONTINUED

 PRACTICE TIME

Have students turn to page 36 in the Practice Section of their book and find Chapter 3, Lesson 3, Practice *(1-2)*. Go over the directions to make sure they understand what to do. Check and discuss the Practices after students have finished. (*Chapter 3, Lesson 3, Practice keys are given below.*)

Chapter 3, Lesson 3, Practice 1: Match the definitions. Write the correct letter beside each numbered concept.

B	1. sentences should begin with	A.	verb
C	2. adjective modifies	B.	capital letter
H	3. verb question	C.	noun or pronoun
A	4. tells what the subject does	D.	person, place, or thing
G	5. subject-noun question (thing)	E.	who
F	6. parts of a complete sentence	F.	subject, verb, complete sense
D	7. noun	G.	what
E	8. subject-noun question (person)	H.	what is being said about
I	9. adverb modifies	I.	verb, adjective, or adverb

Chapter 3, Lesson 3, Practice 2: Write *a* or *an* in the blanks.

1. Alex took **a** bath.
2. Sue bought **an** outfit.
3. Mother picked **an** iris.
4. I ate **a** cup of yogurt.
5. Fred visited **an** old museum.
6. Laura has **a** headache.
7. **a** boat
8. **a** freckle
9. **an** owl
10. **a** cloud
11. **an** insect
12. **an** eagle

 ACTIVITY / ASSIGNMENT TIME

Cut different colors of construction paper into 16 small squares. (Sticky notes would be ideal for this activity.) Write the word "A" on eight pieces and "An" on the other eight pieces. Double roll scotch tape and place one piece of the tape on the back of each square. Place the squares upside down (with the tape side up) on a desk or table and let your student choose one square.

The rules of this game are simple. Students must choose a label and search the house for a noun object to correspond with the label. For instance, if students choose an "A" label, then they must search for an object that begins with a consonant sound (such as: book, telephone, rug, soap, etc.). They will then place their "A" label on that object and return for another label. If they choose an "An" label, then they must find a noun object that begins with a vowel sound (such as: apple, umbrella, aluminum foil, oatmeal, etc.). They will then place their "An" label on that object and return for another label.

This process will continue until all labels have been used. Once students have had time to practice this game, you might time them to see how quickly they can finish. Encourage students to choose different nouns each time.

<u>Variation</u>: Students could write "a" or "an" on objects in coloring books, old magazines, etc.

(End of lesson.)

CHAPTER 3   LESSON 4

Objectives: Jingles, Grammar (Practice Sentences), Skill (Parts of Speech), and Practice Exercise.

 **JINGLE TIME**

Have students turn to the Jingle Section of their books. The teacher will lead the students in reciting the previously-taught jingles.

 GRAMMAR TIME

Put the Practice Sentences from the box below on the board or on notebook paper. Use these sentences as you practice the concepts that have been taught. For the greatest benefit, students must participate orally with the teacher.

Chapter 3, Practice Sentences for Lesson 4
1. _____ Two magnificent eagles flew effortlessly.
2. _____ Four strong gorillas advanced cautiously.
3. _____ Three suspicious policemen stepped cautiously inside.

TEACHING SCRIPT FOR PRACTICE SENTENCES

We will classify three different sentences to practice the grammar concepts in the Question and Answer Flows. We will classify the sentences together. Begin. (*You might have students write the labels above the sentences at this time.*)

Question and Answer Flow for Sentence 1: Two magnificent eagles flew effortlessly.
1. What flew effortlessly? eagles - SN (subject noun)   4. What kind of eagles? magnificent - Adj (adjective)
2. What is being said about eagles? eagles flew - V (verb)   5. How many eagles? two - Adj (adjective)
3. Flew how? effortlessly - Adv (adverb)
Classified Sentence: Adj   Adj   SN   V   Adv
Two magnificent eagles flew effortlessly.

CHAPTER 3 LESSON 4 CONTINUED

> **Question and Answer Flow for Sentence 2: Four strong gorillas advanced cautiously.**
>
> 1. What advanced cautiously? gorillas - SN (subject noun)
> 2. What is being said about gorillas?
>   gorillas advanced - V (verb)
> 3. Advanced how? cautiously - Adv (Adverb)
> 4. What kind of gorillas? strong - Adj (adjective)
> 5. How many gorillas? four - Adj (adjective)
>
> **Classified Sentence:**   Adj   Adj   SN   V   Adv
>   Four strong gorillas advanced cautiously.

> **Question and Answer Flow for Sentence 3: Three suspicious policemen stepped cautiously inside.**
>
> 1. Who stepped cautiously inside? policemen - SN (subject noun)
> 2. What is being said about policemen?
>   policemen stepped - V (verb)
> 3. Stepped how? cautiously - Adv (adverb)
> 4. Stepped where? inside - Adv (adverb)
> 5. What kind of policemen?
>   suspicious - Adj (adjective)
> 6. How many policemen? three - Adj (adjective)
>
> **Classified Sentence:**   Adj   Adj   SN   V   Adv   Adv
>   Three suspicious policemen stepped cautiously inside.

SKILL TIME

TEACHING SCRIPT FOR THE PARTS OF SPEECH

Vocabulary is important in every subject you study. Vocabulary helps you communicate in any given area. English is no different. In fact, there are several areas in English where vocabulary is important. Grammar is the vocabulary for the sentences used in writing. We can talk to each other about writing and editing when we know how to talk about the sentences we write and how we put them together in paragraphs.

We will now discuss the eight parts of speech. Do you know that all words in the English language have been put into eight groups called the **Parts of Speech**? How a word is used in a sentence determines its part of speech. The sentences you have been classifying are made from four parts of speech. Do you know the names of these four parts of speech? *(noun, verb, adjective, and adverb)*

These first four parts of speech are easy to remember because you are using them every day. Make sure you remember them because you will also have them on your test. You will learn the other parts of speech later. *(Have students repeat the four parts of speech four or five times together, orally, and in a rhythmic fashion.)*

Level 2—Shurley English—Homeschool Edition

CHAPTER 3 LESSON 4 CONTINUED

 PRACTICE TIME

Have students turn to pages 36 and 37 in the Practice Section of their books and find Chapter 3, Lesson 4, Practice (*1-3*). Go over the directions to make sure they understand what to do. Check and discuss the Practices after students have finished. (*Chapter 3, Lesson 4, Practice keys are given below.*)

Chapter 3, Lesson 4, Practice 1: Name the four parts of speech that you have studied. (*You may use abbreviations.*)
(The order of the answers may vary.)

1. __noun__   2. __verb__   3. __adjective__   4. __adverb__

Chapter 3, Lesson 4, Practice 2: Match the definitions. Write the correct letter beside each numbered concept.

__C__	1. sentences should begin with	A.	noun or pronoun
__A__	2. adjective modifies	B.	verb
__E__	3. verb question	C.	capital letter
__B__	4. tells what the subject does	D.	person, place, or thing
__G__	5. subject-noun question (thing)	E.	what is being said about
__H__	6. parts of a complete sentence	F.	verb, adjective, or adverb
__D__	7. noun	G.	what
__I__	8. subject-noun question (person)	H.	subject, verb, complete sense
__F__	9. adverb modifies	I.	who

Chapter 3, Lesson 4, Practice 3: Write *a* or *an* in the blanks.

1. Henry was __a__ poet.   4. He caught __a__ fish.   7. __a__ house   10. __a__ pickle
2. Beth found __an__ acorn.   5. She ate __an__ olive.   8. __a__ diamond   11. __an__ almond
3. They lived in __an__ igloo. 6. We carved __a__ pumpkin. 9. __an__ eyelash 12. __an__ ocean

(End of lesson.)

Level 2—Shurley English—Homeschool Edition

CHAPTER 3   LESSON 5

Objectives: Jingles, Study, Test, Check, Writing (Journal), State Activity, and Sentence Time.

 JINGLE TIME

Have students turn to the Jingle Section of their books. The teacher will lead the students in reciting the previously-taught jingles.

 STUDY TIME

Have students study the vocabulary words in their vocabulary notebooks. Remind students that any vocabulary word in their notebooks could be on their test. Also, have students study any of the skills in the different sections that they need to review.

 TEST TIME

Have students turn to page 82 in the Test Section of their books and find Chapter 3 Test. Go over the directions to make sure they understand what to do. (*Chapter 3 Test key is on the next page.*)

 CHECK TIME

After students have finished, check and discuss their test papers. Make sure they understand why their answers are right or wrong. (*For total points, count each required answer as a point.*)

 STATE ACTIVITY TIME

(*Have a recipe box and a package of lined index cards ready for your children to use for this activity.*) Find a map of the United States. Draw or trace the state of Arizona on the blank side of an index card. On the lined side of the card, write the following questions and answers.

1. What is the state on the front of this card? **Arizona**
2. What is the capital of Arizona? **Phoenix**
3. What is the postal abbreviation of Arizona? **AZ**

Color this state. Use the card to quiz family members, friends, and relatives. You may want to time the responses to your questions. Scatter your cards and see how long it takes you to put them in alphabetical order. For a higher level of difficulty, see if you can alphabetize your cards only by the picture of each state.

Level 2—Shurley English—Homeschool Edition

Chapter 3 Test
(Student Page 82)

41 pts

Exercise 1: Classify each sentence.

       Adj   Adj   SN   V   Adv   Adv
1. Four brown squirrels looked cautiously around.

       Adj   SN   V   Adv
2. Six firemen worked carefully.

Exercise 2: Name the four parts of speech that you have studied. (*You may use abbreviations.*)
(The order of the answers may vary.)

1. __noun__   2. __verb__   3. __adjective__   4. __adverb__

Exercise 3: Identify each pair of words as synonyms or antonyms by putting parentheses ( ) around *syn* or *ant*.

1. splendid, magnificent	**(syn)** ant	3. brisk, sluggish	syn **(ant)**	5. enthusiastic, eager	**(syn)** ant
2. impolite, respectful	syn **(ant)**	4. soar, fly	**(syn)** ant	6. hasty, cautious	syn **(ant)**

Exercise 4: Write *a* or *an* in the blanks.

1. Molly saw __a__ squirrel today.   4. She is __a__ nurse.   7. __an__ organ   10. __a__ rabbit

2. He was __an__ astronaut.   5. We have __an__ easy job.   8. __a__ sack   11. __an__ outlet

3. They own __an__ ostrich.   6. He wants __a__ trumpet.   9. __an__ item   12. __a__ bath

Exercise 5: Match the definitions. Write the correct letter beside each numbered concept.

__I__	1. sentences should begin with	A.	subject, verb, complete sense
__C__	2. adjective modifies	B.	verb, adjective, or adverb
__F__	3. verb question	C.	noun or pronoun
__D__	4. tells what the subject does	D.	verb
__H__	5. subject-noun question (thing)	E.	who
__A__	6. parts of a complete sentence	F.	what is being said about
__G__	7. noun	G.	person, place, or thing
__E__	8. subject-noun question (person)	H.	what
__B__	9. adverb modifies	I.	capital letter

Exercise 6: In your journal, write a paragraph summarizing what you have learned this week.

Level 2—Shurley English—Homeschool Edition

CHAPTER 3 LESSON 5 CONTINUED

TEACHER INSTRUCTIONS

Use the Question and Answer Flows below for the sentences on the Chapter 3 Test.

Question and Answer Flow for Sentence 1: Four brown squirrels looked cautiously around.

1. What looked cautiously around? squirrels - SN (subject noun)
2. What is being said about squirrels? squirrels looked - V (verb)
3. Looked how? cautiously - Adv (adverb)
4. Looked where? around - Adv (adverb)
5. What kind of squirrels? brown - Adj (adjective)
6. How many squirrels? four - Adj (adjective)

Classified Sentence: Adj   Adj   SN   V   Adv   Adv
Four brown squirrels looked cautiously around.

Question and Answer Flow for Sentence 2: Six firemen worked carefully.

1. Who worked carefully? firemen - SN (subject noun)
2. What is being said about firemen? firemen worked - V (verb)
3. Worked how? carefully - Adv (adverb)
4. How many firemen? six - Adj (adjective)

Classified Sentence: Adj   SN   V   Adv
Six firemen worked carefully.

 SENTENCE TIME

Chapter 3, Lesson 5, Sentence: Use colored markers to match each label with the correct sentence part by drawing a line from one to the other. Then, use the labels to arrange the sentence parts into a sentence that you will write on the sentence line below. *(The order of the words in your sentence should be in the same sequence as the vertical list of sentence labels.)* Create other labels and scrambled sentence parts on notebook paper for family members to solve. You may color code the sentence parts. *(See page 109 in the student book.)*

Labels for Order of Sentence	Scrambled Sentence Parts
Adj	today
Adj	landed
SN	jumbo
V	jets
Adv	big
Adv	safely

Sentence: Big jumbo jets landed safely today.

(End of lesson.)

CHAPTER 4   LESSON 1

Objectives: Jingle (Article Adjective), Grammar (Introductory Sentences, Article Adjective), and Vocabulary #1.

 **JINGLE TIME**

Have students turn to the Jingle Section in their books and recite the previously-taught jingles. Then, lead students in reciting the Article Adjective Jingle below. Practice the new jingle several times until students can recite it smoothly. Emphasize reciting with a rhythm. Students and teacher should be together! (*Do not try to explain the new jingle. Just have fun reciting it. Add motions for more fun and laughter.*)

Jingle 6: Article Adjective Jingle
We are the article adjectives, Teeny, tiny adjectives: **A, AN, THE - A, AN, THE.** We are called article adjectives and noun markers; We are memorized and used every day. So, if you spot us, you can mark us With the label A. We are the article adjectives, Teeny, tiny adjectives: **A, AN, THE - A, AN, THE.**

 GRAMMAR TIME

Put the introductory sentences from the box below on the board. Use these sentences as you go through the new concepts covered in your teaching scripts. For the greatest benefit, students must participate orally with the teacher. (*You might put the introductory sentences on notebook paper if you are doing one-on-one instruction with your students.*)

Chapter 4, Introductory Sentences for Lesson 1
1. A lively little pony galloped wildly yesterday. 2. The beautiful American flags flew proudly. 3. The huge white clouds moved briskly away.

TEACHING SCRIPT FOR THE ARTICLE ADJECTIVE

Today, we have another adjective to identify. This new adjective is known as the article adjective. There are only three article adjectives. Let's recite the Article Adjective Jingle again to learn more about the article adjectives. (*Recite the Article Adjective Jingle with your students.*)

CHAPTER 4 LESSON 1 CONTINUED

Article Adjectives are the three most commonly-used adjectives. The three article adjectives are *a*, *an*, and *the*. Everyone recite the words *article adjective* three times. (*article adjective, article adjective, article adjective*) Article adjectives are sometimes called noun markers because they tell that a noun is close by. The article adjectives must be <u>memorized</u> because there are no questions in the Question and Answer Flow to find the article adjectives. Article adjectives are labeled with an **A**. This is how you would identify an article adjective in the Question and Answer Flow: **The - article adjective** (*Write **A** above the word **The**.*) Now, we will classify a set of sentences together to practice the new concepts. Begin.

Question and Answer Flow for Sentence 1: A lively little pony galloped wildly yesterday.

1. What galloped wildly yesterday? pony - SN (subject noun)
2. What is being said about pony? pony galloped - V (verb)
3. Galloped how? wildly - Adv (adverb)
4. Galloped when? yesterday - Adv (adverb)
5. What kind of pony? little - Adj (adjective)
6. What kind of pony? lively - Adj (adjective)
7. A - A (*Say: Article Adjective.*)

Classified Sentence: A   Adj   Adj   SN   V   Adv   Adv
A lively little pony galloped wildly yesterday.

Question and Answer Flow for Sentence 2: The beautiful American flags flew proudly.

1. What flew proudly? flags - SN (subject noun)
2. What is being said about flags? flags flew - V (verb)
3. Flew how? proudly - Adv (adverb)
4. What kind of flags? American - Adj (adjective)
5. What kind flags? beautiful - Adj (adjective)
6. The - A (*Say: Article Adjective.*)

Classified Sentence: A   Adj   Adj   SN   V   Adv
The beautiful American flags flew proudly.

Question and Answer Flow for Sentence 3: The huge white clouds moved briskly away.

1. What moved briskly away? clouds - SN (subject noun)
2. What is being said about clouds? clouds moved - V (verb)
3. Moved how? briskly - Adv (adverb)
4. Moved where? away - Adv (adverb)
5. What kind of clouds? white - Adj (adjective)
6. What kind of clouds? huge - Adj (adjective)
7. The - A (*Say: Article Adjective.*)

Classified Sentence: A   Adj   Adj   SN   V   Adv   Adv
The huge white clouds moved briskly away.

VOCABULARY TIME

Assign Chapter 4, Vocabulary Words **#1** on page 6 in the Reference Section for students to define in their Vocabulary notebooks. Tell students they are to use a dictionary or thesaurus to look up the meanings of the vocabulary words.

Chapter 4, Vocabulary Words #1
(clumsy, graceful, often, frequent)

(End of lesson.)

Level 2—Shurley English—Homeschool Edition

CHAPTER 4   LESSON 2

Objectives: Jingles, Grammar (Practice Sentences), Skill (Three Kinds of Sentences), Practice Exercise, and Vocabulary #2.

 **JINGLE TIME**

Have students turn to the Jingle Section of their books. The teacher will lead the students in reciting the previously-taught jingles.

 GRAMMAR TIME

Put the Practice Sentences from the box below on the board or on notebook paper. Use these sentences as you practice the concepts that have been taught. For the greatest benefit, students must participate orally with the teacher.

Chapter 4, Practice Sentences for Lesson 2
1. _____ The pretty little girl danced gracefully around.
2. _____ The giant blue kite soared high yesterday.
3. _____ The two unhappy puppies barked frequently today.

TEACHING SCRIPT FOR PRACTICE SENTENCES

We will classify three different sentences to practice the new concepts in the Question and Answer Flows. We will classify the sentences together. Begin. (*You might have students write the labels above the sentences at this time.*)

Teacher's Notes: At this time, your manual will no longer have the entire name written out for each part of speech used in the Question and Answer Flow. Instead of *adverb*, you will see **Adv**. You will continue to say *adverb* even though you see only the abbreviation **Adv**. You will say *subject noun* whenever you see the abbreviation **SN**. Always say *verb* whenever you see the abbreviation **V**, etc.

Question and Answer Flow for Sentence 1: The pretty little girl danced gracefully around.
1. Who danced gracefully around? girl - SN   5. What kind of girl? little - Adj
2. What is being said about girl? girl danced - V   6. What kind of girl? pretty - Adj
3. Danced how? gracefully - Adv   7. The - A
4. Danced where? around - Adv
A   Adj   Adj   SN   V   Adv   Adv
Classified Sentence: The pretty little girl danced gracefully around.

CHAPTER 4 LESSON 2 CONTINUED

Question and Answer Flow for Sentence 2: The giant blue kite soared high yesterday.

1. What soared high yesterday? kite - SN
2. What is being said about kite? kite soared - V
3. Soared how? high - Adv
4. Soared when? yesterday - Adv
5. What kind of kite? blue - Adj
6. What kind of kite? giant - Adj
7. The - A

```
                    A  Adj  Adj  SN   V    Adv   Adv
Classified Sentence:  The giant blue kite soared high yesterday.
```

Question and Answer Flow for Sentence 3: The two unhappy puppies barked frequently today.

1. What barked frequently today? puppies - SN
2. What is being said about puppies? puppies barked - V
3. Barked how? frequently - Adv
4. Barked when? today - Adv
5. What kind of puppies? unhappy - Adj
6. How many puppies? two - Adj
7. The - A

```
                    A  Adj   Adj    SN     V     Adv     Adv
Classified Sentence:  The two unhappy puppies barked frequently today.
```

Teacher's Notes: <u>Options Available for Classifying Sentences</u>:

- **Option 1:** If this is your student's first year in Shurley English, the program should stay teacher-student oriented. Students should classify all Introductory and Practice Sentences with the teacher to reinforce the new concepts.

- **Option 2:** If your student is experiencing no difficulty with the Practice Sentences, allow him/her to classify them independently on notebook paper. Use the Practice Sentence keys in the teacher's manual to check student's practice work.

- **Note:** Practice Booklets and Practice CDs are available as an alternative to putting the Introductory and Practice Sentences on the board or notebook paper. These booklets and CDs are supplemental and can be purchased separately.

I want you to look at Reference 7 on page 12 in the Reference Section of your book. You are given a Question and Answer Flow as an example so it will be easy for you to study. Let's read it together. Remember, we always begin by reading the sentence. (*Read and discuss the Question and Answer Flow in the reference box on the next page with your students.*)

CHAPTER 4 LESSON 2 CONTINUED

Reference 7: Question and Answer Flow Sentence
Question and Answer Flow Sentence: The three young lions roared loudly.
1. What roared loudly? lions - SN
2. What is being said about lions? lions roared - V
3. Roared how? loudly - Adv
4. What kind of lions? young - Adj
5. How many lions? three - Adj
6. The - A
Classified Sentence: A   Adj   Adj   SN   V   Adv The three young lions roared loudly.

SKILL TIME

TEACHING SCRIPT FOR THREE KINDS OF SENTENCES

In Level 3, there are four kinds of sentences that are introduced, but in this level, we will study only three of them. They are declarative, interrogative, and exclamatory. Let's recite these three kinds of sentences together five times. Go. (*Have your students recite "declarative, interrogative,* and *exclamatory" with you at least five times. This will help them remember the vocabulary necessary for discussing kinds of sentences.*)

These sentences each have a purpose: to tell, to ask, or to show strong feeling. Now, you will learn more about these three kinds of sentences. Look at Reference 8 on page 12 in the Reference Section of your book. (*Read and discuss the information in the left portion of the reference box below with your students.*)

Reference 8: Three Kinds of Sentences and the End Mark Flows	

1. A **declarative** sentence makes a statement.
   It is labeled with a **D**.
   Example: Beth looked hungrily at the cookies.
   (Period, statement, declarative sentence)
	Directions: Read each sentence, recite the end-mark flow in parentheses, and put the end mark and the abbreviation for the sentence type in the blank at the end of each sentence.

2. An **interrogative** sentence asks a question.
   It is labeled with an **Int**.
   Example: Did you swim in the ocean?
   (Question mark, question, interrogative sentence)
	1. Sarah collects stamps **. D**
	(*Period, statement, declarative sentence*)
	
	2. How old are you **? Int**
	(*Question mark, question, interrogative sentence*)

3. An **exclamatory** sentence expresses strong feeling.
   It is labeled with an **E**.
   Example: That huge tree fell on his garage!
   (Exclamation point, strong feeling, exclamatory sentence)
	3. Our team won the race **! E**
	(*Exclamation point, strong feeling, exclamatory sentence*)

Level 2—Shurley English—Homeschool Edition

CHAPTER 4 LESSON 2 CONTINUED

Go to the shaded portion in the top right corner of your reference box. Follow along as I read the directions. Then, I will show you how to identify each sentence by reciting the end-mark flow. Remember, the end-mark flow identifies three things: the punctuation mark, the definition of the sentence, and the kind of sentence. (*Read the examples with your students and recite the end-mark flow that is provided in parentheses.*)

 PRACTICE TIME

Have students turn to pages 37 and 38 in the Practice Section of their book and find the skills under Chapter 4, Lesson 2, Practice *(1-3)*. Go over the directions to make sure they understand what to do. Check and discuss the Practices after students have finished. (*Chapter 4, Lesson 2, Practice keys are given below.*)

Chapter 4, Lesson 2, Practice 1: Put the end mark and the abbreviation for each kind of sentence in the blanks below.

1. Did you see the game last night   ? Int
2. That huge tree branch fell on my new car   ! E
3. Stephanie ate a hamburger for lunch   . D

Chapter 4, Lesson 2, Practice 2: Match the definitions. Write the correct letter beside each numbered concept.

A	1. expresses strong feeling	A.	exclamatory sentence
I	2. makes a statement	B.	interrogative sentence
C	3. adjective modifies	C.	noun or pronoun
H	4. article adjectives can be called	D.	verb, adjective, or adverb
E	5. subject question	E.	who or what
B	6. asks a question	F.	person, place, or thing
F	7. noun	G.	verb
G	8. tells what the subject does	H.	noun markers
D	9. adverb modifies	I.	declarative sentence

Chapter 4, Lesson 2, Practice 3: On notebook paper, write a sentence to demonstrate each of these three kinds of sentences: (1) Declarative, (2) Interrogative, and (3) Exclamatory. Write the correct punctuation and the abbreviation that identifies it at the end. Use these abbreviations: **D, Int, E.**

 VOCABULARY TIME

Assign Chapter 4, Vocabulary Words **#2** on page 6 in the Reference Section for students to define in their Vocabulary notebooks. Tell students they are to use a dictionary or thesaurus to look up the meanings of the vocabulary words.

Chapter 4, Vocabulary Words #2
(dangle, suspend, modern, antique)

(End of lesson.)

Level 2—Shurley English—Homeschool Edition

CHAPTER 4   LESSON 3
Objectives: Jingles, Grammar (Practice Sentences), Skills (Skill Builder Checks, Noun Checks), and Practice Exercise.

 **JINGLE TIME**

Have students turn to the Jingle Section of their books. The teacher will lead the students in reciting the previously-taught jingles.

 GRAMMAR TIME

Put the Practice Sentences from the box below on the board or on notebook paper. Use these sentences as you practice the concepts that have been taught. For the greatest benefit, students must participate orally with the teacher.

Chapter 4, Practice Sentences for Lesson 3
1. _____ The antique lamp broke yesterday.
2. _____ The morning dew evaporates quickly.
3. _____ The suspended bridge swayed suddenly.

TEACHING SCRIPT FOR CLASSIFYING PRACTICE SENTENCES

We will classify three different sentences to practice the grammar skills in the Question and Answer Flows. We will classify the sentences together. Begin. (*You might have students write the labels above the sentences at this time.*)

Question and Answer Flow for Sentence 1: The antique lamp broke yesterday.
1. What broke yesterday? lamp - SN   4. What kind of lamp? antique - Adj
2. What is being said about lamp? lamp broke - V   5. The - A
3. Broke when? yesterday - Adv
Classified Sentence: A   Adj   SN   V   Adv
The antique lamp broke yesterday.

Level 2 Homeschool Teacher's Manual

Level 2—Shurley English—Homeschool Edition

CHAPTER 4 LESSON 3 CONTINUED

Question and Answer Flow for Sentence 2: The morning dew evaporates quickly.

1. What evaporates quickly? dew - SN
2. What is being said about dew? dew evaporates - V
3. Evaporates how? quickly - Adv
4. What kind of dew? morning - Adj
5. The - A

Classified Sentence: A   Adj   SN   V   Adv
The morning dew evaporates quickly.

Question and Answer Flow for Sentence 3: The suspended bridge swayed suddenly.

1. What swayed suddenly? bridge - SN
2. What is being said about bridge? bridge swayed - V
3. Swayed how? suddenly - Adv
4. What kind of bridge? suspended - Adj
5. The - A

Classified Sentence: A   Adj   SN   V   Adv
The suspended bridge swayed suddenly.

SKILL TIME

TEACHING SCRIPT FOR INTRODUCING SKILL BUILDER CHECKS AND NOUN CHECKS

Now that we have classified all three sentences, I am going to use them to do a Skill Builder Check. A **Skill Builder Check** is an oral review of certain skills. Skill Builder Checks are designed to make sure you keep basic skills sharp and automatic. The first skill that will be covered by the Skill Builder Check is the **Noun Check**. Even though a noun is only one part of speech, a noun can do many jobs in a sentence. The first noun job you have learned is that a noun can function as the subject of a sentence. The first noun job will be the subject noun.

Look at Sentences 1-3. In a Noun Check, we will identify the nouns in all three sentences by drawing circles around them. It will be easy today because we have only one noun job at this point. I will use Sentence 1 to demonstrate the four things that you say: **Number 1** (*You say the sentence number.*) **Subject Noun:** *lamp* (*You say the noun job and the noun used for the noun job.*) **Yes** (*You say the word "yes" to verify that the word lamp is a noun, not a pronoun.*) So it will not be confusing, I will repeat number 1 again. We will say, "Number 1: subject noun *lamp*, yes." I will circle *lamp* because we have identified it as a noun.

Level 2—Shurley English—Homeschool Edition

CHAPTER 4 LESSON 3 CONTINUED

Let's start with number 1 again and do a Noun Check. Begin. (*Circle the nouns for all three sentences as your students recite the Noun Check with you: Number 1: subject noun **lamp**, yes. Number 2: subject noun **dew**, yes. Number 3: subject noun **bridge**, yes.*)

 PRACTICE TIME

Have students turn to pages 38 and 39 in the Practice Section of their book and find the skills under Chapter 4, Lesson 3, Practice *(1-4)*. Go over the directions to make sure they understand what to do. Check and discuss the Practices after students have finished. (*Chapter 4, Lesson 3, Practice keys are given below.*)

Chapter 4, Lesson 3, Practice 1: Put the end mark and the abbreviation for each kind of sentence in the blanks below.

1. My green marker fell on the floor   **. D**
2. How old is your brother   **? Int**
3. I spilled grape juice on my best suit   **! E**

Chapter 4, Lesson 3, Practice 2: Match the definitions. Write the correct letter beside each numbered concept.

D	1. sentences should begin with	A.	noun marker
B	2. article adjectives	B.	a, an, the
J	3. adjective modifies	C.	what
F	4. verb question	D.	a capital letter
E	5. tells what the subject does	E.	verb
C	6. subject-noun question (thing)	F.	what is being said about
A	7. article adjective can be called	G.	person, place, or thing
I	8. parts of a complete sentence	H.	verb, adjective, or adverb
G	9. noun	I.	subject, verb, complete sense
K	10. subject-noun question (person)	J.	noun or pronoun
H	11. adverb modifies	K.	who

Chapter 4, Lesson 3, Practice 3: Write *a* or *an* in the blanks.

1. Kate read **a** magazine.   3. He built **a** tree house.   5. **an** orphan   7. **a** picture
2. We found **an** empty bottle.   4. Joe saw **a** raccoon.   6. **an** umbrella   8. **an** oatmeal pie

Chapter 4, Lesson 3, Practice 4: Name the four parts of speech that you have studied. (*You may use abbreviations.*) **(The order of answers may vary.)**

1. **noun**   2. **verb**   3. **adjective**   4. **adverb**

(End of lesson.)

Level 2—Shurley English—Homeschool Edition

CHAPTER 4   LESSON 4

Objectives: Jingles, Study, Test, Check, Writing (Journal), State Activity, and Sentence Time.

 JINGLE TIME

Have students turn to the Jingle Section in their books. The teacher will lead the students in reciting the previously-taught jingles.

 STUDY TIME

Have students study the vocabulary words in their vocabulary notebooks. Remind students that any vocabulary word in their notebooks could be on their test. Also, have students study any of the skills in the Practice Section they need to review.

 TEST TIME

Have students turn to page 83 in the Test Section of their books and find Chapter 4 Test. Go over the directions to make sure they understand what to do. (*Chapter 4 Test key is on the next page.*)

 CHECK TIME

After students have finished, check and discuss their test papers. Make sure they understand why their answers are right or wrong. (*For total points, count each required answer as a point.*)

 STATE ACTIVITY TIME

(*Have a recipe box and a package of lined index cards ready for your children to use for this activity.*) Find a map of the United States. Draw or trace the state of Arkansas on the blank side of an index card. On the lined side of the card, write the following questions and answers.

1. What is the state on the front of this card? **Arkansas**
2. What is the capital of Arkansas? **Little Rock**
3. What is the postal abbreviation of Arkansas? **AR**

Color this state. Use the card to quiz family members, friends, and relatives. You may want to time the responses to your questions. Scatter your cards and see how long it takes you to put them in alphabetical order. For a higher level of difficulty, see if you can alphabetize your cards only by the picture of each state.

(End of lesson.)

Chapter 4 Test
(Student Page 83)

49 pts

Exercise 1: Classify each sentence.

      A   Adj   Adj   SN   V   Adv Adv
1. The huge military plane flew low today.

      A   Adj   Adj   SN V   Adv
2. The crisp morning air blew gently.

Exercise 2: Identify each pair of words as synonyms or antonyms by putting parentheses ( ) around **syn** or **ant**.

1. clumsy, graceful	syn **(ant)**	4. cautious, hasty	syn **(ant)**	7. often, frequent	**(syn)** ant
2. suspend, dangle	**(syn)** ant	5. antique, modern	syn **(ant)**	8. enthusiastic, eager	**(syn)** ant
3. salute, tribute	**(syn)** ant	6. gallop, crawl	syn **(ant)**	9. soar, fly	**(syn)** ant

Exercise 3: Put the end mark and the abbreviation for each kind of sentence in the blanks below.

1. Mom's favorite vase tumbled off the top shelf   **! E**
2. What was the answer to her question   **? Int**
3. Will you wash the dishes   **? Int**
4. My new shoes are brown   **. D**

Exercise 4: Match the definitions. Write the correct letter beside each numbered concept.

H	1. subject-noun question (person)	A.	a, an, the
J	2. verb question	B.	verb
A	3. article adjectives	C.	noun marker
K	4. sentences should begin with	D.	what
E	5. adverb modifies	E.	verb, adjective, or adverb
G	6. noun	F.	subject, verb, complete sense
C	7. article adjective can be called	G.	person, place, or thing
D	8. subject-noun question (thing)	H.	who
I	9. adjective modifies	I.	noun or pronoun
B	10. tells what the subject does	J.	what is being said about
F	11. parts of a complete sentence	K.	a capital letter

Exercise 5: Write *a* or *an* in the blanks.

1. Jim went to **an** auction.   3. He flew **an** airplane.   5. **a** battery   7. **a** spoon
2. Peter baked **a** pizza.   4. The queen wore **a** crown.   6. **a** star   8. **an** orchid

Exercise 6: Name the four parts of speech that you have studied. (*You may use abbreviations.*) **(The order of answers may vary.)**

1. **noun**   2. **verb**   3. **adjective**   4. **adverb**

Exercise 7: In your journal, write a paragraph summarizing what you have learned this week.

Level 2—Shurley English—Homeschool Edition

CHAPTER 4 LESSON 4 CONTINUED

TEACHER INSTRUCTIONS

Use the Question and Answer Flows below for the sentences on the Chapter 4 Test.

Question and Answer Flow for Sentence 1: The huge military plane flew low today.

1. What flew low today? plane - SN
2. What is being said about plane? plane flew - V
3. Flew how? low - Adv
4. Flew when? today - Adv
5. What kind of plane? military - Adj
6. What kind of plane? huge - Adj
7. The - A

Classified Sentence: A   Adj   Adj   SN   V   Adv   Adv
The huge military plane flew low today.

Question and Answer Flow for Sentence 2: The crisp morning air blew gently.

1. What blew gently? air - SN
2. What is being said about air? air blew - V
3. Blew how? gently - Adv
4. What kind of air? morning - Adj
5. What kind of air? crisp - Adj
6. The - A

Classified Sentence: A   Adj   Adj   SN   V   Adv
The crisp morning air blew gently.

SENTENCE TIME

Chapter 4, Lesson 4, Sentence: Use colored markers to match each label with the correct sentence part by drawing a line from one to the other. Then, use the labels to arrange the sentence parts into a sentence that you will write on the sentence line below. *(The order of the words in your sentence should be in the same sequence as the vertical list of sentence labels.)* Create other labels and scrambled sentence parts on notebook paper for family members to solve. You may color code the sentence parts. *(See page 109 in the student book.)*

Labels for Order of Sentence	Scrambled Sentence Parts
A	ran
Adj	the
Adj	yesterday
SN	shiny
V	perfectly
Adv	engine
Adv	new

Sentence: The shiny new engine ran perfectly yesterday.

(End of lesson.)

Level 2—Shurley English—Homeschool Edition

CHAPTER 4   LESSON 5
Objectives: Writing (Practice and Improved Sentence), and Activity.

 **WRITING TIME**

TEACHING SCRIPT FOR THE PRACTICE SENTENCE

Sentences are the foundation of writing; so, you must first learn how sentences are put together. Next, you will learn how to improve and expand sentences, and then you will learn to combine sentences into paragraphs.

The first two areas we will address are how sentences are put together and how to improve them. In order to talk about sentences, we must know the vocabulary that is used to build sentences. If you are building a house, you need to know about hammers and nails. You need to know the names of the tools and materials that you will be using.

In the same way, when you are building or writing sentences, you need to know the names of the parts you will be using and what to do with them. Your writing vocabulary will develop as you learn all the parts of a sentence. We will start by learning how to write a sentence from a given set of English labels. This is called a **Practice Sentence**.

A **Practice Sentence** is a sentence that is written following certain sentence labels (**A**, **Adj**, **SN**, **V**, **Adv**, etc.). The difficulty level of the sentence labels will increase as your ability increases. To write a Practice Sentence, you will follow the labels given to you in your assignment. You must think of words that fit the labels and that make sense.

Look at the Practice Sentence in Reference 9 on page 12 in your Reference Section. Since we have learned only four parts of a sentence so far, the Practice Sentence will demonstrate only these four parts. Notice that by using these sentence parts (*article adjective / adjective, subject noun, verb,* and *adverb*), we can make a seven-word sentence: **The little green snake crawled away quickly**.

Reference 9: Practice Sentence						
Labels:	A	Adj	Adj	SN	V	Adv	Adv
Practice:	**The**	**little**	**green**	**snake**	**crawled**	**away**	**quickly.**

There are three adjectives used in this sentence: *the, little,* and *green*. There are two adverbs: *away* and *quickly*. And, of course, there is the subject noun *snake*, and there is the verb *crawled*. We could just as easily have written a sentence with the bare essentials: *The snake crawled*. That is a correct sentence, but, by adding more parts, we are able to make the picture of the snake even clearer.

Level 2—Shurley English—Homeschool Edition

CHAPTER 4 LESSON 5 CONTINUED

As you learn how to use more sentence parts to expand your sentences, you will use them automatically because they make your writing better.

Put these labels on the board: **A Adj SN V Adv**

Look at the sentence labels on the board: **A Adj SN V Adv**. Now, I am going to guide you through the process of writing a sentence using all the parts that you have learned thus far. Most of these steps will become automatic in a very short time.

Get out a sheet of notebook paper. On the top line of your notebook paper, write the title *Practice Sentence*. Copy the sentence labels from the board onto your notebook paper. Be sure to leave plenty of writing space between each label. Now, I will guide you through the process you will use whenever you write a Practice Sentence.

1. Go to the **SN** label for the subject noun. Think of a noun that you want to use as your subject. Write the noun you have chosen on the line *under* the **SN** label.

2. Go to the **V** label for the verb. Think of a verb that tells what your subject does. Make sure that your verb makes sense with the subject noun. Write the verb you have chosen on the line *under* the **V** label.

3. Go to the **Adv** label for the adverb. Go to the verb in your sentence and ask an adverb question. What are the adverb questions? (*How? When? Where?*) Choose one adverb question to ask and write your adverb answer *under* the **Adv** label.

4. Go to the **Adj** label for the adjective. Go to the subject noun of your sentence and ask an adjective question. What are the adjective questions? (*What kind? Which one? How many?*) Choose one adjective question to ask and write your adjective answer *under* the **Adj** label next to the subject noun. Always check to make sure your answers are making sense in the sentence.

5. Go to the **A** label for the article adjective. What are the three article adjectives? (*a*, *an*, and *the*) You will choose the article adjective that makes the best sense in your sentence. Write the article adjective you have chosen *under* the **A** label.

6. Finally, check the Practice Sentence to make sure it has the necessary parts to be a complete sentence. What are the five parts of a complete sentence? (*subject, verb, complete sense, capital letter, and an end mark*) Does this Practice Sentence have all the parts necessary to make a complete sentence? (*Allow time for students' responses and for any corrections that need to be made on the board or on students' papers.*)

Level 2—Shurley English—Homeschool Edition

CHAPTER 4 LESSON 5 CONTINUED

<u>TEACHING SCRIPT FOR AN IMPROVED SENTENCE</u>

Now that we have written a correct sentence using all the parts that we have studied, we must concentrate on improving what we have written. The result is called an **Improved Sentence**. An **Improved Sentence** is a sentence made from the Practice Sentence that is improved through the use of synonyms, antonyms, or complete word changes. Writing Improved Sentences will help you make better word choices as you write because your writing vocabulary increases.

Look at the Improved Sentence in Reference 10 on page 12 in your Reference Section. The original English labels are on the first line. The sample Practice Sentence is on the second line. On the last line, you see an Improved Sentence made from synonyms, antonyms, and complete word changes. Knowing how to make improvements in what you have written means that you are beginning to revise and edit. *(Read the Practice and Improved Sentences in the box as your students follow along. Make sure students see the difference that improving sentences can make.)*

Reference 10: Improved Sentence						
Labels: **A**	**Adj**	**Adj**	**SN**	**V**	**Adv**	**Adv**
Practice: The	little	green	snake	crawled	away	quickly.
Improved: **A**	**large**	**hissing**	**reptile**	**slithered**	**away**	**slowly.**
(word change)	(antonym)	(word change)	(synonym)	(synonym)	(no change)	(antonym)

Put these directions on the board or on notebook paper:
Make at <u>least</u> one synonym change, one antonym change, and one complete word change.

The directions on the board tell you to make these changes in your Practice Sentence: **Make at <u>least</u> one synonym change, one antonym change, and one complete word change.** I am going to show you how to improve your Practice Sentence by making synonym, antonym, and complete word changes with some of the words.

The changed sentence will be called an **Improved Sentence** because you will make several improvements. Most of these steps will become automatic in a very short time. Now, on another line, under your Practice Sentence, write the title *Improved Sentence*.

1. Look at our Practice Sentence on the board. Let's find a word that can be improved with an antonym. *(Identify the word to be changed.)* Give me an antonym suggestion, and I will write your suggested antonym to improve, or change, the word.

   Remember, antonyms are powerful because they completely change the direction or meaning of your sentence. *(Discuss several antonym suggestions from students.)* Let's write the antonym we have chosen *under* the word we want to change in the Practice Sentence. *(Write the antonym choice on the board and have students write it on their papers.)*

CHAPTER 4 LESSON 5 CONTINUED

2. Let's find a word in the Practice Sentence that can be improved with a synonym. *(Identify the word to be changed.)* Give me a synonym suggestion, and I will write your suggested synonym to improve the word. Remember, synonyms improve your writing vocabulary faster because they give you more word choices. *(Discuss several synonym suggestions from students.)* Let's write the synonym we have chosen *under* the word we want to improve in the Practice Sentence. *(Write the synonym choice on the board and have students write it on their papers.)*

3. Sometimes, you will think of a better word to use to improve your sentence that is not a synonym or antonym. We call this type of improvement a complete word change. It will give you more flexibility as you work to improve your sentences. Look at the Practice Sentence again. Is there another word that we want to change by simply making a complete word change? *(Discuss several complete word change suggestions from students.)* Let's write the complete word change we have chosen *under* the word we want to change in the Practice Sentence. *(Write the complete word change on the board and have students write it on their papers.)* If you cannot think of a complete word change, you can always use a synonym or antonym change.

4. Let's look at our Improved Sentence. Do you want to make any more improvements or changes? *(Discuss and then make extra improvements or changes as indicated by student participation.)*

5. Finally, let's check the Improved Sentence to make sure it has the necessary parts to be a complete sentence. Does our Improved Sentence have all the parts necessary to make a complete sentence? *(Allow time for students' responses and for corrections to be made on the board and on students' papers.)*

I want you to write your own Practice and Improved Sentences. You may use the same English labels that I listed on the board: **A Adj SN V Adv**. Make sure you follow the procedures we have just gone through. Remember, any time you write an Improved Sentence, you are actually editing your writing, and that's why it is so important that you learn to write Improved Sentences. *(Check and discuss students' Practice and Improved Sentences after they have finished. They will add more adjectives and adverbs to their Practice Sentence in the next chapter, but if they want to add them now, allow them to do so.)*

ACTIVITY / ASSIGNMENT TIME

Find 3 large trash cans from around the house. *(Laundry baskets or empty buckets will do fine for this activity.)* You will label each trash can with a type of sentence. *(A "declarative" can, an "exclamatory" can, and an "interrogative" can.)* Then, blow up six balloons. Write one of the six sample sentences below on each balloon with a magic marker.

1. Jeffery wants to borrow my new sweater.
2. Do you want to eat lunch with us?
3. My dog has fleas!
4. Judy ate a worm!
5. She laughed at Peter's joke.
6. Can you pass the mustard?

Line up the three trash cans on one side of the room. Make a line on the floor with a small strip of masking tape about 4 feet away from the cans. Have students stand behind the line. As students correctly identify the type of sentence on each balloon, allow them to toss the balloon into the correct can, run across the room to put the balloon into the appropriate can, or pop the balloon by sitting on it.

(End of lesson.)

CHAPTER 5   LESSON 1

Objectives: Jingles, Grammar (Practice Sentences), Skills (Reviewing Noun Check, Singular and Plural Nouns), Practice Exercise, Vocabulary #1, and Activity.

 **JINGLE TIME**

Have students turn to the Jingle Section of their books. The teacher will lead the students in reciting the previously-taught jingles.

 GRAMMAR TIME

Put the Practice Sentences from the box below on the board or on notebook paper. Use these sentences as you practice the concepts that have been taught. For the greatest benefit, students must participate orally with the teacher.

Chapter 5, Practice Sentences for Lesson 1
1. _____ The surprised pilot landed unexpectedly!
2. _____ The beautiful spring flowers bloomed early.
3. _____ The frightened horse raced quickly away.

TEACHING SCRIPT FOR CLASSIFYING PRACTICE SENTENCES

We will classify three different sentences to practice the grammar skills in the Question and Answer Flows. We will classify the sentences together. Begin. (*You might have students write the labels above the sentences at this time.*)

Question and Answer Flow for Sentence 1: The surprised pilot landed unexpectedly!
1. Who landed unexpectedly? pilot - SN   4. What kind of pilot? surprised - Adj
2. What is being said about pilot? pilot landed - V   5. The - A
3. Landed how? unexpectedly - Adv
A   Adj   SN   V   Adv
Classified Sentence: The surprised pilot landed unexpectedly!

Level 2—Shurley English—Homeschool Edition

CHAPTER 5 LESSON 1 CONTINUED

Question and Answer Flow for Sentence 2: The beautiful spring flowers bloomed early.

1. What bloomed early? flowers - SN
2. What is being said about flowers? flowers bloomed - V
3. Bloomed when? early - Adv
4. What kind of flowers? spring - Adj
5. What kind of flowers? beautiful - Adj
6. The - A

```
                    A    Adj   Adj    SN     V      Adv
Classified Sentence:   The beautiful spring flowers bloomed early.
```

Question and Answer Flow for Sentence 3: The frightened horse raced quickly away.

1. What raced quickly away? horse - SN
2. What is being said about horse? horse raced - V
3. Raced how? quickly - Adv
4. Raced where? away - Adv
5. What kind of horse? frightened - Adj
6. The - A

```
                    A    Adj     SN    V    Adv   Adv
Classified Sentence:   The frightened horse raced quickly away.
```

SKILL TIME

TEACHING SCRIPT FOR REVIEWING A NOUN CHECK

Now that we have classified all three sentences, I am going to use them to do a **Noun Check** during Skill Builder Time. Look at Sentences 1-3. We will identify the nouns in all three sentences by drawing circles around them. Let's start with number 1 and do a Noun Check. Begin. (*Circle the nouns for all three sentences as your students recite the Noun Check with you. Number 1: subject noun **pilot**, yes. Number 2: subject noun **flowers**, yes. Number 3: subject noun **horse**, yes.*)

TEACHING SCRIPT FOR IDENTIFYING NOUNS AS SINGULAR OR PLURAL

We will learn two new skills and then use them during Skill Builder Time. These skills are singular and plural. After we discuss the definitions, we will learn how to identify nouns as singular or plural. This is an easy skill, but you would be surprised at the number of people who have trouble with it. Find Reference 11 on page 13 in the Reference Section of your book. (*Reference 11 is located on the next page.*) Number 1 reminds us that a noun names a person, place, or thing. We will be using the definition quite often as we do Noun Checks. Look at number 2 and number 3 and follow along as I read the definitions for singular and plural in your reference box.

A **singular noun** usually does not end in *s* or *es* and means only one. (*fan, doll, brush*) There are a few exceptions: Some nouns that end in s are singular and mean only one. (*address, mess*)

A **plural noun** usually ends in *s* or *es* and means more than one. (*fans, dolls, brushes*) Again, there are a few exceptions: Some nouns are made plural by changing their spelling. (*ox - oxen, mouse - mice*)

Level 2—Shurley English—Homeschool Edition

CHAPTER 5 LESSON 1 CONTINUED

Reference 11: Definitions for a Skill Builder Check
1. A **noun** names a person, place, or thing.
2. A **singular noun** usually does not end in *s* or *es* and means only one. (*fan, doll, brush*) Exception: Some nouns that end in s are singular and mean only one. (*address, mess*)
3. A **plural noun** usually ends in *s* or *es* and means more than one. (*fans, dolls, brushes*) Exception: Some nouns are made plural by changing their spelling. (*ox - oxen, mouse - mice*)
4. A **common noun** names ANY person, place, or thing. A common noun is not capitalized because it does not name a specific person, place, or thing. (*principal, lake*)
5. A **proper noun** is a noun that names a specific, or particular, person, place, or thing. Proper nouns are always capitalized no matter where they are located in the sentence. (*Thomas, Alaska*)

You can always go back to this reference box if you need to review the definitions for singular and plural nouns. We will now identify each circled noun in Sentences 1-3 as singular or plural. I will write **S** for singular or **P** for plural above each noun as we identify it. We will say "pilot - singular," and I will write **S** above *pilot*. Begin. (*pilot – singular, flowers – plural, horse – singular. Mark the nouns with the letter "S" or "P" in all three sentences. Discuss why the nouns are singular or plural.*)

Let's review the general rules. A noun is usually singular when it does not end in s or es, and it means only one. That's easy, isn't it? A noun is usually plural when it ends in s or es, and it means more than one. As you can see, when you are identifying nouns as singular or plural, it is important to remember a few simple rules.

PRACTICE TIME

Have students turn to pages 39 and 40 in the Practice Section of their book and find the skills under Chapter 5, Lesson 1, Practice *(1-4)*. Go over the directions to make sure they understand what to do. Check and discuss the Practices after students have finished. (*Chapter 5, Lesson 1, Practice keys are given below and on the next page.*)

Chapter 5, Lesson 1, Practice 1: For each noun listed below, write **S** for singular or **P** for plural.

Noun	S or P	Noun	S or P	Noun	S or P
1. cake	S	4. soup	S	7. shells	P
2. telephones	P	5. flags	P	8. grass	S
3. mice	P	6. street	S	9. buttons	P

Chapter 5, Lesson 1, Practice 2: Write *a* or *an* in the blanks.

1. We stayed at **a** hotel.   3. The waiter dropped **a** spoon.   5. **a** boulder   7. **an** eraser

2. That is just **an** excuse.   4. They live in **a** country cottage.   6. **an** agency   8. **an** object

Level 2 Homeschool Teacher's Manual   Page 59

CHAPTER 5 LESSON 1 CONTINUED

Chapter 5, Lesson 1, Practice 3: Put the end mark and the abbreviation for each kind of sentence in the blanks below.

1. William moved to Vermont   **. D**
2. Is it dark outside   **? Int**
3. The wind just blew our candle out **! E**

Chapter 5, Lesson 1, Practice 4: Name the four parts of speech that you have studied. (*You may use abbreviations.*) **(The order of answers may vary.)**

1. __noun__   2. __verb__   3. __adjective__   4. __adverb__

VOCABULARY TIME

Assign Chapter 5, Vocabulary Words **#1** on page 6 in the Reference Section for students to define in their Vocabulary notebooks. Tell students they are to use a dictionary or thesaurus to look up the meanings of the vocabulary words.

Chapter 5, Vocabulary Words #1
(vanish, disappear, mournful, delightful)

ACTIVITY / ASSIGNMENT TIME

Provide students with several paper plates and different colored markers. Tell students that you have prepared an imaginary meal and are inviting them to a Singular & Plural Noun Feast. Give students a list of the menu items below. Read the menu together to make sure they know the vocabulary. Tell students that they must fill their plates with only six food nouns at a time. To fill their plates, students must write the name of each food noun on their paper plates. Three of these nouns must be singular and three must be plural nouns. After they have filled their plates, have students decorate their plates and go back for a second helping with a new plate. The food list and a sample are given below.

Food list			Sample
chips	biscuits	candied yams	hamburger
roll	pudding	salad	French fries
tater tots	French fries	carrots	pudding
brownie	baked potato	pecan pie	chips
sugar cookies	turkey	hamburger	carrots
			brownie

(End of lesson.)

Level 2—Shurley English—Homeschool Edition

CHAPTER 5 LESSON 2

Objectives: Jingles, Grammar (Practice Sentences), Skills (Skill Builder Check, Common and Proper Nouns), Practice Exercise, Vocabulary #2, and Activity.

 JINGLE TIME

Have students turn to the Jingle Section of their books. The teacher will lead the students in reciting the previously-taught jingles.

 GRAMMAR TIME

Put the Practice Sentences from the box below on the board or on notebook paper. Use these sentences as you practice the concepts that have been taught. For the greatest benefit, students must participate orally with the teacher.

Chapter 5, Practice Sentences for Lesson 2
1. _____ That large alligator turned quickly around!
2. _____ A hungry wolf howled mournfully.
3. _____ The winter gloves disappeared mysteriously.

TEACHING SCRIPT FOR CLASSIFYING PRACTICE SENTENCES

We will classify three different sentences to practice the grammar skills in the Question and Answer Flows. We will classify the sentences together. Begin. (*You might have students write the labels above the sentences at this time.*)

Question and Answer Flow for Sentence 1: That large alligator turned quickly around!
1. What turned quickly around? alligator - SN   4. Turned where? around - Adv
2. What is being said about alligator?   5. What kind of alligator? large - Adj
alligator turned - V   6. Which alligator? that - Adj
3. Turned how? quickly - Adv
Adj Adj SN   V   Adv   Adv
Classified Sentence: That large alligator turned quickly around!

Level 2—Shurley English—Homeschool Edition

CHAPTER 5 LESSON 2 CONTINUED

Question and Answer Flow for Sentence 2: A hungry wolf howled mournfully.

1. What howled mournfully? wolf - SN
2. What is being said about wolf? wolf howled - V
3. Howled how? mournfully - Adv
4. What kind of wolf? hungry - Adj
5. A - A

                         A   Adj   SN   V   Adv
Classified Sentence: A hungry wolf howled mournfully.

Question and Answer Flow for Sentence 3: The winter gloves disappeared mysteriously.

1. What disappeared mysteriously? gloves - SN
2. What is being said about gloves?
   gloves disappeared - V
3. Disappeared how? mysteriously - Adv
4. What kind of gloves? winter - Adj
5. The - A

                         A   Adj   SN   V   Adv
Classified Sentence: The winter gloves disappeared mysteriously.

SKILL TIME

<u>TEACHING SCRIPT FOR A SKILL BUILDER CHECK</u>

Now that we have classified all three sentences, we will use them to do a Skill Builder Check. We have already learned two skills that we can apply during our Skill Builder Check. We will do a Noun Check, and then we will identify the nouns as singular or plural. Where do we go to find nouns? (*subject noun*) We know to go to the subject noun because we know that we can find nouns in the subject job. The subject noun is the first <u>noun</u> job that we have studied.

For a Noun Check, you say four things: the sentence number (*Number 1*), the noun job (*subject noun*), the noun used for the noun job (***alligator***), and the word *yes* to verify that it is a noun, not a pronoun. I will circle the nouns as we identify them. Begin. (*Circle the nouns for all three sentences as your students recite the Noun Check with you: Number 1: subject noun **alligator**, yes. Number 2: subject noun **wolf**, yes. Number 3: subject noun **gloves**, yes.*)

We will now identify each noun as singular or plural. Before we begin, let's review the singular and plural skills. Look at Reference 11 on page 13 in the Reference Section of your book. We will read and discuss numbers 2 and 3 about singular and plural nouns. (*Read and discuss the singular and plural nouns that are located in Reference 11 on the next page.*)

We will identify each circled noun in Sentences 1-3 as singular or plural. I will write **S** for singular or **P** for plural above each noun as we identify it. Begin. (*alligator – singular, wolf – singular, gloves – plural. Mark the nouns with the letter "S" or "P" in all three sentences. Discuss why the nouns are singular or plural.*)

CHAPTER 5 LESSON 2 CONTINUED

Reference 11: Definitions for a Skill Builder Check
1. A **noun** names a person, place, or thing.
2. A **singular noun** usually does not end in *s* or *es* and means only one. (*fan, doll, brush*) Exception: Some nouns that end in s are singular and mean only one. (*address, mess*)
3. A **plural noun** usually ends in *s* or *es* and means more than one. (*fans, dolls, brushes*) Exception: Some nouns are made plural by changing their spelling. (*ox - oxen, mouse - mice*)
4. A **common noun** names ANY person, place, or thing. A common noun is not capitalized because it does not name a specific person, place, or thing. (*principal, lake*)
5. A **proper noun** is a noun that names a specific, or particular, person, place, or thing. Proper nouns are always capitalized no matter where they are located in the sentence. (*Thomas, Alaska*)

TEACHING SCRIPT FOR IDENTIFYING NOUNS AS COMMON OR PROPER

We will now learn two more skills that we will use during Skill Builder Checks. Look at Reference 11 again and follow along as I read the information in numbers 4 and 5 about common and proper nouns. (*Read and discuss numbers 4 and 5 in the reference box above with your students.*)

First, we will look at the nouns that are circled in the three sentences. Then, we tell whether they are common or proper. How do we recognize a proper noun? (*It begins with a capital letter no matter where it is located in the sentence.*) Do we have any proper nouns in our sentences? (*No.*) How do you know? (*None of the nouns that are circled begins with a capital letter.*) Since we do not have a proper noun in the three sentences that we have just classified, I want you to think of a proper noun. (*Get several responses and discuss why the nouns named are proper nouns.*)

Do we have any common nouns in our sentences? (*Yes.*) Are all the nouns common? (*Yes.*) How do you know? (*All the nouns that are circled begin with a lowercase, or small, letter.*)

 PRACTICE TIME

Have students turn to pages 40 and 41 in the Practice Section of their book and find Chapter 5, Lesson 2, Practice *(1-4)*. Go over the directions to make sure they understand what to do. Check and discuss the Practices after students have finished. (*Chapter 5, Lesson 2, Practice keys are given below and on the next page.*)

Chapter 5, Lesson 2, Practice 1: For each noun listed below, write **C** for common or **P** for proper.

Noun	C or P	Noun	C or P	Noun	C or P
1. book	C	4. April	P	7. Thanksgiving	P
2. Italian	P	5. Tuesday	P	8. tractor	C
3. sock	C	6. month	C	9. holiday	C

Level 2—Shurley English—Homeschool Edition

CHAPTER 5 LESSON 2 CONTINUED

Chapter 5, Lesson 2, Practice 2: For each noun listed below, write **S** for singular or **P** for plural.

Noun	S or P	Noun	S or P	Noun	S or P
1. mountain	S	4. olive	S	7. nose	S
2. parks	P	5. caves	P	8. spoons	P
3. statues	P	6. hole	S	9. stripes	P

Chapter 5, Lesson 2, Practice 3: Write *a* or *an* in the blanks.

1. They are building **a** bank.   3. Dad built **a** fire.   5. **a** bag   7. **an** acre

2. He drives **an** orange truck.   4. We had **a** pop quiz.   6. **an** index   8. **a** flake

Chapter 5, Lesson 2, Practice 4: Name the four parts of speech that you have studied. (*You may use abbreviations.*)
(The order of answers may vary.)

1. **noun**   2. **verb**   3. **adjective**   4. **adverb**

VOCABULARY TIME

Assign Chapter 5, Vocabulary Words #2 on page 6 in the Reference Section for students to define in their Vocabulary notebooks. Tell students they are to use a dictionary or thesaurus to look up the meanings of the vocabulary words.

Chapter 5, Vocabulary Words #2
(calm, excited, annoy, irritate)

ACTIVITY / ASSIGNMENT TIME

Tell students that they are about to take a short stroll down Common & Proper Street. (*Before you begin, review common and proper in Reference 11 in their student book if necessary.*) Have them close their eyes and imagine that they are walking down a street. They notice that things on the left side of the street are very different from the things on the right side. All of the nouns (people, places, and things) on the left are common. They see a store, a car, a tall building, a man walking a dog, and a doctor. On the right side of the street they see Save-A-Lot Grocery Store, a Honda, the Empire State Building, Mr. Jones walking Fido, and Dr. Peterson. All of the nouns on the right are proper! Have students take out a sheet of paper and draw a street down the middle. Have them label the left side of the street "common" and the right side of the street "proper". Have students write nouns that they might see on each side of the street.
(*Extension: Students could find different nouns in old magazines.*)

(End of lesson.)

Level 2—Shurley English—Homeschool Edition

CHAPTER 5   LESSON 3
Objectives: Jingles, Grammar (Practice Sentences), Skills (Practice and Improved Sentence).

 **JINGLE TIME**

Have students turn to the Jingle Section of their books. The teacher will lead the students in reciting the previously-taught jingles.

 GRAMMAR TIME

Put the Practice Sentences from the box below on the board or on notebook paper. Use these sentences as you practice the concepts that have been taught. For the greatest benefit, students must participate orally with the teacher.

Chapter 5, Practice Sentences for Lesson 3
1. _____ The delightful holidays passed quickly.
2. _____ The excited hunters shot carefully.
3. _____ The dangerous wasps attacked unexpectedly!

TEACHING SCRIPT FOR CLASSIFYING PRACTICE SENTENCES

We will classify three different sentences to practice the grammar skills in the Question and Answer Flows. We will classify the sentences together. Begin. (*You might have students write the labels above the sentences at this time.*)

Question and Answer Flow for Sentence 1: The delightful holidays passed quickly.	
1. What passed quickly? holidays - SN	3. Passed how? quickly - Adv
2. What is being said about holidays? holidays passed - V	4. What kind of holidays? delightful - Adj
	5. The - A

                         A   Adj   SN   V   Adv
Classified Sentence: The delightful holidays passed quickly.

Level 2 Homeschool Teacher's Manual

CHAPTER 5 LESSON 3 CONTINUED

Question and Answer Flow for Sentence 2: The excited hunters shot carefully.

1. Who shot carefully? hunters - SN
2. What is being said about hunters? hunters shot - V
3. Shot how? carefully - Adv
4. What kind of hunters? excited - Adj
5. The - A

```
                    A    Adj   SN   V    Adv
Classified Sentence:   The excited hunters shot carefully.
```

Question and Answer Flow for Sentence 3: The dangerous wasps attacked unexpectedly!

1. What attacked unexpectedly? wasps - SN
2. What is being said about wasps? wasps attacked - V
3. Attacked how? unexpectedly - Adv
4. What kind of wasps? dangerous - Adj
5. The - A

```
                    A    Adj      SN    V       Adv
Classified Sentence:   The dangerous wasps attacked unexpectedly!
```

SKILL TIME

TEACHING SCRIPT FOR A PRACTICE SENTENCE

Put these labels on the board: **A Adj Adj SN V Adv Adv**

In the previous lesson, I guided you through the process of writing a Practice Sentence and an Improved Sentence for the first time. Today, I am going to guide you through the same process again, but this time you will write an expanded sentence by adding a few more sentence labels. Writing a sentence using English labels is total sentence control. It is very easy if you know how, but it is also something very few people can do without training. Look at the new sentence labels on the board. Let's repeat the labels together: **A Adj Adj SN V Adv Adv.** You will now write a seven-word sentence.

Get out a sheet of notebook paper. On the top line of your notebook paper, write the title *Practice Sentence*. Copy the sentence labels from the board onto your notebook paper. Be sure to leave plenty of writing space between each label. Now, I will guide you through the process you will use whenever you write a Practice Sentence. We will begin with the subject noun.

CHAPTER 5 LESSON 3 CONTINUED

1. Go to the **SN** label for the subject noun. Think of a noun that you want to use as your subject. Write the noun you have chosen on the line *under* the **SN** label.

2. Go to the **V** label for the verb. Think of a verb that tells what your subject does. Make sure that your verb makes sense with the subject noun. Write the verb you have chosen on the line *under* the **V** label.

3. Go to the **Adv** label for the adverb. Go to the verb in your sentence and ask an adverb question. What are the adverb questions? (*How, When, Where*) Choose one adverb question to ask and write your adverb answer *under* the first **Adv** label.

4. Go to the **Adv** label for another adverb. Go to the verb again and ask another adverb question. You can ask the same adverb question, or you can ask a different adverb question. Write another adverb *under* the second **Adv** label.

5. Go to the **Adj** label for the adjective. Go to the subject noun of your sentence and ask an adjective question. What are the adjective questions? (*What kind, Which one, How many*) Choose one adjective question to ask and write your adjective answer *under* the **Adj** label next to the subject noun. Always check to make sure your answers are making sense in the sentence.

6. Go to the next **Adj** label for another adjective. Go to the subject noun again and ask another adjective question. You can ask the same adjective question, or you can ask a different adjective question. Write another adjective *under* the second **Adj** label.

7. Go to the **A** label for the article adjective. What are the three article adjectives? (*a, an,* and *the*) Choose the article adjective that makes the best sense in your sentence. Write the article adjective you have chosen *under* the **A** label.

8. Finally, check your Practice Sentence to make sure it has the necessary parts to be a complete sentence. What are the five parts of a complete sentence? (*subject, verb, complete sense, capital letter, and an end mark*) Does your Practice Sentence have the five parts of a complete sentence? (*Allow time for students to read over their sentences and to make any necessary corrections.*)

9. Under your Practice Sentence, write the title *Improved Sentence* on another line. To improve your Practice Sentence, you will make two synonym changes, one antonym change, and your choice of a complete word change or another synonym or antonym change.

Since it is harder to find words that can be changed to an antonym, it is usually wise to go through your sentence to find an antonym change first. Then, look through your sentence again to find words that can be improved with synonyms. Finally, make a decision about whether your last change will be a complete word change, another synonym change, or another antonym change. I will give you time to write your Improved Sentence. (*Encourage students to use a thesaurus, synonym-antonym book, or a dictionary to help them develop an interesting and improved writing vocabulary. After students have finished, check and discuss students' Practice and Improved Sentences.*)

(End of lesson.)

Level 2—Shurley English—Homeschool Edition

CHAPTER 5   LESSON 4
Objectives: Jingles, Study, Test, Check, Writing (Journal), State Activity, and Sentence Time.

 JINGLE TIME

Have students turn to the Jingle Section in their books. The teacher will lead the students in reciting the previously-taught jingles.

 STUDY TIME

Have students study the vocabulary words in their vocabulary notebooks. Remind students that any vocabulary word in their notebooks could be on their test. Also, have students study any of the skills in the Practice Section they need to review.

 TEST TIME

Have students turn to page 84 in the Test Section of their books and find Chapter 5 Test. Go over the directions to make sure they understand what to do. (*Chapter 5 Test key is on the next page.*)

 CHECK TIME

After students have finished, check and discuss their test papers. Make sure they understand why their answers are right or wrong. (*For total points, count each required answer as a point.*)

 STATE ACTIVITY TIME

(*Have a recipe box and a package of lined index cards ready for your children to use for this activity.*) Find a map of the United States. Draw or trace the state of California on the blank side of an index card. On the lined side of the card, write the following questions and answers.

      1. What is the state on the front of this card? **California**
      2. What is the capital of California? **Sacramento**
      3. What is the postal abbreviation of California? **CA**

Color this state. Use the card to quiz family members, friends, and relatives. You may want to time the responses to your questions.

(End of lesson.)

Chapter 5 Test
(Student Page 84)

52 pts

Exercise 1: Classify each sentence.

       Adj   SN   V   Adv
1. Wild ducks descend gracefully.

     A   Adj   Adj   SN   V   Adv
2. The thick, annoying smoke drifted upward.

Exercise 2: Identify each pair of words as synonyms or antonyms by putting parentheses ( ) around *syn* or *ant*.

1. often, frequent	**(syn)** ant	4. annoy, irritate	**(syn)** ant	7. disappear, vanish	**(syn)** ant
2. excited, calm	syn **(ant)**	5. antique, modern	syn **(ant)**	8. dangle, suspend	**(syn)** ant
3. soar, fly	**(syn)** ant	6. mournful, delightful	syn **(ant)**	9. graceful, clumsy	syn **(ant)**

Exercise 3: Put the end mark and the abbreviation for each kind of sentence in the blanks below.

1. James tripped over the water hose   **! E**
2. The waiter poured the coffee   **. D**
3. Do you have a pet rabbit   **? Int**

Exercise 4: For each noun listed below, write **C** for common or **P** for proper.

Noun	C or P	Noun	C or P	Noun	C or P
1. Walter	P	4. city	C	7. yellow	C
2. St. Peter	P	5. tuna	C	8. poster	C
3. painting	C	6. Texas	P	9. Paula	P

Exercise 5: For each noun listed below, write **S** for singular or **P** for plural.

Noun	S or P	Noun	S or P	Noun	S or P
1. board	S	4. stores	P	7. matches	P
2. dress	S	5. birds	P	8. nails	P
3. planets	P	6. brother	S	9. spider	S

Exercise 6: Write *a* or *an* in the blanks.

1. That is **an** adorable puppy.   3. She made **a** mistake.   5. **a** point   7. **an** ounce
2. Chad listened for **an** echo.   4. Sewing is **a** hobby.   6. **an** approval   8. **a** gym

Exercise 7: Name the four parts of speech that you have studied. (*You may use abbreviations.*)
(The order of answers may vary.)

1. **noun**   2. **verb**   3. **adjective**   4. **adverb**

Exercise 8: In your journal, write a paragraph summarizing what you have learned this week.

Level 2—Shurley English—Homeschool Edition

CHAPTER 5 LESSON 4 CONTINUED

TEACHER INSTRUCTIONS

Use the Question and Answer Flows below for the sentences on the Chapter 5 Test.

Question and Answer Flow for Sentence 1: Wild ducks descend gracefully.

1. What descend gracefully? ducks - SN
2. What is being said about ducks? ducks descend - V
3. Descend how? gracefully - Adv
4. What kind of ducks? wild - Adj

                          Adj   SN   V   Adv
Classified Sentence: Wild ducks descend gracefully.

Question and Answer Flow for Sentence 2: The thick, annoying smoke drifted upward.

1. What drifted upward? smoke - SN
2. What is being said about smoke? smoke drifted - V
3. Drifted where? upward - Adv
4. What kind of smoke? annoying - Adj
5. What kind of smoke? thick - Adj
6. The - A

                      A   Adj   Adj   SN   V   Adv
Classified Sentence: The thick, annoying smoke drifted upward.

 SENTENCE TIME

Chapter 5, Lesson 4, Sentence: Use colored markers to match each label with the correct sentence part by drawing a line from one to the other. Then, use the labels to arrange the sentence parts into a sentence that you will write on the sentence line below. *(The order of the words in your sentence should be in the same sequence as the vertical list of sentence labels.)* Create other labels and scrambled sentence parts on notebook paper for family members to solve. You may color code the sentence parts. *(See page 110 in the student book.)*

Labels for Order of Sentence	Scrambled Sentence Parts
A	squirrel
Adj	loudly
Adj	a
SN	complained
V	grumpy
Adv	old

Sentence: A grumpy old squirrel complained loudly.

(End of lesson.)

CHAPTER 5 LESSON 5

Objectives: Writing (Finding a Topic, Supporting and Non-Supporting Ideas and Sentences), Practice Exercise, and Activity.

 **WRITING TIME**

TEACHING SCRIPT FOR FINDING A TOPIC

You have been learning the parts of a sentence so you can write sentences and paragraphs correctly. Today we will learn the meaning of the word **paragraph**. A paragraph is a group of sentences that tells about one topic. The **topic** tells what things are about. That means that the topic tells what a paragraph is about, and the topic also tells what a group of words is about. So, we see that the topic tells what anything is about. That is why the topic is sometimes called the **subject** because it tells what something is about.

Since it is very important to know all we can about topics, we will find the topic of different sets of words. Remember, a topic tells what something is about. Turn to page 13 in your Reference section. Look at the first section in Reference 12 as I go over it with you. (*Read and discuss the information in the reference box below.*)

Reference 12: The Topic

The topic tells what something is about. The topic can tell what a paragraph or what a group of words is about. The topic is sometimes called the subject because it tells what something is about.

Directions for finding the topic: Write the name of the topic that best describes what each row of words is about. Choose from these topics: **Sports**   **Clothing**   **Animals**   **Colors**

(1) Sports	(2) Colors	(3) Clothing
basketball	purple	sweater
tennis	red	pants
baseball	yellow	socks
soccer	blue	shorts

TEACHING SCRIPT FOR SUPPORTING AND NON-SUPPORTING IDEAS AND SENTENCES

When a topic has been selected, all sentences and ideas should tell about that topic. A sentence or idea that tells about the topic is called **supporting** and can be used for that topic. A sentence or idea that does not support the topic is called **non-supporting** and cannot be used for that topic. Now look at Reference 13 as I read the information about supporting and non-supporting ideas and sentences. (*Read and discuss the information in the reference box on the next page.*)

CHAPTER 5 LESSON 5 CONTINUED

Reference 13: Supporting and Non-Supporting Ideas and Sentences

Words that support the topic: In each row, cross out the one idea that does not support the underlined topic at the top.

(1) Animals	(2) Food	(3) Transportation
bear	cake	truck
rabbit	broccoli	~~lake~~
hippopotamus	~~purple~~	helicopter
chipmunk	biscuit	boat
~~onion~~	potato	bus

Sentences that support the topic: Read the topic. Then, cross out the one sentence that does not support the topic.

Topic: A Furry Little Bunny

1. The bunny was covered with white fur.
2. His tail looked like a cotton ball.
3. ~~I like bunnies and ostriches.~~
4. His ears were long and floppy.

 PRACTICE TIME

Have students turn to pages 41 and 42 in the Practice Section of their book and find Chapter 5, Lesson 5, Practice *(1-3)*. Go over the directions to make sure they understand what to do. Check and discuss the Practices after students have finished. *(Chapter 5, Lesson 5, Practice keys are given below and on the next page.)*

Chapter 5, Lesson 5, Practice 1: Finding the topic: Write the name of the topic that best describes what each row of words is about. Choose from these topics:

    Colors   Sweets   Animals   Seasons   Kitchen Things   Holidays

(1) Holidays	(2) Sweets	(3) Kitchen Things
Easter	cake	spoon
Christmas	cookies	bowl
Labor Day	ice cream	pan
Thanksgiving	pie	oven

CHAPTER 5 LESSON 5 CONTINUED

Chapter 5, Lesson 5, Practice 2: Words that support the topic: In each row, cross out the one idea that does not support the underlined topic at the top.

(1) Farm Animals	(2) Pets	(3) Vegetables
horse	dog	green bean
~~shoe~~	cat	squash
cow	goldfish	~~valley~~
pig	~~peach~~	potato
chicken	parrot	okra

Chapter 5, Lesson 5, Practice 3: Sentences that support the topic: Read each topic. Then, cross out the one sentence that does not support the topic.

Topic: A Marvelous Fairy Tale

1. The prince saves the princess.
2. The prince lives in a large castle.
3. ~~My sister loves to read fairy tales.~~
4. The prince and princess live happily ever after.

Topic: Signs of Spring

1. The grass in the yard turns green.
2. ~~Spring and summer are my favorite seasons.~~
3. The weather turns warmer.
4. Flowers begin to bloom.

ACTIVITY / ASSIGNMENT TIME

   Tell students that they are to create an imaginary character and write a detailed description of the character. They should describe every detail from the head to the feet of their imaginary character. Tell students to have fun and be creative. Remind them to include color, size, shape, arms, hands, legs, feet, eyes, eyebrows, nose, ears, tongue, etc.
   After students finish their descriptions, have them illustrate their characters on another sheet of paper. Their written description must match their illustration. They cannot draw anything if it has not been described in writing. (*Example: If they did not mention eyes, they cannot draw eyes; if they did not include color in their written description, then their drawing must be black and white. If they mentioned feet, but not legs, then their character must only have feet.*) It may take several attempts to get the written descriptions detailed enough for a good illustration. (*Extension: Write written descriptions of their rooms, the kitchen, favorite parts of a book, different family members.*)

(End of lesson.)

Level 2—Shurley English—Homeschool Edition

CHAPTER 6   LESSON 1
Objectives: Jingles, Grammar (Practice Sentences), Skills (Skill Builder Check, Simple Subject, Simple Predicate, Complete Subject, Complete Predicate), Practice Exercise, and Vocabulary #1.

 JINGLE TIME

Have students turn to the Jingle Section of their books. The teacher will lead the students in reciting the previously-taught jingles.

 GRAMMAR TIME

Put the Practice Sentences from the box below on the board or on notebook paper. Use these sentences as you practice the concepts that have been taught. For the greatest benefit, students must participate orally with the teacher.

Chapter 6, Practice Sentences for Lesson 1
1. _____ The brown spotted pony galloped quickly away.
2. _____ Those glass plates break easily.
3. _____ An enormous turtle traveled slowly onward.

TEACHING SCRIPT FOR CLASSIFYING PRACTICE SENTENCES

We will classify three different sentences to practice the grammar skills in the Question and Answer Flows. We will classify the sentences together. Begin. (*You might have students write the labels above the sentences at this time.*)

Question and Answer Flow for Sentence 1: The brown spotted pony galloped quickly away.
1. What galloped quickly away? pony - SN   5. What kind of pony? spotted - Adj
2. What is being said about pony?   6. What kind of pony? brown - Adj
pony galloped - V   7. The - A
3. Galloped how? quickly - Adv
4. Galloped where? away - Adv
A   Adj   Adj   SN   V   Adv   Adv
Classified Sentence: The brown spotted pony galloped quickly away.

CHAPTER 6 LESSON 1 CONTINUED

Question and Answer Flow for Sentence 2: Those glass plates break easily.

1. What break easily? plates - SN
2. What is being said about plates? plates break - V
3. Break how? easily - Adv
4. What kind of plates? glass - Adj
5. Which plates? those - Adj

                Adj   Adj   SN   V   Adv

Classified Sentence: Those glass plates break easily.

Question and Answer Flow for Sentence 3: An enormous turtle traveled slowly onward.

1. What traveled slowly onward? turtle - SN
2. What is being said about turtle? turtle traveled - V
3. Traveled how? slowly - Adv
4. Traveled where? onward - Adv
5. What kind of turtle? enormous - Adj
6. An - A

              A   Adj   SN   V   Adv   Adv

Classified Sentence: An enormous turtle traveled slowly onward.

SKILL TIME

TEACHING SCRIPT FOR A SKILL BUILDER CHECK

Now that we have classified all three sentences, we will use them to do a Skill Builder Check. We have already learned three skills that we can do during our Skill Builder Check. We will do a Noun Check, and then we will identify the nouns as singular or plural and as common or proper. We will start with a Noun Check. Where do we go to find nouns? (*subject job*)

Look at Sentences 1-3. We will identify the nouns in all three sentences by drawing circles around them. Let's start with number 1 and do a Noun Check. Begin. (*Circle the nouns for all three sentences as your students recite the Noun Check with you. Number 1: subject noun **pony**, yes. Number 2: subject noun **plates**, yes. Number 3: subject noun **turtle**, yes.*)

We will now identify each noun as singular or plural. Before we begin, let's review the singular and plural skills. Look at Reference 11 on page 13 in the Reference Section of your book. We will read and discuss numbers 2 and 3 about singular and plural nouns. (*Read and discuss the singular and plural nouns that are located in Reference 11 on the next page.*)

We will identify each circled noun in Sentences 1-3 as singular or plural. I will write **S** for singular or **P** for plural above each noun as we identify it. Begin. (*pony – singular, plates – plural, turtle – singular. Mark the nouns with the letter "**S**" or "**P**" in all three sentences. Discuss why the nouns are singular or plural.*)

CHAPTER 6 LESSON 1 CONTINUED

Reference 11: Definitions for a Skill Builder Check
1. A **noun** names a person, place, or thing.
2. A **singular noun** usually does not end in *s* or *es* and means only one. (*fan, doll, brush*)   Exception: Some nouns that end in s are singular and mean only one. (*address, mess*)
3. A **plural noun** usually ends in *s* or *es* and means more than one. (*fans, dolls, brushes*)   Exception: Some nouns are made plural by changing their spelling. (*ox - oxen, mouse - mice*)
4. A **common noun** names ANY person, place, or thing. A common noun is not capitalized because it does not name a specific person, place, or thing. (*principal, lake*)
5. A **proper noun** is a noun that names a specific, or particular, person, place, or thing. Proper nouns are always capitalized no matter where they are located in the sentence. (*Thomas, Alaska*)

Next, we will identify each noun as common or proper. Look at Reference 11 so we can review these skills again. (*Read and discuss the common and proper nouns in Reference 11 above.*) How do we recognize a proper noun? (*It begins with a capital letter no matter where it is located in the sentence.*) Look at each noun in each sentence. (*Say each noun together.*) Do we have any proper nouns in our sentences? (*No.*) How do you know? (*None of the nouns that are circled begins with a capital letter.*) Since we do not have a proper noun in the three sentences that we have just classified, I want you to think of a proper noun. (*Get several responses and discuss why the nouns named are proper nouns.*)

Do we have any common nouns in our sentences? (*Yes.*) Are all the nouns common? (*Yes.*) How do you know? (*All the nouns that are circled begin with a lowercase, or small, letter.*)

TEACHING SCRIPT FOR IDENTIFYING THE SIMPLE SUBJECT AND THE SIMPLE PREDICATE

We will now learn two very simple concepts: the simple subject and the simple predicate. Look at Reference 14 on page 14. Let's read the definition for the simple subject. "The **simple subject** is another name for the **subject**." Whenever you hear the term **simple subject**, it means someone is talking about the subject of the sentence. The subject noun can also be called the **simple subject**. The simple subject does not include other words in the sentence.

Look at number 2. Let's read the definition for the simple predicate. "The **simple predicate** is another name for the **verb**." Whenever you hear the term **simple predicate**, it means someone is talking about the verb of the sentence. The verb can also be called the **simple predicate**. The simple predicate does not include other words in the sentence.

Reference 14: Simple Subject, Simple Predicate, Complete Subject, Complete Predicate
1. The **simple subject** is another name for the subject.
2. The **simple predicate** is another name for the verb.
3. The **complete subject** is the subject and all the words that modify the subject.
4. The **complete predicate** is the verb and all the words that modify the verb.

Level 2—Shurley English—Homeschool Edition

CHAPTER 6 LESSON 1 CONTINUED

<u>TEACHING SCRIPT FOR THE COMPLETE SUBJECT AND THE COMPLETE PREDICATE</u>

You are learning new vocabulary words that will help you understand English terms. You have learned that the **simple subject** is another word for the subject or subject noun, and the **simple predicate** is another word for the verb.

The next step is to learn about the complete subject and the complete predicate. Look at number 3 in your reference box. Follow along as I read the definition to you. "The **complete subject** is the subject and all the words that modify the subject." The complete subject usually starts at the beginning of the sentence and includes every word up to the verb of the sentence. The subject parts usually end at the verb, and the predicate parts begin with the verb. We will underline subject parts one time because subject parts are generally indicated by only one line.

Look at number 4. Follow along as I read the definition to you. "The **complete predicate** is the verb and all the words that modify the verb." The complete predicate usually starts with the verb and includes every word after the verb. We will underline the predicate parts two times because predicate parts are generally indicated by two lines.

Now, we will use the three sentences that we have classified to practice what you have just learned. Let's read Sentence 1 again. (*The brown spotted pony galloped quickly away.*) I want you to tell me the complete subject in Sentence 1, and I will underline it once. What is the <u>complete</u> subject? (*The brown spotted pony*)

I want you to tell me the complete predicate in Sentence 1, and I will underline it twice. What is the complete predicate? (*galloped quickly away*) (*Mark the answers for Sentences 2-3 in the same way. <u>Those glass plates</u> <u>break easily</u>. <u>An enormous turtle</u> <u>traveled slowly onward</u>.*)

Look at Sentence 1 again. Now, we will identify the simple subject and simple predicate. Usually, I would draw one line under the simple subject and two lines under the simple predicate. But since I have already underlined the complete subject and complete predicate, I will just darken the lines under the words that need to be identified.

I will show you how I want you to respond when I ask for the simple subject. **What is the simple subject?** (*the subject noun, pony*) Notice that I responded with the words **the subject noun** before I actually named the subject. Now, I want you to respond after I ask the question. I will help you at the beginning if you need it. Here is the question: **What is the simple subject?** (*the subject noun, **pony***) I will darken the one line under the simple subject **pony** so you can tell the difference between the simple subject and the complete subject.

We will identify the simple predicate the same way, except we will say "*the verb*" before we name the verb. Here is the question: **What is the simple predicate?** (*the verb, **galloped***) I will darken the two lines under the simple predicate ***galloped*** so you can tell the difference between the simple predicate and the complete predicate. (*Mark the answers for Sentences 2-3 in the same way. Those glass <u>plates</u> <u>break</u> easily. An enormous <u>turtle</u> <u>traveled</u> slowly onward.*)

Level 2—Shurley English—Homeschool Edition

CHAPTER 6 LESSON 1 CONTINUED

TEACHER INSTRUCTIONS

From this time forward, the skills for a Skill Builder Check and a short explanation will be listed in a Skill Builder box. As more skills are covered, they will be added to the skill box. These guidelines will help you know the skills you have covered.

Skill Builder Check	
1. **Noun check.** (Say the job and then say the noun. Circle each noun.)	4. **Identify the complete subject and the complete predicate.** (Underline the complete subject once and the complete predicate twice.)
2. **Identify the nouns as singular or plural.** (Write **S** or **P** above each noun.)	5. **Identify the simple subject and simple predicate.** (Underline the simple subject once and the simple predicate twice. Bold, or highlight, the lines to distinguish them from the complete subject and complete predicate.)
3. **Identify the nouns as common or proper.** (Follow established procedure for oral identification.)	

Teacher's Notes: During a Skill Builder Check, the teacher asks a series of questions designed to enhance students' knowledge and understanding of different skills on a regular basis. This exercise helps students identify sentence parts and types of nouns easily and provides effective vocabulary work for new concepts.

PRACTICE TIME

Have students turn to page 42 in the Practice Section of their book and find Chapter 6, Lesson 1, Practice (*1-2*). Go over the directions to make sure they understand what to do. Check and discuss the Practices after students have finished. (*Chapter 6, Lesson 1, Practice keys are given below.*)

Chapter 6, Lesson 1, Practice 1: Underline the complete subject once and the complete predicate twice.
1. Several little puppies played happily.
2. The old bus stopped suddenly.
3. A giant toad hopped away.
4. The tiny tadpoles darted quickly around.

Chapter 6, Lesson 1, Practice 2: Underline the simple subject once and the simple predicate twice.
1. A baby robin chirped loudly.
2. The two toddlers played tirelessly.
3. The black kettle fell.
4. The new student sat quietly.

VOCABULARY TIME

Assign Chapter 6, Vocabulary Words **#1** on page 6 in the Reference Section for students to define in their Vocabulary notebooks. Tell students they are to use a dictionary or thesaurus to look up the meanings of the vocabulary words.

Chapter 6, Vocabulary Words #1
(scamper, scurry, simple, complex)

(End of lesson.)

CHAPTER 6 LESSON 2

Objectives: Jingles, Grammar (Practice Sentences), Skill (Noun Job Chart), Practice Exercise, and Vocabulary #2.

 **JINGLE TIME**

Have students turn to the Jingle Section of their books. The teacher will lead the students in reciting the previously-taught jingles.

 GRAMMAR TIME

Put the Practice Sentences from the box below on the board or on notebook paper. Use these sentences as you practice the concepts that have been taught. For the greatest benefit, students must participate orally with the teacher.

Chapter 6, Practice Sentences for Lesson 2
1. _____ Two energetic squirrels scampered quickly outside.
2. _____ The complex computer ran daily.
3. _____ The talented soloist sang beautifully.

TEACHING SCRIPT FOR CLASSIFYING PRACTICE SENTENCES

We will classify three different sentences to practice the grammar skills in the Question and Answer Flows. We will classify the sentences together. Begin. (*You might have students write the labels above the sentences at this time.*)

Question and Answer Flow for Sentence 1: Two energetic squirrels scampered quickly outside.
1. What scampered quickly outside? squirrels - SN   4. Scampered where? outside - Adv
2. What is being said about squirrels?   5. What kind of squirrels? energetic - Adj
squirrels scampered - V   6. How many squirrels? two - Adj
3. Scampered how? quickly - Adv
Adj   Adj   SN   V   Adv   Adv
Classified Sentence: Two energetic squirrels scampered quickly outside.

CHAPTER 6 LESSON 2 CONTINUED

Question and Answer Flow for Sentence 2: The complex computer ran daily.

1. What ran daily? computer - SN
2. What is being said about computer? computer ran - V
3. Ran when? daily - Adv
4. What kind of computer? complex - Adj
5. The - A

	A	Adj	SN	V	Adv

Classified Sentence: The complex computer ran daily.

Question and Answer Flow for Sentence 3: The talented soloist sang beautifully.

1. Who sang beautifully? soloist - SN
2. What is being said about soloist? soloist sang - V
3. Sang how? beautifully - Adv
4. What kind of soloist? talented - Adj
5. The - A

	A	Adj	SN	V	Adv

Classified Sentence: The talented soloist sang beautifully.

SKILL TIME

Today, you will use a new format to practice the skills that you have learned. Look at Reference 15 on page 14 in the Reference section. This is a Noun Job Chart. You will also have a Noun Job Chart on your weekly tests. This chart is very easy to fill out, but you must read the directions carefully so you do not miss anything. I will explain the Noun Job Chart in Reference 15. It will show you what is expected and how to do it. (*Read the directions to your students and then go through the sentence, showing them how to find the answers in the Noun Job Chart in Reference 15 below.*)

Reference 15: Noun Job Chart

Directions: Classify the sentence below. Underline the complete subject once and the complete predicate twice. Then, complete the table.

A Adj SN   V   Adv   Adv
The small raft drifted lazily downstream.

List the Noun Used	List the Noun Job	Singular or Plural	Common or Proper	Simple Subject	Simple Predicate
raft	SN	S	C	raft	drifted

Level 2—Shurley English—Homeschool Edition

CHAPTER 6 LESSON 2 CONTINUED

 PRACTICE TIME

Have students turn to pages 42 and 43 in the Practice Section of their book and find Chapter 6, Lesson 2, Practice *(1-5)*. Go over the directions to make sure they understand what to do. Check and discuss the Practices after students have finished. (*Chapter 6, Lesson 2, Practice keys are given below.*)

Chapter 6, Lesson 2, Practice 1

Directions: Classify the sentence below. Underline the complete subject once and the complete predicate twice. Then, complete the table below.

A   Adj   SN   V   Adv
The Christmas ornaments sparkled brightly.

List the Noun Used	List the Noun Job	Singular or Plural	Common or Proper	Simple Subject	Simple Predicate
ornaments	SN	P	C	ornaments	sparkled

Chapter 6, Lesson 2, Practice 2: Underline the complete subject once and the complete predicate twice.
1. The new toy broke suddenly.
2. The office staff laughed loudly.
3. A wildfire burned brightly ahead.
4. The jet airliner flew away.

Chapter 6, Lesson 2, Practice 3: Underline the simple subject once and the simple predicate twice.
1. An empty bottle broke.
2. The three red tulips bloomed.
3. The tomatoes ripened quickly.
4. Many horses trot contentedly.

Chapter 6, Lesson 2, Practice 4: For each noun listed below, write **C** for common or **P** for proper.

Noun	C or P	Noun	C or P	Noun	C or P
1. jacket	C	3. month	C	5. pizza	C
2. Phillip	P	4. insect	C	6. October	P

Chapter 6, Lesson 2, Practice 5: For each noun listed below, write **S** for singular or **P** for plural.

Noun	S or P	Noun	S or P	Noun	S or P
1. plants	P	3. tractors	P	5. socks	P
2. mop	S	4. glass	S	6. lions	P

 VOCABULARY TIME

Assign Chapter 6, Vocabulary Words **#2** on page 6 in the Reference Section for students to define in their Vocabulary notebooks. Tell students they are to use a dictionary or thesaurus to look up the meanings of the vocabulary words.

Chapter 6, Vocabulary Words #2
(brilliant, dull, rage, anger)

(End of lesson.)

Level 2 Homeschool Teacher's Manual   Page 81

Level 2—Shurley English—Homeschool Edition

CHAPTER 6   LESSON 3
Objectives: Jingles, Grammar (Practice Sentences), Skills (Practice and Improved Sentences).

 **JINGLE TIME**

Have students turn to the Jingle Section of their books. The teacher will lead the students in reciting the previously-taught jingles.

 GRAMMAR TIME

Put the Practice Sentences from the box below on the board or on notebook paper. Use these sentences as you practice the concepts that have been taught. For the greatest benefit, students must participate orally with the teacher.

Chapter 6, Practice Sentences for Lesson 3
1. _____ The eager catfish ate hungrily.
2. _____ The brilliant scientist left unexpectedly.
3. _____ The raging waters rushed wildly downstream.

TEACHING SCRIPT FOR CLASSIFYING PRACTICE SENTENCES

We will classify three different sentences to practice the grammar skills in the Question and Answer Flows. We will classify the sentences together. Begin. (*You might have students write the labels above the sentences at this time.*)

Question and Answer Flow for Sentence 1: The eager catfish ate hungrily.
1. What ate hungrily? catfish - SN   4. What kind of catfish? eager - Adj
2. What is being said about catfish? catfish ate - V   5. The - A
3. Catfish ate how? hungrily - Adv
Classified Sentence: A   Adj   SN   V   Adv
The eager catfish ate hungrily.

CHAPTER 6 LESSON 3 CONTINUED

Question and Answer Flow for Sentence 2: The brilliant scientist left unexpectedly.

1. Who left unexpectedly? scientist - SN
2. What is being said about scientist? scientist left - V
3. Left how? unexpectedly - Adv
4. What kind of scientist? brilliant - Adj
5. The - A

```
                    A    Adj   SN   V    Adv
Classified Sentence:  The brilliant scientist left unexpectedly.
```

Question and Answer Flow for Sentence 3: The raging waters rushed wildly downstream.

1. What rushed wildly downstream? waters - SN
2. What is being said about waters? waters rushed - V
3. Rushed how? wildly - Adv
4. Rushed where? downstream - Adv
5. What kind of waters? raging - Adj
6. The - A

```
                    A    Adj   SN   V    Adv   Adv
Classified Sentence:  The raging waters rushed wildly downstream.
```

 SKILL TIME

TEACHING SCRIPT FOR A PRACTICE SENTENCE

> Put these labels on the board: **A Adj Adj SN V Adv Adv**

Today, I will guide you as you write a Practice Sentence and an Improved Sentence. Look at the sentence labels on the board. Let's repeat the labels together: **A Adj Adj SN V Adv Adv**. You will now write a seven-word sentence.

Get out a sheet of notebook paper. On the top line of your notebook paper, write the title *Practice Sentence*. Copy the sentence labels from the board onto your notebook paper. Be sure to leave plenty of writing space between each label. We will begin with the subject noun.

1. Go to the **SN** label for the subject noun. Think of a noun that you want to use as your subject. Write the noun you have chosen on the line *under* the **SN** label.

2. Go to the **V** label for the verb. Think of a verb that tells what your subject does. Make sure that your verb makes sense with the subject noun. Write the verb you have chosen on the line *under* the **V** label.

Level 2—Shurley English—Homeschool Edition

CHAPTER 6 LESSON 3 CONTINUED

3. Go to the **Adv** label for the adverb. Go to the verb in your sentence and ask an adverb question. What are the adverb questions? (*How, When, Where*) Choose one adverb question to ask and write your adverb answer *under* the first **Adv** label.

4. Go to the **Adv** label for another adverb. Go to the verb again and ask another adverb question. You can ask the same adverb question, or you can ask a different adverb question. Write another adverb *under* the second **Adv** label.

5. Go to the **Adj** label for the adjective. Go to the subject noun of your sentence and ask an adjective question. What are the adjective questions? (*What kind, Which one, How many*) Choose one adjective question to ask and write your adjective answer *under* the **Adj** label next to the subject noun. Always check to make sure your answers are making sense in the sentence.

6. Go to the next **Adj** label for another adjective. Go to the subject noun again and ask another adjective question. You can ask the same adjective question, or you can ask a different adjective question. Write another adjective *under* the second **Adj** label.

7. Go to the **A** label for the article adjective. What are the three article adjectives? (*a*, *an*, and *the*) Choose the article adjective that makes the best sense in your sentence. Write the article adjective you have chosen *under* the **A** label.

8. Finally, check your Practice Sentence to make sure it has the necessary parts to be a complete sentence. What are the five parts of a complete sentence? (*subject, verb, complete sense, capital letter, and an end mark*) Does your Practice Sentence have the five parts of a complete sentence? (*Allow time for students to read over their sentences and to make any necessary corrections.*)

9. Under your Practice Sentence, write the title *Improved Sentence* on another line. To improve your Practice Sentence, you will make two synonym changes, one antonym change, and your choice of a complete word change or another synonym or antonym change.

Since it is harder to find words that can be changed to an antonym, it is usually wise to go through your sentence to find an antonym change first. Then, look through your sentence again to find words that can be improved with synonyms. Finally, make a decision about whether your last change will be a complete word change, another synonym change, or another antonym change. I will give you time to write your Improved Sentence. (*Always encourage students to use a thesaurus, synonym-antonym book, or a dictionary to help them develop an interesting and improved writing vocabulary. After students have finished, check and discuss students' Practice and Improved Sentences.*)

(End of lesson.)

CHAPTER 6   LESSON 4

Objectives: Jingles, Study, Test, Check, Writing (Journal), State Activity, and Sentence Time.

JINGLE TIME

Have students turn to the Jingle Section in their books. The teacher will lead the students in reciting the previously-taught jingles.

STUDY TIME

Have students study the vocabulary words in their vocabulary notebooks. Remind students that any vocabulary word in their notebooks could be on their test. Also, have students study any of the skills in the Practice Section they need to review.

TEST TIME

Have students turn to page 85 in the Test Section of their books and find Chapter 6 Test. Go over the directions to make sure they understand what to do. *(Chapter 6 Test key is on the next page.)*

CHECK TIME

After students have finished, check and discuss their test papers. Make sure they understand why their answers are right or wrong. *(For total points, count each required answer as a point.)*

STATE ACTIVITY TIME

(Have a recipe box and a package of lined index cards ready for your children to use for this activity.) Find a map of the United States. Draw or trace the state of Colorado on the blank side of an index card. On the lined side of the card, write the following questions and answers.

1. What is the state on the front of this card? **Colorado**
2. What is the capital of Colorado? **Denver**
3. What is the postal abbreviation of Colorado? **CO**

Color this state. Use the card to quiz family members, friends, and relatives. You may want to time the responses to your questions.

(End of lesson.)

Level 2—Shurley English—Homeschool Edition

Chapter 6 Test
(Student Page 85)

53 pts

Exercise 1: Classify each sentence.

       A   Adj   SN   V   Adv   Adv
1. The thick fog disappeared rapidly today.

       A   Adj Adj   SN   V   Adv
2. <u>The fresh hot pizza</u> <u>arrived unexpectedly</u>.

Exercise 2: Use Sentence 2 to underline the complete subject once and the complete predicate twice and to complete the table below.

List the Noun Used	List the Noun Job	Singular or Plural	Common or Proper	Simple Subject	Simple Predicate
1. pizza	2. SN	3. S	4. C	5. pizza	6. arrived

Exercise 3: Identify each pair of words as synonyms or antonyms by putting parentheses ( ) around **syn** or **ant**.

1. irritate, annoy	**(syn)** ant	4. disappear, vanish	**(syn)** ant	7. scamper, scurry	**(syn)** ant
2. brilliant, dull	syn **(ant)**	5. simple, complex	syn **(ant)**	8. frequent, often	**(syn)** ant
3. anger, rage	**(syn)** ant	6. mournful, delightful	syn **(ant)**	9. excited, calm	syn **(ant)**

Exercise 4: Put the end mark and the abbreviation for each kind of sentence in the blanks below.

1. My new shoes are covered in mud   **!**   **E**
2. The bread is on the cabinet   **.**   **D**
3. May I help you   **?**   **Int**

Exercise 5: Write **S** for singular or **P** for plural.

Noun	S or P
1. paper	S
2. voices	P
3. swing	S

Exercise 6: Write **C** for Common or **P** for proper.

Noun	C or P
1. Mississippi	P
2. George	P
3. patio	C

Exercise 7: Write *a* or *an* in the blanks.

1. Uncle Joe owns **a** motel.
2. We did **an** activity.
3. The priest said **a** prayer.
4. The ship dropped **an** anchor.
5. **a** wolf
6. **an** axe
7. **a** hunter
8. **an** ostrich

Exercise 8: Name the four parts of speech that you have studied. (*You may use abbreviations*.) **(The order of answers may vary.)**

1. **noun**   2. **verb**   3. **adjective**   4. **adverb**

Exercise 9: In your journal, write a paragraph summarizing what you have learned this week.

Level 2—Shurley English—Homeschool Edition

CHAPTER 6 LESSON 4 CONTINUED

TEACHER INSTRUCTIONS

Use the Question and Answer Flows below for the sentences on the Chapter 6 Test.

Question and Answer Flow for Sentence 1: The thick fog disappeared rapidly today.

1. What disappeared rapidly today? fog - SN
2. What is being said about fog? fog disappeared - V
3. Disappeared how? rapidly - Adv
4. Disappeared when? today - Adv
5. What kind of fog? thick - Adj
6. The - A

Classified Sentence: A   Adj   SN   V   Adv   Adv
  The thick fog disappeared rapidly today.

Question and Answer Flow for Sentence 2: The fresh hot pizza arrived unexpectedly.

1. What arrived unexpectedly? pizza - SN
2. What is being said about pizza? pizza arrived - V
3. Arrived how? unexpectedly - Adv
4. What kind of pizza? hot - Adj
5. What kind of pizza? fresh - Adj
6. The - A

Classified Sentence: A   Adj   Adj   SN   V   Adv
  The fresh hot pizza arrived unexpectedly.

SENTENCE TIME

Chapter 6, Lesson 4, Sentence: Use colored markers to match each label with the correct sentence part by drawing a line from one to the other. Then, use the labels to arrange the sentence parts into a sentence that you will write on the sentence line below. *(The order of the words in your sentence should be in the same sequence as the vertical list of sentence labels.)* Create other labels and scrambled sentence parts on notebook paper for family members to solve. You may color code the sentence parts. *(See page 110 in the student book.)*

Labels for Order of Sentence	Scrambled Sentence Parts
A	young
Adj	today
SN	the
V	excitedly
Adv	whispered
Adv	children

Sentence: The young children whispered excitedly today.

(End of lesson.)

CHAPTER 6   LESSON 5

Objectives: Writing (Reviewing Topics, Supporting and Non-Supporting Ideas and Sentences), Practice Exercise, and Activity.

 **WRITING TIME**

TEACHING SCRIPT FOR REVIEWING TOPICS AND SUPPORTING AND NON-SUPPORTING IDEAS AND SENTENCES

We will practice writing-related activities again in this lesson. These skills will help you when you begin writing paragraphs. Since you will begin writing paragraphs in Chapter 7, it is important that we review the terms from last week: *topic*, *supporting*, and *non-supporting*. We will review the information about each term in your Reference Section. Turn to page 13 and look at Reference 12 as I go over it again with you. (*Read and discuss the information in Reference 12 on page 71 in the teacher's manual.*)

Now, look at Reference 13 on page 14 as I review the information about supporting and non-supporting ideas and sentences. (*Read and discuss the information in Reference 13 on page 72 in the teacher's manual.*)

 PRACTICE TIME

Have students turn to pages 43 and 44 in the Practice Section of their book and find Chapter 6, Lesson 5, Practice *(1-3)*. Go over the directions to make sure they understand what to do. Check and discuss the Practices after students have finished. (*Chapter 6, Lesson 5, Practice keys are given below and on the next page.*)

Chapter 6, Lesson 5, Practice 1: Finding the topic: Write the name of the topic that best describes what each row of words is about. Choose from these topics:

Colors   Food   Animals   Seasons   Kitchen Things   Transportation.

(1) Food	(2) Transportation	(3) Kitchen Things
pizza	motorcycle	pan
taco	car	refrigerator
hamburger	scooter	sink
burrito	truck	knife

CHAPTER 6 LESSON 5 CONTINUED

Chapter 6, Lesson 5, Practice 2: Words that support the topic: In each row, cross out the one idea that does not support the underlined topic at the top.

(1) Zoo Animals	(2) Shapes	(3) Colors
tiger	oval	red
~~clown~~	rectangle	green
ostrich	square	~~valley~~
ape	~~pepperoni~~	brown
tortoise	circle	pink

Chapter 6, Lesson 5, Practice 3: Sentences that support the topic: Read each topic. Then, cross out the one sentence that does not support the topic.

Topic: A Trip to the Circus

1. Dad took me to the circus yesterday.
2. Dad gave our tickets to the lady in the booth.
3. ~~My dad took me to the movies last week.~~
4. We found our seats and waited patiently for the show to begin.

Topic: An Exciting New Game Show

1. The contestants stand nervously in front of the cameras.
2. ~~My uncle is a newscaster on channel eight.~~
3. The host asks each player a different question.
4. The player with the highest score wins a new car.

ACTIVITY / ASSIGNMENT TIME

Have students get out four sheets of paper and trace the outline of their hand on each one. Have students write one of the sentences below under each hand. Provide a copy of the code below. Using the code, students should color one finger for each of the sentence parts in the key. A sample is provided below. *(Students may make a new color code for each sentence.)*

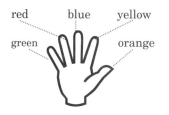

Color Code	
Article Adjective	orange
Adjective	yellow
Noun	blue
Verb	red
Adverb	green

Sentences
1. The sweet baby slept soundly.
2. A colorful butterfly flew away.
3. A tiny frog croaked loudly.
4. The happy fans cheered excitedly.

       A   Adj   SN   V   Adv
Sample: The hairy caterpillar crawled slowly.

(End of lesson.)

Level 2—Shurley English—Homeschool Edition

CHAPTER 7   LESSON 1
Objectives: Jingles, Grammar (Introductory Sentences, Pattern 1, End Punctuation, Skill Builder Check), Practice Exercise, and Vocabulary #1.

 **JINGLE TIME**

Have students turn to the Jingle Section of their books. The teacher will lead the students in reciting the previously-taught jingles.

 GRAMMAR TIME

Put the introductory sentences from the box below on the board. Use these sentences as you go through the new concepts covered in your teaching scripts. For the greatest benefit, students must participate orally with the teacher. (*You might put the introductory sentences on notebook paper if you are doing one-on-one instruction with your students.*)

Chapter 7, Introductory Sentences for Lesson 1
1. _____ The magnificent rainbow appeared brilliantly overhead.
2. _____ The powerful truck crashed suddenly!
3. _____ The graceful white swan swam here daily.

TEACHING SCRIPT FOR PATTERN 1 AND END PUNCTUATION

We will now classify Sentence 1. This time, there will be more information added to the Question and Answer Flow. You will classify the sentence with me until we get to the new part. The new part will be at the end of the Question and Answer Flow. Begin.

Sentence 1: The magnificent rainbow appeared brilliantly overhead.
What appeared brilliantly overhead? rainbow - SN
What is being said about rainbow? rainbow appeared - V
Appeared how? brilliantly - Adv
Appeared where? overhead - Adv
What kind of rainbow? magnificent - Adj
The - A

I will now explain the new parts and show you how to add them to the Question and Answer Flow. First, I will say the new parts in the Question and Answer Flow, and then I will explain each new part to you. Listen carefully as I repeat the two new parts in the Question and Answer Flow.

CHAPTER 7 LESSON 1 CONTINUED

1. Subject Noun Verb Pattern 1 Check. (*Write **SN V P1** in the blank in front of the sentence. Be sure to say **check**. You will use the check to identify any new skill that is added to the Question and Answer Flow.*)
2. Period, statement, declarative sentence. (*Write a **D** at the end of the sentence.*)

> **Note:** Your sentence should look like this:
>
> | | A | Adj | SN | V | Adv | Adv | |
> |-------|---|-----|----|----|-----|-----|---|
> | SN V P1 | The | magnificent | rainbow | appeared | brilliantly | overhead. | D |

I will explain each new part, one at a time. Listen to the definition for a Pattern 1 sentence. The pattern of a sentence is the **order of the main parts** in that sentence. **Pattern 1** has only two main parts: the subject and the verb. Adjectives and adverbs add information to sentences, but they are not part of a sentence pattern. A **Pattern 1** sentence is labeled ***SN V P1***. (*Put the SN V P1 on the board for your students to see.*) When you see or write the ***SN V P1*** labels, you will say, "Subject Noun, Verb, Pattern 1."

You will also add a <u>check</u> to the sentence pattern to check for any additional skills to be identified. You will say, **"Subject Noun, Verb, Pattern 1, Check."** The word **check** will be explained again as you use it.

Now, I will review the information that you just learned to make sure you understand it correctly. You may be a little uncertain at first, but the more we practice, the easier it will be. Listen carefully to the review.

1. The pattern of a sentence is <u>the order of its main parts</u>. <u>The subject and the verb are the main parts of a Pattern 1 sentence</u>.

2. Adjectives and adverbs are extra words that are not considered main parts of a sentence pattern because they are used freely with all sentence patterns.

3. To identify a Pattern 1 sentence, you will write ***SN V P1*** on the line in front of the sentence and say, "Subject Noun, Verb, Pattern 1, Check."

The second part that we will add to the Question and Answer Flow is to identify the sentence as a declarative, interrogative, or exclamatory sentence. As soon as you say **check**, you will check for the kind of sentence. To do this, you will go to the end of the sentence, identify the end mark, give the definition of the sentence, and the kind of sentence. I will demonstrate this for you in Sentence 1. You will say, ***"Period, statement, declarative sentence."*** After you have identified the sentence as a declarative sentence, you will write a ***D*** after the period, but you will always say, "Period, statement, declarative sentence."

I will classify Sentence 1 again, and you will classify it with me this time. We will add the two new parts at the end of the Question and Answer Flow. Then, we will classify sentences 2-3 together.

Level 2—Shurley English—Homeschool Edition

CHAPTER 7 LESSON 1 CONTINUED

Question and Answer Flow for Sentence 1: The magnificent rainbow appeared brilliantly overhead.

1. What appeared brilliantly overhead? rainbow - SN
2. What is being said about rainbow? rainbow appeared - V
3. Appeared how? brilliantly - Adv
4. Appeared where? overhead - Adv
5. What kind of rainbow? magnificent - Adj
6. The - A
7. SN V P1 Check (Say: Subject Noun, Verb, Pattern 1, Check.)
   (Write *SN V P1* in the blank beside the sentence.)
8. Period, statement, declarative sentence
   (Write *D* at the end of the sentence.)

```
                            A    Adj       SN       V     Adv    Adv
Classified Sentence:   SN V    The magnificent rainbow appeared brilliantly overhead.  D
                       P1
```

Question and Answer Flow for Sentence 2: The powerful truck crashed suddenly!

1. What crashed suddenly? truck - SN
2. What is being said about truck? truck crashed - V
3. Crashed how? suddenly - Adv
4. What kind of truck? powerful - Adj
5. The - A
6. SN V P1 Check (Say: Subject Noun, Verb, Pattern 1, Check.)
   (Write *SN V P1* in the blank beside the sentence.)
7. Exclamation point, strong feeling, exclamatory sentence
   (Write *E* at the end of the sentence.)

```
                            A    Adj    SN      V     Adv
Classified Sentence:   SN V    The powerful truck crashed suddenly!  E
                       P1
```

Question and Answer Flow for Sentence 3: The graceful white swan swam here daily.

1. What swam here daily? swan - SN
2. What is being said about swan? swan swam - V
3. Swam where? here - Adv
4. Swam when? daily - Adv
5. What kind of swan? white - Adj
6. What kind of swan? graceful - Adj
7. The - A
8. SN V P1 Check (Say: Subject Noun, Verb, Pattern 1, Check.)
   (Write *SN V P1* in the blank beside the sentence.)
9. Period, statement, declarative sentence
   (Write *D* at the end of the sentence.)

```
                            A    Adj    Adj    SN     V    Adv   Adv
Classified Sentence:   SN V    The graceful white swan swam here daily.  D
                       P1
```

TEACHER INSTRUCTIONS

Use sentences 1-3 that you just classified with your students to do a Skill Builder Check. Use the guidelines on the next page. Use the same procedure that you used in the previous lessons. You have five Skill Builder Checks to do. It should not take you long, but explain or review whenever necessary.

Level 2—Shurley English—Homeschool Edition

CHAPTER 7 LESSON 1 CONTINUED

Skill Builder Check	
1. **Noun check.** (Say the job and then say the noun. Circle each noun.) 2. **Identify the nouns as singular or plural.** (Write **S** or **P** above each noun.) 3. **Identify the nouns as common or proper.** (Follow established procedure for oral identification.)	4. **Identify the complete subject and the complete predicate.** (Underline the complete subject once and the complete predicate twice.) 5. **Identify the simple subject and simple predicate.** (Underline the simple subject once and the simple predicate twice. Bold, or highlight, the lines to distinguish them from the complete subject and complete predicate.)

PRACTICE TIME

Have students turn to page 44 in the Practice Section of their book and find Chapter 7, Lesson 1, Practice. Go over the directions to make sure they understand what to do. Check and discuss the Practice after students have finished. (*Chapter 7, Lesson 1, Practice key is given below.*)

Chapter 7, Lesson 1, Practice					
Directions: Classify the sentence below. Underline the complete subject once and the complete predicate twice. Then, complete the table below.					
SN V — P1	A Adj Adj SN V Adv The large helium balloon floated freely. D				
List the Noun Used	List the Noun Job	Singular or Plural	Common or Proper	Simple Subject	Simple Predicate
balloon	SN	S	C	balloon	floated

VOCABULARY TIME

Assign Chapter 7, Vocabulary Words **#1** on page 6 in the Reference Section for students to define in their Vocabulary notebooks. Tell students they are to use a dictionary or thesaurus to look up the meanings of the vocabulary words.

Chapter 7, Vocabulary Words #1
(cargo, freight, arrive, depart)

(End of lesson.)

Level 2—Shurley English—Homeschool Edition

CHAPTER 7   LESSON 2
Objectives: Jingles, Grammar (Introductory Sentences, Complete Subject, Complete Predicate), Skill (Add Vocabulary Check to Skill Builder Time), and Vocabulary #2.

 **JINGLE TIME**

Have students turn to the Jingle Section of their books. The teacher will lead the students in reciting the previously-taught jingles.

 GRAMMAR TIME

Put the introductory sentences from the box below on the board. Use these sentences as you go through the new concepts covered in your teaching scripts. For the greatest benefit, students must participate orally with the teacher. (*You might put the introductory sentences on notebook paper if you are doing one-on-one instruction with your students.*)

Chapter 7, Introductory Sentences for Lesson 2
1. _____ The small rabbit scurried quickly away.
2. _____ The freight train departed loudly.
3. _____ The two little calves jumped around friskily.

TEACHING SCRIPT FOR COMPLETE SUBJECT AND COMPLETE PREDICATE

As we classify today's sentences, we will have more information added to the end of the Question and Answer Flow. You will classify the sentence with me until we get to the new part. Then, I will explain the new part to you. We will now classify Sentence 1 together. Begin.

Sentence 1: The small rabbit scurried quickly away.
What scurried quickly away? rabbit - SN
What is being said about rabbit? rabbit scurried - V
Scurried how? quickly - Adv
Scurried where? away - Adv
What kind of rabbit? small - Adj
The - A
SN V P1 Check (Subject Noun, Verb, Pattern 1 Check)
Period, statement, declarative sentence

I will now explain the new part and show you how to add it to the Question and Answer Flow. First, I will say the new part in the Question and Answer Flow, and then I will explain it to you. Listen carefully as I say the new part.

Page 94 Level 2 Homeschool Teacher's Manual

CHAPTER 7 LESSON 2 CONTINUED

Go back to the verb - divide the complete subject from the complete predicate.
(*As you say **divide**, put a slash mark before your verb.*)

> **Note:** Your sentence should look like this:
>
> ```
>              A   Adj  SN     V    Adv   Adv
> SN V         The small rabbit / scurried quickly away.  D
> P1
> ```

Listen carefully as I repeat the new part again. *"Go back to the verb - divide the complete subject from the complete predicate."* Since this new part contains information about the complete subject and the complete predicate, I will review these skills first. Look at Reference 14 on page 14. Follow along as I read the definitions for the complete subject and the complete predicate. (*Follow the script below.*)

The **complete subject** is the subject and all the words that modify the subject. The complete subject usually starts at the beginning of the sentence and includes every word up to the verb of the sentence. The slash mark in front of the verb shows where the subject parts end and the predicate parts begin.

The **complete predicate** is the verb and all the words that modify the verb. The complete predicate usually starts with the verb and includes every word after the verb. The slash mark in front of the verb shows where the predicate parts start. The vertical line is a dividing line that divides, or separates, all the subject parts from all the predicate parts in the sentence.

Remember, the words you say in the Question and Answer Flow are these: *Go back to the verb - divide the complete subject from the complete predicate.* Then, you will put a slash mark in front of the verb to indicate that the verb and everything after the verb is the complete predicate, and everything in front of the verb is the complete subject. (*Exceptions to this general rule are addressed in Levels 4-6.*) This is an easy way to identify all the subject parts and all the predicate parts. I will classify Sentence 1 again, and you will classify it with me this time. Then, we will classify Sentences 2-3 together.

Teacher's Notes: Make sure students are reciting each Question and Answer Flow orally, with you. They learn the concepts so much faster and retain them longer if they say the Question and Answer Flows orally!

> **Question and Answer Flow for Sentence 1: The small rabbit scurried quickly away.**
>
> 1. What scurried quickly away? rabbit - SN
> 2. What is being said about rabbit? rabbit scurried - V
> 3. Scurried how? quickly - Adv
> 4. Scurried where? away - Adv
> 5. What kind of rabbit? small - Adj
> 6. The - A
>
> 7. SN V P1 (Subject Noun Verb Pattern 1) Check
>   (Write *SN V P1* in the blank beside the sentence.)
> 8. Period, statement, declarative sentence
>   (Write *D* at the end of the sentence.)
> 9. Go back to the verb - divide the complete subject from the complete predicate.
>   (As you say <u>divide</u>, put a slash mark before the verb.)
>
> **Classified Sentence:**
> ```
>                    A   Adj  SN     V    Adv  Adv
>         SN V       The small rabbit / scurried quickly away.  D
>         P1
> ```

Level 2—Shurley English—Homeschool Edition

CHAPTER 7 LESSON 2 CONTINUED

Question and Answer Flow for Sentence 2: The freight train departed loudly.

1. What departed loudly? train - SN
2. What is being said about train? train departed - V
3. Departed how? loudly - Adv
4. What kind of train? freight - Adj
5. The - A
6. SN V P1 (Subject Noun Verb Pattern 1) Check
    (Write *SN V P1* in the blank beside the sentence.)
7. Period, statement, declarative sentence
    (Write *D* at the end of the sentence.)
8. Go back to the verb - divide the complete subject from the complete predicate.
    (As you say <u>divide</u>, put a slash mark before the verb.)

```
                         A    Adj   SN        V    Adv
Classified Sentence:   SN V    The freight train / departed loudly.  D
                       P1
```

Question and Answer Flow for Sentence 3: The two little calves jumped around friskily.

1. What jumped around friskily? calves - SN
2. What is being said about calves? calves jumped - V
3. Jumped where? around - Adv
4. Jumped how? friskily - Adv
5. What kind of calves? little - Adj
6. How many calves? two - Adj
7. The - A
8. SN V P1 (Subject Noun Verb Pattern 1) Check
    (Write *SN V P1* in the blank beside the sentence.)
9. Period, statement, declarative sentence
    (Write *D* at the end of the sentence.)
10. Go back to the verb - divide the complete subject from the complete predicate.
    (As you say <u>divide</u>, put a slash mark before the verb.)

```
                          A   Adj  Adj   SN        V     Adv    Adv
Classified Sentence:   SN V    The two little calves / jumped around friskily.  D
                       P1
```

SKILL TIME

<u>*TEACHING SCRIPT FOR ADDING A VOCABULARY CHECK TO SKILL BUILDER TIME*</u>

We will use the three sentences that we just classified to learn a new Skill Builder. We will add a Vocabulary Check to the Skill Builder Check time. The Vocabulary Check will give me an opportunity to expand your vocabulary. I will select several words from the three sentences that we classified together for a Vocabulary Check. We will define the words, use them in new sentences, and name synonyms and antonyms for them.

<u>*TEACHER INSTRUCTIONS*</u>

Look over the words in the classified sentences. Select any words you think your students may not understand or words for which you want students to develop a broader understanding. Use the guidelines on the next page for a Vocabulary Check. (*For some words, you might use all the guidelines presented for a Vocabulary Check. For the reinforcement of other words, you might ask only for synonyms and antonyms. Talk about how synonym and antonym changes can affect the meaning of the original sentence. Show your students that synonyms and antonyms are powerful writing tools, and they must learn to use them well. It is very important that each child has a thesaurus of his/her own.*)

CHAPTER 7 LESSON 2 CONTINUED

Guidelines for a Vocabulary Check
1. Give a definition for the word.
2. Use the word correctly in a sentence.
3. Think of a synonym for the word.
4. Think of an antonym for the word.

TEACHER INSTRUCTIONS

Use sentences 1-3 that you just classified with your students to do a Skill Builder Check. Use the guidelines below. Notice that a vocabulary check has been added to the checklist. You now have 6 checks to do. Read the information contained in the guidelines below. It will help keep you on track. This is a valuable skill, and you do not want to skip it.

Skill Builder Check	
1. Noun check. (Say the job and then say the noun. Circle each noun.)	**5. Identify the complete subject and the complete predicate.** (Underline the complete subject once and the complete predicate twice.)
2. Identify the nouns as singular or plural. (Write **S** or **P** above each noun.)	**6. Identify the simple subject and simple predicate.** (Underline the simple subject once and the simple predicate twice. Bold, or highlight, the lines to distinguish them from the complete subject and complete predicate.)
3. Identify the nouns as common or proper. (Follow established procedure for oral identification.)	
4. Do a vocabulary check. (Follow established procedure for oral identification.)	

VOCABULARY TIME

Assign Chapter 7, Vocabulary Words **#2** on page 6 in the Reference Section for students to define in their Vocabulary notebooks. Tell students they are to use a dictionary or thesaurus to look up the meanings of the vocabulary words.

Chapter 7, Vocabulary Words #2
(build, collapse, overhead, above)

(End of lesson.)

CHAPTER 7   LESSON 3
Objectives: Jingles, Grammar (Practice Sentences, Practice and Improved Sentence).

 **JINGLE TIME**

Have students turn to the Jingle Section of their books. The teacher will lead the students in reciting the previously-taught jingles.

 GRAMMAR TIME

Put the Practice Sentences from the box below on the board or on notebook paper. Use these sentences as you practice the concepts that have been taught. For the greatest benefit, students must participate orally with the teacher.

Chapter 7, Practice Sentences for Lesson 3
1. _____ The wind blew briskly today.
2. _____ The cloth hammock collapsed suddenly.
3. _____ An ugly green moth flew overhead.

TEACHING SCRIPT FOR CLASSIFYING PRACTICE SENTENCES

We will classify three different sentences to practice the grammar skills in the Question and Answer Flows. We will classify the sentences together. Begin. (*You might have students write the labels above the sentences at this time.*)

Question and Answer Flow for Sentence 1: The wind blew briskly today.
1. What blew briskly today? wind - SN   6. SN V P1 Check
2. What is being said about wind? wind blew - V   7. Period, statement, declarative sentence
3. Blew how? briskly - Adv   8. Go back to the verb - divide the complete subject
4. Blew when? today - Adv   from the complete predicate.
5. The - A
A   SN   V   Adv   Adv
Classified Sentence: SN V   The wind / blew briskly today.   D
P1

CHAPTER 7 LESSON 3 CONTINUED

Question and Answer Flow for Sentence 2: The cloth hammock collapsed suddenly.

1. What collapsed suddenly? hammock - SN
2. What is being said about hammock? hammock collapsed - V
3. Collapsed how? suddenly - Adv
4. What kind of hammock? cloth - Adj
5. The - A
6. SN V P1 Check
7. Period, statement, declarative sentence
8. Go back to the verb - divide the complete subject from the complete predicate.

```
                          A   Adj    SN      V     Adv
Classified Sentence:   SN V    The cloth hammock / collapsed suddenly.  D
                       P1
```

Question and Answer Flow for Sentence 3: An ugly green moth flew overhead.

1. What flew overhead? moth - SN
2. What is being said about moth? moth flew - V
3. Flew where? overhead - Adv
4. What kind of moth? green - Adj
5. What kind of moth? ugly - Adj
6. An - A
7. SN V P1 Check
8. Period, statement, declarative sentence
9. Go back to the verb - divide the complete subject from the complete predicate.

```
                          A  Adj  Adj   SN    V    Adv
Classified Sentence:   SN V    An ugly green moth / flew overhead.  D
                       P1
```

TEACHING SCRIPT FOR A PRACTICE SENTENCE

Put these labels on the board: **A   Adj   Adj   SN   V   Adv   Adv**

Today, I will guide you as you write a Practice Sentence and an Improved Sentence. Look at the sentence labels on the board. Let's repeat the labels together: **A Adj Adj SN V Adv Adv**. You will now write a seven-word sentence.

Get out a sheet of notebook paper. On the top line of your notebook paper, write the title *Practice Sentence*. Copy the sentence labels from the board onto your notebook paper. Be sure to leave plenty of writing space between each label. We will begin with the subject noun.

1. Go to the **SN** label for the subject noun. Think of a noun that you want to use as your subject. Write the noun you have chosen on the line *under* the **SN** label.

2. Go to the **V** label for the verb. Think of a verb that tells what your subject does. Make sure that your verb makes sense with the subject noun. Write the verb you have chosen on the line *under* the **V** label.

CHAPTER 7 LESSON 3 CONTINUED

3. Go to the **Adv** label for the adverb. Go to the verb in your sentence and ask an adverb question. What are the adverb questions? (*How, When, Where*) Choose one adverb question to ask and write your adverb answer *under* the first **Adv** label.

4. Go to the **Adv** label for another adverb. Go to the verb again and ask another adverb question. You can ask the same adverb question, or you can ask a different adverb question. Write another adverb *under* the second **Adv** label.

5. Go to the **Adj** label for the adjective. Go to the subject noun of your sentence and ask an adjective question. What are the adjective questions? (*What kind, Which one, How many*) Choose one adjective question to ask and write your adjective answer *under* the **Adj** label next to the subject noun. Always check to make sure your answers are making sense in the sentence.

6. Go to the next **Adj** label for another adjective. Go to the subject noun again and ask another adjective question. You can ask the same adjective question, or you can ask a different adjective question. Write another adjective *under* the second **Adj** label.

7. Go to the **A** label for the article adjective. What are the three article adjectives? (*a, an,* and *the*) Choose the article adjective that makes the best sense in your sentence. Write the article adjective you have chosen *under* the **A** label.

8. Finally, check your Practice Sentence to make sure it has the necessary parts to be a complete sentence. What are the five parts of a complete sentence? (*subject, verb, complete sense, capital letter, and an end mark*) Does your Practice Sentence have the five parts of a complete sentence? (*Allow time for students to read over their sentences and to make any necessary corrections.*)

9. Under your Practice Sentence, write the title *Improved Sentence* on another line. To improve your Practice Sentence, you will make two synonym changes, one antonym change, and your choice of a complete word change or another synonym or antonym change.

Since it is harder to find words that can be changed to an antonym, it is usually wise to go through your sentence to find an antonym change first. Then, look through your sentence again to find words that can be improved with synonyms. Finally, make a decision about whether your last change will be a complete word change, another synonym change, or another antonym change. I will give you time to write your Improved Sentence.

(*Always encourage students to use a thesaurus, synonym-antonym book, or a dictionary to help them develop an interesting and improved writing vocabulary. After students have finished, check and discuss students' Practice and Improved Sentences.*)

(End of lesson.)

CHAPTER 7   LESSON 4
Objectives: Jingles, Study, Test, Check, Writing (Journal), State Activity, and Sentence Time.

 JINGLE TIME

Have students turn to the Jingle Section in their books. The teacher will lead the students in reciting the previously-taught jingles.

 STUDY TIME

Have students study the vocabulary words in their vocabulary notebooks. Remind students that any vocabulary word in their notebooks could be on their test. Also, have students study any of the skills in the Practice Section they need to review.

 TEST TIME

Have students turn to page 86 in the Test Section of their books and find Chapter 7 Test. Go over the directions to make sure they understand what to do. (*Chapter 7 Test key is on the next page.*)

 CHECK TIME

After students have finished, check and discuss their test papers. Make sure they understand why their answers are right or wrong. (*For total points, count each required answer as a point.*)

 STATE ACTIVITY TIME

(*Have a recipe box and a package of lined index cards ready for your children to use for this activity.*) Find a map of the United States. Draw or trace the state of Connecticut on the blank side of an index card. On the lined side of the card, write the following questions and answers.

      1. What is the state on the front of this card? **Connecticut**
      2. What is the capital of Connecticut? **Hartford**
      3. What is the postal abbreviation of Connecticut? **CT**

Color this state. Use the card to quiz family members, friends, and relatives. You may want to time the responses to your questions.

(End of lesson.)

Level 2—Shurley English—Homeschool Edition

Chapter 7 Test
(Student Page 86)

52 pts

Exercise 1: Classify each sentence.

```
              A    Adj    Adj     SN       V     Adv
1. SN  V      The antique copper teakettle / whistled loudly.  D
   P1

              A   Adj    Adj    SN     V    Adv   Adv
2. SN  V      A little brown snail / crawled slowly away.  D
   P1
```

Exercise 2: Use Sentence 1 to underline the complete subject once and the complete predicate twice and to complete the table below.

List the Noun Used	List the Noun Job	Singular or Plural	Common or Proper	Simple Subject	Simple Predicate
1. teakettle	2. SN	3. S	4. C	5. teakettle	6. whistled

Exercise 3: Identify each pair of words as synonyms or antonyms by putting parentheses ( ) around **syn** or **ant**.

1. annoy, irritate	**(syn)** ant	4. above, overhead	**(syn)** ant	7. disappear, vanish	**(syn)** ant
2. depart, arrive	syn **(ant)**	5. complex, simple	syn **(ant)**	8. freight, cargo	**(syn)** ant
3. graceful, clumsy	syn **(ant)**	6. collapse, build	syn **(ant)**	9. brilliant, dull	syn **(ant)**

Exercise 4: Write **S** for singular or **P** for plural.

Noun	S or P
1. mice	P
2. windows	P
3. caterpillar	S

Exercise 5: Write **C** for Common or **P** for proper.

Noun	C or P
1. Sandy	P
2. pepper	C
3. December	P

Exercise 6: Write *a* or *an* in the blanks.

1. We heard a strange voice.   3. This is a bitter apple.   5. a glass   7. an arm
2. Three is an odd number.   4. Kelly is an only child.   6. a watch   8. an octopus

Exercise 7: Name the four parts of speech that you have studied. (*You may use abbreviations.*) **(The order of answers may vary.)**

1. noun   2. verb   3. adjective   4. adverb

Exercise 8: In your journal, write a paragraph summarizing what you have learned this week.

CHAPTER 7 LESSON 4 CONTINUED

TEACHER INSTRUCTIONS

Use the Question and Answer Flows below for the sentences on the Chapter 7 Test.

Question and Answer Flow for Sentence 1: The antique copper teakettle whistled loudly.

1. What whistled loudly? teakettle - SN
2. What is being said about teakettle? teakettle whistled - V
3. Whistled how? loudly - Adv
4. What kind of teakettle? copper - Adj
5. What kind of teakettle? antique - Adj
6. The - A
7. SN V P1 Check
8. Period, statement, declarative sentence
9. Go back to the verb - divide the complete subject from the complete predicate.

```
                         A   Adj    Adj      SN       V      Adv
Classified Sentence:  SN V   The antique copper teakettle / whistled loudly.  D
                      P1
```

Question and Answer Flow for Sentence 2: A little brown snail crawled slowly away.

1. What crawled slowly away? snail - SN
2. What is being said about snail? snail crawled - V
3. Crawled how? slowly - Adv
4. Crawled where? away - Adv
5. What kind of snail? brown - Adj
6. What kind of snail? little - Adj
7. A - A
8. SN V P1 Check
9. Period, statement, declarative sentence
10. Go back to the verb - divide the complete subject from the complete predicate.

```
                         A   Adj    Adj    SN       V      Adv    Adv
Classified Sentence:  SN V   A  little  brown  snail / crawled  slowly  away.  D
                      P1
```

 SENTENCE TIME

Chapter 7, Lesson 4, Sentence: Use colored markers to match each label with the correct sentence part by drawing a line from one to the other. Then, use the labels to arrange the sentence parts into a sentence that you will write on the sentence line below. *(The order of the words in your sentence should be in the same sequence as the vertical list of sentence labels.)* Create other labels and scrambled sentence parts on notebook paper for family members to solve. You may color code the sentence parts. *(See page 110 in the student book.)*

Labels for Order of Sentence	Scrambled Sentence Parts
A	silently
Adj	eagle
SN	overhead
V	the
Adv	flew
Adv	magnificent

Sentence: The magnificent eagle flew silently overhead.

(End of lesson.)

Level 2—Shurley English—Homeschool Edition

CHAPTER 7   LESSON 5

Objectives: Writing (Expository, Writing Definitions, Two Point Paragraph) and Writing Assignment #1.

 **WRITING TIME**

Teacher's Notes:
As students write their two-point paragraphs, it is very important that they follow the exact writing pattern that this lesson teaches. If this is done consistently, the students will learn to organize their writing by learning how to do these things: write a topic sentence for any given topic, write sentences that support the topic, and write a concluding sentence that summarizes their paragraph.

Teaching students how to write a two-point paragraph gives students several advantages:

1. It gives students a definite, concrete pattern to follow when asked to write a paragraph.
2. It gives students the practice they need in organizing their writing.
3. It gives students a chance to greatly improve their self-confidence because, as they advance in the program, they become stronger and more independent in all areas of their grammar and writing skills.

TEACHER INSTRUCTIONS

Put the following writing definitions on the board:

> 1. **Paragraph** - a group of sentences that is written about one particular subject or topic.
> 2. **Topic** - the subject of the paragraph; the topic tells what the paragraph is about.
> 3. **Expository writing** - the discussion or telling of ideas by giving facts, directions, explanations, definitions, and examples.

TEACHING SCRIPT FOR INTRODUCING EXPOSITORY WRITING AND WRITING DEFINITIONS

As a second grade student, you want to be prepared to be a good writer. As a part of that preparation, today, we are going to learn about expository writing and how to organize your writing by writing a two-point paragraph. First, let's look at some key definitions to be sure that we know what we are talking about.

Look at the first two definitions. A **paragraph** is a group of sentences that is written about one particular subject or topic. A **topic** is the subject of the paragraph; the topic tells what the paragraph is about.

Now, let's look at the last definition: **expository writing**. I want you to say "expository writing" with me so we can feel this type of writing on our tongues: **Expository writing**! Expository writing is the discussion or telling of ideas by giving facts, directions, explanations, definitions, and examples.

CHAPTER 7 LESSON 5 CONTINUED

In other words, expository writing is informational. Its purpose is to inform, to give facts, to give directions, to explain, or to define something. Remember, expository writing is informational.

Since expository writing deals with information of some kind, it is very important to focus on making the meaning clear and understandable. The reader must be able to understand exactly what the writer means.

Now that we know what expository writing is, we must learn more about it because the first type of paragraph that we learn to write is an EXPOSITORY paragraph. Knowing exactly what to do when you are given a writing assignment makes any type of writing easy. The first thing you will learn to do is organize your writing.

Expository writing may be organized in different ways. One of the most common ways to write an expository paragraph is by using a **two-point paragraph** format. The two-point paragraph format is a way of organizing the sentences in your expository paragraph that will help make your meaning clear and understandable.

Now, you will learn how to write a two-point expository paragraph. I am going to give you a topic about which you are to write your paragraph. Remember that a topic tells what the paragraph is about; it is the subject of the paragraph. In order to make sure you understand, we are going to write a two-point expository paragraph together, following specific steps.

<u>TEACHING SCRIPT FOR SELECTING THE TWO POINTS OF THE PARAGRAPH</u>

The first thing we learn is how to select and list the points that we are going to write about. Let's begin with our topic. Remember that a topic is a subject. The topic about which we are going to write our paragraph is "My Favorite Colors." I will write this on the board under "Topic" (*Demonstrate by writing on the board.*)

Topic: My Favorite Colors

Do you have some favorite colors that you could write about? (*Discuss some of the students' favorite colors.*) Now, let's see how we are going to write this paragraph. Remember that I told you this paragraph is called a two-point paragraph. First, we are going to look at our topic, "My Favorite Colors," and see if we can list two favorite colors about which we can write.

Teacher's Note:
Even though students have named their favorite colors, the teaching sample will use red and brown.

Level 2—Shurley English—Homeschool Edition

CHAPTER 7 LESSON 5 CONTINUED

Red and brown. These are two good favorite colors. I will list these two colors on the board under "Two points about the topic." They will be the two points for our two-point expository paragraph. (*Demonstrate by writing on the board.*)

Two points about the topic:

1. _____red_____   2. _____brown_____

Now, let's set them aside for a minute and begin our paragraph. We are going to use these two items shortly.

Teacher's Notes: The simplified outline below will give you a quick view of what you will be covering with your students in your discussion of the two-point expository paragraph. Write each part on the board only as it is being discussed so that your students will not be overwhelmed by the amount of written work that they see on the board.

The Two-Point Expository Paragraph Outline
Topic
2 points about the topic
Sentence #1: Topic sentence
Sentence #2: A two-point sentence
Sentence #3: A **first**-point sentence
Sentence #4: A **supporting** sentence for the first point
Sentence #5: A **second**-point sentence
Sentence #6: A **supporting** sentence for the second point
Sentence #7: A concluding sentence

Teacher's Notes: As you work through the steps, be sure to show students how the sentences are divided into three categories: the introduction (*topic and two-point sentence*), the body (*the two main points and their supporting sentences*), and the conclusion (*the concluding sentence*).

TEACHING SCRIPT FOR WRITING THE TOPIC SENTENCE

First, we must write what is called a topic sentence. A topic sentence is very important because it tells the main idea of our paragraph. We are going to let the topic sentence be the first sentence in our paragraph because it tells everyone what our paragraph is going to be about. In many paragraphs, it is not the first sentence. Later, we can learn to put the topic sentence in other places in the paragraph, but, for now, it is important that we make it the first sentence in our two-point paragraph.

CHAPTER 7 LESSON 5 CONTINUED

The topic sentence for a two-point paragraph needs three things:

1. It needs to tell the main idea of the paragraph.
2. It needs to be general because the other sentences in the paragraph must tell about the topic sentence.
3. It needs to tell the number of points that will be discussed in the paragraph.

When you write a topic sentence for a two-point paragraph, follow these two easy steps:

1. You will use all or some of the words in the topic.
2. You will tell the number of points, or ideas, you will discuss in your paragraph.

Now, we are going to write a topic sentence by following the two easy steps we have just discussed. Look at our topic, "My Favorite Colors." Without actually listing the two specific points – red and brown – let's write a sentence that makes a general statement about the main idea of our topic and tells the number of points we will list later.

How about using "I have two favorite colors" as the topic sentence? I will write this on the board under "Sentence #1: Topic sentence." (*Demonstrate by writing on the board. Read the sentence to the students.*)

Sentence #1. Topic sentence: I have two favorite colors.

Look at the topic sentence on the board. Notice that in this sentence, we have mentioned our topic, "My Favorite Colors," and we have stated that there are two of these colors; we will tell what the two are in the two-point sentence that follows.

Also, notice that we did not say, "I am going to tell you about my two favorite colors." We do not need to tell the reader we are going to tell him/her something; we simply do it. To say "I am going to tell you" is called "writing about your writing," and it is not effective writing. Do not "write about your writing."

TEACHING SCRIPT FOR WRITING THE TWO-POINT SENTENCE

Now that we have our topic sentence, our next sentence will list the two specific points our paragraph will discuss. Our next sentence could be, "These colors are red and brown." I will write this on the board under "Sentence #2: A two-point sentence." (*Demonstrate by writing the information below on the board. Read the sentence to the students.*)

Sentence #2. A two-point sentence: These colors are red and brown.

Look at the order in which I have listed the two subjects. You must always be aware of the order in which you put your points because that will be the order in which you discuss these points in your paragraph.

I have chosen to place these in this order: red and brown. I did not have any particular reason for placing red first. Depending upon your two points as well as your purpose in writing, you will select the order of your two points.

CHAPTER 7 LESSON 5 CONTINUED

Notice three things we have done here:

1. We have put our two items in the order we have chosen, remembering that we will be discussing these points in this order later in our paragraph. (*red and brown*)

2. We have written our first sentence, and our first sentence tells us the number of points that will be discussed in the rest of the paragraph. (*I have two favorite colors.*)

3. We have started our listing sentence with words that helped us connect it to our first sentence. (*These colors are **red** and **brown**.*)

Notice how we have used repetition to link our two sentences. Our first sentence mentions **"favorite colors"** by stating **"I have two favorite colors."** Sentence number two, **"These colors are red and brown,"** refers to sentence number one by stating **"These colors,"** meaning the favorite colors just mentioned in sentence number one. Although you will not want to use repetition in every sentence to link sentences, repetition is a good device for making your paragraph flow smoothly.

TEACHING SCRIPT FOR DEVELOPING AND SUPPORTING THE POINTS OF THE PARAGRAPH

After you have stated the general topic sentence and then followed it by the more specific two-point sentence, you will begin to discuss each of the two points, one at a time. DO NOT FORGET: You are going to discuss them in the order in which you listed them in sentence number two. You will begin your third sentence by stating, "My first favorite color is red." This is your first listed point. I will write this on the board under "Sentence #3: A first-point sentence." (*Demonstrate by writing the information below on the board. Read the sentence to the students.*)

Sentence #3. A first-point sentence: My first favorite color is red.

Next, you will write one sentence about red. It can be a descriptive sentence about red. It can be a reason why you like red, but it must be about red being your favorite color. This is called a supporting sentence. I will now write a supporting sentence on the board under "Sentence #4: A supporting sentence for the first point." You can use this sentence or make up your own: "I like red because it reminds me of a special patchwork quilt that my grandmother made." (*Demonstrate by writing the information below on the board. Read the sentence to the students.*)

Sentence #4. A supporting sentence for the first point: I like red because it reminds me of a special patchwork quilt that my grandmother made.

When you keep your writing targeted to the topic you are assigned, your paragraph will have what we call "unity," or will be a "unified" paragraph. In a unified paragraph, all sentences work together to form one idea about the subject, or topic.

As you get more skilled at two-point writing, you may write two or more sentences about each of your listed points, but, for now, stay with one sentence for each point. Each of the sentences that you write following your points should support what you have stated in that point. Use only ideas that support. Discard non-supporting ideas.

CHAPTER 7 LESSON 5 CONTINUED

So far, we have introduced our topic and listed our two specific points. We have begun to discuss our two points and have completed the first point along with a sentence that supports the first point. So far, we have four sentences.

Your fifth sentence will introduce the second point of the two-point paragraph. Your second point is "brown." Since "brown" is the second item you listed, your fifth sentence should state, "My second favorite color is brown." I will write this on the board under "Sentence #5: A second-point sentence." (*Demonstrate by writing the information below on the board. Read the sentence to the students.*)

Sentence #5. A second-point sentence: My second favorite color is brown.

Just as you wrote the sentence supporting the statement of your first point, now you must write a sentence supporting your statement about brown being your second favorite color. I will write the next supporting sentence on the board under "Sentence #6: A supporting sentence for the second point." (*Demonstrate by writing the information below on the board. Read the sentence to the students.*)

Sentence #6. A supporting sentence for the second point: Brown reminds me of the hot fudge brownies that Grandma used to make for me.

By now, you can begin to see a pattern to your paragraph. So far, you have written six sentences in your paragraph. Your seventh sentence will be your last, or final, sentence.

TEACHING SCRIPT FOR WRITING THE CONCLUSION OF THE PARAGRAPH

We have now introduced our topic, or subject, listed each of our two points, and made one supporting statement about each point. Now, we need to complete our paragraph, leaving the reader with the impression that he/she has read a finished product. In order to complete our paragraph, we need a conclusion, or final sentence.

There are different ways to write a concluding sentence, but one of the best and simplest is the summary statement. This means that the main points of the paragraph are stated again, briefly, in one sentence.

When you write a concluding sentence, follow these two easy steps:
   1. You will use some of the words in your topic sentence.
   2. You will add an extra, or concluding, thought about your paragraph.

You might try a good concluding sentence, such as, "My two favorite colors, red and brown, bring back wonderful memories of my grandmother." I will write this on the board under "Sentence #7: A concluding sentence." (*Demonstrate by writing the information below on the board. Read the sentence again to the students.*)

Sentence #7. A concluding sentence: My two favorite colors, red and brown, bring back wonderful memories of my grandmother.

Level 2—Shurley English—Homeschool Edition

CHAPTER 7 LESSON 5 CONTINUED

TEACHING SCRIPT FOR CHECKING THE FINISHED PARAGRAPH

It is good to get in the habit of checking over your writing after you have finished. Just reading your finished paragraph aloud several times slowly will help you see and hear things that you may want to correct. It also helps to have a checklist that tells specific areas to check to make sure you do not lose points for careless mistakes.

Turn to page 15 and look at Reference 16 as I read what it tells you to do as you write each sentence of your two-point paragraph. (*Read and discuss each section of the two-point paragraph example in Reference 16. Tell students to use this reference page if they need it when they write a two-point paragraph. It will help them organize their writing, and it will help them see the pattern of a two-point expository paragraph.*) (*Reference 16 is reproduced for you on the next page.*)

Teacher's Notes: Guidelines are not provided for writing a title for a paragraph. Single paragraphs are often written without titles; the decision is left to the teacher or writer. Remind students that this is an expository paragraph, which means that its purpose is to inform or explain. The two-point format is a way of <u>organizing</u> an expository paragraph.

TEACHER INSTRUCTIONS FOR WRITING ASSIGNMENT #1

Give Writing Assignment #1 from the box below. Remind students to use the two-point paragraph example in Reference 16 on page 15 in the Reference Section if they need it. **If this is their first year in the program, tell students that this writing assignment will be done on a writing page in their books.** The writing page is already set up in a two-point format that will help them follow the form of the two-point paragraph. Direct students to page 45 in the Practice Section of their books. (*The practice page is reproduced for you at the end of this lesson on page 113.*)

Writing Assignment Box

Writing Assignment #1: Two-Point Expository Paragraph

Writing topic choices: My Favorite Colors   or   My Favorite Flowers/Trees   or   My Favorite Holidays

---

After students have filled out the two-point practice page, have them transfer their paragraph to a sheet of notebook paper or type it on a computer. Before students begin, go over the Writing Checklist on page 16 so they will know how to arrange their writing assignment on notebook paper or on the computer.

CHAPTER 7 LESSON 5 CONTINUED

Reference 16: Two-Point Paragraph Sample
Topic: **My favorite colors** Two main points: 1. **red** 2. **brown** Sentence #1 – Topic Sentence (*Use words in the topic and tell how many points will be used.*) **I have two favorite colors.** Sentence #2 – 2-Point Sentence (*List the 2 points in the order you will present them.*) **These colors are red and brown.** Sentence #3 – First Point **My first favorite color is red.** Sentence #4 – Supporting Sentence for the first point. **I like red because it reminds me of a special patchwork quilt that my grandmother made.** Sentence #5 – Second Point **My second favorite color is brown.** Sentence #6 – Supporting Sentence for the second point. **Brown reminds me of the hot fudge brownies that Grandma used to make for me.** Sentence #7 – Concluding (final) Sentence (*Restate the topic sentence and add an extra thought.*) **My two favorite colors, red and brown, bring back wonderful memories of my grandmother.**
SAMPLE PARAGRAPH <u>My Favorite Colors</u>   I have two favorite colors. These colors are red and brown. My first favorite color is red. I like red because it reminds me of a special patchwork quilt that my grandmother made. My second favorite color is brown. Brown reminds me of the hot fudge brownies that Grandma used to make for me. My two favorite colors, red and brown, bring back wonderful memories of my grandmother.

Level 2—Shurley English—Homeschool Edition

CHAPTER 7 LESSON 5 CONTINUED

TEACHING SCRIPT FOR WRITING GUIDELINES

Today, we will go through some guidelines for your writing. Turn to page 16 in your book and look at Reference 17. You will use this writing checklist every time you are given a writing assignment. (*Read and discuss the Writing Checklist with your students.*)

Reference 17: Writing Checklist

1. Label your writing assignment in the top right-hand corner of your page with the following information:
   A. Your Name
   B. The Writing Assignment Number. *(Examples: WA#1, WA#2, etc.)*

2. Write the title of the writing on the top of the first line.
3. Have you followed the pattern for the type of writing assigned?
   (Is your assignment a 2-point paragraph, a 3-point paragraph, a descriptive paragraph, or a letter?)
4. Do you have complete sentences?
5. Have you capitalized the first word and put an end mark at the end of every sentence?
6. Have you checked your sentences for other capitalization and punctuation mistakes?
7. Have you checked for misspelled words and incorrect homonym choices?
8. Have you indented each paragraph?

TEACHING SCRIPT FOR WRITING ASSIGNMENT #1

As you begin this writing assignment, you will use the writing checklist discussed in Reference 17. After you have finished, you will then give the finished writing assignment to me.

TEACHER INSTRUCTIONS FOR CHECKING WRITING ASSIGNMENT #1

Read, check, and discuss Writing Assignment #1 after students have finished their final paper. Use the writing checklist (*Reference 17 on student's page 16*) as you check and discuss students' papers. Make sure students are using the checklist correctly. In the beginning, you must also check students' papers carefully for <u>form</u> mistakes. This will ensure that students are learning the two-point format correctly.

Teacher's Notes: It's okay for students to pattern their sentences after the examples. As they get stronger in this system and as the topics change, you will see more independent sentences. In fact, you will see a lot of variety in these paragraphs because students will probably choose at least two different points and write different supporting sentences. Remind students to add adjectives and adverbs to make their sentences more interesting.

CHAPTER 7 LESSON 5 CONTINUED

Chapter 7, Lesson 5, Practice Writing Page: Use the two-point outline form below to guide you as you write a two-point expository paragraph.

Write a topic: _____

List 2 points about the topic:

1. _____ 2. _____

Sentence #1   Topic sentence (*Use words in the topic and tell how many points will be used.*)

_____

_____

Sentence #2   2-point sentence (*List your 2 points in the order that you will present them.*)

_____

_____

Sentence #3   State your first point in a complete sentence.

_____

_____

Sentence #4   Write a supporting sentence for the first point.

_____

_____

Sentence #5   State your second point in a complete sentence.

_____

_____

Sentence #6   Write a supporting sentence for the second point.

_____

_____

Sentence #7   Concluding sentence (*Restate the topic sentence and add an extra thought.*)

_____

_____

Student Notes: Rewrite your seven-sentence paragraph on notebook paper. Be sure to indent and use the checklists to help you edit your paragraph. Make sure you re-read your paragraph slowly several times.

(End of lesson.)

Level 2—Shurley English—Homeschool Edition

CHAPTER 8   LESSON 1
Objectives: Jingles (Preposition, Object of the Preposition), Grammar (Practice Sentences), Skills (Skill Builder Check, Practice and Improved Sentence), Vocabulary #1, and Activity.

 JINGLE TIME

Have students turn to the Jingle Section in their books and recite the previously-taught jingles. Then, lead students in reciting the new jingles (*Preposition and Object of the Preposition*) below. Practice the new jingles several times until students can recite them smoothly. Emphasize reciting with rhythm. (*Do not try to explain the jingles at this time. Just have fun reciting them. Add motions for more fun and laughter.*)

Teacher's Notes: Again, do not spend a large amount of time practicing the new jingles. Students learn the jingles best by spending a small amount of time consistently, **every** day.

Jingle 7: Preposition Jingle
A PREP PREP PREPOSITION Is a special group of words That connects a NOUN, NOUN, NOUN Or a PRO, PRO, PRONOUN To the rest of the sentence.

Jingle 8:   Object of the Prep Jingle
Dum De Dum Dum! An O-P is a N-O-U-N or a P-R-O After the P-R-E-P In a S-E-N-T-E-N-C-E. Dum De Dum Dum - DONE!

 GRAMMAR TIME

Put the Practice Sentences from the box below on the board or on notebook paper. Use these sentences as you practice the concepts that have been taught. For the greatest benefit, students must participate orally with the teacher.

Chapter 8, Practice Sentences for Lesson 1
1. _____ The delightful young dentist worked here yesterday. 2. _____ A cold, bitter wind howled shrilly. 3. _____ The cute little hummingbirds fly effortlessly.

TEACHING SCRIPT FOR CLASSIFYING PRACTICE SENTENCES

We will classify three different sentences to practice the grammar skills in the Question and Answer Flows. We will classify the sentences together. Begin. (*You might have students write the labels above the sentences at this time.*)

CHAPTER 8 LESSON 1 CONTINUED

Question and Answer Flow for Sentence 1: The delightful young dentist worked here yesterday.

1. Who worked here yesterday? dentist - SN
2. What is being said about dentist? dentist worked - V
3. Worked where? here - Adv
4. Worked when? yesterday - Adv
5. What kind of dentist? young - Adj
6. What kind of dentist? delightful - Adj
7. The - A
8. SN V P1 Check
9. Period, statement, declarative sentence
10. Go back to the verb - divide the complete subject from the complete predicate.

```
                              A    Adj    Adj    SN    V    Adv    Adv
Classified Sentence:   SN  V     The delightful young dentist / worked here yesterday.  D
                       P1
```

Question and Answer Flow for Sentence 2: A cold, bitter wind howled shrilly.

1. What howled shrilly? wind - SN
2. What is being said about wind? wind howled - V
3. Howled how? shrilly - Adv
4. What kind of wind? bitter - Adj
5. What kind of wind? cold - Adj
6. A - A
7. SN V P1 Check
8. Period, statement, declarative sentence
9. Go back to the verb - divide the complete subject from the complete predicate.

```
                              A   Adj   Adj   SN    V     Adv
Classified Sentence:   SN  V     A cold, bitter wind / howled shrilly.  D
                       P1
```

Question and Answer Flow for Sentence 3: The cute little hummingbirds fly effortlessly.

1. What fly effortlessly? hummingbirds - SN
2. What is being said about hummingbirds? hummingbirds fly - V
3. Fly how? effortlessly - Adv
4. What kind of hummingbirds? little - Adj
5. What kind of hummingbirds? cute - Adj
6. The - A
7. SN V P1 Check
8. Period, statement, declarative sentence
9. Go back to the verb - divide the complete subject from the complete predicate.

```
                              A   Adj    Adj        SN         V      Adv
Classified Sentence:   SN  V     The cute little hummingbirds / fly effortlessly.  D
                       P1
```

SKILL TIME

Use Sentences 1-3 that you just classified with your students to do a Skill Builder Check. Use the guidelines on the next page.

CHAPTER 8 LESSON 1 CONTINUED

Skill Builder Check	
1. **Noun check.** (Say the job and then say the noun. Circle each noun.)	5. **Identify the complete subject and the complete predicate.** (Underline the complete subject once and the complete predicate twice.)
2. **Identify the nouns as singular or plural.** (Write **S** or **P** above each noun.)	6. **Identify the simple subject and simple predicate.** (Underline the simple subject once and the simple predicate twice. Bold, or highlight, the lines to distinguish them from the complete subject and complete predicate.)
3. **Identify the nouns as common or proper.** (Follow established procedure for oral identification.)	
4. **Do a vocabulary check.** (Follow established procedure for oral identification.)	

TEACHING SCRIPT FOR A PRACTICE SENTENCE

Put these labels on the board: **A Adj Adj SN V Adv Adv**

Today, I will guide you as you write a Practice Sentence and an Improved Sentence. Look at the sentence labels on the board. Let's repeat the labels together: **A Adj Adj SN V Adv Adv**. You will now write a seven-word sentence.

Get out a sheet of notebook paper. On the top line of your notebook paper, write the title *Practice Sentence*. Copy the sentence labels from the board onto your notebook paper. Be sure to leave plenty of writing space between each label. We will begin with the subject noun.

1. Go to the **SN** label for the subject noun. Think of a noun that you want to use as your subject. Write the noun you have chosen on the line *under* the **SN** label.

2. Go to the **V** label for the verb. Think of a verb that tells what your subject does. Make sure that your verb makes sense with the subject noun. Write the verb you have chosen on the line *under* the **V** label.

3. Go to the **Adv** label for the adverb. Go to the verb in your sentence and ask an adverb question. What are the adverb questions? (*How, When, Where*) Choose one adverb question to ask and write your adverb answer *under* the first **Adv** label.

4. Go to the **Adv** label for another adverb. Go to the verb again and ask another adverb question. You can ask the same adverb question, or you can ask a different adverb question. Write another adverb *under* the second **Adv** label.

5. Go to the **Adj** label for the adjective. Go to the subject noun of your sentence and ask an adjective question. What are the adjective questions? (*What kind, Which one, How many*) Choose one adjective question to ask and write your adjective answer *under* the **Adj** label next to the subject noun. Always check to make sure your answers are making sense in the sentence.

CHAPTER 8 LESSON 1 CONTINUED

6. Go to the next **Adj** label for another adjective. Go to the subject noun again and ask another adjective question. You can ask the same adjective question, or you can ask a different adjective question. Write another adjective *under* the second **Adj** label.

7. Go to the **A** label for the article adjective. What are the three article adjectives? (*a*, *an*, and *the*) Choose the article adjective that makes the best sense in your sentence. Write the article adjective you have chosen *under* the **A** label.

8. Finally, check your Practice Sentence to make sure it has the necessary parts to be a complete sentence. What are the five parts of a complete sentence? (*subject, verb, complete sense, capital letter, and an end mark*) Does your Practice Sentence have the five parts of a complete sentence? (*Allow time for students to read over their sentences and to make any necessary corrections.*)

9. Under your Practice Sentence, write the title *Improved Sentence* on another line. To improve your Practice Sentence, you will make two synonym changes, one antonym change, and your choice of a complete word change or another synonym or antonym change.

    I will give you time to write your Improved Sentence. (*Always encourage students to use a thesaurus, synonym-antonym book, or a dictionary to help them develop an interesting and improved writing vocabulary. After students have finished, check and discuss students' Practice and Improved Sentences.*)

 VOCABULARY TIME

Assign Chapter 8, Vocabulary Words #1 on page 6 in the Reference Section for students to define in their Vocabulary notebooks. Tell students they are to use a dictionary or thesaurus to look up the meanings of the vocabulary words.

Chapter 8, Vocabulary Words #1
(weary, energetic, nibble, munch)

 ACTIVITY / ASSIGNMENT TIME

Make a list of four people in your family (and/or extended family/friends). Write each family member's name on an index card. On the back of each index card, write a descriptive sentence about the person listed on the front. Be sure to include as many adjectives and adverbs as possible. Finally, play a guessing game with different members of your family. Read aloud or hold up the side of the card with the description and let family members guess whose name is written on the other side. Discuss the family members that were the hardest and easiest to guess. Also, discuss which family members were the hardest and easiest to describe.

(End of lesson.)

Level 2—Shurley English—Homeschool Edition

CHAPTER 8 LESSON 2
Objectives: Jingles, Grammar (Introductory Sentences, Preposition, Object of the Preposition, Prepositional Phrase, Add the Preposition to the Parts of Speech), and Vocabulary #2.

 **JINGLE TIME**

Have students turn to the Jingle Section in their books. The teacher will lead the students in reciting the previously-taught jingles.

 GRAMMAR TIME

Put the introductory sentences from the box below on the board. Use these sentences as you go through each new concept covered in your teaching script. For the greatest benefit, students must participate orally with the teacher. (*You might put the introductory sentences on notebook paper if you are doing one-on-one instruction with your students.*)

Chapter 8, Introductory Sentences for Lesson 2
1. _____ The grasshoppers nibbled on the brown leaves.
2. _____ The old house shook during the earthquake!
3. _____ That bull stomped angrily inside the barn!

<u>TEACHING SCRIPT FOR PREPOSITION, OBJECT OF THE PREPOSITION, AND PREPOSITIONAL PHRASE</u>

We will now learn an especially fun part of English. We are going to learn about prepositions! The preposition jingle has already told you a lot about prepositions, but now we are going to learn even more. I will give you the new information about prepositions. Then, I will show you how each part works in a sentence, so listen carefully.

A **preposition** is a joining word. It joins a noun to the rest of the sentence. Prepositions are memory words, just like article adjectives. But you have an easy way to recognize whether a word is a preposition. To know whether a word is a preposition, say the word and ask *What* or *Whom*. If the answer is a noun, then the word is a preposition. Prepositions are labeled with a *P*. (*The pronoun will not be addressed as an object of the preposition at this time because it has not been introduced.*)

When you ask *What* or *Whom* after a preposition and the answer is a noun, the noun is called the **object of the preposition**. An object of the preposition always comes after the preposition and answers the question *What* or *Whom*. An object of the preposition is labeled with an *OP*. Look at Reference 18 on page 16 as I go over the information you need to know about prepositions.

CHAPTER 8 LESSON 2 CONTINUED

Reference 18: How to Find a Preposition and an Object of the Preposition
SN   V   Matthew fell **down the steps**.
To find a preposition, find the word with a noun after it. The word **down** has the noun **steps** after it. Now, it is time to ask the question *What* or *Whom*. We will ask *What* since the noun is a thing and not a person: **Down what? steps** – object of the preposition. Now we know that the word **down** is a preposition because it has the noun **steps** (the object of the preposition) after it. To find the preposition and object of the preposition in the Question and Answer Flow, say: **Down – Preposition** **Down what? steps – Object of the Preposition**

It is also important for you to know the difference between prepositions and adverbs. Look at Reference 19 on page 16 as I explain how you can tell the difference between prepositions and adverbs.

Many words can be either a <u>preposition</u> or an <u>adverb</u>, depending on how they are used in a sentence. For example, the word *down* can be an adverb or a preposition. How do you decide if the word *down* is an adverb or a preposition? If *down* is used alone, without a noun after it, it is an adverb. If *down* has a noun after it that answers the question *what* or *whom*, then *down* is a preposition, and the noun after *down* is an object of the preposition. (*Have students follow along as you read and discuss the information in the reference box below.*)

Reference 19: Knowing the Difference Between Prepositions and Adverbs
SN   V   Adv   SN   V   P   A   OP 1. Matthew fell **down**.   2. Matthew fell **down the steps**.
In the <u>first sentence</u>, *Matthew fell **down***, the word **down** is an adverb because it does not have a noun after it.
In the <u>second sentence</u>, *Matthew fell **down the steps***, the word **down** is a preposition because it has the noun **steps** (an object of the preposition) after it.

Remember, to find the preposition and object of the preposition in the Question and Answer Flow, say the words below.
           Down – Preposition
           Down what? steps – Object of the Preposition

You will learn one more interesting term. It is **prepositional phrase**. Let's say "prepositional phrase" several times together. (*Say "prepositional phrase" several times in a rhythmic manner.*) A **prepositional phrase** starts with the preposition and ends with the object of the preposition. It includes any words between the preposition and the object of the preposition. A prepositional phrase adds meaning to a sentence and can be located anywhere in the sentence.

Teacher's Notes: A single word that modifies a verb is called an adverb. A prepositional phrase that modifies a verb is called an adverb, or adverbial, phrase. For example, the prepositional phrase (*down the steps*) tells *where* Matthew fell. Prepositional phrases can also modify like adjectives. (*Students are not required to identify adjectival and adverbial phrases in sentences until seventh grade.*)

Level 2—Shurley English—Homeschool Edition

CHAPTER 8 LESSON 2 CONTINUED

Prepositional phrases are identified in the Question and Answer Flow after you say the word *Check*. When you say *Check*, you are now looking for prepositional phrases in the sentence. If you find a prepositional phrase, you will read the whole prepositional phrase and put parentheses around it.

You will learn prepositional phrases very quickly simply by identifying and using them every day. I will show you how quick and easy it is to identify prepositional phrases by using the Question and Answer Flow. Remember, the Question and Answer Flow will make learning prepositional phrases easy and fun. Listen as I classify the first sentence. I will show you how to identify a prepositional phrase. (*Classify Sentence 1 to demonstrate a prepositional phrase in the Question and Answer Flow.*)

Question and Answer Flow for Sentence 1: The grasshoppers nibbled on the brown leaves.

1. What nibbled on the brown leaves? grasshoppers - SN
2. What is being said about grasshoppers? grasshoppers nibbled - V
3. On - P (Preposition)
4. On what? leaves - OP (Object of the Preposition)
5. What kind of leaves? brown - Adj
6. The - A
7. The - A

Note: To test whether a word is a preposition, say your preposition and ask "what" or "whom." If your answer is a noun or pronoun, you will have a preposition. All prepositions will have a noun or pronoun object. (When the object of the preposition is a person use "whom" instead of "what.")

8. SN V P1 Check
9. (On the brown leaves) - Prepositional phrase

Note: Say "on the brown leaves - Prepositional phrase" as you put parentheses around the words. This also teaches your students how to read in complete phrases, so keep it smooth.

10. Period, statement, declarative sentence
11. Go back to the verb - divide the complete subject from the complete predicate.

Classified Sentence:

```
                    A    SN        V     P  A  Adj   OP
   SN V     The grasshoppers / nibbled (on the brown leaves). D
   P1
```

I will now classify Sentence 1 again, but this time you classify it with me. I will lead you as we say the questions and answers together. Remember, it is very important that you say the **questions** with me as well as the **answers**. (*Classify Sentence 1 again with your students.*)

We will classify Sentences 2 and 3 together to practice the new grammar concepts in the Question and Answer Flows. By asking and answering the questions orally, you will learn everything faster because you see it, hear it, say it, and then do it. Begin.

CHAPTER 8 LESSON 2 CONTINUED

Question and Answer Flow for Sentence 2: The old house shook during the earthquake!

1. What shook during the earthquake? house - SN
2. What is being said about house? house shook - V
3. During - P (preposition)
4. During what? earthquake - OP (object of the preposition)
5. The - A
6. What kind of house? old - Adj
7. The - A
8. SN V P1 Check
9. (During the earthquake) - Prepositional phrase
10. Exclamation point, strong feeling, exclamatory sentence
11. Go back to the verb - divide the complete subject from the complete predicate.

Classified Sentence: SN V / P1   A Adj SN V P A OP
The old house / shook (during the earthquake)! E

Question and Answer Flow for Sentence 3: That bull stomped angrily inside the barn!

1. What stomped angrily inside the barn? bull - SN
2. What is being said about bull? bull stomped - V
3. Stomped how? angrily - Adv
4. Inside - P (preposition)
5. Inside what? barn - OP (object of the preposition)
6. The - A
7. Which bull? that - Adj
8. SN V P1 Check
9. (Inside the barn) - Prepositional phrase
10. Exclamation point, strong feeling, exclamatory sentence
11. Go back to the verb - divide the complete subject from the complete predicate.

Classified Sentence: SN V / P1   Adj SN V Adv P A OP
That bull / stomped angrily (inside the barn)! E

TEACHING SCRIPT FOR ADDING THE PREPOSITION TO THE PARTS OF SPEECH

Until now, we have had only four parts of speech. Do you remember the names of the four parts of speech we have already learned? *(noun, verb, adjective,* and *adverb)* Today, we have learned about prepositions. A preposition is also a part of speech; so, we will add it to our list. We do not add the object of the preposition because it is a noun, and nouns are already on our list. Now, you know five of the eight parts of speech. What are the five parts of speech we have studied? *(noun, verb, adjective, adverb,* and *preposition)* *(Recite the five parts of speech several times. Now, have students write the five parts of speech on notebook paper.)*

 VOCABULARY TIME

Assign Chapter 8, Vocabulary Words **#2** on page 6 in the Reference Section for students to define in their Vocabulary notebooks. Tell students they are to use a dictionary or thesaurus to look up the meanings of the vocabulary words.

Chapter 8, Vocabulary Words #2
(gush, trickle, flicker, flash)

(End of lesson.)

Level 2—Shurley English—Homeschool Edition

CHAPTER 8   LESSON 3
Objectives: Jingles, Grammar (Practice Sentences), and Skills (Add Object of the Preposition to the Noun Check, Skill Builder Check).

 **JINGLE TIME**

Have students turn to the Jingle Section in their books and recite the previously-taught jingles.

 GRAMMAR TIME

Put the Practice Sentences from the box below on the board or on notebook paper. Use these sentences as you practice the concepts that have been taught. For the greatest benefit, students must participate orally with the teacher.

Chapter 8, Practice Sentences for Lesson 3
1. _____ The weary sailors sailed for several months.
2. _____ Water gushed wildly from the pipe.
3. _____ The new community pool opens in June.

TEACHING SCRIPT FOR CLASSIFYING PRACTICE SENTENCES

We will classify three different sentences to practice using prepositional phrases in the Question and Answer Flows. We will classify the sentences together. Begin.

Question and Answer Flow for Sentence 1: The weary sailors sailed for several months.	
1. Who sailed for several months? sailors - SN	7. The - A
2. What is being said about sailors? sailors sailed - V	8. SN V P1 Check
3. For - P	9. (For several months) - Prepositional phrase
4. For what? months - OP	10. Period, statement, declarative sentence
5. How many months? several - Adj	11. Go back to the verb - divide the complete subject
6. What kind of sailors? weary - Adj	from the complete predicate.

Classified Sentence:
　　　　　　　　　　　　A　Adj　SN　　V　P　Adj　OP
　　　　　SN V　The weary sailors / sailed (for several months). D
　　　　　P1

CHAPTER 8 LESSON 3 CONTINUED

Question and Answer Flow for Sentence 2: Water gushed wildly from the pipe.

1. What gushed wildly from the pipe? water - SN
2. What is being said about water? water gushed - V
3. Gushed how? wildly - Adv
4. From - P
5. From what? pipe - OP
6. The - A
7. SN V P1 Check
8. (From the pipe) - Prepositional phrase
9. Period, statement, declarative sentence
10. Go back to the verb - divide the complete subject from the complete predicate.

```
                           SN   V   Adv   P   A   OP
Classified Sentence:   SN V    Water / gushed wildly (from the pipe).   D
                       ----
                        P1
```

Question and Answer Flow for Sentence 3: The new community pool opens in June.

1. What opens in June? pool - SN
2. What is being said about pool? pool opens - V
3. In - P
4. In what? June - OP
5. What kind of pool? community - Adj
6. What kind of pool? new - Adj
7. The - A
8. SN V P1 Check
9. (In June) - Prepositional phrase
10. Period, statement, declarative sentence
11. Go back to the verb - divide the complete subject from the complete predicate.

```
                           A   Adj   Adj   SN   V   P   OP
Classified Sentence:   SN V    The new community pool / opens (in June).   D
                       ----
                        P1
```

SKILL TIME

TEACHING SCRIPT FOR ADDING THE OBJECT OF THE PREPOSITION TO THE NOUN CHECK

We are going to use the sentences we have just classified to do a Skill Builder Check. You have already learned how to do a Noun Check with the subject of the sentence. Today, we are going to add a new noun job, the object of the preposition, to the Noun Check. We will learn to identify nouns in the object of the preposition job. Therefore, to find nouns, you will go to the words marked SN and OP in the classified sentences.

Look at Sentences 1-3 that we have just classified on the board. Remember, we will go to the subject nouns **and** the objects of the prepositions to find nouns. We will circle each noun as we find it.

CHAPTER 8 LESSON 3 CONTINUED

Look at Sentence 1. You will say, "Number 1: subject noun *sailors, yes;* object of the preposition *months, yes.*" I will circle each noun as you identify it. *(Have students repeat number 1 with you as you circle each noun identified.)* We will find and circle the nouns in Sentences 2 and 3 the same way.

(Work through the rest of the sentences, identifying and circling the subject nouns and object-of-the-preposition nouns.) *(Number 1:* subject noun *sailors, yes;* object of the preposition *months, yes;.* Number 2: subject noun *water, yes;* object of the preposition *pipe; yes.* Number 3: subject noun *pool, yes;* object of the preposition *June, yes.)*

Use the same Skill Builder procedures that were taught in previous chapters to have students identify each noun as singular or plural. Ask students to tell which nouns are common and which are proper. Check the vocabulary words used for each sentence. Select the words your students may not know and do a Vocabulary Check. For each word selected, make sure it is defined, used in a new sentence, and given a synonym and/or an antonym. You might also ask for synonyms and antonyms of several words just to check students' understanding of different words.

Now that you have finished the Noun Check, the Singular/Plural Check, the Common/Proper Check, and the Vocabulary Check, continue using Sentences 1-3 to do the rest of the Skill Builders from the checklist below. This checklist will always be given to you every time you do a Skill Builder Check.

Teacher's Notes: You will be given directions for a Skill Builder Check only with one set of sentences in a chapter. You could do Skill Builder Checks with every set of sentences, but it is usually not necessary. Your time allotment and the needs of your students will influence your decision.

Skill Builder Check	
1. **Noun check.** (Say the job and then say the noun. Circle each noun.)	5. **Identify the complete subject and the complete predicate.** (Underline the complete subject once and the complete predicate twice.)
2. **Identify the nouns as singular or plural.** (Write **S** or **P** above each noun.)	6. **Identify the simple subject and simple predicate.** (Underline the simple subject once and the simple predicate twice. Bold, or highlight, the lines to distinguish them from the complete subject and complete predicate.)
3. **Identify the nouns as common or proper.** (Follow established procedure for oral identification.)	
4. **Do a vocabulary check.** (Follow established procedure for oral identification.)	

(End of lesson.)

Level 2—Shurley English—Homeschool Edition

CHAPTER 8   LESSON 4
Objectives: Jingles, Study, Test, Check, Writing (Journal), and State Activity.

 **JINGLE TIME**

Have students turn to the Jingle Section in their books and recite the previously-taught jingles.

 STUDY TIME

Have students study the vocabulary words in their vocabulary notebooks. Remind students that any vocabulary word in their notebooks could be on their test. Also, have students study any of the skills in the Practice Section that they need to review.

 TEST TIME

Have students turn to page 87 in the Test Section of their book and find Chapter 8 Test. Go over the directions to make sure they understand what to do. (*Chapter 8 Test key is on the next page.*)

 CHECK TIME

After students have finished, check and discuss their test papers. Make sure they understand why their answers are right or wrong. (*For total points, count each required answer as a point.*)

 STATE ACTIVITY TIME

(*Have a recipe box and a package of lined index cards ready for your children to use for this activity.*) Find a map of the United States. Draw or trace the state of Delaware on the blank side of an index card. On the lined side of the card, write the following questions and answers.

1. What is the state on the front of this card? **Delaware**
2. What is the capital of Delaware? **Dover**
3. What is the postal abbreviation of Delaware? **DE**

Color this state. Use the card to quiz family members, friends, and relatives. You may want to time the responses to your questions.

(End of lesson.)

Level 2—Shurley English—Homeschool Edition

Chapter 8 Test
(Student Page 87)

61 pts

Exercise 1: Classify each sentence.

```
          A    Adj   SN        V           P   A    OP
1. SN V   The swim team / competed (in the finals).  D
   P1

          A     SN       V       Adv    P   A   OP
2. SN V   The candles / flickered softly (in the dark).  D
   P1
```

Exercise 2: Use Sentence 1 to underline the complete subject once and the complete predicate twice and to complete the table below.

List the Noun Used	List the Noun Job	Singular or Plural	Common or Proper	Simple Subject	Simple Predicate
1. team	2. SN	3. S	4. C	5. team	6. competed
7. finals	8. OP	9. P	10. C		

Exercise 3: Name the five parts of speech that you have studied. (*You may use abbreviations.*)
(The order of answers may vary.)

1. **Noun**   2. **Verb**   3. **Adjective**   4. **Adverb**   5. **Preposition**

Exercise 4: Identify each pair of words as synonyms or antonyms by putting parentheses ( ) around *syn* or *ant*.

1. flicker, flash	**(syn)** ant	4. nibble, munch	**(syn)** ant	7. energetic, weary	syn **(ant)**
2. depart, arrive	syn **(ant)**	5. brilliant, dull	syn **(ant)**	8. anger, rage	**(syn)** ant
3. scamper, scurry	**(syn)** ant	6. build, collapse	syn **(ant)**	9. gush, trickle	syn **(ant)**

Exercise 5: Write **S** for singular or **P** for plural.

Noun	S or P
1. toads	P
2. women	P
3. coffee	S

Exercise 6: Write **C** for Common or **P** for proper.

Noun	C or P
1. juice	C
2. store	C
3. Mexico	P

Exercise 7: Write *a* or *an* in the blanks.

1. The chef cut **an** onion.   3. Terry lives by **a** swamp.   5. **a** tulip   7. **a** radish
2. We went on **a** walk.   4. Frank planted **an** oak tree.   6. **an** apology   8. **a** castle

Exercise 8: In your journal, write a paragraph summarizing what you have learned this week.

CHAPTER 8 LESSON 4 CONTINUED

TEACHER INSTRUCTIONS

Use the Question and Answer Flows below for the sentences on the Chapter 8 Test.

Question and Answer Flow for Sentence 1: The swim team competed in the finals.

1. What competed in the finals? team - SN
2. What is being said about team? team competed - V
3. In - P
4. In what? finals - OP
5. The - A
6. What kind of team? swim - Adj
7. The - A
8. SN V P1 Check
9. (In the finals) - Prepositional phrase
10. Period, statement, declarative sentence
11. Go back to the verb - divide the complete subject from the complete predicate.

```
                          A   Adj   SN      V      P  A   OP
Classified Sentence:   SN  V    The swim team / competed (in the finals).   D
                       ——
                       P1
```

Question and Answer Flow for Sentence 2: The candles flickered softly in the dark.

1. What flickered softly in the dark? candles - SN
2. What is being said about candles? candles flickered - V
3. Flickered how? softly - Adv
4. In - P
5. In what? dark - OP
6. The - A
7. The - A
8. SN V P1 Check
9. (In the dark) - Prepositional phrase
10. Period, statement, declarative sentence
11. Go back to the verb - divide the complete subject from the complete predicate.

```
                          A    SN       V      Adv    P  A   OP
Classified Sentence:   SN  V    The candles / flickered softly (in the dark).   D
                       ——
                       P1
```

Level 2—Shurley English—Homeschool Edition

CHAPTER 8   LESSON 5
Objectives: Writing Assignment #2, and Sentence Time.

 WRITING TIME

<u>*TEACHER INSTRUCTIONS FOR WRITING ASSIGNMENT #2*</u>

Give Writing Assignment #2 from the box below. Remind students to use the Writing Checklist in Reference 17 to check their finished writing assignment.

Read, check, and discuss Writing Assignment #2 after students have finished their final papers. Use the Writing Checklist (*Reference 17 on teacher's page 112*) as you check and discuss students' papers. Make sure students are using the checklist correctly. In the beginning, you must also check students' papers carefully for <u>form</u> mistakes. This will ensure that students are learning the two-point format correctly.

Writing Assignment Box

Writing Assignment #2: Two-Point Expository Paragraph

Writing topic choices: My Favorite Places   or   Things to Do With a Friend   or   My Favorite Books

---

 SENTENCE TIME

Chapter 8, Lesson 5, Sentence: Use colored markers to match each label with the correct sentence part by drawing a line from one to the other. Then, use the labels to arrange the sentence parts into a sentence that you will write on the sentence line below. *(The order of the words in your sentence should be in the same sequence as the vertical list of sentence labels.)* Create other labels and scrambled sentence parts on notebook paper for family members to solve. You may color code the sentence parts. *(See page 111 in the student book.)*

Labels for Order of Sentence	Scrambled Sentence Parts
A	children
Adj	performed
SN	funny
V	the
P	clowns
A	for
OP	the

Sentence: The funny clowns performed for the children.

(End of lesson.)

CHAPTER 9   LESSON 1
Objectives: Jingles, Grammar (Practice Sentences), Skills (Skill Builder Check, Homonyms), Practice Exercise, Vocabulary #1, and Activity.

 **JINGLE TIME**

Have students turn to the Jingle Section in their books and recite the previously-taught jingles.

 GRAMMAR TIME

Put the Practice Sentences from the box below on the board or on notebook paper. Use these sentences as you practice the concepts that have been taught. For the greatest benefit, students must participate orally with the teacher.

Chapter 9, Practice Sentences for Lesson 1
1. _____ The loud thunder rumbled noisily in the distance.
2. _____ Eight girls went to the movie on Friday night.
3. _____ The huge brown crate fell off the truck today.

TEACHING SCRIPT FOR CLASSIFYING PRACTICE SENTENCES

We will classify three different sentences to practice the grammar skills in the Question and Answer Flows. We will classify the sentences together. Begin. (*You might have students write the labels above the sentences at this time.*)

Question and Answer Flow for Sentence 1: The loud thunder rumbled noisily in the distance.
1. What rumbled noisily in the distance? thunder - SN   8. The - A
2. What is being said about thunder? thunder rumbled - V   9. SN V P1 Check
3. Rumbled how? noisily - Adv   10. (In the distance) - Prepositional phrase
4. In - P   11. Period, statement, declarative sentence
5. In what? distance - OP   12. Go back to the verb - divide the complete
6. The - A   subject from the complete predicate.
7. What kind of thunder? loud - Adj
A   Adj   SN   V   Adv   P   A   OP
Classified Sentence: <u>SN V</u>   The loud thunder **/** rumbled noisily (in the distance).   D
P1

CHAPTER 9 LESSON 1 CONTINUED

Question and Answer Flow for Sentence 2: Eight girls went to the movie on Friday night.

1. Who went to the movie on Friday night? girls - SN
2. What is being said about girls? girls went - V
3. To - P
4. To what? movie - OP
5. The - A
6. On - P
7. On what? night - OP
8. Which night? Friday - Adj
9. How many girls? eight - Adj
10. SN V P1 Check
11. (To the movie) - Prepositional phrase
12. (On Friday night) - Prepositional phrase
13. Period, statement, declarative sentence
14. Go back to the verb - divide the complete subject from the complete predicate.

Classified Sentence: SN V / P1   Adj SN V P A OP P Adj OP
Eight girls / went (to the movie) (on Friday night). D

Question and Answer Flow for Sentence 3: The huge brown crate fell off the truck today.

1. What fell off the truck today? crate - SN
2. What is being said about crate? crate fell - V
3. Off - P
4. Off what? truck - OP
5. The - A
6. Fell when? today - Adv
7. What kind of crate? brown - Adj
8. What kind of crate? huge - Adj
9. The - A
10. SN V P1 Check
11. (Off the truck) - Prepositional phrase
12. Period, statement, declarative sentence
13. Go back to the verb - divide the complete subject from the complete predicate.

Classified Sentence: SN V / P1   A Adj Adj SN V P A OP Adv
The huge brown crate / fell (off the truck) today. D

SKILL TIME

Use Sentences 1-3 that you just classified with your students to do a Skill Builder Check. Use the guidelines below.

Skill Builder Check	
1. Noun check. (Say the job and then say the noun. Circle each noun.)	**5. Identify the complete subject and the complete predicate.** (Underline the complete subject once and the complete predicate twice.)
2. Identify the nouns as singular or plural. (Write **S** or **P** above each noun.)	**6. Identify the simple subject and simple predicate.** (Underline the simple subject once and the simple predicate twice. Bold, or highlight, the lines to distinguish them from the complete subject and complete predicate.)
3. Identify the nouns as common or proper. (Follow established procedure for oral identification.)	
4. Do a vocabulary check. (Follow established procedure for oral identification.)	

CHAPTER 9 LESSON 1 CONTINUED

SKILL TIME

TEACHING SCRIPT FOR HOMONYMS

Today, we will learn about homonyms. Look at Reference 20 on page 17 in the Reference section of your book. The definition says that homonyms are words that sound the same but have different meanings and different spellings. You should study the Homonym Chart until you are familiar enough with each homonym that you can choose the correct form easily. Since this is only a partial listing, you must look up any homonyms that you do not know and that are not listed on the chart. (*The homonym chart is located below.*)

Look at the examples for choosing the right homonyms at the bottom of the reference box. The directions say to underline the correct homonym. Read number 1. Look at the homonyms *right* and *write*. Go to the Homonym Chart and read the definition for each spelling. How do we spell the homonym that means *correct*? (*r-i-g-h-t*) How do we spell the homonym that means *to form letters*? (*w-r-i-t-e*)

Which homonym would you choose to complete the first sentence correctly? (*write*) How did you decide? It makes sense for Jennifer *to form letters* with her left hand. The word *write* means the same thing as *to form letters*.

Now, look at number 2. Which homonym would you choose to complete the second sentence correctly? (*right*) How did you decide? It makes sense for the contestant to have the *correct* answer. The word *right* means the same thing as *correct*. Always check the Homonym Chart or use a dictionary if you have a question about which homonym to use.

Reference 20: Homonym Chart		
Homonyms are words that sound the same but have different meanings and different spellings.		
1. **capital** - upper part, main	15. **lead** - metal	29. **their** - belonging to them
2. **capitol** - statehouse	16. **led** - guided	30. **there** - in that place
3. **coarse** - rough	17. **no** - not so	31. **they're** - they are
4. **course** - route	18. **know** - to understand	32. **threw** - did throw
5. **council** - assembly	19. **right** - correct, opposite of left	33. **through** - from end to end
6. **counsel** - advice	20. **write** - to form letters	34. **to** - toward (a preposition)
7. **forth** - forward	21. **principle** - a truth/rule/law	35. **too** - denoting excess
8. **fourth** - ordinal number	22. **principal** - chief/head person	36. **two** - a couple
9. **its** - possessive pronoun	23. **stationary** - motionless	37. **your** - belonging to you
10. **it's** - it is	24. **stationery** - paper	38. **you're** - you are
11. **hear** - to listen	25. **peace** - quiet	39. **weak** - not strong
12. **here** - in this place	26. **piece** - a part	40. **week** - seven days
13. **knew** - understood	27. **sent** - caused to go	41. **days** - more than one day
14. **new** - not old	28. **scent** - odor	42. **daze** - a confused state
Directions: Underline the correct homonym.		
1. Jennifer learned to (right, **write**) with her left hand.		
2. Contestant number two had the (**right**, write) answer.		

CHAPTER 9 LESSON 1 CONTINUED

 PRACTICE TIME

Now, have students turn to page 46 in the Practice Section of their book and find Chapter 9, Lesson 1, Practice. Go over the directions to make sure they understand what to do. Check and discuss the Practice after students have finished. Discuss strong areas as well as weak areas. (*Chapter 9, Lesson 1, Practice key is given below.*)

Chapter 9, Lesson 1, Practice: Underline the correct homonym in each sentence.

1. He (<u>threw</u>, through) the ball to Alex.
2. I want to travel (<u>to</u>, too, two) Alaska.
3. Jeremy walked (threw, <u>through</u>) the front door.
4. Shelly had (to, too, <u>two</u>) new dresses.
5. The ship sank (to, <u>too</u>, two) quickly.
6. You need to stand in line over (hear, <u>here</u>).
7. Mom (<u>sent</u>, scent) me to the store.
8. I didn't (<u>hear</u>, here) the alarm clock.

 VOCABULARY TIME

Assign Chapter 9, Vocabulary Words #1 on page 6 in the Reference Section for students to define in their Vocabulary notebooks. Tell students they are to use a dictionary or thesaurus to look up the meanings of the vocabulary words.

Chapter 9, Vocabulary Words #1
(expert, beginner, unchanging, constant)

 ACTIVITY / ASSIGNMENT TIME

Have students draw a very simple flower with a round center and petals surrounding the center. Have students classify the sample sentence below. Next, students should write the type of sentence in the center of the flower and each sentence label used in the petals. Have students make up and classify more sentences. Then, have them draw flowers for their sentence labels and type of sentences. They could draw more petals to accommodate longer sentences.

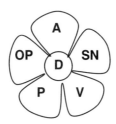

Sample:
A   SN   V   P   OP
The fishermen searched for worms. D

(End of lesson.)

CHAPTER 9   LESSON 2

Objectives: Jingles, Grammar (Practice Sentences), Skills (Practice and Improved Sentence), Practice Exercise, and Vocabulary #2.

 **JINGLE TIME**

Have students turn to the Jingle Section in their books and recite the previously-taught jingles.

 GRAMMAR TIME

Put the Practice Sentences from the box below on the board or on notebook paper. Use these sentences as you practice the concepts that have been taught. For the greatest benefit, students must participate orally with the teacher.

Chapter 9, Practice Sentences for Lesson 2
1. _____ The expert fireman spoke to the students at the elementary school.
2. _____ A statue of a famous American soldier stood in the hallway.
3. _____ The children played in the snow with the sleds.

TEACHING SCRIPT FOR CLASSIFYING PRACTICE SENTENCES

We will classify three different sentences to practice the grammar skills in the Question and Answer Flows. We will classify the sentences together. Begin. (*You might have students write the labels above the sentences at this time.*)

Question and Answer Flow for Sentence 1: The expert fireman spoke to the students at the elementary school.
1. Who spoke to the students at the elementary school? fireman - SN
2. What is being said about fireman? fireman spoke - V
3. To - P
4. To whom? students - OP
5. The - A
6. At - P
7. At what? school - OP
8. What kind of school? elementary - Adj
9. The - A
10. What kind of fireman? expert - Adj
11. The - A
12. SN V P1 Check
13. (To the students) - Prepositional phrase
14. (At the elementary school) - Prepositional phrase
15. Period, statement, declarative sentence
16. Go back to the verb - divide the complete subject from the complete predicate.

```
                          A  Adj  SN    V    P A    OP    P  A   Adj   OP
Classified Sentence:     SN V    The expert fireman / spoke (to the students) (at the elementary school).  D
                          P1
```

CHAPTER 9 LESSON 2 CONTINUED

Question and Answer Flow for Sentence 2: A statue of a famous American soldier stood in the hallway.

1. What stood in the hallway? statue - SN
2. What is being said about statue? statue stood - V
3. In - P
4. In what? hallway - OP
5. The - A
6. Of - P
7. Of whom? soldier - OP
8. What kind of soldier? American - Adj
9. What kind of soldier? famous - Adj
10. A - A
11. A - A
12. SN V P1 Check
13. (Of a famous American soldier) - Prepositional phrase
14. (In the hallway) - Prepositional phrase
15. Period, statement, declarative sentence
16. Go back to the verb - divide the complete subject from the complete predicate.

```
                        A  SN    P A   Adj        Adj      OP     V   P A   OP
Classified Sentence:    SN V     A statue (of a famous American soldier) / stood (in the hallway).   D
                        P1
```

Question and Answer Flow for Sentence 3: The children played in the snow with the sleds.

1. Who played in the snow with the sleds? children - SN
2. What is being said about children? children played - V
3. In - P
4. In what? snow - OP
5. The - A
6. With - P
7. With what? sleds - OP
8. The - A
9. The - A
10. SN V P1 Check
11. (In the snow) - Prepositional phrase
12. (With the sleds) - Prepositional phrase
13. Period, statement, declarative sentence
14. Go back to the verb - divide the complete subject from the complete predicate.

```
                        A   SN       V    P A  OP   P  A   OP
Classified Sentence:    SN V   The children / played (in the snow) (with the sleds).   D
                        P1
```

TEACHING SCRIPT FOR A PRACTICE SENTENCE WITH PREPOSITIONAL PHRASES

Put these labels on the board: **A Adj Adj SN V Adv P A Adj OP**

Look at the new sentence labels on the board: **A Adj Adj SN V Adv P A Adj OP**. I will guide you again through the process of writing a sentence to practice all the parts that you have learned.

Get out a sheet of notebook paper. On the top line of your notebook paper, write the title *Practice Sentence*. Copy the sentence labels from the board onto your notebook paper. Be sure to leave plenty of writing space between each label. Now, I will guide you through the process you will use whenever you write a Practice Sentence with a prepositional phrase.

1. Go to the **SN** label for the subject noun. Think of a noun that you want to use as your subject. Write the noun you have chosen on the line *under* the **SN** label.

CHAPTER 9 LESSON 2 CONTINUED

2. Go to the **V** label for the verb. Think of a verb that tells what your subject does. Make sure that your verb makes sense with the subject noun. Write the verb you have chosen on the line *under* the **V** label.

3. Go to the **Adv** label for the adverb. Immediately go to the verb in your sentence and ask an adverb question. What are the adverb questions? (*How, When, Where*) Choose one adverb question to ask and write your adverb answer *under* the **Adv** label.

4. Go to the **P** label for the preposition. Think of a preposition word that tells something about your verb. You must be careful to choose a preposition word that makes sense with the noun you will choose for the object of the preposition in your next step. Write the word you have chosen for a preposition *under* the **P** label.

5. Go to the **OP** label for the object of the preposition. If you like the noun you thought of while thinking of a preposition, write it down under the **OP** label. If you prefer, think of another noun by asking **what** or **whom** after your preposition. Check to make sure the preposition and object of the preposition make sense together and also make sense with the rest of the sentence. Remember, the object of the preposition will always answer the question **what** or **whom** after the preposition. Write the word you have chosen for the object of the preposition *under* the **OP** label.

6. Go to the **Adj** label for the adjective. Go to the object of the preposition that you just wrote and ask an adjective question to describe the object-of-the-preposition noun. What are the adjective questions? (*What kind, Which one, How many*) Choose one adjective question to ask and write your adjective answer *under* the **Adj** label next to the object of the preposition. Always check to make sure your answers are making sense in the sentence.

7. Go to the **A** label for the article adjective that is part of your prepositional phrase. What are the three article adjectives? (*a, an,* and *the*) Choose the article adjective that makes the best sense in your sentence. Write the article adjective you have chosen *under* the **A** label.

8. Go to the **Adj** label for another adjective. Go to the subject noun of your sentence and ask an adjective question. What are the adjective questions again? (*What kind, Which one, How many*) Choose one adjective question to ask and write your adjective answer *under* the **Adj** label next to the subject noun.

9. Go to the **Adj** label for the third adjective. Go to the subject noun again and ask another adjective question. You can ask the same adjective question, or you can ask a different adjective question. Write another adjective *under* the third **Adj** label.

10. Go to the **A** label for the article adjective in the subject area. What are the three article adjectives again? (*a, an,* and *the*) Choose the article adjective that makes the best sense in your sentence. Write the article adjective you have chosen *under* the **A** label.

11. Finally, check your Practice Sentence to make sure it has the necessary parts to be a complete sentence. What are the five parts of a complete sentence? (*subject, verb, complete sense, capital letter, and an end mark*) Does your Practice Sentence have the five parts of a complete sentence? (*Allow time for students to read over their sentences and to make any corrections they need to make.*)

Level 2—Shurley English—Homeschool Edition

CHAPTER 9 LESSON 2 CONTINUED

TEACHING SCRIPT FOR THE IMPROVED SENTENCE

Under your Practice Sentence, write the title *Improved Sentence* on another line. To improve your Practice Sentence, you will make two synonym changes, one antonym change, and your choice of a complete word change or another synonym or antonym change.

Since it is harder to find words that can be changed to an antonym, it is usually wise to go through your sentence to find an antonym change first. Then, look through your sentence again to find words that can be improved with synonyms. Finally, make a decision about whether your last change will be a complete word change, another synonym change, or another antonym change.

I will give you time to write your Improved Sentence. *(Always encourage students to use a thesaurus, synonym-antonym book, or a dictionary to help them develop an interesting and improved writing vocabulary. After students have finished, check and discuss students' Practice and Improved Sentences.)*

 PRACTICE TIME

Have students turn to page 46 in the Practice Section of their book and find Chapter 9, Lesson 2, Practice. Go over the directions to make sure they understand what to do. Check and discuss the Practice after students have finished. *(Chapter 9, Lesson 2, Practice key is given below.)*

Chapter 9, Lesson 2, Practice: Underline the correct homonym in each sentence.

1. The (led, <u>lead</u>) pipes were replaced.
2. These are my (knew, <u>new</u>) boots.
3. She (<u>led</u>, lead) me to my classroom.
4. My dad (<u>knew</u>, new) your grandfather.
5. The church (<u>council</u>, counsel) cast the final vote.
6. The doctor gave (council, <u>counsel</u>) to his patients.
7. There are seven (<u>days</u>, daze) in a week.
8. The excitement left me in a (days, <u>daze</u>).

 VOCABULARY TIME

Assign Chapter 9, Vocabulary Words **#2** on page 6 in the Reference Section for students to define in their Vocabulary notebooks. Tell students they are to use a dictionary or thesaurus to look up the meanings of the vocabulary words.

Chapter 9, Vocabulary Words #2
(keep, abandon, immerse, plunge)

(End of lesson.)

CHAPTER 9   LESSON 3
Objectives: Jingles, Grammar (Practice Sentences), Practice Exercise, and Activity.

 **JINGLE TIME**

Have students turn to the Jingle Section in their books and recite the previously-taught jingles.

 GRAMMAR TIME

Put the Practice Sentences from the box below on the board or on notebook paper. Use these sentences as you practice the concepts that have been taught.

Chapter 9, Practice Sentences for Lesson 3
1. _____ An Olympic skater trains constantly for competition.
2. _____ An abandoned pup looks aimlessly for food.
3. _____ Carol went to the wedding yesterday.

TEACHING SCRIPT FOR CLASSIFYING PRACTICE SENTENCES

We will classify three different sentences to practice the grammar skills in the Question and Answer Flows. We will classify the sentences together. Begin.

Question and Answer Flow for Sentence 1: An Olympic skater trains constantly for competition.
1. Who trains constantly for competition? skater - SN   7. An - A
2. What is being said about skater? skater trains - V   8. SN V P1 Check
3. Trains how? constantly - Adv   9. (For competition) - Prepositional phrase
4. For - P   10. Period, statement, declarative sentence
5. For what? competition - OP   11. Go back to the verb - divide the complete subject
6. What kind of skater? Olympic - Adj   from the complete predicate.
A   Adj   SN   V   Adv   P   OP
Classified Sentence: SN V   An Olympic skater / trains constantly (for competition). D
P1

Question and Answer Flow for Sentence 2: An abandoned pup looks aimlessly for food.
1. What looks aimlessly for food? pup - SN   7. An - A
2. What is being said about pup? pup looks - V   8. SN V P1 Check
3. Looks how? aimlessly - Adv   9. (For food) - Prepositional phrase
4. For - P   10. Period, statement, declarative sentence
5. For what? food - OP   11. Go back to the verb - divide the complete subject
6. What kind of pup? abandoned - Adj   from the complete predicate.
A   Adj   SN   V   Adv   P   OP
Classified Sentence: SN V   An abandoned pup / looks aimlessly (for food). D
P1

CHAPTER 9 LESSON 3 CONTINUED

> **Question and Answer Flow for Sentence 3: Carol went to the wedding yesterday.**
>
> 1. Who went to the wedding yesterday? Carol - SN
> 2. What is being said about Carol? Carol went - V
> 3. To - P
> 4. To what? wedding - OP
> 5. The - A
> 6. Went when? yesterday - Adv
> 7. SN V P1 Check
> 8. (To the wedding) - Prepositional phrase
> 9. Period, statement, declarative sentence
> 10. Go back to the verb - divide the complete subject from the complete predicate.
>
> ```
>                              SN   V   P  A   OP     Adv
> Classified Sentence:    SN V  Carol / went (to the wedding) yesterday.  D
>                          P1
> ```

 PRACTICE TIME

Have students turn to page 46 in the Practice Section of their book and find Chapter 9, Lesson 3, Practice. Go over the directions to make sure they understand what to do. Check and discuss the Practice after students have finished. (*Chapter 9, Lesson 3, Practice key is given below.*)

Chapter 9, Lesson 3, Practice: Underline the correct homonym in each sentence.

1. Is this (<u>your</u>, you're) book?
2. The group went (<u>to</u>, too, two) the mall.
3. I need some (<u>peace</u>, piece) and quiet.
4. (Your, <u>You're</u>) Katie's partner.
5. She ate another (peace, <u>piece</u>) of pizza.
6. We placed (forth, <u>fourth</u>) in the tournament.
7. They were gone for an entire (<u>week</u>, weak).
8. My knees felt (<u>weak</u>, week) during the recital.

 ACTIVITY / ASSIGNMENT TIME

To practice prepositions, make an obstacle course for your students. Your course can be as simple as a chair in the middle of the floor, or as elaborate as a course that continues throughout the entire house and into the yard. Incorporate as many prepositions as possible to make up directions for the course. Once your students have finished following the directions to your obstacle course, have them design one of their own. Encourage them to use as many prepositions as possible.

> **Sample directions:**
>
> around the couch, behind the door, between the chairs, out the door, down the stairs, through the gate, past the mailbox, around the yard, up the stairs, in the house, under the table, in your seat

(End of lesson.)

CHAPTER 9 LESSON 4

Objectives: Jingles, Study, Test, Check, Writing (Journal), and State Activity.

JINGLE TIME

Have students turn to the Jingle Section in their books and recite the previously-taught jingles.

STUDY TIME

Have students study the vocabulary words in their vocabulary notebooks. Remind students that any vocabulary word in their notebooks could be on their test. Also, have students study any of the skills in the Practice Section that they need to review.

TEST TIME

Have students turn to page 88 in the Test Section of their book and find Chapter 9 Test. Go over the directions to make sure they understand what to do. (*Chapter 9 Test key is on the next page.*)

CHECK TIME

After students have finished, check and discuss their test papers. Make sure they understand why their answers are right or wrong. (*For total points, count each required answer as a point.*)

STATE ACTIVITY TIME

(*Beginning with Chapter 9, two states will be introduced. If more time is needed, continue working in the next lesson.*)
Students will continue to draw or trace the states and to write the following questions and answers.

Florida	Georgia
1. What is the state on the front of this card? **Florida**	1. What is the state on the front of this card? **Georgia**
2. What is the capital of Florida? **Tallahassee**	2. What is the capital of Georgia? **Atlanta**
3. What is the postal abbreviation of Florida? **FL**	3. What is the postal abbreviation of Georgia? **GA**

Color these states. Use the cards to quiz family members, friends, and relatives. You may want to time the responses to your questions.

(End of lesson.)

Level 2—Shurley English—Homeschool Edition

Chapter 9 Test
(Student Page 88)

67 pts

Exercise 1: Classify each sentence.

```
           A    Adj         Adj       SN      V      Adv       P   A    OP       P       OP
1. SN V    The frightened student pilot / landed carefully (on the runway) (before sundown).  D
   P1

           A   Adj    SN        V       Adv      P   A   Adj  OP
2. SN V    The stunt driver / plunged fearlessly (down the steep hill)!  E
   P1
```

Exercise 2: Use Sentence 1 to underline the complete subject once and the complete predicate twice and to complete the table below.

List the Noun Used	List the Noun Job	Singular or Plural	Common or Proper	Simple Subject	Simple Predicate
1. **pilot**	2. **SN**	3. **S**	4. **C**	5. **pilot**	6. **landed**
7. **runway**	8. **OP**	9. **S**	10. **C**		
11. **sundown**	12. **OP**	13. **S**	14. **C**		

Exercise 3: Name the five parts of speech that you have studied. (*You may use abbreviations.*)
(The order of answers may vary.)

1. **Noun**   2. **Verb**   3. **Adjective**   4. **Adverb**   5. **Preposition**

Exercise 4: Identify each pair of words as synonyms or antonyms by putting parentheses ( ) around **syn** or **ant**.

1. plunge, immerse	**(syn)** ant	4. collapse, build	syn **(ant)**	7. weary, energetic	syn **(ant)**
2. gush, trickle	syn **(ant)**	5. abandon, keep	syn **(ant)**	8. constant, unchanging	**(syn)** ant
3. overhead, above	**(syn)** ant	6. rage, anger	**(syn)** ant	9. expert, beginner	syn **(ant)**

Exercise 5: Underline the correct homonym in each sentence.

1. My cold made me feel (**weak**, week).
2. We placed our jackets over (**there**, their).
3. I want to (**hear**, here) the choir sing.
4. He (**led**, lead) the troops into battle.
5. Mr. Paul (**sent**, scent) me a birthday card.
6. Christmas is only a (weak, **week**) away.
7. The state (counsel, **council**) met yesterday.
8. We lost one (**piece**, peace) of our puzzle.

Exercise 6: In your journal, write a paragraph summarizing what you have learned this week.

CHAPTER 9 LESSON 4 CONTINUED

TEACHER INSTRUCTIONS

Use the Question and Answer Flows below for the sentences on the Chapter 9 Test.

Question and Answer Flow for Sentence 1: The frightened student pilot landed carefully on the runway before sundown.

1. Who landed carefully on the runway before sundown? pilot - SN
2. What is being said about pilot? pilot landed - V
3. Landed how? carefully - Adv
4. On - P
5. On what? runway - OP
6. The - A
7. Before - P
8. Before what? sundown - OP
9. What kind of pilot? student - Adj
10. What kind of pilot? frightened - Adj
11. The - A
12. SN V P1 Check
13. (On the runway) - Prepositional phrase
14. (Before sundown) - Prepositional phrase
15. Period, statement, declarative sentence
16. Go back to the verb - divide the complete subject from the complete predicate.

```
                          A   Adj       Adj      SN       V       Adv     P  A   OP        P      OP
Classified Sentence:   SN V    The frightened student pilot / landed carefully (on the runway) (before sundown).  D
                       P1
```

Question and Answer Flow for Sentence 2: The stunt driver plunged fearlessly down the steep hill!

1. Who plunged fearlessly down the steep hill? driver - SN
2. What is being said about driver? driver plunged - V
3. Plunged how? fearlessly - Adv
4. Down - P
5. Down what? hill - OP
6. What kind of hill? steep - Adj
7. The - A
8. What kind of driver? stunt - Adj
9. The - A
10. SN V P1 Check
11. (Down the steep hill) - Prepositional phrase
12. Exclamation point, strong feeling, exclamatory sentence
13. Go back to the verb - divide the complete subject from the complete predicate.

```
                          A   Adj    SN        V         Adv      P   A   Adj   OP
Classified Sentence:   SN V    The stunt driver / plunged fearlessly (down the steep hill)!  E
                       P1
```

CHAPTER 9   LESSON 5

Objectives: Writing Assignment #3 and Sentence Time.

 WRITING TIME

TEACHER INSTRUCTIONS FOR WRITING ASSIGNMENT #3

Give Writing Assignment #3 from the box below. Remind students to use the Writing Checklist in Reference 17 to check their finished writing assignment.

Read, check, and discuss Writing Assignment #3 after students have finished their final papers. Use the Writing Checklist (*Reference 17 on teacher's page 112*) as you check and discuss students' papers. Make sure students are using the checklist correctly. In the beginning, you must also check students' papers carefully for <u>form</u> mistakes. This will ensure that students are learning the two-point format correctly.

Writing Assignment Box
Writing Assignment #3: Two-Point Expository Paragraph
Writing topic choices: My Favorite Snacks   or   My Favorite Sports   or   Things I Wonder About

 SENTENCE TIME

Chapter 9, Lesson 5, Sentence: Use colored markers to match each label with the correct sentence part by drawing a line from one to the other. Then, use the labels to arrange the sentence parts into a sentence that you will write on the sentence line below. *(The order of the words in your sentence should be in the same sequence as the vertical list of sentence labels.)* Create other labels and scrambled sentence parts on notebook paper for family members to solve. You may color code the sentence parts. *(See page 111 in the student book.)*

Labels for Order of Sentence	Scrambled Sentence Parts
A	huge
SN	in
V	family
P	mall
A	shopped
Adj	the
OP	the

Sentence: The family shopped in the huge mall.

(End of lesson.)

CHAPTER 10   LESSON 1

Objectives: Jingles, Grammar (Practice Sentences), Skills (Skill Builder Check, Subject-Verb Agreement), Practice Exercise, and Vocabulary #1.

 **JINGLE TIME**

Have students turn to the Jingle Section in their books and recite the previously-taught jingles.

 GRAMMAR TIME

Put the Practice Sentences from the box below on the board or on notebook paper. Use these sentences as you practice the concepts that have been taught. For the greatest benefit, students must participate orally with the teacher.

Chapter 10, Practice Sentences for Lesson 1
1. _____ The six frisky kittens lived in the old wooden shed.
2. _____ The man in the room prayed quietly in the dark.
3. _____ The huge elephants plodded carefully down the steep hill.

TEACHING SCRIPT FOR CLASSIFYING PRACTICE SENTENCES

We will classify three different sentences to practice the grammar skills in the Question and Answer Flows. We will classify the sentences together. Begin. (*You might have students write the labels above the sentences at this time.*)

Question and Answer Flow for Sentence 1: The six frisky kittens lived in the old wooden shed.

1. What lived in the old wooden shed? kittens - SN
2. What is being said about kittens? kittens lived - V
3. In - P
4. In what? shed - OP
5. What kind of shed? wooden - Adj
6. What kind of shed? old - Adj
7. The - A
8. What kind of kittens? frisky - Adj
9. How many kittens? six - Adj
10. The - A
11. SN V P1 Check
12. (In the old wooden shed) - Prepositional phrase
13. Period, statement, declarative sentence
14. Go back to the verb - divide the complete subject from the complete predicate.

```
                          A  Adj  Adj   SN      V    P  A  Adj   Adj    OP
Classified Sentence:  SN V   The six frisky kittens / lived (in the old wooden shed).  D
                      P1
```

CHAPTER 10 LESSON 1 CONTINUED

Question and Answer Flow for Sentence 2: The man in the room prayed quietly in the dark.

1. Who prayed quietly in the dark? man - SN
2. What is being said about man? man prayed - V
3. Prayed how? quietly - Adv
4. In - P
5. In what? dark - OP
6. The - A
7. In - P
8. In what? room - OP
9. The - A
10. The - A
11. SN V P1 Check
12. (In the room) - Prepositional phrase
13. (In the dark) - Prepositional phrase
14. Period, statement, declarative sentence
15. Go back to the verb - divide the complete subject from the complete predicate.

```
                       A   SN   P  A   OP    V    Adv   P  A   OP
Classified Sentence:   SN V   The man (in the room) / prayed quietly (in the dark).  D
                       ----
                       P1
```

Question and Answer Flow for Sentence 3: The huge elephants plodded carefully down the steep hill.

1. What plodded carefully down the steep hill? elephants - SN
2. What is being said about elephants? elephants plodded - V
3. Plodded how? carefully - Adv
4. Down - P
5. Down what? hill - OP
6. What kind of hill? steep - Adj
7. The - A
8. What kind of elephants? huge - Adj
9. The - A
10. SN V P1 Check
11. (Down the steep hill) - Prepositional phrase
12. Period, statement, declarative sentence
13. Go back to the verb - divide the complete subject from the complete predicate.

```
                       A  Adj    SN       V      Adv    P  A  Adj  OP
Classified Sentence:   SN V   The huge elephants / plodded carefully (down the steep hill).  D
                       ----
                       P1
```

 SKILL TIME

Use Sentences 1-3 that you just classified with your students to do a Skill Builder Check. Use the guidelines below.

Skill Builder Check	
1. Noun check. (Say the job and then say the noun. Circle each noun.)	**5. Identify the complete subject and the complete predicate.** (Underline the complete subject once and the complete predicate twice.)
2. Identify the nouns as singular or plural. (Write **S** or **P** above each noun.)	**6. Identify the simple subject and simple predicate.** (Underline the simple subject once and the simple predicate twice. Bold, or highlight, the lines to distinguish them from the complete subject and complete predicate.)
3. Identify the nouns as common or proper. (Follow established procedure for oral identification.)	
4. Do a vocabulary check. (Follow established procedure for oral identification.)	

CHAPTER 10 LESSON 1 CONTINUED

SKILL TIME

<u>TEACHING SCRIPT FOR SUBJECT-VERB AGREEMENT</u>

A sentence must have correct subject-verb agreement. The word **agreement** means to work together; therefore, subject-verb agreement means the special way in which the subject and verb work together to make the sentence correct.

We will use the following sentence to demonstrate the subject-verb agreement concept: **The little chipmunk gathered acorns.** *(Put the sample sentence on the board.)* Whenever you work with subject-verb agreement, you must remember to work only with the subject and verb. Therefore, you must isolate the subject and verb before you begin. What are the subject and verb in the sample sentence? (*chipmunk gathered*)

I will write the subject and verb *chipmunk gathered* on a different section of the board so we can concentrate on what we need to do for subject-verb agreement. *(Write "chipmunk gathered" on a clean area of the board so you will have room to work without other sentences distracting students.)*

You only worry about subject-verb agreement with present tense verbs. When a verb is past tense or ends with -ed, it doesn't matter if the subject is singular or plural; the verb remains the same: past tense.

Example: Chipmunk gathered.   Chipmunks gathered.

The example clearly demonstrates that we must change a past tense verb to present tense in order to work with singular and plural forms. How do we change *gathered* to present tense? (*Take off the* **-ed**.) Now that *gather* is in present tense, we must check whether it agrees with its subject. If the subject is singular, we must use a singular verb form. If the subject is plural, we must use a plural verb form.

Is the subject *chipmunk* singular or plural? (*singular*) Since the subject *chipmunk* is singular, we must choose the singular form of the verb *gather*. How do we make a verb singular? (*Add an* **s** *or* **es** *to the plain form to make the word* **gathers**.)

Since we have checked to make sure the subject and verb are both singular, we know the subject agrees with the verb. Let's say both singular forms together so we can hear the singular combination as we say them. *(Have students say "chipmunk gathers" several times to hear the subject-verb agreement.)*

Now, we will form the plural forms of the subject and verb. Since the subject *chipmunk* is singular, how do we make it plural? (*Add an* **s** *to make the word* **chipmunks**.) We must also change the verb to a plural form. The plural form of a present tense verb is called the <u>plain form</u> because it does not end in *s* or *es*.

How would we write the plural form of the verb *gather*? (*gather*) The verb *gather* is plural because it does not end in *s* or *es*. Since we have changed both the subject and verb to plural forms, we know the subject agrees with the verb. Let's say both plural forms together so we can hear the plural combinations as we say them. *(Have students say "chipmunks gather" several times to hear the subject-verb agreement.)*

CHAPTER 10 LESSON 1 CONTINUED

Sometimes, a word does not follow the regular rules because of spelling form. These are called exceptions. One such exception is the word *mouse*. In the sentence, *The mouse nibbled*, what are the subject and verb? *(mouse nibbled)* What is the present tense of the verb *nibbled*? *(nibble)* Is the subject *mouse* singular or plural? *(singular)* Since the subject is singular, we must use the singular verb form. How do we make the verb *nibble* singular? *(Add an **s** or **es** to the plain form to make the word **nibbles**.)*

Since our subject and verb are both singular, we know the subject agrees with the verb. Let's say both singular forms together so we can hear the singular combination as we say them. *(Have students say "mouse nibbles" several times to hear the subject-verb agreement.)*

Now, we will form the plurals of the subject and verb. Since the subject *mouse* is singular, how do we make it plural? This is one of the exceptions. Some words are made plural by changing the spelling form, not by adding an "s" or "es". To make *mouse* plural, we must make a spelling change to make the plural word *mice*. We must also change the verb to a plural form.

Remember, the plural form of a present tense verb is called the plain form because it does not end in *s* or *es*. What is the plural form of the verb *nibble*? *(nibble)* The verb *nibble* is plural because it does not end in *s* or *es*. Since we have changed both the subject and verb to plural forms, we know the subject agrees with the verb. Let's say both plural forms together so we can hear the plural combination as we say them. *(Have students say "mice nibble" several times to hear the subject-verb agreement.)*

We will now discuss a set of rules that will also help you make the right subject-verb agreement choice with different kinds of verbs. Look at Reference 21 on page 17 in the Reference Section of your book. Rule 1 says that if you have a singular subject, you must use a singular verb form that ends in *s*: **is, was, has, does, or verbs ending with s or es**. Notice that singular verb forms end in *s*. The "s" stands for singular verb forms. Remember, a singular subject agrees with a singular verb form that ends in ***s or es***.

Reference 21: Subject-Verb Agreement Rules
Rule 1: A singular subject must use a singular verb form that ends in **s**: *is, was, has, does,* or verbs ending with **es**.
Rule 2: A plural subject, a compound subject, or the subject **YOU** must use a plural verb form that has **no s** ending: *are, were, do, have,* or verbs without **s** or **es** endings. (A plural verb form is also called the *plain form*.)
Directions: For each sentence, do these four things: (1) Write the subject. (2) Write **S** if the subject is singular or **P** if the subject is plural. (3) Write the rule number. (4) Underline the correct verb in the sentence.

Subject	S or P	Rule	
kitten	S	1	1. The **kitten** (**licks**, lick) his paws.
pie and cake	P	2	2. The **pie** and **cake** (**are**, is) in the oven.
You	P	2	3. **You** (watches, **watch**) for the deliveryman.

Rule 2 says that if you have a plural subject, a compound subject, or the subject *YOU*, you must use these verbs: **are, were, do, have, or verbs without *s* or *es* endings** because these verbs are plural verb forms. Any time the pronoun YOU is the subject of a sentence, you do not have to decide whether it is singular or plural. The subject pronoun YOU always uses a plural verb, and you MUST choose a plural verb form. Remember, a plural subject agrees with a plural verb form that does not end in ***s or es***.

CHAPTER 10 LESSON 1 CONTINUED

Look at the examples under the rules. The directions say you must write the subject, then write **S** if the subject is singular or write **P** if the subject is plural. You must also write the rule number (Rule 1 or 2) from the rule box and then underline the correct verb in the sentence. What is the subject in Sentence 1? (*kitten*) Is the subject *kitten* singular or plural? (*singular*)

Since the subject is singular, you will go to the rule box and find the rule that tells you which verb to choose if you have a singular subject. Which rule do we put in the blank? (*Rule 1*) Notice that a number 1 has been written in the blank for Rule 1. Using the list of singular verbs in Rule 1, which verb would we choose to agree with the singular subject *kitten*? (*licks, the verb with the s or es ending*) The verb *licks* has been underlined as the correct verb choice.

What is the subject in Sentence 2? (*pie and cake*) Is the subject *pie* and *cake* singular or plural? (*plural - because it is compound*) Since the subject is plural, you will go to the rule box and find the rule that tells you which verb to choose if you have a plural subject. Which rule do we put in the blank? (*Rule 2*) A number 2 has been written in the blank for Rule 2. Using the list of plural verbs in Rule 2, which verb would we choose to agree with the plural subject *pie* and *cake*? (*are*) The verb *are* has been underlined as the correct verb choice.

What is the subject in Sentence 3? (*You*) Is the subject *you* singular or plural? (*Plural*) Since the subject is plural, you will go to the rule box and find the rule that tells you which verb to choose if you have a plural subject. Which rule do we put in the blank? (*Rule 2*) A number 2 has been written in the blank for Rule 2. Using the list of plural verbs in Rule 2, which verb would we choose to agree with the plural subject *you*? (*watch*) The verb *watch* has been underlined as the correct verb choice.

Choosing verbs to agree with the subjects in the sentences on your test will be easy if you follow the rules you have just learned. Remember, first you must decide if the subject of the sentence is singular or plural. Next, you must look at the verb choices in parentheses in the sentence. Last, you must choose the verb that is listed under the singular or plural rule in the box. (*Discuss the subject **I** as an exception. The subject **I** takes a plural verb form. Examples: I have, I want, I walk, I talk, etc.*)

Teacher's Notes: The singular subject **I** and the verb **be** present a special case of subject-verb agreement. Use the following examples to demonstrate the verb forms used with the pronoun **I**.
Examples: I am. I was. I have. I walk. I talk.

 PRACTICE TIME

Have students turn to page 47 in the Practice Section of their book and find Chapter 10, Lesson 1, Practice *(1-2)*. Go over the directions to make sure they understand what to do. Check and discuss the Practices after students have finished. (*Chapter 10, Lesson 1, Practice keys are given on the next page.*)

CHAPTER 10 LESSON 1 CONTINUED

Chapter 10, Lesson 1, Practice 1: For each sentence, do these four things: (1) Write the subject. (2) Write **S** if the subject is singular or **P** if the subject is plural. (3) Write the rule number. (4) Underline the correct verb in the sentence.

Rule 1: A singular subject must use a singular verb form that ends in **s**: *is, was, has, does,* or verbs ending with **es**.

Rule 2: A plural subject, a compound subject, or the subject **YOU** must use a plural verb form that has **no s** ending: *are, were, do, have,* or verbs without **s** or **es** endings. (A plural verb form is also called the *plain form*.)

Subject	S or P	Rule	
penguins	P	2	1. The **penguins** (shuffles, <u>shuffle</u>) across the ice.
lemonade and tea	P	2	2. The **lemonade** and **tea** (is, <u>are</u>) in the refrigerator.
boat	S	1	3. Tyler's **boat** (<u>glides</u>, glide) across the lake.
Larry	S	1	4. **Larry** (play, <u>plays</u>) in the sandbox.
you	P	2	5. **You** (washes, <u>wash</u>) your hands.
stomach	S	1	6. Her **stomach** (<u>growls</u>, growl) loudly.
curtains	P	2	7. The **curtains** (<u>flutter</u>, flutters) in the breeze.
chefs	P	2	8. The **chefs** (prepares, <u>prepare</u>) the dinner.
Tom and Jennifer	P	2	9. **Tom** and **Jennifer** (takes, <u>take</u>) the dog on a walk.
women	P	2	10. Several **women** (<u>quilt</u>, quilts) happily.

Chapter 10, Lesson 1, Practice 2: Underline the correct homonym in each sentence.

1. She said to turn (<u>right</u>, write).
2. I didn't (<u>know</u>, no) the answer.
3. The steel wool felt (course, <u>coarse</u>).
4. We ate a five (coarse, <u>course</u>) meal.
5. She will (<u>write</u>, right) on the board.
6. Peter answered (<u>no</u>, know) to her question.

 VOCABULARY TIME

Assign Chapter 10, Vocabulary Words **#1** on page 6 in the Reference Section for students to define in their Vocabulary notebooks. Tell students they are to use a dictionary or thesaurus to look up the meanings of the vocabulary words.

Chapter 10, Vocabulary Words #1
(old, youthful, canyon, gorge)

(End of lesson.)

Level 2—Shurley English—Homeschool Edition

CHAPTER 10 LESSON 2

Objectives: Jingles, Grammar (Practice Sentences, Practice and Improved Sentence) Practice Exercise, and Vocabulary #2.

 **JINGLE TIME**

Have students turn to the Jingle Section in their books and recite the previously-taught jingles.

 GRAMMAR TIME

Put the Practice Sentences from the box below on the board or on notebook paper. Use these sentences as you practice the concepts that have been taught. For the greatest benefit, students must participate orally with the teacher.

Chapter 10, Practice Sentences for Lesson 2
1. _____ The four puppets danced happily across the stage.
2. _____ The tourists rode through the canyon on mules.
3. _____ The bewildered players sat on the dugout steps.

TEACHING SCRIPT FOR CLASSIFYING PRACTICE SENTENCES

We will classify three different sentences to practice the grammar skills in the Question and Answer Flows. We will classify the sentences together. Begin. (*You might have students write the labels above the sentences at this time.*)

Question and Answer Flow for Sentence 1: The four puppets danced happily across the stage.

1. What danced happily across the stage?
   puppets - SN
2. What is being said about puppets?
   puppets danced - V
3. Danced how? happily - Adv
4. Across - P
5. Across what? stage - OP
6. The - A
7. How many puppets? four - Adj
8. The - A
9. SN V P1 Check
10. (Across the stage) - Prepositional phrase
11. Period, statement, declarative sentence
12. Go back to the verb - divide the complete subject from the complete predicate.

```
                        A   Adj  SN     V       Adv      P   A   OP
Classified Sentence:   SN V   The four puppets / danced happily (across the stage).  D
                       P1
```

Level 2 Homeschool Teacher's Manual

Page 149

CHAPTER 10 LESSON 2 CONTINUED

Question and Answer Flow for Sentence 2: The tourists rode through the canyon on mules.

1. Who rode through the canyon on mules? tourists - SN
2. What is being said about tourists? tourists rode - V
3. Through - P
4. Through what? canyon - OP
5. The - A
6. On - P
7. On what? mules - OP
8. The - A
9. SN V P1 Check
10. (Through the canyon) - Prepositional phrase
11. (On mules) - Prepositional phrase
12. Period, statement, declarative sentence
13. Go back to the verb - divide the complete subject from the complete predicate.

                              A   SN   V   P   A   OP   P   OP

Classified Sentence: SN V / P1   The tourists / rode (through the canyon) (on mules). D

Question and Answer Flow for Sentence 3: The bewildered players sat on the dugout steps.

1. Who sat on the dugout steps? players - SN
2. What is being said about players? players sat - V
3. On - P
4. On what? steps - OP
5. What kind of steps? dugout - Adj
6. The - A
7. What kind of players? bewildered - Adj
8. The - A
9. SN V P1 Check
10. (On the dugout steps) - Prepositional phrase
11. Period, statement, declarative sentence
12. Go back to the verb - divide the complete subject from the complete predicate.

                            A   Adj   SN   V   P   A   Adj   OP

Classified Sentence: SN V / P1   The bewildered players / sat (on the dugout steps). D

TEACHING SCRIPT FOR A PRACTICE SENTENCE WITH PREPOSITIONAL PHRASES

Put these labels on the board: **A Adj Adj SN V Adv P A Adj OP**

Look at the new sentence labels on the board: **A Adj Adj SN V Adv P A Adj OP**. Get out a sheet of notebook paper. On the top line of your notebook paper, write the title *Practice Sentence*. Copy the sentence labels from the board onto your notebook paper. Be sure to leave plenty of writing space between each label. Now, I will guide you through the process you will use whenever you write a Practice Sentence with a prepositional phrase.

1. Go to the **SN** label for the subject noun. Think of a noun that you want to use as your subject. Write the noun you have chosen on the line *under* the **SN** label.

2. Go to the **V** label for the verb. Think of a verb that tells what your subject does. Make sure that your verb makes sense with the subject noun. Write the verb you have chosen on the line *under* the **V** label.

3. Go to the **Adv** label for the adverb. Immediately go to the verb in your sentence and ask an adverb question. What are the adverb questions? (*How, When, Where*) Choose one adverb question to ask and write your adverb answer *under* the **Adv** label.

CHAPTER 10 LESSON 2 CONTINUED

4. Go to the **P** label for the preposition. Think of a preposition word that tells something about your verb. You must be careful to choose a preposition word that makes sense with the noun you will choose for the object of the preposition in your next step. Write the word you have chosen for a preposition *under* the **P** label.

5. Go to the **OP** label for the object of the preposition. If you like the noun you thought of while thinking of a preposition, write it down under the **OP** label. If you prefer, think of another noun by asking **what** or **whom** after your preposition. Check to make sure the preposition and object of the preposition make sense together and also make sense with the rest of the sentence. Remember, the object of the preposition will always answer the question **what** or **whom** after the preposition. Write the word you have chosen for the object of the preposition *under* the **OP** label.

6. Go to the **Adj** label for the adjective. Go to the object of the preposition that you just wrote and ask an adjective question to describe the object-of-the-preposition noun. What are the adjective questions? (*What kind, Which one, How many*) Choose one adjective question to ask and write your adjective answer *under* the **Adj** label next to the object of the preposition. Always check to make sure your answers are making sense in the sentence.

7. Go to the **A** label for the article adjective that is part of your prepositional phrase. What are the three article adjectives? (*a*, *an*, and *the*) Choose the article adjective that makes the best sense in your sentence. Write the article adjective you have chosen *under* the **A** label.

8. Go to the **Adj** label for another adjective. Go to the subject noun of your sentence and ask an adjective question. What are the adjective questions again? (*What kind, Which one, How many*) Choose one adjective question to ask and write your adjective answer *under* the **Adj** label next to the subject noun.

9. Go to the **Adj** label for the third adjective. Go to the subject noun again and ask another adjective question. You can ask the same adjective question, or you can ask a different adjective question. Write another adjective *under* the third **Adj** label.

10. Go to the **A** label for the article adjective in the subject area. What are the three article adjectives again? (*a*, *an*, and *the*) Choose the article adjective that makes the best sense in your sentence. Write the article adjective you have chosen *under* the **A** label.

11. Finally, check your Practice Sentence to make sure it has the necessary parts to be a complete sentence. What are the five parts of a complete sentence? (*subject, verb, complete sense, capital letter, and an end mark*) Does your Practice Sentence have the five parts of a complete sentence? (*Allow time for students to read over their sentences and to make any corrections they need to make.*)

TEACHING SCRIPT FOR THE IMPROVED SENTENCE

Under your Practice Sentence, write the title *Improved Sentence* on another line. To improve your Practice Sentence, you will make two synonym changes, one antonym change, and your choice of a complete word change or another synonym or antonym change.

I will give you time to write your Improved Sentence. (*Always encourage students to use a thesaurus, synonym-antonym book, or a dictionary to help them develop an interesting and improved writing vocabulary. After students have finished, check and discuss students' Practice and Improved Sentences.*)

CHAPTER 10 LESSON 2 CONTINUED

 PRACTICE TIME

Have students turn to page 48 in the Practice Section of their book and find Chapter 10, Lesson 2, Practice (1-2). Go over the directions to make sure they understand what to do. Check and discuss the Practices after students have finished. (*Chapter 10, Lesson 2, Practice keys are given below.*)

Chapter 10, Lesson 2, Practice 1: For each sentence, do these four things: (1) Write the subject. (2) Write **S** if the subject is singular or **P** if the subject is plural. (3) Write the rule number. (4) Underline the correct verb in the sentence.

Rule 1: A singular subject must use a singular verb form that ends in **s**: *is, was, has, does,* or verbs ending with **es**.

Rule 2: A plural subject, a compound subject, or the subject **YOU** must use a plural verb form that has **no s** ending: *are, were, do, have,* or verbs without **s** or **es** endings. (A plural verb form is also called the *plain form*.)

Subject	S or P	Rule	
bugs	P	2	1. The **bugs** (swarms, <u>swarm</u>) the chocolate cake.
Josh and Steven	P	2	2. **Josh** and **Steven** (plays, <u>play</u>) soccer.
cloud	S	1	3. The **cloud** (<u>covers</u>, cover) the bright sun.
aunt	S	1	4. My **aunt** (work, <u>works</u>) at a bank.
you	P	2	5. **You** (helps, <u>help</u>) gather the trash.
we	P	2	6. **We** (rakes, <u>rake</u>) the leaves into a pile.
bus	S	1	7. The **bus** (stop, <u>stops</u>) at the railroad tracks.
buckets	P	2	8. The **buckets** (leaks, <u>leak</u>) onto the floor.
Tony	S	1	9. **Tony** (<u>asks</u>, ask) politely for permission.

Chapter 10, Lesson 2, Practice 2: Underline the correct homonym in each sentence.

1. Our school's (<u>principal</u>, principle) won the award.
2. We learned the basic (<u>principles</u>, principals).
3. Please direct your attention over (their, <u>there</u>).
4. The group visited the (capital, <u>capitol</u>) building.
5. Georgia's (capitol, <u>capital</u>) is Atlanta.
6. She showed us a (<u>capital</u>, capitol) letter.
7. I wanted to visit (<u>their</u>, there) new home.
8. Timothy ran (<u>to</u>, too, two) the bus stop.

 VOCABULARY TIME

Assign Chapter 10, Vocabulary Words **#2** on page 6 in the Reference Section for students to define in their Vocabulary notebooks. Tell students they are to use a dictionary or thesaurus to look up the meanings of the vocabulary words.

Chapter 10, Vocabulary Words #2
(dangerous, harmless, bewilder, confuse)

(End of lesson.)

CHAPTER 10   LESSON 3

Objectives: Jingles, Grammar (Practice Sentences), Practice Exercise, and Activity.

 **JINGLE TIME**

Have students turn to the Jingle Section in their books and recite the previously-taught jingles.

 GRAMMAR TIME

Put the Practice Sentences from the box below on the board or on notebook paper. Use these sentences as you practice the concepts that have been taught. For the greatest benefit, students must participate orally with the teacher.

Chapter 10, Practice Sentences for Lesson 3
1. _____ The avalanche raced toward the tiny village!
2. _____ A youthful swimmer drifts on the waves at sea.
3. _____ The baby elephant rests comfortably in the corner.

TEACHING SCRIPT FOR CLASSIFYING PRACTICE SENTENCES

We will classify three different sentences to practice the grammar skills in the Question and Answer Flows. We will classify the sentences together. Begin. (*You might have students write the labels above the sentences at this time.*)

Question and Answer Flow for Sentence 1:   The avalanche raced toward the tiny village!
1. What raced toward the tiny village? avalanche - SN
2. What is being said about avalanche? avalanche raced - V
3. Toward - P
4. Toward what? village - OP
5. What kind of village? tiny - Adj
6. The - A
7. The - A
8. SN V P1 Check
9. (Toward the tiny village) - Prepositional phrase
10. Exclamation point, strong feeling, exclamatory sentence
11. Go back to the verb - divide the complete subject from the complete predicate.

```
                              A    SN      V     P   A  Adj  OP
Classified Sentence:    SN V     The avalanche / raced (toward the tiny village)!  E
                        P1
```

CHAPTER 10 LESSON 3 CONTINUED

Question and Answer Flow for Sentence 2: A youthful swimmer drifts on the waves at sea.

1. Who drifts on the waves at sea? swimmer - SN
2. What is being said about swimmer? swimmer drifts - V
3. On - P
4. On what? waves - OP
5. The - A
6. At - P
7. At what? sea - OP
8. What kind of swimmer? youthful - Adj
9. A - A
10. SN V P1 Check
11. (On the waves) - Prepositional phrase
12. (At sea) - Prepositional phrase
13. Period, statement, declarative sentence
14. Go back to the verb - divide the complete subject from the complete predicate.

Classified Sentence: SN V / P1   A Adj SN V P A OP P OP
A youthful swimmer / drifts (on the waves) (at sea). D

Question and Answer Flow for Sentence 3: The baby elephant rests comfortably in the corner.

1. What rests comfortably in the corner? elephant - SN
2. What is being said about elephant? elephant rests - V
3. Rests how? comfortably - Adv
4. In - P
5. In what? corner - OP
6. The - A
7. What kind of elephant? baby - Adj
8. The - A
9. SN V P1 Check
10. (In the corner) - Prepositional phrase
11. Period, statement, declarative sentence
12. Go back to the verb - divide the complete subject from the complete predicate.

Classified Sentence: SN V / P1   A Adj SN V Adv P A OP
The baby elephant / rests comfortably (in the corner). D

PRACTICE TIME

Have students turn to page 49 in the Practice Section of their book and find Chapter 10, Lesson 3, Practice (1-2). Go over the directions to make sure they understand what to do. Check and discuss the Practices after students have finished. *(Chapter 10, Lesson 3, Practice keys are given below and on the next page.)*

Chapter 10, Lesson 3, Practice 1: Underline the correct homonym in each sentence.

1. Todd placed (<u>fourth</u>, forth) in the race.
2. We'll meet (<u>here</u>, hear) in one hour.
3. Jackie (<u>knew</u>, new) where to shop.
4. Patsy (lead, <u>led</u>) me to the door.
5. The lion jumped (threw, <u>through</u>) the hoops.
6. The nation's (piece, <u>peace</u>) was not long-lasting.
7. The mayor appointed Jim to the (counsel, <u>council</u>).
8. There are only three (<u>days</u>, daze) until my birthday.

Level 2—Shurley English—Homeschool Edition

CHAPTER 10 LESSON 3 CONTINUED

Chapter 10, Lesson 3, Practice 2: For each sentence, do these four things: (1) Write the subject. (2) Write **S** if the subject is singular or **P** if the subject is plural. (3) Write the rule number. (4) Underline the correct verb in the sentence.

Rule 1: A singular subject must use a singular verb form that ends in **s**: *is*, *was*, *has*, *does*, or verbs ending with **es**.

Rule 2: A plural subject, a compound subject, or the subject **YOU** must use a plural verb form that has **no s** ending: *are*, *were*, *do*, *have*, or verbs without **s** or **es** endings. (A plural verb form is also called the *plain form*.)

Subject	S or P	Rule
pineapples	P	2
squirrels	P	2
lunchbox	S	1
ship	S	1
you	P	2
socks	P	2
firemen	P	2
helicopter	S	1
trumpets	P	2

1. The **pineapples** (ripens, <u>ripen</u>) in the hot sun.
2. The **squirrels** (enjoys, <u>enjoy</u>) our bird bath.
3. My **lunchbox** (<u>falls</u>, fall) off the counter top.
4. The **ship** (dock, <u>docks</u>) quickly at the port.
5. **You** (needs, <u>need</u>) to drink more milk.
6. Her **socks** (clings, <u>cling</u>) tightly to her ankles.
7. The **firemen** (<u>rush</u>, rushes) quickly to the scene.
8. The **helicopter** (land, <u>lands</u>) safely on the pad.
9. The **trumpets** (plays, <u>play</u>) the melody.

ACTIVITY / ASSIGNMENT TIME

Part 1:
The first part of this activity will strengthen your understanding of subject-verb agreement. I will give you a list of subjects. Write these words on a sheet of paper. (*Have the subject words below on the board for students to copy.*) Then, you will write a present tense verb beside each subject word. A present tense verb does not end in *ed*. Be sure to check for subject-verb agreement as you write your sentences.

        Subject Words
        1. Birds
        2. Boat
        3. Flowers
        4. Kite

Part 2:
The next portion of your activity is a little more challenging. After you have finished writing your subject-verb sentences, you will follow the four steps below. You are allowed to change some of the verbs in your sentences if you wish.

1. Choose one sentence to expand by adding adjectives, adverbs, and prepositional phrases.
2. Choose one sentence to illustrate.
3. Choose one sentence to change a singular subject and verb to a plural subject and verb.
4. Choose one sentence to remain the same.

(End of lesson.)

Level 2 Homeschool Teacher's Manual

Level 2—Shurley English—Homeschool Edition

CHAPTER 10   LESSON 4

Objectives: Jingles, Study, Test, Check, Writing (Journal), and State Activity.

 JINGLE TIME

Have students turn to the Jingle Section in their books and recite the previously-taught jingles.

 STUDY TIME

Have students study the vocabulary words in their vocabulary notebooks. Remind students that any vocabulary word in their notebooks could be on their test. Also, have students study any of the skills in the Practice Section that they need to review.

 TEST TIME

Have students turn to page 89 in the Test Section of their book and find Chapter 10 Test. Go over the directions to make sure they understand what to do. (*Chapter 10 Test key is on the next page.*)

 CHECK TIME

After students have finished, check and discuss their test papers. Make sure they understand why their answers are right or wrong. (*For total points, count each required answer as a point.*)

 STATE ACTIVITY TIME

Students will continue to draw or trace the states and to write the following questions and answers.

Hawaii	Idaho
1. What is the state on the front of this card? **Hawaii**	1. What is the state on the front of this card? **Idaho**
2. What is the capital of Hawaii? **Honolulu**	2. What is the capital of Idaho? **Boise**
3. What is the postal abbreviation of Hawaii? **HI**	3. What is the postal abbreviation of Idaho? **ID**

Color these states. Use the cards to quiz family members, friends, and relatives. You may want to time the responses to your questions.

(End of lesson.)

Level 2—Shurley English—Homeschool Edition

Chapter 10 Test
(Student Page 89)

84 pts

Exercise 1: Classify each sentence.

```
              A   Adj    SN       V       Adv      P  A   OP    P  A   OP
1. SN V       An ugly crocodile / lies harmlessly (on the bank) (of the river).  D
   P1
              SN   V   P    OP    P   A   Adj  OP   Adv
2. SN V       Ann / rode (to school) (in the yellow bus) today.  D
   P1
```

Exercise 2: Use Sentence 2 to underline the complete subject once and the complete predicate twice and to complete the table below.

List the Noun Used	List the Noun Job	Singular or Plural	Common or Proper	Simple Subject	Simple Predicate
1. Ann	2. SN	3. S	4. P	5. Ann	6. rode
7. school	8. OP	9. S	10. C		
11. bus	12. OP	13. S	14. C		

Exercise 3: Name the five parts of speech that you have studied. (*You may use abbreviations.*) **(The order may vary.)**

1. **Noun**   2. **Verb**   3. **Adjective**   4. **Adverb**   5. **Preposition**

Exercise 4: Identify each pair of words as synonyms or antonyms by putting parentheses ( ) around **syn** or **ant**.

1. canyon, gorge	(syn) ant	4. expert, beginner	syn (ant)	7. nibble, munch	(syn) ant
2. abandon, keep	syn (ant)	5. weary, energetic	syn (ant)	8. bewilder, confuse	(syn) ant
3. flicker, flash	(syn) ant	6. youthful, old	syn (ant)	9. harmless, dangerous	syn (ant)

Exercise 5: Underline the correct homonym in each sentence.

1. That light is (to, <u>too</u>, two) bright.
2. The quarterback (<u>threw</u>, through) the ball.
3. The perfume had a marvelous (sent, <u>scent</u>).
4. Robert felt (week, <u>weak</u>) after the marathon.

Exercise 6: For each sentence, do these four things: (1) Write the subject. (2) Write **S** if the subject is singular or **P** if the subject is plural. (3) Write the rule number. (4) Underline the correct verb in the sentence.

Rule 1 and Rule 2 are located in Reference 21 on page 17 in your student book.

Subject	S or P	Rule	
shelter	S	1	1. The **shelter** (provide, <u>provides</u>) dinners for the homeless.
campers	P	2	2. The **campers** (casts, <u>cast</u>) their tent near the fire.
beam	S	1	3. The **beam** (<u>supports</u>, support) the building.
snow	S	1	4. The **snow** (cover, <u>covers</u>) the ground.
you	P	2	5. **You** (cleans, <u>clean</u>) your room.

Exercise 7: In your journal, write a paragraph summarizing what you have learned this week.

Level 2 Homeschool Teacher's Manual

Level 2—Shurley English—Homeschool Edition

CHAPTER 10 LESSON 4 CONTINUED

TEACHER INSTRUCTIONS

Use the Question and Answer Flows below for the sentences on the Chapter 10 Test.

Question and Answer Flow for Sentence 1: An ugly crocodile lies harmlessly on the bank of the river.

1. What lies harmlessly on the bank of the river? crocodile - SN
2. What is being said about crocodile? crocodile lies - V
3. Lies how? harmlessly - Adv
4. On - P
5. On what? bank - OP
6. The - A
7. Of - P
8. Of what? river - OP
9. The - A
10. What kind of crocodile? ugly - Adj
11. An - A
12. SN V P1 Check
13. (On the bank) - Prepositional phrase
14. (Of the river) - Prepositional phrase
15. Period, statement, declarative sentence
16. Go back to the verb - divide the complete subject from the complete predicate.

```
                            A  Adj   SN     V     Adv    P  A  OP   P  A  OP
Classified Sentence:   SN V  An ugly crocodile / lies harmlessly (on the bank) (of the river).  D
                       P1
```

Question and Answer Flow for Sentence 2: Ann rode to school in the yellow bus today.

1. Who rode to school in the yellow bus today? Ann - SN
2. What is being said about Ann? Ann rode - V
3. To - P
4. To what? school - OP
5. In - P
6. In what? bus - OP
7. What kind of bus? yellow - Adj
8. The - A
9. Rode when? today - Adv
10. SN V P1 Check
11. (To school) - Prepositional phrase
12. (In the yellow bus) - Prepositional phrase
13. Period, statement, declarative sentence
14. Go back to the verb - divide the complete subject from the complete predicate.

```
                            SN    V    P   OP    P  A  Adj   OP   Adv
Classified Sentence:   SN V  Ann / rode (to school) (in the yellow bus) today.  D
                       P1
```

Level 2—Shurley English—Homeschool Edition

CHAPTER 10   LESSON 5

Objectives: Writing Assignment #4 and Sentence Time.

 WRITING TIME

TEACHER INSTRUCTIONS FOR WRITING ASSIGNMENT # 4

Give Writing Assignment #4 from the box below. Remind students to use the Writing Checklist in Reference 17 to check their finished writing assignment.

Read, check, and discuss Writing Assignment #4 after students have finished their final papers. Use the Writing Checklist (*Reference 17 on teacher's page 112*) as you check and discuss students' papers. Make sure students are using the checklist correctly. In the beginning, you must also check students' papers carefully for <u>form</u> mistakes. This will ensure that students are learning the two-point format correctly.

Writing Assignment Box

Writing Assignment #4: Two-Point Expository Paragraph

Writing topic choices: My Favorite Cartoons   or   My Favorite Pets   or   Why Computers Are Important

---

 SENTENCE TIME

Chapter 10, Lesson 5, Sentence: Use colored markers to match each label with the correct sentence part by drawing a line from one to the other. Then, use the labels to arrange the sentence parts into a sentence that you will write on the sentence line below. *(The order of the words in your sentence should be in the same sequence as the vertical list of sentence labels.)* Create other labels and scrambled sentence parts on notebook paper for family members to solve. You may color code the sentence parts. *(See page 111 in the student book.)*

Labels for Order of Sentence	Scrambled Sentence Parts
A	along
Adj	garden
Adj	hopped
SN	a
V	the
P	edge
A	rabbit
OP	brown
P	of
A	curious
OP	the

Sentence: A curious brown rabbit hopped along the edge of the garden.

(End of lesson.)

Level 2 Homeschool Teacher's Manual

© SHURLEY INSTRUCTIONAL MATERIALS, INC.

Level 2—Shurley English—Homeschool Edition

CHAPTER 11   LESSON 1
Objectives: Jingles, Grammar (Practice Sentences), Skill (Skill Builder Check), Practice Exercise, and Vocabulary #1.

 **JINGLE TIME**

Have students turn to the Jingle Section in their books and recite the previously-taught jingles.

 GRAMMAR TIME

Put the Practice Sentences from the box below on the board or on notebook paper. Use these sentences as you practice the concepts that have been taught. For the greatest benefit, students must participate orally with the teacher.

Chapter 11, Practice Sentences for Lesson 1
1. _____ The three brown ponies in the field galloped to the big red barn.
2. _____ The wounded soldier waited patiently for the medical team.
3. _____ The feisty alligator lunged suddenly toward the playful otters.

TEACHING SCRIPT FOR CLASSIFYING PRACTICE SENTENCES

We will classify three different sentences to practice the grammar skills in the Question and Answer Flows. We will classify the sentences together. Begin. (*You might have students write the labels above the sentences at this time.*)

Question and Answer Flow for Sentence 1: The three brown ponies in the field galloped to the big red barn.
1. What galloped to the big red barn? ponies - SN   11. What kind of ponies? brown - Adj
2. What is being said about ponies? ponies galloped - V   12. How many ponies? three - Adj
3. To - P   13. The - A
4. To what? barn - OP   14. SN V P1 Check
5. What kind of barn? red - Adj   15. (In the field) - Prepositional phrase
6. What kind of barn? big - Adj   16. (To the big red barn) - Prepositional phrase
7. The - A   17. Period, statement, declarative sentence
8. In - P   18. Go back to the verb - divide the complete subject
9. In what? field - OP   from the complete predicate
10. The - A
Classified Sentence: A   Adj Adj SN   P A OP   V   P A Adj Adj OP
SN V   The three brown ponies (in the field) / galloped (to the big red barn). D
P1

CHAPTER 11 LESSON 1 CONTINUED

Question and Answer Flow for Sentence 2: The wounded soldier waited patiently for the medical team.

1. Who waited patiently for the medical team? soldier - SN
2. What is being said about soldier? soldier waited - V
3. Waited how? patiently - Adv
4. For - P
5. For what? team - OP
6. What kind of team? medical - Adj
7. The - A
8. What kind of soldier? wounded - Adj
9. The - A
10. SN V P1 Check
11. (For the medical team) - Prepositional phrase
12. Period, statement, declarative sentence
13. Go back to the verb - divide the complete subject from the complete predicate.

Classified Sentence:

```
                     A    Adj    SN     V      Adv    P   A    Adj   OP
    SN V      The wounded soldier / waited patiently (for the medical team).  D
    ─────
     P1
```

Question and Answer Flow for Sentence 3: The feisty alligator lunged suddenly toward the playful otters.

1. What lunged suddenly toward the playful otters? alligator - SN
2. What is being said about alligator? alligator lunged - V
3. Lunged how? suddenly - Adv
4. Toward - P
5. Toward what? otters - OP
6. What kind of otters? playful - Adj
7. The - A
8. What kind of alligator? feisty - Adj
9. The - A
10. SN V P1 Check
11. (Toward the playful otters) - Prepositional phrase
12. Period, statement, declarative sentence
13. Go back to the verb - divide the complete subject from the complete predicate.

Classified Sentence:

```
                     A    Adj    SN      V     Adv    P    A    Adj   OP
    SN V      The feisty alligator / lunged suddenly (toward the playful otters).  D
    ─────
     P1
```

SKILL TIME

Use Sentences 1-3 that you just classified with your students to do a Skill Builder Check. Use the guidelines below.

Skill Builder Check	
1. Noun check. (Say the job and then say the noun. Circle each noun.)	**5. Identify the complete subject and the complete predicate.** (Underline the complete subject once and the complete predicate twice.)
2. Identify the nouns as singular or plural. (Write **S** or **P** above each noun.)	
3. Identify the nouns as common or proper. (Follow established procedure for oral identification.)	**6. Identify the simple subject and simple predicate.** (Underline the simple subject once and the simple predicate twice. Bold, or highlight, the lines to distinguish them from the complete subject and complete predicate.)
4. Do a vocabulary check. (Follow established procedure for oral identification.)	

CHAPTER 11 LESSON 1 CONTINUED

 PRACTICE TIME

Have students turn to page 50 in the Practice Section of their book and find Chapter 11, Lesson 1, Practice. Go over the directions to make sure they understand what to do. Check and discuss the Practice after students have finished. (*Chapter 11, Lesson 1, Practice key is given below.*)

Chapter 11, Lesson 1, Practice: For each sentence, do these four things: (1) Write the subject. (2) Write **S** if the subject is singular or **P** if the subject is plural. (3) Write the rule number. (4) Underline the correct verb in the sentence.

Rule 1: A singular subject must use a singular verb form that ends in **s**: *is, was, has, does,* or verbs ending with **es**.
Rule 2: A plural subject, a compound subject, or the subject **YOU** must use a plural verb form that has **no s** ending: *are, were, do, have,* or verbs without **s** or **es** endings. (A plural verb form is also called the *plain form*.)

Subject	S or P	Rule	
stars	P	2	1. The **stars** (shines, <u>shine</u>) brightly in the night sky.
Peter and Jerry	P	2	2. **Peter** and **Jerry** (lives, <u>live</u>) on the same street.
we	P	2	3. **We** (<u>visit</u>, visits) the new theme park.
Josh	S	1	4. **Josh** (think, <u>thinks</u>) about the questions on the test.
teacher	S	1	5. The piano **teacher** (speak, <u>speaks</u>) quietly to the new student.
flowers	P	2	6. The **flowers** (<u>wilt</u>, wilts) in the dry summer months.
he	S	1	7. **He** (<u>sends</u>, send) the letter to the company.
cookies	P	2	8. The **cookies** (sits, <u>sit</u>) on a plate in the kitchen.
triplets	P	2	9. The **triplets** (plays, <u>play</u>) under the sprinkler.
scout	S	1	10. The **scout** (find, <u>finds</u>) the enemy base.
men	P	2	11. The **men** (<u>board</u>, boards) the trolley car.
gophers	P	2	12. Several **gophers** (<u>tunnel</u>, tunnels) underground.

 VOCABULARY TIME

Assign Chapter 11, Vocabulary Words **#1** on page 6 in the Reference Section for students to define in their Vocabulary notebooks. Tell students they are to use a dictionary or thesaurus to look up the meanings of the vocabulary words.

Chapter 11, Vocabulary Words #1
(clog, block, exhausted, refreshed)

(End of lesson.)

Level 2—Shurley English—Homeschool Edition

CHAPTER 11   LESSON 2
Objectives: Jingles, Grammar (Practice Sentences, Practice and Improved Sentence), Practice Exercise, Vocabulary #2, and Activity.

 **JINGLE TIME**

Have students turn to the Jingle Section in their books and recite the previously-taught jingles.

 GRAMMAR TIME

Put the Practice Sentences from the box below on the board or on notebook paper. Use these sentences as you practice the concepts that have been taught. For the greatest benefit, students must participate orally with the teacher.

Chapter 11, Practice Sentences for Lesson 2
1. _____ The young monkeys climbed awkwardly through the trees in the dense jungle.
2. _____ The exhausted repairman worked for hours on the clogged drain today.
3. _____ The express train stopped daily at the station for several passengers during the summer.

TEACHING SCRIPT FOR CLASSIFYING PRACTICE SENTENCES

We will classify three different sentences to practice the grammar skills in the Question and Answer Flows. We will classify the sentences together. Begin. (*You might have students write the labels above the sentences at this time.*)

Question and Answer Flow for Sentence 1: The young monkeys climbed awkwardly through the trees in the dense jungle.
1. What climbed awkwardly through the trees in the dense jungle? monkeys - SN
2. What is being said about monkeys? monkeys climbed - V
3. Climbed how? awkwardly - Adv
4. Through - P
5. Through what? trees - OP
6. The - A
7. In - P
8. In what? jungle - OP
9. What kind of jungle? dense - Adj
10. The - A
11. What kind of monkeys? young - Adj
12. The - A
13. SN V P1 Check
14. (Through the trees) - Prepositional phrase
15. (In the dense jungle) - Prepositional phrase
16. Period, statement, declarative sentence
17. Go back to the verb - divide the complete subject from the complete predicate.

Classified Sentence:
A Adj SN   V   Adv   P   A   OP   P   A   Adj   OP
SN V   The young monkeys / climbed awkwardly (through the trees) (in the dense jungle).   D
P1

CHAPTER 11 LESSON 2 CONTINUED

Question and Answer Flow for Sentence 2: The exhausted repairman worked for hours on the clogged drain today.

1. Who worked for hours on the clogged drain today? repairman - SN
2. What is being said about repairman? repairman worked - V
3. For - P
4. For what? hours - OP
5. On - P
6. On what? drain - OP
7. What kind of drain? clogged - Adj
8. The - A
9. Worked when? today - Adv
10. What kind of repairman? exhausted - Adj
11. The - A
12. SN V P1 Check
13. (For hours) - Prepositional phrase
14. (On the clogged drain) - Prepositional phrase
15. Period, statement, declarative sentence
16. Go back to the verb - divide the complete subject from the complete predicate.

Classified Sentence:

```
                       A    Adj        SN       V   P  OP    P  A    Adj    OP   Adv
          SN  V    The exhausted repairman / worked (for hours) (on the clogged drain) today.  D
          P1
```

Question and Answer Flow for Sentence 3: The express train stopped daily at the station for several passengers during the summer.

1. What stopped daily at the station for several passengers during the summer? train - SN
2. What is being said about train? train stopped - V
3. Stopped when? daily - Adv
4. At - P
5. At what? station - OP
6. The - A
7. For - P
8. For what? passengers - OP
9. How many passengers? several - Adj
10. During - P
11. During what? summer - OP
12. The - A
13. What kind of train? express - Adj
14. The - A
15. SN V P1 Check
16. (At the station) - Prepositional phrase
17. (For several passengers) - Prepositional phrase
18. (During the summer) - Prepositional phrase
19. Period, statement, declarative sentence
20. Go back to the verb - divide the complete subject from the complete predicate.

Classified Sentence:

```
                       A   Adj    SN       V    Adv  P A    OP      P   Adj       OP
          SN  V    The express train / stopped daily (at the station) (for several passengers)
          P1        P    A    OP
                  (during the summer).  D
```

TEACHING SCRIPT FOR A PRACTICE SENTENCE WITH PREPOSITIONAL PHRASES

Put these labels on the board: **A Adj Adj SN V Adv P A Adj OP**

Look at the new sentence labels on the board: **A Adj Adj SN V Adv P A Adj OP**. Get out a sheet of notebook paper. On the top line of your notebook paper, write the title *Practice Sentence*. Copy the sentence labels from the board onto your notebook paper. Be sure to leave plenty of writing space between each label. Now, I will guide you through the process you will use whenever you write a Practice Sentence with a prepositional phrase.

CHAPTER 11 LESSON 2 CONTINUED

1. Go to the **SN** label for the subject noun. Think of a noun that you want to use as your subject. Write the noun you have chosen on the line *under* the **SN** label.

2. Go to the **V** label for the verb. Think of a verb that tells what your subject does. Make sure that your verb makes sense with the subject noun. Write the verb you have chosen on the line *under* the **V** label.

3. Go to the **Adv** label for the adverb. Immediately go to the verb in your sentence and ask an adverb question. What are the adverb questions? (*How, When, Where*) Choose one adverb question to ask and write your adverb answer *under* the **Adv** label.

4. Go to the **P** label for the preposition. Think of a preposition word that tells something about your verb. You must be careful to choose a preposition word that makes sense with the noun you will choose for the object of the preposition in your next step. Write the word you have chosen for a preposition *under* the **P** label.

5. Go to the **OP** label for the object of the preposition. If you like the noun you thought of while thinking of a preposition, write it down under the **OP** label. If you prefer, think of another noun by asking **what** or **whom** after your preposition. Check to make sure the preposition and object of the preposition make sense together and also make sense with the rest of the sentence. Remember, the object of the preposition will always answer the question **what** or **whom** after the preposition. Write the word you have chosen for the object of the preposition *under* the **OP** label.

6. Go to the **Adj** label for the adjective. Go to the object of the preposition that you just wrote and ask an adjective question to describe the object-of-the-preposition noun. What are the adjective questions? (*What kind, Which one, How many*) Choose one adjective question to ask and write your adjective answer *under* the **Adj** label next to the object of the preposition. Always check to make sure your answers are making sense in the sentence.

7. Go to the **A** label for the article adjective that is part of your prepositional phrase. What are the three article adjectives? (*a, an*, and *the*) Choose the article adjective that makes the best sense in your sentence. Write the article adjective you have chosen *under* the **A** label.

8. Go to the **Adj** label for another adjective. Go to the subject noun of your sentence and ask an adjective question. What are the adjective questions again? (*What kind? Which one? How many?*) Choose one adjective question to ask and write your adjective answer *under* the **Adj** label next to the subject noun.

9. Go to the **Adj** label for the third adjective. Go to the subject noun again and ask another adjective question. You can ask the same adjective question, or you can ask a different adjective question. Write another adjective *under* the third **Adj** label.

10. Go to the **A** label for the article adjective in the subject area. What are the three article adjectives again? (*a, an*, and *the*) Choose the article adjective that makes the best sense in your sentence. Write the article adjective you have chosen *under* the **A** label.

CHAPTER 11 LESSON 2 CONTINUED

11. Finally, check your Practice Sentence to make sure it has the necessary parts to be a complete sentence. What are the five parts of a complete sentence? (*subject, verb, complete sense, capital letter, and an end mark*) Does your Practice Sentence have the five parts of a complete sentence? (*Allow time for students to read over their sentences and to make any corrections they need to make.*)

TEACHING SCRIPT FOR THE IMPROVED SENTENCE

Under your Practice Sentence, write the title *Improved Sentence* on another line. To improve your Practice Sentence, you will make two synonym changes, one antonym change, and your choice of a complete word change or another synonym or antonym change.

Since it is harder to find words that can be changed to an antonym, it is usually wise to go through your sentence to find an antonym change first. Then, look through your sentence again to find words that can be improved with synonyms. Finally, make a decision about whether your last change will be a complete word change, another synonym change, or another antonym change.

I will give you time to write your Improved Sentence. (*Always encourage students to use a thesaurus, synonym-antonym book, or a dictionary to help them develop an interesting and improved writing vocabulary. After students have finished, check and discuss students' Practice and Improved Sentences.*)

 PRACTICE TIME

Have students turn to pages 50 and 51 in the Practice Section of their book and find Chapter 11, Lesson 2, Practice *(1-2)*. Go over the directions to make sure they understand what to do. Check and discuss the Practices after students have finished. (*Chapter 11, Lesson 2, Practice keys are given below and on the next page.*)

Chapter 11, Lesson 2, Practice 1: Underline the correct homonym in each sentence.

1. Debbie has (to, too, <u>two</u>) sisters.
2. The desert is (to, <u>too</u>, two) hot.
3. She bought new (<u>stationery</u>, stationary).
4. (<u>Their</u>, There) meeting started at five.
5. The ball went (threw, <u>through</u>) the window.
6. May I come to (<u>your</u>, you're) birthday party.
7. I found the last (<u>piece</u>, peace) of the puzzle.
8. The train stood (stationery, <u>stationary</u>) yesterday.

CHAPTER 11 LESSON 2 CONTINUED

Chapter 11, Lesson 2, Practice 2: For each sentence, do these four things: (1) Write the subject. (2) Write **S** if the subject is singular or **P** if the subject is plural. (3) Write the rule number. (4) Underline the correct verb in the sentence.

Rule 1: A singular subject must use a singular verb form that ends in **s**: *is, was, has, does,* or verbs ending with **es**.

Rule 2: A plural subject, a compound subject, or the subject **YOU** must use a plural verb form that has **no s** ending: *are, were, do, have,* or verbs without **s** or **es** endings. (A plural verb form is also called the *plain form*.)

Subject	S or P	Rule		
brother	S	1	1.	My **brother** (climb, <u>climbs</u>) the big oak tree.
scarf	S	1	2.	The woman's **scarf** (drape, <u>drapes</u>) around her neck.
whales	P	2	3.	The **whales** (<u>move</u>, moves) slowly through the ocean.
light	S	1	4.	The **light** (flash, <u>flashes</u>) on top of the tower.
you	P	2	5.	**You** (moves, <u>move</u>) your truck over there.
peaches	P	2	6.	The ripened **peaches** (falls, <u>fall</u>) from the tree.
vine	S	1	7.	The **vine** (grow, <u>grows</u>) up the side of the building.
voices	P	2	8.	The **voices** (echoes, <u>echo</u>) in the tunnel.
campfire	S	1	9.	Our **campfire** (<u>burns</u>, burn) brightly.

VOCABULARY TIME

Assign Chapter 11, Vocabulary Words **#2** on page 6 in the Reference Section for students to define in their Vocabulary notebooks. Tell students they are to use a dictionary or thesaurus to look up the meanings of the vocabulary words.

Chapter 11, Vocabulary Words #2
(alert, aware, tardy, punctual)

ACTIVITY / ASSIGNMENT TIME

Make a list of four different animals. Write the name of each animal on an index card. On the back of each index card, write descriptive sentences about the animal listed on the front. Be sure to include as many adjectives and adverbs as possible. Finally, play a guessing game with different members of your family. Read aloud or hold up the side of the card with the description and let family members guess which animal's name is written on the other side. Discuss which animals were the hardest and easiest to guess. Also, discuss which animals were the hardest and easiest to describe.

(End of lesson.)

Level 2—Shurley English—Homeschool Edition

CHAPTER 11   LESSON 3
Objectives: Jingles, Grammar (Practice Sentences), Practice Exercise, and Activity.

 **JINGLE TIME**

Have students turn to the Jingle Section in their books and recite the previously-taught jingles.

 GRAMMAR TIME

Put the Practice Sentences from the box below on the board or on notebook paper. Use these sentences as you practice the concepts that have been taught. For the greatest benefit, students must participate orally with the teacher.

Chapter 11, Practice Sentences for Lesson 3
1. _____ A shrill whistle sounded through the woods during the snowstorm.
2. _____ An alert policeman sped quickly to the accident.
3. _____ Two tardy students reported quickly to the principal.

TEACHING SCRIPT FOR CLASSIFYING PRACTICE SENTENCES

We will classify three different sentences to practice the grammar skills in the Question and Answer Flows. We will classify the sentences together. Begin. (*You might have students write the labels above the sentences at this time.*)

Question and Answer Flow for Sentence 1: A shrill whistle sounded through the woods during the snowstorm.	
1. What sounded through the woods during the snowstorm? whistle - SN	8. The - A
2. What is being said about whistle? whistle sounded - V	9. What kind of whistle? shrill - Adj
3. Through - P	10. A - A
4. Through what? woods - OP	11. SN V P1 Check
5. The - A	12. (Through the woods) - Prepositional phrase
6. During - P	13. (During the snowstorm) - Prepositional phrase
7. During what? snowstorm - OP	14. Period, statement, declarative sentence
	15. Go back to the verb - divide the complete subject from the complete predicate.

```
                              A  Adj  SN         V       P   A   OP      P    A    OP
Classified Sentence:  SN V    A shrill whistle / sounded (through the woods) (during the snowstorm).  D
                      P1
```

CHAPTER 11 LESSON 3 CONTINUED

Question and Answer Flow for Sentence 2: An alert policeman sped quickly to the accident.

1. Who sped quickly to the accident? policeman - SN
2. What is being said about policeman?
   policeman sped - V
3. Sped how? quickly - Adv
4. To - P
5. To what? accident - OP
6. The - A

7. What kind of policeman? alert - Adj
8. An - A
9. SN V P1 Check
10. (To the accident) - Prepositional phrase
11. Period, statement, declarative sentence
12. Go back to the verb - divide the complete subject from the complete predicate.

Classified Sentence: SN V / P1
 A   Adj   SN   V   Adv   P A   OP
An alert policeman / sped quickly (to the accident). D

Question and Answer Flow for Sentence 3: Two tardy students reported quickly to the principal.

1. Who reported quickly to the principal? students - SN
2. What is being said about students?
   students reported - V
3. Reported how? quickly - Adv
4. To - P
5. To whom? principal - OP
6. The - A

7. What kind of students? tardy - Adj
8. How many students? two - Adj
9. SN V P1 Check
10. (To the principal) - Prepositional phrase
11. Period, statement, declarative sentence
12. Go back to the verb - divide the complete subject from the complete predicate.

Classified Sentence: SN V / P1
 Adj Adj   SN   V   Adv   P A   OP
Two tardy students / reported quickly (to the principal). D

PRACTICE TIME

Have students turn to pages 51 and 52 in the Practice Section of their book and find Chapter 11, Lesson 3, Practice *(1-2)*. Go over the directions to make sure they understand what to do. Check and discuss the Practices after students have finished. *(Chapter 11, Lesson 3, Practice keys are given below and on the next page.)*

Chapter 11, Lesson 3, Practice 1: Underline the correct homonym in each sentence.

1. Try our (knew, <u>new</u>) milkshake.
2. That is the (<u>right</u>, write) answer.
3. I (<u>knew</u>, new) you could do it!
4. Place your hand (<u>here</u>, hear).

5. The girls ran (threw, <u>through</u>) the sprinkler.
6. The waiter (through, <u>threw</u>) down his apron.
7. Can you (<u>hear</u>, here) my heartbeat?
8. I should (<u>write</u>, right) a letter to the company.

CHAPTER 11 LESSON 3 CONTINUED

Chapter 11, Lesson 3, Practice 2: For each sentence, do these four things: (1) Write the subject. (2) Write **S** if the subject is singular or **P** if the subject is plural. (3) Write the rule number. (4) Underline the correct verb in the sentence.

Rule 1: A singular subject must use a singular verb form that ends in **s**: *is, was, has, does,* or verbs ending with **es**.

Rule 2: A plural subject, a compound subject, or the subject **YOU** must use a plural verb form that has **no s** ending: *are, were, do, have,* or verbs without **s** or **es** endings. (A plural verb form is also called the *plain form*.)

Subject	S or P	Rule
newscasters	P	2
games	P	2
Jill	S	1
wind	S	1
you	P	2
conferences	P	2
dew	S	1
bills	P	2
billboards	P	2

1. The **newscasters** (reports, <u>report</u>) the forest fire.
2. The **games** (begins, <u>begin</u>) tomorrow.
3. **Jill** (<u>searches</u>, search) for her purse.
4. The **wind** (gust, <u>gusts</u>) across the plains.
5. **You** (turns, <u>turn</u>) left at the stoplight.
6. The **conferences** (was, <u>were</u>) held in the new arena.
7. The **dew** (<u>covers</u>, cover) the lawn.
8. Several **bills** quickly (passes, <u>pass</u>) through Congress.
9. The **billboards** (dots, <u>dot</u>) the highway.

ACTIVITY / ASSIGNMENT TIME

Give students the list of subjects and verbs below. Have them write the correct subject number that matches the verb in the verb blank. Then, have students underline the correct verb. Remind them to pay attention to subject-verb agreement rules.

Subjects	Verbs
1. A farmer	__3__ (purr, <u>purrs</u>).
2. The horses	__7__ (blow, <u>blows</u>).
3. The kittens	__1__ (plow, <u>plows</u>).
4. My mother	__5__ (sting, <u>stings</u>).
5. The bees	__6__ (<u>hop</u>, hops).
6. Rabbits	__2__ (<u>gallop</u>, gallops).
7. The fan	__8__ (crawl, <u>crawls</u>).
8. The worm	__4__ (cook, <u>cooks</u>).

(End of lesson.)

CHAPTER 11   LESSON 4

Objectives: Jingles, Study, Test, Check, Writing (Journal), State Activity, and Sentence Time.

 JINGLE TIME

Have students turn to the Jingle Section in their books and recite the previously-taught jingles.

 STUDY TIME

Have students study the vocabulary words in their vocabulary notebooks. Remind students that any vocabulary word in their notebooks could be on their test. Also, have students study any of the skills in the Practice Section that they need to review.

 TEST TIME

Have students turn to page 90 in the Test Section of their book and find Chapter 11 Test. Go over the directions to make sure they understand what to do. (*Chapter 11 Test key is on the next page.*)

 CHECK TIME

After students have finished, check and discuss their test papers. Make sure they understand why their answers are right or wrong. (*For total points, count each required answer as a point.*)

 STATE ACTIVITY TIME

Students will continue to draw or trace the states and to write the following questions and answers.

Illinois	Indiana
1. What is the state on the front of this card? **Illinois**	1. What is the state on the front of this card? **Indiana**
2. What is the capital of Illinois? **Springfield**	2. What is the capital of Indiana? **Indianapolis**
3. What is the postal abbreviation of Illinois? **IL**	3. What is the postal abbreviation of Indiana? **IN**

Color these states. Use the cards to quiz family members, friends, and relatives. You may want to time the responses to your questions.

(End of lesson.)

Level 2—Shurley English—Homeschool Edition

Chapter 11 Test
(Student Page 90)

91 pts

Exercise 1: Classify each sentence.

1. SN V / P1 — A Adj SN V P OP P A Adj OP P A OP
   The young students / screamed (with delight) (at the splendid costumes) (for the parade)! E

2. SN V / P1 — A SN P Adj OP V P Adj OP
   The hillside (of mixed flowers) / exploded (with brilliant colors). D

35 pts

Exercise 2: Use Sentence 1 to underline the complete subject once and the complete predicate twice and to complete the table below.

List the Noun Used	List the Noun Job	Singular or Plural	Common or Proper	Simple Subject	Simple Predicate
1. students	2. SN	3. P	4. C	5. students	6. screamed
7. delight	8. OP	9. S	10. C		
11. costumes	12. OP	13. P	14. C		
15. parade	16. OP	17. S	18. C		

Exercise 3: Name the five parts of speech that you have studied. (*You may use abbreviations.*) (The order of answers may vary.)

1. Noun   2. Verb   3. Adjective   4. Adverb   5. Preposition

Exercise 4: Identify each pair of words as synonyms or antonyms by putting parentheses ( ) around *syn* or *ant*.

1. clog, block	(syn) ant	4. exhausted, refreshed	syn (ant)	7. constant, unchanging	(syn) ant
2. youthful, old	syn (ant)	5. tardy, punctual	syn (ant)	8. bewilder, confuse	(syn) ant
3. alert, aware	(syn) ant	6. plunge, immerse	(syn) ant	9. harmless, dangerous	syn (ant)

Exercise 5: For each sentence, do these four things: (1) Write the subject. (2) Write **S** if the subject is singular or **P** if the subject is plural. (3) Write the rule number. (4) Underline the correct verb in the sentence.

Rule 1 and Rule 2 are located in Reference 21 on page 17 in your student book.

Subject	S or P	Rule	
you	P	2	1. **You** (sings, <u>sing</u>) very well.
Bill and Linda	P	2	2. **Bill** and **Linda** (helps, <u>help</u>) their new neighbors.
clock	S	1	3. The **clock** (<u>chimes</u>, chime) every hour.
clothes	P	2	4. The **clothes** (wrinkles, <u>wrinkle</u>) in the dryer.
scientist	S	1	5. The **scientist** (<u>discovers</u>, discover) a new cure.

Exercise 6: Underline the correct homonym in each sentence.

1. Mallory is my (<u>new</u>, knew) friend.
2. He ran (<u>to</u>, too, two) the finish line.
3. We live by a golf (coarse, <u>course</u>).
4. She (<u>sent</u>, scent) the letter via airmail.

Exercise 7: In your journal, write a paragraph summarizing what you have learned this week.

CHAPTER 11 LESSON 4 CONTINUED

TEACHER INSTRUCTIONS

Use the Question and Answer Flows below for the sentences on the Chapter 11 Test.

Question and Answer Flow for Sentence 1: The young students screamed with delight at the splendid costumes for the parade!

1. Who screamed with delight at the splendid costumes for the parade? students - SN
2. What is being said about students? students screamed - V
3. With - P
4. With what? delight - OP
5. At - P
6. At what? costumes - OP
7. What kind of costumes? splendid - Adj
8. The - A
9. For - P
10. For what? parade - OP
11. The - A
12. What kind of students? young - Adj
13. The - A
14. SN V P1 Check
15. (With delight) - Prepositional phrase
16. (At the splendid costumes) - Prepositional phrase
17. (For the parade) - Prepositional phrase
18. Exclamation point, strong feeling, exclamatory sentence
19. Go back to the verb - divide the complete subject from the complete predicate.

Classified Sentence:
A Adj SN V P OP P A Adj OP P A OP
SN V The young students / screamed (with delight) (at the splendid costumes) (for the parade)! E
P1

Question and Answer Flow for Sentence 2: The hillside of mixed flowers exploded with brilliant colors.

1. What exploded with brilliant colors? hillside - SN
2. What is being said about hillside? hillside exploded - V
3. With - P
4. With what? colors - OP
5. What kind of colors? brilliant - Adj
6. Of - P
7. Of what? flowers - OP
8. What kind of flowers? mixed - Adj
9. The - A
10. SN V P1 Check
11. (Of mixed flowers) - Prepositional phrase
12. (With brilliant colors) - Prepositional phrase
13. Period, statement, declarative sentence
14. Go back to the verb - divide the complete subject from the complete predicate.

Classified Sentence:
A SN P Adj OP V P Adj OP
SN V The hillside (of mixed flowers) / exploded (with brilliant colors). D
P1

 SENTENCE TIME

Chapter 11, Lesson 4, Sentence: For this assignment, make your own labels and scrambled sentence parts on notebook paper. You may still use colored markers to match each label with the correct sentence part by drawing a line from one to the other. Then, use the labels to arrange the sentence parts into a sentence that you will use for an answer key on your paper. Have family members unscramble your sentences according to the grammar labels. You may color code the sentence parts. *(See page 112 in the student book.)*

Labels for Order of Sentence	Scrambled Sentence Parts
Independent sentence assignment.	

(End of lesson.)

CHAPTER 11   LESSON 5

Objectives: Writing (Changing Plural Categories to Singular Points) and Writing Assignment #5.

 WRITING TIME

TEACHING SCRIPT FOR CHANGING PLURAL CATEGORIES TO SINGULAR POINTS

When you have a topic such as *My favorite desserts*, you will usually name your favorite desserts by categories, or groups, like chocolate cakes and peach cobblers. When this happens, you need to know how to change plural points to singular points. I will demonstrate how this is done in a paragraph. Look at Reference 22 on page 18 as I read the paragraph to you. Then, I will show you how to change each of the two points in the paragraph. *(Read the paragraph to your students from beginning to end. Then, go through the teaching script given for each sentence in the paragraph.)*

Reference 22: Singular and Plural Points

Two-Point Expository Paragraph

Topic: My favorite desserts
2-points: 1. chocolate cakes   2. peach cobblers

   I have two favorite desserts. These desserts are chocolate cakes and peach cobblers. My first favorite dessert is a chocolate cake. I like chocolate cakes loaded with lots of sugary frosting. My second favorite dessert is a peach cobbler. I love cobblers made with fresh peaches picked from my grandfather's orchard. I enjoy eating all kinds of desserts, but my favorites will always be chocolate cakes and peach cobblers.

Notice that the topic is written first because it is the subject of the paragraph. Having the topic written first will help us focus on what the paragraph is about. Next, the two points that we will discuss are listed. Again, having the two points written down before we start will help us focus on what we will say in the paragraph.

We are now ready to begin our paragraph because we are clear about our topic and about the points we will cover as we write. We start with a topic sentence because it tells the reader what the paragraph is about: *I have two favorite desserts.* Knowing what the paragraph is about helps the reader focus on the main points as the reader progresses through the paragraph.

Our next sentence is the two-point sentence: *These desserts are chocolate cakes and peach cobblers.* The two-point sentence lists the two main points that will be discussed in the paragraph. So, in this paragraph, we know the two main points are *chocolate cakes* and *peach cobblers*. Now, I want you to notice that each of the two points listed is plural (*cakes* and *cobblers*). These main points are actually categories, or groups, of desserts, and that is why they are listed in plural form.

CHAPTER 11 LESSON 5 CONTINUED

Let's look at the sentence written for the first point. The sentence for the first point starts out like this: *My first favorite dessert is.* Since this phrase is singular, we could change the plural listing to a singular listing to agree with the type of sentence that is written. To do this, we will change *cakes* from plural to singular: *My first favorite dessert is a chocolate cake.* Usually, an article adjective is needed to make the sentence sound better.

Just remember: If your two points are plural, you usually make them singular as you name them for your first point and second point. Use an article adjective with your singular form to make it sound better. Notice that the second main point follows this same format. Look at the form as I read the sentence to you. (**2nd point:** *My second favorite dessert is a peach cobbler.*)

After each main point, there is a supporting sentence. Supporting sentences make each point clearer by telling extra information about each main point. Remember, we have stated in the main points that chocolate cakes and peach cobblers are two of our favorite desserts. Each supporting sentence should state some kind of information that proves each of the main points. (**1st Supporting sentence:** *I like chocolate cakes loaded with lots of sugary frosting.* **2nd Supporting sentence:** *I love cobblers made with fresh peaches picked from my grandfather's orchard.*) Notice that we also used the plural forms in the supporting sentences.

Our last sentence is a concluding sentence. It summarizes our two points by restating some of the words in the topic sentence and by adding an extra thought that finalizes the paragraph. (**Concluding sentence:** *I enjoy eating all kinds of desserts, but my favorites will always be chocolate cakes and peach cobblers.*)

TEACHER INSTRUCTIONS FOR WRITING ASSIGNMENT #5

Give Writing Assignment #5 from the box below. Tell students that this assignment is a two-point paragraph that demonstrates the use of singular and plural points. Remind them to use the Writing Checklist in Reference 17 to check their finished writing assignment.

Read, check, and discuss Writing Assignment #5 after students have finished their final papers. Use the Writing Checklist (*Reference 17 on teacher's page 112*) as you check and discuss students' papers. Make sure students are using the checklist correctly. In the beginning, you must also check students' papers carefully for <u>form</u> mistakes. This will ensure that students are learning the two-point format correctly.

Writing Assignment Box

Writing Assignment #5: Two-Point Expository Paragraph, demonstrating singular/plural points

Writing topics: My Favorite Animals or **My Favorite Games** or **Foods That I Don't Like**

(End of lesson.)

Level 2—Shurley English—Homeschool Edition

CHAPTER 12   LESSON 1
Objectives: Jingles (Pronoun, Subject Pronoun), Grammar (Introductory Sentences, Noun Check with Pronouns, Add Pronouns to the Parts of Speech, Skill Builder Check), and Vocabulary #1.

 **JINGLE TIME**

Have students turn to the Jingle Section in their books and recite the previously-taught jingles. Then, lead students in reciting the new jingles (*Pronoun, Subject Pronoun*) below. Practice the new jingles several times until students can recite them smoothly. Emphasize reciting with a rhythm. Students and teacher should be together! (*Do not try to explain the jingles at this time. Just have fun reciting them. Remember, add motions for more fun and laughter.*)

Jingle 9: Pronoun Jingle
This little pronoun, Floating around, Takes the place of a little old noun. With a knick knack, paddy wack, These are English rules. Isn't language fun and cool!

Jingle 10: Subject Pronoun Jingle
There are seven subject pronouns That are easy as can be: I and we,   (clap 2 times) He and she,   (clap 2 times) It and they and you. (clap 3 times)

 GRAMMAR TIME

Put the introductory sentences from the box below on the board. Use these sentences as you go through each new concept covered in your teaching script. For the greatest benefit, students must participate orally with the teacher. (*You might put the introductory sentences on notebook paper if you are doing one-on-one instruction with your students.*)

Chapter 12, Introductory Sentences for Lesson 1
1. _____ We went to the zoo on the city bus yesterday. 2. _____ They stopped at a country store for lunch. 3. _____ He jumped quickly into the refreshing pool.

TEACHING SCRIPT FOR THE PRONOUN AND THE SUBJECT PRONOUN

Today, we will learn about pronouns and the different kinds of pronouns. Let's look at the Pronoun Jingle again. It tells us that a **pronoun** takes the place of a noun. A pronoun may take the place of a person, place, or thing in a sentence. Without pronouns, everyone would be forced to repeat the same nouns again and again. Frequently-used pronouns are usually memorized.

CHAPTER 12 LESSON 1 CONTINUED

The first kind of pronoun we will study is the subject pronoun. Look at Reference 23 on page 18 as I explain the five things you should know about the subject pronoun.

Reference 23: Subject Pronoun
1. A **subject pronoun** takes the place of a noun that is used as the subject of a sentence.
2. These are the most common subject pronouns: *I, we, he, she, it, they,* and *you.* Use the Subject Pronoun Jingle to remember the common subject pronouns.
3. To find a subject pronoun, ask the subject question *who* or *what.*
4. Label a subject pronoun with an **SP**.
5. Call the **SP** abbreviation a subject pronoun.

If you are ever in doubt about whether the subject is a noun or pronoun, just recite the Subject Pronoun Jingle. If the subject is one of the pronouns in the Subject Pronoun Jingle, it is a subject pronoun. (*Have students recite the Subject Pronoun Jingle.*)

We will use this information as you classify Sentence 1 with me to find the subject pronoun. Remember, you use the same subject question, starting with *who* or *what*, to find the subject pronoun. Begin.

Question and Answer Flow for Sentence 1: We went to the zoo on the city bus yesterday.

1. Who went to the zoo on the city bus yesterday?
   we - SP (subject pronoun)
2. What is being said about we? we went - V
3. To - P
4. To what? zoo - OP
5. The - A
6. On - P
7. On what? bus - OP
8. What kind of bus? city - Adj
9. The - A
10. Went when? yesterday - Adv
11. SN V P1 Check
12. (To the zoo) - Prepositional phrase
13. (On the city bus) - Prepositional phrase
14. Period, statement, declarative sentence
15. Go back to the verb - divide the complete subject from the complete predicate.

```
                        SP   V   P A OP  P A Adj OP    Adv
Classified Sentence:   SN V  We / went (to the zoo) (on the city bus) yesterday.  D
                       P1
```

Teacher's Notes: Each sentence pattern is still identified with an **SN** even though the actual subject is identified and labeled as **SP** in the sentence. The **SN** is part of the pattern identification, not the actual identification of the subject in the sentence.

Remember, you use the same subject question, starting with *who* or *what*, to find the subject pronoun. You should never have trouble with subject pronouns because if you are not sure if the subject is a pronoun, just recite the Subject Pronoun Jingle to check the subject pronoun list. Now, we will classify the next two sentences together. Begin.

Level 2—Shurley English—Homeschool Edition

CHAPTER 12 LESSON 1 CONTINUED

Question and Answer Flow for Sentence 2: They stopped at a country store for lunch.

1. Who stopped at a country store for lunch?
   they - SP (subject pronoun)
2. What is being said about they? they stopped - V
3. At - P
4. At what? store - OP
5. What kind of store? country - Adj
6. A - A
7. For - P
8. For what? lunch - OP
9. SN V P1 Check
10. (At a country store) - Prepositional phrase
11. (For lunch) - Prepositional phrase
12. Period, statement, declarative sentence
13. Go back to the verb - divide the complete subject from the complete predicate.

```
                          SP    V    P A  Adj    OP   P   OP
Classified Sentence:    SN V    They / stopped (at a country store) (for lunch).  D
                        P1
```

Question and Answer Flow for Sentence 3: He jumped quickly into the refreshing pool.

1. Who jumped quickly into the refreshing pool?
   he - SP (subject pronoun)
2. What is being said about he? he jumped - V
3. Jumped how? quickly - Adv
4. Into - P
5. Into what? pool - OP
6. What kind of pool? refreshing - Adj
7. The - A
8. SN V P1 Check
9. (Into the refreshing pool) - Prepositional phrase
10. Period, statement, declarative sentence
11. Go back to the verb - divide the complete subject from the complete predicate.

```
                          SP    V      Adv    P  A   Adj    OP
Classified Sentence:    SN V    He / jumped quickly (into the refreshing pool).  D
                        P1
```

Teacher's Notes: Question and Answer Flow Notice.

For consistency, the Question and Answer Flow will use the verb form that is written in each sentence to complete the subject question, regardless of whether the verb is singular or plural.
   Example: They <u>are</u> laughing. Q & A: Who <u>are</u> laughing?
If you prefer using the singular verb form, just make the necessary change whenever it occurs.

TEACHING SCRIPT FOR A NOUN CHECK WHEN PRONOUNS ARE IN THE SENTENCES

A Noun Check is a check for nouns. Since nouns are located in noun jobs, it is essential to know the noun jobs so that you know where to go to find nouns. You have had two noun jobs so far: the subject noun job and the object-of-the-preposition noun job.

Since we are looking for nouns, we will say the noun job, say the noun or pronoun, and then say *yes* if it is a noun or *no* if it is a pronoun. Let's start with number one and go through the Noun Check for sentences 1-3, identifying nouns by using the procedure on the next page.

Level 2—Shurley English—Homeschool Edition

CHAPTER 12 LESSON 1 CONTINUED

Sentence 1: Subject pronoun *we*, no. Object of the preposition *zoo*, yes. *(Circle **zoo** because it is a noun.)*
Object of the preposition *bus*, yes. *(Circle **bus** because it is a noun.)*

Sentence 2: Subject pronoun *they*, no. Object of the preposition *store*, yes. *(Circle **store** because it is a noun.)*
Object of the preposition *lunch*, yes. *(Circle **lunch** because it is a noun.)*

Sentence 3: Subject pronoun *he*, no. Object of the preposition *pool*, yes. *(Circle **pool** because it is a noun.)*

Use sentences 1-3 that you just classified with your students to do a Skill Builder Check. Use the guidelines below.

Skill Builder Check	
1. Noun check. (Say the job and then say the noun. Circle each noun.)	**5. Identify the complete subject and the complete predicate.** (Underline the complete subject once and the complete predicate twice.)
2. Identify the nouns as singular or plural. (Write **S** or **P** above each noun.)	**6. Identify the simple subject and simple predicate.** (Underline the simple subject once and the simple predicate twice. Bold, or highlight, the lines to distinguish them from the complete subject and complete predicate.)
3. Identify the nouns as common or proper. (Follow established procedure for oral identification.)	
4. Do a vocabulary check. (Follow established procedure for oral identification.)	

<u>TEACHING SCRIPT FOR ADDING THE PRONOUN TO THE PARTS OF SPEECH</u>

Do you remember that all words in the English language have been put into one of eight groups called the **Parts of Speech**? We learned that how a word is used in a sentence determines its part of speech. Do you remember the names of the five parts of speech we have already studied? *(noun, verb, adjective, adverb,* and *preposition)*

Today, we have learned about pronouns. A pronoun is also a part of speech; so, we will add it to our list. Now, we know six of the eight parts of speech. What are the six parts of speech that we have covered? *(noun, verb, adjective, adverb, preposition,* and *pronoun)* *(Chant the six parts of speech that the students have learned several times for immediate reinforcement and for fun.)*

 VOCABULARY TIME

Assign Chapter 12, Vocabulary Words **#1** on page 6 in the Reference Section for students to define in their Vocabulary notebooks. Tell students they are to use a dictionary or thesaurus to look up the meanings of the vocabulary words.

Chapter 12, Vocabulary Words #1
(stride, waddle, beneath, below)

(End of lesson.)

CHAPTER 12   LESSON 2
Objectives: Jingles, Grammar (Practice Sentences), Skill (Capitalization Rules), Practice Exercise, and Vocabulary #2.

 **JINGLE TIME**

Have students turn to the Jingle Section in their books and recite the previously-taught jingles.

 GRAMMAR TIME

Put the Practice Sentences from the box below on the board or on notebook paper. Use these sentences as you practice the concepts that have been taught. For the greatest benefit, students must participate orally with the teacher.

Chapter 12, Practice Sentences for Lesson 2
1. _____ They jumped joyfully into the pile of leaves.
2. _____ An enormous American flag flew proudly over the new library.
3. _____ I ran after the bus today.

TEACHING SCRIPT FOR CLASSIFYING PRACTICE SENTENCES

We will classify three different sentences to practice the grammar skills in the Question and Answer Flows. We will classify the sentences together. Begin. (*You might have students write the labels above the sentences at this time.*)

Question and Answer Flow for Sentence 1: They jumped joyfully into the pile of leaves.	
1. Who jumped joyfully into the pile of leaves? they - SP	8. Of what? leaves - OP
2. What is being said about they? they jumped - V	9. SN V P1 Check
3. Jumped how? joyfully - Adv	10. (Into the pile) - Prepositional phrase
4. Into - P	11. (Of leaves) - Prepositional phrase
5. Into what? pile - OP	12. Period, statement, declarative sentence
6. The - A	13. Go back to the verb - divide the complete subject
7. Of - P	from the complete predicate.

```
                              SP   V    Adv     P  A  OP   P   OP
Classified Sentence:    SN V  They / jumped joyfully (into the pile) (of leaves).  D
                        ___
                        P1
```

Page 180   Level 2 Homeschool Teacher's Manual

© SHURLEY INSTRUCTIONAL MATERIALS, INC.

CHAPTER 12 LESSON 2 CONTINUED

Question and Answer Flow for Sentence 2: An enormous American flag flew proudly over the new library.

1. What flew proudly over the new library? flag - SN
2. What is being said about flag? flag flew - V
3. Flew how? proudly - Adv
4. Over - P
5. Over what? library - OP
6. What kind of library? new - Adj
7. The - A
8. What kind of flag? American - Adj
9. What kind of flag? enormous - Adj
10. An - A
11. SN V P1 Check
12. (Over the new library) - Prepositional phrase
13. Period, statement, declarative sentence
14. Go back to the verb - divide the complete subject from the complete predicate.

Classified Sentence: SN V / P1   A Adj Adj SN V Adv P A Adj OP
An enormous American flag / flew proudly (over the new library). D

Question and Answer Flow for Sentence 3: I ran after the bus today.

1. Who ran after the bus today? I - SP
2. What is being said about I? I ran - V
3. After - P
4. After what? bus - OP
5. The - A
6. Ran when? today - Adv
7. SN V P1 Check
8. (After the bus) - Prepositional phrase
9. Period, statement, declarative sentence
10. Go back to the verb - divide the complete subject from the complete predicate.

Classified Sentence: SN V / P1   SP V P A OP Adv
I / ran (after the bus) today. D

SKILL TIME

TEACHING SCRIPT FOR CAPITALIZATION RULES

You are ready to learn how to use the rules for capitalization to correct capitalization mistakes in sentences. It is important for you to know how to capitalize sentences correctly. Look on page 18 at Reference 24 for the capitalization rules that you will use. Let's read over the capitalization rules together. Begin. (*Go over the different rules together.*) I'm going to show you how to use these capitalization rules to correct capitalization mistakes in sentences.

Look at the sample at the bottom of Reference 24. First, we must look at the editing guide that is located at the end of each sentence. This tells us how many capitalization mistakes we must correct in the sentence. It tells us that there are four capitalization mistakes to correct. For each correction, we must also have a rule number from the rule box. The rule number tells us why the correction was necessary. Let's go over the sample so you can see how to make the correction and how to write the rule number above the correction. (*Go over the sample on the next page.*)

Level 2—Shurley English—Homeschool Edition

CHAPTER 12 LESSON 2 CONTINUED

Reference 24: Capitalization Rules
1. Capitalize the first word of a sentence. 2. Capitalize the pronoun I. 3. Capitalize the names of people and the names of pets. (*Alan, Molly*) 4. Capitalize titles used with people's names and people's initials. (*Ms., Uncle, Dr., T. S.*) 5. Capitalize names of streets, cities, states, and countries. (*Main Street, Atlanta, Georgia, Germany*) 6. Capitalize the days of the week and the months of the year. (*Friday, April*)

Sample: Correct the capitalization mistakes and put the rule number above each correction.
 	
   1(or 3)   2   5   6   (capitalization rule numbers)
    S   I   O   T
1. sarah and i drove to ohio on tuesday.   (Editing Guide: 4 capitalization mistakes)

 PRACTICE TIME

Have students turn to page 52 in the Practice Section of their book and find Chapter 12, Lesson 2, Practice. Go over the directions to make sure they understand what to do. Check and discuss the Practice after students have finished. (*Chapter 12, Lesson 2, Practice key is given below.*)

Chapter 12, Lesson 2, Practice: Correct the capitalization mistakes and put the rule number above each correction. Use the rule numbers in Reference 24 on page 18 in the Reference Section of your book.

1 (or 3)   4   3   6   (capitalization rule numbers)
   J   D J   T
1. jan has an appointment with dr. jones on tuesday. (Editing Guide: 4 capitalization mistakes)
 	
  1 (or 2)   4   3   4   3   (capitalization rule numbers)
   I   A   M   U   J
2. i took a picture of aunt mary and uncle james. (Editing Guide: 5 capitalization mistakes)

 VOCABULARY TIME

Assign Chapter 12, Vocabulary Words #2 on page 6 in the Reference Section for students to define in their Vocabulary notebooks. Tell students they are to use a dictionary or thesaurus to look up the meanings of the vocabulary words.

Chapter 12, Vocabulary Words #2
(cranky, grouchy, nimble, slow)

(End of lesson.)

Level 2—Shurley English—Homeschool Edition

CHAPTER 12   LESSON 3

Objectives: Jingles, Grammar (Practice Sentences, Practice and Improved Sentence), and Practice Exercise.

JINGLE TIME

Have students turn to the Jingle Section in their books and recite the previously-taught jingles.

GRAMMAR TIME

Put the Practice Sentences from the box below on the board or on notebook paper. Use these sentences as you practice the concepts that have been taught. For the greatest benefit, students must participate orally with the teacher.

Chapter 12, Practice Sentences for Lesson 3
1. _____ She gave about twenty dollars for that gift.
2. _____ They walked slowly along the edge of the water.
3. _____ A miniature collie waded carefully in the shallow water.

TEACHING SCRIPT FOR CLASSIFYING PRACTICE SENTENCES

We will classify three different sentences to practice the grammar skills in the Question and Answer Flows. We will classify the sentences together. Begin. (*You might have students write the labels above the sentences at this time.*)

Question and Answer Flow for Sentence 1: She gave about twenty dollars for that gift.
1. Who gave about twenty dollars for that gift? she - SP
2. What is being said about she? she gave - V
3. About - P
4. About what? dollars - OP
5. How many dollars? twenty - Adj
6. For - P
7. For what? gift - OP
8. Which gift? that - Adj
9. SN V P1 Check
10. (About twenty dollars) - Prepositional phrase
11. (For that gift) - Prepositional phrase
12. Period, statement, declarative sentence
13. Go back to the verb - divide the complete subject from the complete predicate.

Classified Sentence:

```
                    SP  V     P    Adj   OP      P   Adj  OP
           SN  V    She / gave (about twenty dollars) (for that gift).  D
           P1
```

Level 2 Homeschool Teacher's Manual

CHAPTER 12 LESSON 3 CONTINUED

Question and Answer Flow for Sentence 2: They walked slowly along the edge of the water.

1. Who walked slowly along the edge of the water? they - SP
2. What is being said about they? they walked - V
3. Walked how? slowly - Adv
4. Along - P
5. Along what? edge - OP
6. The - A
7. Of - P
8. Of what? water - OP
9. The - A
10. SN V P1 Check
11. (Along the edge) - Prepositional phrase
12. (Of the water) - Prepositional phrase
13. Period, statement, declarative sentence
14. Go back to the verb - divide the complete subject from the complete predicate.

```
                          SP   V   Adv   P  A  OP   P  A  OP
Classified Sentence:  SN V   They / walked slowly (along the edge) (of the water).  D
                      P1
```

Question and Answer Flow for Sentence 3: A miniature collie waded carefully in the shallow water.

1. What waded carefully in the shallow water? collie - SN
2. What is being said about collie? collie waded - V
3. Waded how? carefully - Adv
4. In - P
5. In what? water - OP
6. What kind of water? shallow - Adj
7. The - A
8. What kind of collie? miniature - Adj
9. A - A
10. SN V P1 Check
11. (In the shallow water) - Prepositional phrase
12. Period, statement, declarative sentence
13. Go back to the verb - divide the complete subject from the complete predicate.

```
                          A  Adj   SN      V    Adv   P  A  Adj  OP
Classified Sentence:  SN V   A miniature collie / waded carefully (in the shallow water).  D
                      P1
```

TEACHING SCRIPT FOR A PRACTICE SENTENCE WITH PREPOSITIONAL PHRASES

> Put these labels on the board: **SP V Adv P A Adj OP**

Look at the new sentence labels on the board: **SP V Adv P A Adj OP**. I will guide you again through the process of writing a sentence to practice all the parts that you have learned.

Get out a sheet of notebook paper. On the top line of your notebook paper, write the title *Practice Sentence*. Copy the sentence labels from the board onto your notebook paper. Be sure to leave plenty of writing space between each label. Now, I will guide you through the process you will use whenever you write a Practice Sentence with a prepositional phrase.

1. Go to the **SP** label for the subject pronoun. Repeat the Subject Pronoun Jingle to help you think of a pronoun that you want to use as your subject. Write the pronoun you have chosen on the line *under* the **SP** label.

CHAPTER 12 LESSON 3 CONTINUED

2. Go to the **V** label for the verb. Think of a verb that tells what your subject does. Make sure that your verb makes sense with the subject pronoun. Write the verb you have chosen on the line *under* the **V** label.

3. Go to the **Adv** label for the adverb. Immediately go to the verb in your sentence and ask an adverb question. What are the adverb questions? (*How, When, Where*) Choose one adverb question to ask and write your adverb answer *under* the **Adv** label.

4. Go to the **P** label for the preposition. Think of a preposition word that tells something about your verb. You must be careful to choose a preposition word that makes sense with the noun you will choose for the object of the preposition in your next step. Write the word you have chosen for a preposition *under* the **P** label.

5. Go to the **OP** label for the object of the preposition. If you like the noun you thought of while thinking of a preposition, write it down under the **OP** label. If you prefer, think of another noun by asking **what** or **whom** after your preposition. Check to make sure the preposition and object of the preposition make sense together and also make sense with the rest of the sentence. Remember, the object of the preposition will always answer the question **what** or **whom** after the preposition. Write the word you have chosen for the object of the preposition *under* the **OP** label.

6. Go to the **Adj** label for the adjective. Go to the object of the preposition that you just wrote and ask an adjective question to describe the object-of-the-preposition noun. What are the adjective questions? (*What kind, Which one, How many*) Choose one adjective question to ask and write your adjective answer *under* the **Adj** label next to the object of the preposition. Always check to make sure your answers are making sense in the sentence.

7. Go to the **A** label for the article adjective that is part of your prepositional phrase. What are the three article adjectives? (*a, an,* and *the*) Choose the article adjective that makes the best sense in your sentence. Write the article adjective you have chosen *under* the **A** label.

8. Finally, check your Practice Sentence to make sure it has the necessary parts to be a complete sentence. What are the five parts of a complete sentence? (*subject, verb, complete sense, capital letter, and an end mark*) Does your Practice Sentence have the five parts of a complete sentence? (*Allow time for students to read over their sentences and to make any corrections they need to make.*)

<u>TEACHING SCRIPT FOR THE IMPROVED SENTENCE</u>

Under your Practice Sentence, write the title *Improved Sentence* on another line. To improve your Practice Sentence, you will make two synonym changes, one antonym change, and your choice of a complete word change or another synonym or antonym change.

Since it is harder to find words that can be changed to an antonym, it is usually wise to go through your sentence to find an antonym change first. Then, look through your sentence again to find words that can be improved with synonyms. Finally, make a decision about whether your last change will be a complete word change, another synonym change, or another antonym change.

I will give you time to write your Improved Sentence. (*Always encourage students to use a thesaurus, synonym-antonym book, or a dictionary to help them develop an interesting and improved writing vocabulary. After students have finished, check and discuss students' Practice and Improved Sentences.*)

CHAPTER 12 LESSON 3 CONTINUED

 PRACTICE TIME

Have students turn to page 53 in the Practice Section of their book and find Chapter 12, Lesson 3, Practice (1-3). Go over the directions to make sure they understand what to do. Check and discuss the Practices after students have finished. (*Chapter 12, Lesson 3, Practice keys are given below*.)

Chapter 12, Lesson 3, Practice 1: For each sentence, do these four things: (1) Write the subject. (2) Write **S** if the subject is singular or **P** if the subject is plural. (3) Write the rule number. (4) Underline the correct verb in the sentence.

Rule 1: A singular subject must use a singular verb form that ends in **s**: *is, was, has, does,* or verbs ending with **es**.

Rule 2: A plural subject, a compound subject, or the subject **YOU** must use a plural verb form that has **no s** ending: *are, were, do, have,* or verbs without **s** or **es** endings. (A plural verb form is also called the *plain form*.)

Subject	S or P	Rule	
mattress	S	1	1. The **mattress** (sag, <u>sags</u>) when we sit on it.
mud	S	1	2. The **mud** (<u>dries</u>, dry) on the edges of the pond.
radishes	P	2	3. The **radishes** (<u>ripen</u>, ripens) in the garden.
taco	S	1	4. My **taco** (taste, <u>tastes</u>) good.
stones	P	2	5. The **stones** (skips, <u>skip</u>) across the pond.

Chapter 12, Lesson 3, Practice 2: Underline the correct homonym in each sentence.

1. The cashier gave me a (<u>new</u>, knew) coin.
2. Can you (here, <u>hear</u>) the robin singing?
3. (<u>No</u>, Know), I don't need your help.
4. (There, <u>They're</u>) going to the movies.
5. A sentence begins with a (<u>capital</u>, capitol) letter.
6. Joey (<u>threw</u>, through) the baseball to Tom.

Chapter 12, Lesson 3, Practice 3: Correct the capitalization mistakes and put the rule number above each correction. Use the rule numbers in Reference 24 on page 18 in the Reference Section of your book.

```
   1     4     3         2                  (capitalization rule numbers)
   M     U     J         I
1. my  uncle john and i like to hunt.   (Editing Guide: 4 capitalization mistakes)


   1(or 3)    3              5        6     (capitalization rule numbers)
   J          S              S        M
2. jared and sam are traveling to spain in may.   (Editing Guide: 4 capitalization mistakes)
```

(End of lesson.)

Level 2—Shurley English—Homeschool Edition

CHAPTER 12   LESSON 4

Objectives: Jingles, Study, Test, Check, Writing (Journal), and State Activity.

 JINGLE TIME

Have students turn to the Jingle Section in their books and recite the previously-taught jingles.

 STUDY TIME

Have students study the vocabulary words in their vocabulary notebooks. Remind students that any vocabulary word in their notebooks could be on their test. Also, have students study any of the skills in the Practice Section that they need to review.

 TEST TIME

Have students turn to page 91 in the Test Section of their book and find Chapter 12 Test. Go over the directions to make sure they understand what to do. (*Chapter 12 Test key is on the next page.*)

 CHECK TIME

After students have finished, check and discuss their test papers. Make sure they understand why their answers are right or wrong. (*For total points, count each required answer as a point.*)

 STATE ACTIVITY TIME

Students will continue to draw or trace the states and to write the following questions and answers.

Iowa	Kansas
1. What is the state on the front of this card? **Iowa**	1. What is the state on the front of this card? **Kansas**
2. What is the capital of Iowa? **Des Moines**	2. What is the capital of Kansas? **Topeka**
3. What is the postal abbreviation of Iowa? **IA**	3. What is the postal abbreviation of Kansas? **KS**

Color these states. Use the cards to quiz family members, friends, and relatives. You may want to time the responses to your questions.

(End of lesson.)

Level 2—Shurley English—Homeschool Edition

Chapter 12 Test
(Student Page 91)

76 pts.

Exercise 1: Classify each sentence.

```
              A   Adj  Adj   Adj   SN    V    P    A    OP    P    A    OP
1. SN V       The tall, slim elderly man / came (to the office) (for an interview).  D
   P1

              SP   V    P   OP    P    A    OP
2. SN V       We / ran (for cover) (during the storm).  D
   P1
```

Exercise 2: Use Sentence 2 to underline the complete subject once and the complete predicate twice and to complete the table below.

List the Noun Used	List the Noun Job	Singular or Plural	Common or Proper	Simple Subject	Simple Predicate
1. cover	2. OP	3. S	4. C	5. we	6. ran
7. storm	8. OP	9. S	10. C		

Exercise 3: Name the six parts of speech that you have studied. (*You may use abbreviations.*)
(The order of answers may vary.)

1. **Noun**   2. **Verb**   3. **Adjective**   4. **Adverb**   5. **Preposition**   6. **Pronoun**

Exercise 4: Identify each pair of words as synonyms or antonyms by putting parentheses ( ) around *syn* or *ant*.

1. beneath, below	**(syn)**	ant	4. tardy, punctual	syn	**(ant)**	7. canyon, gorge	**(syn)**	ant
2. waddle, stride	syn	**(ant)**	5. clog, block	**(syn)**	ant	8. cranky, grouchy	**(syn)**	ant
3. aware, alert	**(syn)**	ant	6. slow, nimble	syn	**(ant)**	9. exhausted, refreshed	syn	**(ant)**

later

Exercise 5: Correct the capitalization mistakes and put the rule number above each correction. Use the rule numbers in Reference 24 on page 18 in the Reference Section of your book.

```
  1(or 3)      3              5         5           (capitalization rule numbers)
     K         S              M         S
1. katie and susan live on maple street.    (Editing Guide: 4 capitalization mistakes)


  1(or 4)     3              5         5           (capitalization rule numbers)
     M        T              P         O
2. miss taylor works in portland, oregon.    (Editing Guide: 4 capitalization mistakes)
```

Exercise 6: Underline the correct homonym in each sentence.

1. Telling the truth is the (<u>right</u>, write) thing to do.
2. September has thirty (daze, <u>days</u>).
3. The dog chased (<u>its</u>, it's) tail.
4. Sara (new, <u>knew</u>) all fifty states.

Exercise 7: In your journal, write a paragraph summarizing what you have learned this week.

CHAPTER 12 LESSON 4 CONTINUED

TEACHER INSTRUCTIONS

Use the Question and Answer Flows below for the sentences on the Chapter 12 Test.

Question and Answer Flow for Sentence 1: The tall, slim elderly man came to the office for an interview.

1. Who came to the office for an interview? man - SN
2. What is being said about man? man came - V
3. To - P
4. To what? office - OP
5. The - A
6. For - P
7. For what? interview - OP
8. An - A
9. What kind of man? elderly - Adj
10. What kind of man? slim - Adj
11. What kind of man? tall - Adj
12. The - A
13. SN V P1 Check
14. (To the office) - Prepositional phrase
15. (For an interview) - Prepositional phrase
16. Period, statement, declarative sentence
17. Go back to the verb - divide the complete subject from the complete predicate.

```
                          A   Adj  Adj   Adj   SN     V    P  A   OP    P  A   OP
Classified Sentence:  SN V     The tall, slim elderly man / came (to the office) (for an interview).  D
                      ―――
                       P1
```

Question and Answer Flow for Sentence 2: We ran for cover during the storm.

1. Who ran for cover during the storm? we - SP
2. What is being said about we? we ran - V
3. For - P
4. For what? cover - OP
5. During - P
6. During what? storm - OP
7. The - A
8. SN V P1 Check
9. (For cover) - Prepositional phrase
10. (During the storm) - Prepositional phrase
11. Period, statement, declarative sentence
12. Go back to the verb - divide the complete subject from the complete predicate.

```
                          SP  V   P   OP      P   A   OP
Classified Sentence:  SN V  We / ran (for cover) (during the storm).  D
                      ―――
                       P1
```

CHAPTER 12   LESSON 5

Objectives: Writing Assignment #6 and Sentence Time.

 WRITING TIME

TEACHER INSTRUCTIONS FOR WRITING ASSIGNMENT #6

Give Writing Assignment #6 from the box below. Remind students to use the Writing Checklist in Reference 17 to check their finished writing assignment.

Read, check, and discuss Writing Assignment #6 after students have finished their final papers. Use the Writing Checklist (*Reference 17 on teacher's page 112*) as you check and discuss students' papers. Make sure students are using the checklist correctly. In the beginning, you must also check students' papers carefully for <u>form</u> mistakes. This will ensure that students are learning the two-point format correctly.

Writing Assignment Box

Writing Assignment #6: Two-Point Expository Paragraph

Writing topic choices: My Favorite Eating Places   or   Special Inventions   or   My Favorite Vacations

---

 SENTENCE TIME

Chapter 12, Lesson 5, Sentence: Use colored markers to match each label with the correct sentence part by drawing a line from one to the other. Then, use the labels to arrange the sentence parts into a sentence that you will write on the sentence line below. *(The order of the words in your sentence should be in the same sequence as the vertical list of sentence labels.)* Create other labels and scrambled sentence parts on notebook paper for family members to solve. You may color code the sentence parts. *(See page 112 in the student book.)*

Labels for Order of Sentence	Scrambled Sentence Parts
SP	along
V	quietly
Adv	the
P	walked
A	path
Adj	in
OP	lovely
P	city
A	the
Adj	we
OP	park

Sentence: We walked quietly along the lovely path in the city park. (Order may vary.)

(End of lesson.)

CHAPTER 13 LESSON 1

Objectives: Jingle (Possessive Pronoun), Grammar (Introductory Sentences, Skill Builder Check, Reviewing the Six Parts of Speech), and Vocabulary #1.

JINGLE TIME

Have students turn to the Jingle Section in their books and recite the previously-taught jingles. Then, lead students in reciting the new jingle (*Possessive Pronoun*) below. Practice the new jingle several times until students can recite it smoothly. Emphasize reciting with a rhythm. Students and teacher should be together! (*Do not try to explain the new jingle at this time. Just have fun reciting it. Remember, add motions for more fun and laughter.*)

Jingle 11: Possessive Pronoun Jingle	
There are seven possessive pronouns	
That are easy as can be:	
My and our,	(clap 2 times)
His and her,	(clap 2 times)
Its and their and your.	(clap 3 times)

GRAMMAR TIME

Put the introductory sentences from the box below on the board. Use these sentences as you go through each new concept covered in your teaching script. For the greatest benefit, students must participate orally with the teacher. (*You might put the introductory sentences on notebook paper if you are doing one-on-one instruction with your students.*)

Chapter 13, Introductory Sentences for Lesson 1
1. _____ We hike through their woods occasionally.
2. _____ The baby ducks waddled behind their mother.
3. _____ A small lizard hid beneath a rock in our yard.

TEACHING SCRIPT FOR THE POSSESSIVE PRONOUN

The next kind of pronoun we will study is the possessive pronoun. Look at Reference 25 on page 19 in the Reference Section of your book. Follow along as I explain the six things you should know about the possessive pronoun. (*Read and discuss the information about possessive pronouns in the reference box on the next page.*)

Level 2—Shurley English—Homeschool Edition

CHAPTER 13 LESSON 1 CONTINUED

Reference 25: Possessive Pronouns
1. A possessive pronoun takes the place of a possessive noun.
2. A possessive pronoun's spelling form makes it possessive. A possessive pronoun does NOT contain an apostrophe. These are the most common possessive pronouns: *my, our, his, her, its, their,* and *your.* Use the Possessive Pronoun Jingle to remember the most common possessive pronouns.
3. A possessive pronoun's main job is to show ownership. (*Her kite*)
4. Use the abbreviation PP (possessive pronoun).
5. Include possessive pronouns when you are asked to identify pronouns, possessives, or adjectives.
6. To find a possessive pronoun, begin with the question *whose*. (*Whose kite? Her - PP*)

You will use this information as you classify Sentence 1 with me to find the possessive pronoun. Remember, you use the question *whose* to find the possessive pronoun. Begin.

Question and Answer Flow for Sentence 1: We hike through their woods occasionally.

1. Who hike through their woods occasionally? we - SP
2. What is being said about we? we hike - V
3. Through - P
4. Through what? woods - OP
5. Whose woods? their - PP (possessive pronoun)
6. Hike when? occasionally - Adv
7. SN V P1 Check
8. (Through their woods) - Prepositional phrase
9. Period, statement, declarative sentence
10. Go back to the verb - divide the complete subject from the complete predicate.

```
                         SP   V    P   PP   OP        Adv
Classified Sentence:  SN V    We / hike (through their woods) occasionally.  D
                      P1
```

Question and Answer Flow for Sentence 2: The baby ducks waddled behind their mother.

1. What waddled behind their mother? ducks - SN
2. What is being said about ducks? ducks waddled - V
3. Behind - P
4. Behind whom? mother - OP
5. Whose mother? their - PP (possessive pronoun)
6. What kind of ducks? baby - Adj
7. The - A
8. SN V P1 Check
9. (Behind their mother) - Prepositional phrase
10. Period, statement, declarative sentence
11. Go back to the verb - divide the complete subject from the complete predicate.

```
                         A   Adj  SN    V        P   PP    OP
Classified Sentence:  SN V    The baby ducks / waddled (behind their mother).  D
                      P1
```

Level 2—Shurley English—Homeschool Edition

CHAPTER 13 LESSON 1 CONTINUED

Question and Answer Flow for Sentence 3: A small lizard hid beneath a rock in our yard.

1. What hid beneath a rock in our yard? lizard - SN
2. What is being said about lizard? lizard hid - V
3. Beneath - P
4. Beneath what? rock - OP
5. A - A
6. In - P
7. In what? yard - OP
8. Whose yard? our - PP (possessive pronoun)
9. What kind of lizard? small - Adj
10. A - A
11. SN V P1 Check
12. (Beneath a rock) - Prepositional phrase
13. (In our yard) - Prepositional phrase
14. Period, statement, declarative sentence
15. Go back to the verb - divide the complete subject from the complete predicate.

Classified Sentence:
    SN V
    P1
       A Adj SN V P A OP P PP OP
       A small lizard / hid (beneath a rock) (in our yard). D

Use Sentences 1-3 that you just classified with your students to do a Skill Builder Check. Use the guidelines below.

Skill Builder Check

1. **Noun check.**
   (Say the job and then say the noun. Circle each noun.)
2. **Identify the nouns as singular or plural.**
   (Write **S** or **P** above each noun.)
3. **Identify the nouns as common or proper.**
   (Follow established procedure for oral identification.)
4. **Do a vocabulary check.**
   (Follow established procedure for oral identification.)
5. **Identify the complete subject and the complete predicate.** (Underline the complete subject once and the complete predicate twice.)
6. **Identify the simple subject and simple predicate.**
   (Underline the simple subject once and the simple predicate twice. Bold, or highlight, the lines to distinguish them from the complete subject and complete predicate.)

TEACHING SCRIPT FOR REVIEWING THE SIX PARTS OF SPEECH

What are the six parts of speech that we have covered? *(noun, verb, adjective, adverb, preposition,* and *pronoun)* *(Chant the six parts of speech that the students have learned several times for reinforcement and fun.)*

 VOCABULARY TIME

Assign Chapter 13, Vocabulary Words **#1** on page 7 in the Reference Section for students to define in their Vocabulary notebooks. Tell students they are to use a dictionary or thesaurus to look up the meanings of the vocabulary words.

Chapter 13, Vocabulary Words #1
(deep, shallow, appear, emerge)

(End of lesson.)

Level 2—Shurley English—Homeschool Edition

CHAPTER 13   LESSON 2
Objectives: Jingles, Grammar (Practice Sentences), Skill (Punctuation Rules), Practice Exercise, and Vocabulary #2.

 **JINGLE TIME**

Have students turn to the Jingle Section in their books and recite the previously-taught jingles.

 GRAMMAR TIME

Put the Practice Sentences from the box below on the board or on notebook paper. Use these sentences as you practice the concepts that have been taught. For the greatest benefit, students must participate orally with the teacher.

Chapter 13, Practice Sentences for Lesson 2
1. _____ That young man drove across the narrow bridge on his motorcycle.
2. _____ The kindergarten teacher spoke kindly to her class on the first day of school.
3. _____ I read in my room with a flashlight underneath my covers until midnight.

TEACHING SCRIPT FOR CLASSIFYING PRACTICE SENTENCES

We will classify three different sentences to practice the grammar skills in the Question and Answer Flows. We will classify the sentences together. Begin. (*You might have students write the labels above the sentences at this time.*)

Question and Answer Flow for Sentence 1: That young man drove across the narrow bridge on his motorcycle.
1. Who drove across the narrow bridge on his motorcycle? man - SN
2. What is being said about man? man drove - V
3. Across - P
4. Across what? bridge - OP
5. What kind of bridge? narrow - Adj
6. The - A
7. On - P
8. On what? motorcycle - OP
9. Whose motorcycle? his - PP
10. What kind of man? young - Adj
11. Which man? that - Adj
12. SN V P1 Check
13. (Across the narrow bridge) - Prepositional phrase
14. (On his motorcycle) - Prepositional phrase
15. Period, statement, declarative sentence
16. Go back to the verb - divide the complete subject from the complete predicate.
Adj Adj   SN   V   P   A   Adj   OP   P PP   OP
Classified Sentence: SN V / P1   That young man / drove (across the narrow bridge) (on his motorcycle). D

CHAPTER 13 LESSON 2 CONTINUED

Question and Answer Flow for Sentence 2: The kindergarten teacher spoke kindly to her class on the first day of school.

1. Who spoke kindly to her class on the first day of school? teacher - SN
2. What is being said about teacher? teacher spoke - V
3. Spoke how? kindly - Adv
4. To - P
5. To what? class - OP
6. Whose class? her - PP
7. On - P
8. On what? day - OP
9. Which day? first - Adj
10. The - A
11. Of - P
12. Of what? school - OP
13. What kind of teacher? kindergarten - Adj
14. The - A
15. SN V P1 Check
16. (To her class) - Prepositional phrase
17. (On the first day) - Prepositional phrase
18. (Of school) - Prepositional phrase
19. Period, statement, declarative sentence
20. Go back to the verb - divide the complete subject from the complete predicate.

Classified Sentence:
```
              A    Adj         SN      V    Adv  P  PP  OP    P  A   Adj   OP    P   OP
SN V          The kindergarten teacher / spoke kindly (to her class) (on the first day) (of school).  D
P1
```

Question and Answer Flow for Sentence 3: I read in my room with a flashlight underneath my covers until midnight.

1. Who read in my room with a flashlight underneath my covers until midnight? I - SP
2. What is being said about I? I read - V
3. In - P
4. In what? room - OP
5. Whose room? my - PP
6. With - P
7. With what? flashlight - OP
8. A - A
9. Underneath - P
10. Underneath what? covers - OP
11. Whose covers? my - PP
12. Until - P
13. Until what? midnight - OP
14. SN V P1 Check
15. (In my room) - Prepositional phrase
16. (With a flashlight) - Prepositional phrase
17. (Underneath my covers) - Prepositional phrase
18. (Until midnight) - Prepositional phrase
19. Period, statement, declarative sentence
20. Go back to the verb - divide the complete subject from the complete predicate.

Classified Sentence:
```
                        SP  V  P PP  OP    P  A   OP       P      PP   OP     P    OP
SN V                    I / read (in my room) (with a flashlight) (underneath my covers) (until midnight).  D
P1
```

 SKILL TIME

TEACHING SCRIPT FOR PUNCTUATION RULES

You have already been using the capitalization rules to find and correct capitalization mistakes in sentences. You will continue correcting capitalization mistakes, but today you will also learn how to use the rules for punctuation to correct punctuation mistakes in sentences.

Look on page 19 at Reference 26 for the punctuation rules that you will use. Let's read over the punctuation rules together. Begin. *(Go over the different rules together.)* Now, I will show you how to use these punctuation rules to correct punctuation mistakes in sentences.

CHAPTER 13 LESSON 2 CONTINUED

Look at the sample at the bottom of Reference 26. First, we must look at the editing guide that is located at the end of each sentence. The editing guide tells us how many capitalization mistakes we must correct by putting that number by the word *capitals*. It also tells how many punctuation mistakes we must correct by putting that number by the word *punctuation*.

As you can see, you have 6 capitalization mistakes and 5 punctuation mistakes to correct. Remember, for each correction, we must also have a rule number from the rule box. The rule numbers tells us why the corrections were necessary. You will go to Reference 24 for the capitalization rule numbers and to Reference 26 for the punctuation rule numbers. Let's go over the sample so you can see how to make the corrections and how to write the rule numbers above the corrections. (*Go over the capitalization and punctuation corrections in the sample below.*)

Reference 26: Punctuation Rules

1. Use a period after initials. (*J. M. Scott*)
2. Use a period after an abbreviation. (*Dr., Mrs., Oct.*)
3. Use a comma to separate the city from the state. (*Nashville, Tennessee*)
4. Use a comma between the day and the year. (*December 25, 2002*)
5. Put an end mark at the end of a sentence. (*period, question mark, or exclamation mark*)

Directions: Correct the capitalization and punctuation mistakes for the sentence below. Write the rule numbers above the capitalization corrections and below the punctuation corrections.

<u>1(or 4) 4 4 3</u>   <u>5   5   </u>   (capitalization rule numbers)
   M   R L T   C   O

1. ms. r. l. thompson called her sister in columbus, ohio. (Editing Guide: 6 capitals & 5 punctuation)

<u>   2 1 1   3   5   </u> (punctuation rule numbers)

 PRACTICE TIME

Have students turn to page 54 in the Practice Section of their book and find Chapter 13, Lesson 2, Practice. Go over the directions to make sure they understand what to do. Check and discuss the Practice after students have finished. (*Chapter 13, Lesson 2, Practice key is given below and on the next page.*)

Chapter 13, Lesson 2, Practice: Correct the capitalization and punctuation mistakes for sentences 1-3. Write the rule numbers above the capitalization corrections and below the punctuation corrections. Use Reference 24 for the capitalization rules and Reference 26 for the punctuation rules. The references are located on pages 18 and 19 in your Reference Section.

<u> 1(or 3)   2   6   </u>   (capitalization rule numbers)
    S   I   J

1. sam and i were both born on january 19, 1992.   (Editing Guide: 3 capitals & 2 punctuation)

<u>   4   5   </u>   (punctuation rule numbers)

CHAPTER 13 LESSON 2 CONTINUED

Chapter 13, Lesson 2, Practice (continued)

```
  1(or 4)  3                  5        5         (capitalization rule numbers)
     D     M                  D        O
2. dr.  murphy  has  a  clinic  in  dayton,  ohio.   (Editing Guide: 4 capitals & 3 punctuation)
      2                              3       5      (punctuation rule numbers)


  1 (or 3)   3                   5      5           (capitalization rule numbers)
     C       J                   W      S
3. chad  and  jeff  rode  their  bikes  down  willow  street.   (Editing Guide: 4 capitals & 1 punctuation)
                                                         5      (punctuation rule numbers)
```

 VOCABULARY TIME

Assign Chapter 13, Vocabulary Words **#2** on page 7 in the Reference Section for students to define in their Vocabulary notebooks. Tell students they are to use a dictionary or thesaurus to look up the meanings of the vocabulary words.

Chapter 13, Vocabulary Words #2
(stable, unsteady, collect, gather)

(End of lesson.)

Level 2—Shurley English—Homeschool Edition

CHAPTER 13   LESSON 3
Objectives: Jingles, Grammar (Practice Sentences, Practice and Improved Sentence), Practice Exercise, and Activity.

 **JINGLE TIME**

Have students turn to the Jingle Section in their books and recite the previously-taught jingles.

 GRAMMAR TIME

Put the Practice Sentences from the box below on the board or on notebook paper. Use these sentences as you practice the concepts that have been taught. For the greatest benefit, students must participate orally with the teacher.

Chapter 13, Practice Sentences for Lesson 3
1. _____ We waded across the shallow stream near my house.
2. _____ The unsteady gate fell on its side during the windy weather.
3. _____ The cranky little boy behaved badly during his birthday party.

TEACHING SCRIPT FOR CLASSIFYING PRACTICE SENTENCES

We will classify three different sentences to practice the grammar skills in the Question and Answer Flows. We will classify the sentences together. Begin. (*You might have students write the labels above the sentences at this time.*)

Question and Answer Flow for Sentence 1: We waded across the shallow stream near my house.
1. Who waded across the shallow stream near my house? we - SP
2. What is being said about we? we waded - V
3. Across - P
4. Across what? stream - OP
5. What kind of stream? shallow - Adj
6. The - A
7. Near - P
8. Near what? house - OP
9. Whose house? my - PP
10. SN V P1 Check
11. (Across the shallow stream) - Prepositional phrase
12. (Near my house) - Prepositional phrase
13. Period, statement, declarative sentence
14. Go back to the verb - divide the complete subject from the complete predicate.
SP   V   P   A   Adj   OP   P PP   OP
Classified Sentence: SN V   We / waded (across the shallow stream) (near my house). D
P1

CHAPTER 13 LESSON 3 CONTINUED

Question and Answer Flow for Sentence 2: The unsteady gate fell on its side during the windy weather.

1. What fell on its side during the windy weather? gate - SN
2. What is being said about gate? gate fell - V
3. On - P
4. On what? side - OP
5. Whose side? its - PP
6. During - P
7. During what? weather - OP
8. What kind of weather? windy - Adj
9. The - A
10. What kind of gate? unsteady - Adj
11. The - A
12. SN V P1 Check
13. (On its side) - Prepositional phrase
14. (During the windy weather) - Prepositional phrase
15. Period, statement, declarative sentence
16. Go back to the verb - divide the complete subject from the complete predicate.

Classified Sentence: SN V P1   A Adj SN V P PP OP P A Adj OP
The unsteady gate / fell (on its side) (during the windy weather). D

Question and Answer Flow for Sentence 3: The cranky little boy behaved badly during his birthday party.

1. Who behaved badly during his birthday party? boy - SN
2. What is being said about boy? boy behaved - V
3. Behaved how? badly - Adv
4. During - P
5. During what? party - OP
6. What kind of party? birthday - Adj
7. Whose party? his - PP
8. What kind of boy? little - Adj
9. What kind of boy? cranky - Adj
10. The - A
11. SN V P1 Check
12. (During his birthday party) - Prepositional phrase
13. Period, statement, declarative sentence
14. Go back to the verb - divide the complete subject from the complete predicate.

Classified Sentence: SN V P1   A Adj Adj SN V Adv P PP Adj OP
The cranky little boy / behaved badly (during his birthday party). D

TEACHING SCRIPT FOR A PRACTICE SENTENCE WITH PRONOUNS

Put these labels on the board: **SP V Adv P PP Adj OP**

Look at the new sentence labels on the board: **SP V Adv P PP Adj OP**. I will guide you through the process of writing a sentence to practice the new parts that you have learned.

Get out a sheet of notebook paper. On the top line of your notebook paper, write the title *Practice Sentence*. Copy the sentence labels from the board onto your notebook paper. Be sure to leave plenty of writing space between each label. I will guide you through the process you will use whenever you write a Practice Sentence with pronouns.

1. Go to the **SP** label for the subject pronoun. Repeat the Subject Pronoun Jingle to help you think of a pronoun that you want to use as your subject. Write the pronoun you have chosen on the line *under* the **SP** label.

CHAPTER 13 LESSON 3 CONTINUED

2. Go to the **V** label for the verb. Think of a verb that tells what your subject does. Make sure that your verb makes sense with the subject pronoun. Write the verb you have chosen on the line *under* the **V** label.

3. Go to the **Adv** label for the adverb. Immediately go to the verb in your sentence and ask an adverb question. What are the adverb questions? (*How, When, Where*) Choose one adverb question to ask and write your adverb answer *under* the **Adv** label.

4. Go to the **P** label for the preposition. Think of a preposition word that tells something about your verb. You must be careful to choose a preposition word that makes sense with the noun you will choose for the object of the preposition in your next step. Write the word you have chosen for a preposition *under* the **P** label.

5. Now, go to the **OP** label for the object of the preposition. If you like the noun you thought of while thinking of a preposition, write it down under the **OP** label. If you prefer, think of another noun by asking **what** or **whom** after your preposition. Check to make sure the preposition and object of the preposition make sense together and also make sense with the rest of the sentence. Remember, the object of the preposition will always answer the question **what** or **whom** after the preposition. Write the word you have chosen for the object of the preposition *under* the **OP** label.

6. Go to the **Adj** label for the adjective. Go to the object of the preposition that you just wrote and ask an adjective question to describe the object-of-the-preposition noun. What are the adjective questions? (*What kind, Which one, How many*) Choose one adjective question to ask and write your adjective answer *under* the **Adj** label next to the object of the preposition. Always check to make sure your answers are making sense in the sentence.

7. Go to the **PP** label for the possessive pronoun that is part of your prepositional phrase. Repeat the Possessive Pronoun Jingle to help you think of a pronoun that you want to use as your possessive pronoun. You will choose one of the possessive pronouns that makes the best sense in your sentence. Write the possessive pronoun you have chosen *under* the **PP** label.

8. Finally, check your Practice Sentence to make sure it has the necessary parts to be a complete sentence. What are the five parts of a complete sentence? (*subject, verb, complete sense, capital letter, and an end mark*) Does your Practice Sentence have the five parts of a complete sentence? (*Allow time for students to read over their sentences and to make any corrections they need to make.*)

Under your Practice Sentence, write the title *Improved Sentence* on another line. To improve your Practice Sentence, you will make two synonym changes, one antonym change, and your choice of a complete word change or another synonym or antonym change.

Since it is harder to find words that can be changed to an antonym, it is usually wise to go through your sentence to find an antonym change first. Look through your sentence again to find words that can be improved with synonyms. Finally, make a decision about whether your last change will be a complete word change, another synonym change, or another antonym change.

I will give you time to write your Improved Sentence. (*Always encourage students to use a thesaurus, synonym-antonym book, or a dictionary to help them develop an interesting and improved writing vocabulary. After students have finished, check and discuss students' Practice and Improved Sentences.*)

CHAPTER 13 LESSON 3 CONTINUED

 PRACTICE TIME

Have students turn to page 54 in the Practice Section of their book and find Chapter 13, Lesson 3, Practice *(1-2)*. Go over the directions to make sure they understand what to do. Check and discuss the Practices after students have finished. *(Chapter 13, Lesson 3, Practice keys are given below.)*

Chapter 13, Lesson 3, Practice 1: Underline the correct homonym in each sentence.

1. I (no, <u>know</u>) how to fix the computer.
2. The cat didn't fit (<u>through</u>, threw) the hole.
3. She received a (<u>fourth</u>, forth) place ribbon.
4. Please raise your (write, <u>right</u>) hand.
5. Allen went (<u>to</u>, too, two) the beach.
6. (<u>It's</u>, Its) so good to see you!

Chapter 13, Lesson 3, Practice 2: Correct the capitalization and punctuation mistakes. Write the rule numbers above the capitalization corrections and below the punctuation corrections. Use Reference 24 for the capitalization rules and Reference 26 for the punctuation rules. The references are located on pages 18 and 19 in your Reference Section.

   1(or 3)   5   5   (capitalization rule numbers)
   C   O   M

1. chris goes to school in oxford, mississippi.   (Editing Guide: 3 capitals & 2 punctuation)
                                       3   5 (punctuation rule numbers)

   1(or 4) 3   6   (capitalization rule numbers)
   M   T   T

2. mr. thorton has a birthday on thursday.   (Editing Guide: 3 capitals & 2 punctuation)
    2   5 (punctuation rule numbers)

 ACTIVITY / ASSIGNMENT TIME

Write the sentences below in very large print on large pieces of butcher paper. (If you don't have butcher paper, you may have to put several pieces of paper together.) Then, give the sentences to your students along with the following items: pennies and macaroni noodles. The students are to punctuate the sentences by using the pennies as periods and the macaroni noodles as commas. *(Students may refer to the punctuation rules for help.)* Then, have students make several sentences of their own, write them in large print, and punctuate them correctly with pennies and macaroni noodles. Have them share their "punctuated" sentences with family members.

Sample Sentences: Mr. E. M. Lawrence helped Mom fix my bicycle.
                        Mrs. Stewart is from St. Paul, Minnesota.
                        I did not know that her dad moved to Enid, Oklahoma.
                        His brother was born on August 18, 2001.

(End of lesson.)

CHAPTER 13   LESSON 4

Objectives: Jingles, Study, Test, Check, Writing (Journal), and State Activity.

JINGLE TIME

Have students turn to the Jingle Section in their books and recite the previously-taught jingles.

STUDY TIME

Have students study the vocabulary words in their vocabulary notebooks. Remind students that any vocabulary word in their notebooks could be on their test. Also, have students study any of the skills in the Practice Section that they need to review.

TEST TIME

Have students turn to page 92 in the Test Section of their book and find Chapter 13 Test. Go over the directions to make sure they understand what to do. (*Chapter 13 Test key is on the next page.*)

CHECK TIME

After students have finished, check and discuss their test papers. Make sure they understand why their answers are right or wrong. (*For total points, count each required answer as a point.*)

STATE ACTIVITY TIME

Students will continue to draw or trace the states and to write the following questions and answers.

Kentucky	Louisiana
1. What is the state on the front of this card? **Kentucky**	1. What is the state on the front of this card? **Louisiana**
2. What is the capital of Kentucky? **Frankfort**	2. What is the capital of Louisiana? **Baton Rouge**
3. What is the postal abbreviation of Kentucky? **KY**	3. What is the postal abbreviation of Louisiana? **LA**

Color these states. Use the cards to quiz family members, friends, and relatives. You may want to time the responses to your questions.

(End of lesson.)

Level 2—Shurley English—Homeschool Edition

90 pts

Chapter 13 Test
(Student Page 92)

Exercise 1: Classify each sentence.

                PP   SN   V   P   A   OP   P Adj   OP

1. **SN V**   Your name **/** appeared (below the picture) (of another person). **D**
   P1

                Adj   Adj   SN   V   P PP Adj Adj OP

2. **SN V**   <u>Many noisy blackbirds</u> **/** <u>gathered (in our large oak tree)</u>. **D**
   P1

Exercise 2: Use Sentence 2 to underline the complete subject once and the complete predicate twice and to complete the table below.

List the Noun Used	List the Noun Job	Singular or Plural	Common or Proper	Simple Subject	Simple Predicate
1. **blackbirds**	2. **SN**	3. **P**	4. **C**	5. **blackbirds**	6. **gathered**
7. **tree**	8. **OP**	9. **S**	10. **C**		

Exercise 3: Name the six parts of speech that you have studied. (*You may use abbreviations.*)
(The order of answers may vary.)

1. **Noun**   2. **Verb**   3. **Adjective**   4. **Adverb**   5. **Preposition**   6. **Pronoun**

Exercise 4: Identify each pair of words as synonyms or antonyms by putting parentheses ( ) around *syn* or *ant*.

1. deep, shallow	syn **(ant)**	4. tardy, punctual	syn **(ant)**	7. gather, collect	**(syn)** ant
2. waddle, stride	syn **(ant)**	5. appear, emerge	**(syn)** ant	8. aware, alert	**(syn)** ant
3. beneath, below	**(syn)** ant	6. nimble, slow	syn **(ant)**	9. unsteady, stable	syn **(ant)**

1 pt ea.

Exercises 5: Correct the capitalization and punctuation mistakes. Write the rule numbers above the capitalization corrections and below the punctuation corrections. Use Reference 24 for the capitalization rules and Reference 26 for the punctuation rules. The references are located on pages 18 and 19 in your Reference Section.

    1(or 4) 4   4   3   5   5   (capitalization rule numbers)
    M   W   R   S   D   C

1. mr. w. r. speer was born in denver, colorado. **(Editing Guide: 6 capitals & 5 punctuation)**
     2   1 1   3   5   (punctuation rule numbers)

    1(or 4) 3   3   6   (capitalization rule numbers)
    M   V   K   J

2. mrs. vines baked kelly a birthday cake on july 4, 2002. **(Editing Guide: 4 capitals & 3 punctuation)**
     2   4   5 (punctuation rule numbers)

Exercise 6: In your journal, write a paragraph summarizing what you have learned this week.

Level 2—Shirley English—Homeschool Edition

CHAPTER 13 LESSON 4 CONTINUED

TEACHER INSTRUCTIONS

Use the Question and Answer Flows below for the sentences on the Chapter 13 Test.

Question and Answer Flow for Sentence 1: Your name appeared below the picture of another person.

1. What appeared below the picture of another person? name - SN
2. What is being said about name? name appeared - V
3. Below - P
4. Below what? picture - OP
5. The - A
6. Of - P
7. Of what? person - OP
8. What kind of person? another - Adj
9. Whose name? your - PP
10. SN V P1 Check
11. (Below the picture) - Prepositional phrase
12. (Of another person) - Prepositional phrase
13. Period, statement, declarative sentence
14. Go back to the verb - divide the complete subject from the complete predicate.

```
                           PP    SN    V       P  A   OP    P  Adj    OP
Classified Sentence:    SN  V      Your name / appeared (below the picture) (of another person).  D
                        P1
```

Question and Answer Flow for Sentence 2: Many noisy blackbirds gathered in our large oak tree.

1. What gathered in our large oak tree? blackbirds - SN
2. What is being said about blackbirds? blackbirds gathered - V
3. In - P
4. In what? tree - OP
5. What kind of tree? oak - Adj
6. What kind of tree? large - Adj
7. Whose tree? our - PP
8. What kind of blackbirds? noisy - Adj
9. How many blackbirds? many - Adj
10. SN V P1 Check
11. (In our large oak tree) - Prepositional phrase
12. Period, statement, declarative sentence
13. Go back to the verb - divide the complete subject from the complete predicate.

```
                           Adj   Adj    SN          V      P  PP  Adj  Adj  OP
Classified Sentence:    SN  V      Many noisy blackbirds / gathered (in our large oak tree).  D
                        P1
```

CHAPTER 13   LESSON 5

Objectives: Writing Assignment #7 and Sentence Time.

 WRITING TIME

<u>*TEACHER INSTRUCTIONS FOR WRITING ASSIGNMENT #7*</u>

Give Writing Assignment #7 from the box below. Remind students to use the Writing Checklist in Reference 17 to check their finished writing assignment.

Read, check, and discuss Writing Assignment #7 after students have finished their final papers. Use the Writing Checklist (*Reference 17 on teacher's page 112*) as you check and discuss students' papers. Make sure students are using the checklist correctly. In the beginning, you must also check students' papers carefully for <u>form</u> mistakes. This will ensure that students are learning the two-point format correctly.

Writing Assignment Box

Writing Assignment #7: Two-Point Expository Paragraph

Writing topic choices: My Favorite Cereals   or I Give Thanks for....   or   My Favorite Stuffed Animals

---

 SENTENCE TIME

Chapter 13, Lesson 5, Sentence: Use colored markers to match each label with the correct sentence part by drawing a line from one to the other. Then, use the labels to arrange the sentence parts into a sentence that you will write on the sentence line below. *(The order of the words in your sentence should be in the same sequence as the vertical list of sentence labels.)* Create other labels and scrambled sentence parts on notebook paper for family members to solve. You may color code the sentence parts. *(See page 112 in the student book.)*

Labels for Order of Sentence	Scrambled Sentence Parts
SP	outside
V	snow
Adv	the
P	in
A	we
OP	new
P	neighbors
PP	our
Adj	with
OP	played

Sentence: We played outside in the snow with our new neighbors. (Order may vary.)

(End of lesson.)

Level 2—Shurley English—Homeschool Edition

CHAPTER 14   LESSON 1
Objectives: Jingles, Grammar (Practice Sentences, Skill Builder Check, Reviewing the Six Parts of Speech), Practice Exercise, and Vocabulary #1.

 **JINGLE TIME**

Have students turn to the Jingle Section in their books and recite the previously-taught jingles.

 GRAMMAR TIME

Put the Practice Sentences from the box below on the board or on notebook paper. Use these sentences as you practice the concepts that have been taught. For the greatest benefit, students must participate orally with the teacher.

Chapter 14, Practice Sentences for Lesson 1
1. _____ David traveled with his family to France.
2. _____ The nimble cat jumped unexpectedly across our kitchen table.
3. _____ The skillful volunteers worked daily for our charity.

TEACHING SCRIPT FOR CLASSIFYING PRACTICE SENTENCES

We will classify three different sentences to practice the grammar skills in the Question and Answer Flows. We will classify the sentences together. Begin. (*You might have students write the labels above the sentences at this time.*)

Question and Answer Flow for Sentence 1: David traveled with his family to France.
1. Who traveled with his family to France? David - SN
2. What is being said about David? David traveled - V
3. With - P
4. With whom? family - OP
5. Whose family? his - PP
6. To - P
7. To what? France - OP
8. SN V P1 Check
9. (With his family) - Prepositional phrase
10. (To France) - Prepositional phrase
11. Period, statement, declarative sentence
12. Go back to the verb - divide the complete subject from the complete predicate.
SN   V   P PP OP   P OP
Classified Sentence: SN V   David / traveled (with his family) (to France). D
P1

CHAPTER 14 LESSON 1 CONTINUED

Question and Answer Flow for Sentence 2: The nimble cat jumped unexpectedly across our kitchen table.

1. What jumped unexpectedly across our kitchen table? cat - SN
2. What is being said about cat? cat jumped - V
3. Jumped how? unexpectedly - Adv
4. Across - P
5. Across what? table - OP
6. What kind of table? kitchen - Adj
7. Whose table? our - PP
8. What kind of cat? nimble - Adj
9. The - A
10. SN V P1 Check
11. (Across our kitchen table) - Prepositional phrase
12. Period, statement, declarative sentence
13. Go back to the verb - divide the complete subject from the complete predicate.

```
                         A   Adj  SN    V         Adv       P  PP  Adj  OP
Classified Sentence:    SN V      The nimble cat / jumped unexpectedly (across our kitchen table).  D
                         P1
```

Question and Answer Flow for Sentence 3: The skillful volunteers worked daily for our charity.

1. Who worked daily for our charity? volunteers - SN
2. What is being said about volunteers? volunteers worked - V
3. Worked when? daily - Adv
4. For - P
5. For what? charity - OP
6. Whose charity? our - PP
7. What kind of volunteers? skillful - Adj
8. The - A
9. SN V P1 Check
10. (For our charity) - Prepositional phrase
11. Period, statement, declarative sentence
12. Go back to the verb - divide the complete subject from the complete predicate.

```
                         A   Adj     SN        V      Adv  P  PP   OP
Classified Sentence:    SN V     The skillful volunteers / worked daily (for our charity).  D
                         P1
```

Use Sentences 1-3 that you just classified with your students to do a Skill Builder Check. Use the guidelines below.

Skill Builder Check

1. **Noun check.**
   (Say the job and then say the noun. Circle each noun.)
2. **Identify the nouns as singular or plural.**
   (Write **S** or **P** above each noun.)
3. **Identify the nouns as common or proper.**
   (Follow established procedure for oral identification.)
4. **Do a vocabulary check.**
   (Follow established procedure for oral identification.)
5. **Identify the complete subject and the complete predicate.** (Underline the complete subject once and the complete predicate twice.)
6. **Identify the simple subject and simple predicate.** (Underline the simple subject once and the simple predicate twice. Bold, or highlight, the lines to distinguish them from the complete subject and complete predicate.)

TEACHING SCRIPT FOR REVIEWING THE SIX PARTS OF SPEECH

What are the six parts of speech that we have covered? *(noun, verb, adjective, adverb, preposition,* and *pronoun)* *(Chant the six parts of speech that the students have learned several times for reinforcement and fun.)*

CHAPTER 14 LESSON 1 CONTINUED

 PRACTICE TIME

Have students turn to page 55 in the Practice Section of their book and find Chapter 14, Lesson 1, Practice (1-2). Go over the directions to make sure they understand what to do. Check and discuss the Practices after students have finished. (*Chapter 14, Lesson 1, Practice keys are given below.*)

Chapter 14, Lesson 1, Practice 1: Underline the correct homonym in each sentence.

1. Mr. Wilson is a high school (principle, <u>principal</u>).
2. The crowd cheered when (<u>their</u>, there) team won.
3. The (week, <u>weak</u>) branch broke off the tree.
4. The water in the tub is (to, <u>too</u>, two) hot.
5. I used a (<u>lead</u>, led) pencil on the test.
6. I would like a (<u>piece</u>, peace) of candy.

Chapter 14, Lesson 1, Practice 2: Correct the capitalization and punctuation mistakes. Write the rule numbers above the capitalization corrections and below the punctuation corrections. Use Reference 24 for the capitalization rules and Reference 26 for the punctuation rules. The references are located on pages 18 and 19 in your Reference Section.

```
   1(or3)                              6           (capitalization rule numbers)
    J                                  A
1. julie  started  the  beautiful  quilt  on  april 2, 2002.  (Editing Guide: 2 capitals & 2 punctuation)
                                                4    5       (punctuation rule numbers)


    1                          5   5        5      (capitalization rule numbers)
    H                          S   A        T
2. his  team  played  in  the  arena  at  san  antonio,  texas.  (Editing Guide: 4 capitals & 2 punctuation)
                                              3         5         (punctuation rule numbers)
```

 VOCABULARY TIME

Assign Chapter 14, Vocabulary Words #1 on page 7 in the Reference Section for students to define in their Vocabulary notebooks. Tell students they are to use a dictionary or thesaurus to look up the meanings of the vocabulary words.

Chapter 14, Vocabulary Words #1
(begin, retire, burrow, tunnel)

(End of lesson.)

CHAPTER 14   LESSON 2

Objectives: Jingles, Grammar (Practice Sentences), Practice Exercise, and Vocabulary #2.

 **JINGLE TIME**

Have students turn to the Jingle Section in their books and recite the previously-taught jingles.

 GRAMMAR TIME

Put the Practice Sentences from the box below on the board or on notebook paper. Use these sentences as you practice the concepts that have been taught. For the greatest benefit, students must participate orally with the teacher.

Chapter 14, Practice Sentences for Lesson 2
1. _____ The snowflakes melted quickly in the hot sun.
2. _____ The frightened groundhog raced quickly toward his burrow.
3. _____ She asked for his advice about the situation.

TEACHING SCRIPT FOR CLASSIFYING PRACTICE SENTENCES

We will classify three different sentences to practice the grammar skills in the Question and Answer Flows. We will classify the sentences together. Begin. (*You might have students write the labels above the sentences at this time.*)

Question and Answer Flow for Sentence 1: The snowflakes melted quickly in the hot sun.
1. What melted quickly in the hot sun? snowflakes - SN   7. The - A
2. What is being said about snowflakes?   8. The - A
snowflakes melted - V   9. SN V P1 Check
3. Melted how? quickly - Adv   10. (In the hot sun) - Prepositional phrase
4. In - P   11. Period, statement, declarative sentence
5. In what? sun - OP   12. Go back to the verb - divide the complete subject
6. What kind of sun? hot - Adj   from the complete predicate.
A   SN   V   Adv   P   A   Adj   OP
Classified Sentence: <u>SN V</u>   The snowflakes / melted quickly (in the hot sun).   D
P1

CHAPTER 14 LESSON 2 CONTINUED

Question and Answer Flow for Sentence 2: The frightened groundhog raced quickly toward his burrow.

1. What raced quickly toward his burrow? groundhog - SN
2. What is being said about groundhog? groundhog raced - V
3. Raced how? quickly - Adv
4. Toward - P
5. Toward what? burrow - OP
6. Whose burrow? his - PP
7. What kind of groundhog? frightened - Adj
8. The - A
9. SN V P1 Check
10. (Toward his burrow) - Prepositional phrase
11. Period, statement, declarative sentence
12. Go back to the verb - divide the complete subject from the complete predicate.

```
                          A   Adj       SN      V    Adv    P   PP   OP
Classified Sentence:   SN V   The frightened groundhog / raced quickly (toward his burrow).  D
                       P1
```

Question and Answer Flow for Sentence 3: She asked for his advice about the situation.

1. Who asked for his advice about the situation? she - SP
2. What is being said about she? she asked - V
3. For - P
4. For what? advice - OP
5. Whose advice? his - PP
6. About - P
7. About what? situation - OP
8. The - A
9. SN V P1 Check
10. (For his advice) - Prepositional phrase
11. (About the situation) - Prepositional phrase
12. Period, statement, declarative sentence
13. Go back to the verb - divide the complete subject from the complete predicate.

```
                          SP    V    P  PP   OP     P   A    OP
Classified Sentence:   SN V   She / asked (for his advice) (about the situation).  D
                       P1
```

 PRACTICE TIME

Have students turn to pages 55 and 56 in the Practice Section of their book and find Chapter 14, Lesson 2, Practice *(1-3)*. Go over the directions to make sure they understand what to do. Check and discuss the Practices after students have finished. *(Chapter 14, Lesson 2, Practice keys are given below and on the next page.)*

Chapter 14, Lesson 2, Practice 1: Underline the correct homonym in each sentence.

1. The runners said the (<u>course</u>, coarse) was difficult.
2. The company invented a (knew, <u>new</u>) product.
3. The (<u>capitol</u>, capital) building was built in 1876.
4. She (scent, <u>sent</u>) cookies to the party.
5. The clowns painted (<u>their</u>, there) faces.
6. I feel like I could sleep for (<u>days</u>, daze).

CHAPTER 14 LESSON 2 CONTINUED

Chapter 14, Lesson 2, Practice 2: Correct the capitalization and punctuation mistakes. Write the rule numbers above the capitalization corrections and below the punctuation corrections. Use Reference 24 for the capitalization rules and Reference 26 for the punctuation rules. The references are located on pages 18 and 19 in your Reference Section.

```
     1     4  4  4     3                5            5      (capitalization rule numbers)
     W     J  R  R     J                A            M
1.  was   j. r. r.   johnson   from   augusta,    maine?    (Editing Guide: 7 capitals & 5 punctuation)
           2  2  2                               3       5  (punctuation rule numbers)
```

Chapter 14, Lesson 2, Practice 3: For each sentence, do these four things: (1) Write the subject. (2) Write **S** if the subject is singular or **P** if the subject is plural. (3) Write the rule number. (4) Underline the correct verb in the sentence.

Rule 1: A singular subject must use a singular verb form that ends in **s**: *is*, *was*, *has*, *does*, or verbs ending with **es**.

Rule 2: A plural subject, a compound subject, or the subject **YOU** must use a plural verb form that has **no s** ending: *are*, *were*, *do*, *have*, or verbs without **s** or **es** endings. (A plural verb form is also called the *plain form*.)

Subject	S or P	Rule		
motorists	P	2	1.	The **motorists** cautiously (<u>drive</u>, drives) through the tunnel.
cows	P	2	2.	**Cows** (grazes, <u>graze</u>) contentedly in the pasture.
cider	S	1	3.	The apple **cider** (<u>cools</u>, cool) in my mug.
duckling	S	1	4.	The **duckling** (hatch, <u>hatches</u>) from the tiny egg.
you	P	2	5.	**You** (catches, <u>catch</u>) the ball.
kites	P	2	6.	Several **kites** (flies, <u>fly</u>) above our heads.
kettle	S	1	7.	The tea **kettle** (<u>whistles</u>, whistle) in the kitchen.
clowns	P	2	8.	The circus **clowns** (carries, <u>carry</u>) balloons.

VOCABULARY TIME

Assign Chapter 14, Vocabulary Words **#2** on page 7 in the Reference Section for students to define in their Vocabulary notebooks. Tell students they are to use a dictionary or thesaurus to look up the meanings of the vocabulary words.

Chapter 14, Vocabulary Words #2
(advice, counsel, junior, senior)

(End of lesson.)

CHAPTER 14 LESSON 3

Objectives: Jingles, Grammar (Practice Sentences, Practice and Improved Sentence), and Practice Exercise.

 **JINGLE TIME**

Have students turn to the Jingle Section in their books and recite the previously-taught jingles.

 GRAMMAR TIME

Put the Practice Sentences from the box below on the board or on notebook paper. Use these sentences as you practice the concepts that have been taught. For the greatest benefit, students must participate orally with the teacher.

Chapter 14, Practice Sentences for Lesson 3
1. _____ Our parents moved to the city after their retirement.
2. _____ He wrote for our newspaper during his senior year.
3. _____ She climbed aboard the train with her ticket in her hand.

TEACHING SCRIPT FOR CLASSIFYING PRACTICE SENTENCES

We will classify three different sentences to practice the grammar skills in the Question and Answer Flows. We will classify the sentences together. Begin. (*You might have students write the labels above the sentences at this time.*)

Question and Answer Flow for Sentence 1: Our parents moved to the city after their retirement.

1. Who moved to the city after their retirement?
   parents - SN
2. What is being said about parents? parents moved - V
3. To - P
4. To what? city - OP
5. The - A
6. After - P
7. After what? retirement - OP
8. Whose retirement? their - PP
9. Whose parents? our - PP
10. SN V P1 Check
11. (To the city) - Prepositional phrase
12. (After their retirement) - Prepositional phrase
13. Period, statement, declarative sentence
14. Go back to the verb - divide the complete subject from the complete predicate.

Classified Sentence:

```
                       PP   SN   V   P  A  OP    P    PP    OP
         SN V    Our parents / moved (to the city) (after their retirement).  D
         P1
```

CHAPTER 14 LESSON 3 CONTINUED

Question and Answer Flow for Sentence 2: He wrote for our newspaper during his senior year.

1. Who wrote for our newspaper during his senior year? he - SP
2. What is being said about he? he wrote - V
3. For - P
4. For what? newspaper - OP
5. Whose newspaper? our - PP
6. During - P
7. During what? year - OP
8. Which year? senior - Adj
9. Whose year? his - PP
10. SN V P1 Check
11. (For our newspaper) - Prepositional phrase
12. (During his senior year) - Prepositional phrase
13. Period, statement, declarative sentence
14. Go back to the verb - divide the complete subject from the complete predicate.

```
                        SP  V   P  PP  OP        P   PP  Adj  OP
Classified Sentence:   SN V    He / wrote (for our newspaper) (during his senior year).  D
                        P1
```

Question and Answer Flow for Sentence 3: She climbed aboard the train with her ticket in her hand.

1. Who climbed aboard the train with her ticket in her hand? she - SP
2. What is being said about she? she climbed - V
3. Aboard - P
4. Aboard what? train - OP
5. The - A
6. With - P
7. With what? ticket - OP
8. Whose ticket? her - PP
9. In - P
10. In what? hand - OP
11. Whose hand? her - PP
12. SN V P1 Check
13. (Aboard the train) - Prepositional phrase
14. (With her ticket) - Prepositional phrase
15. (In her hand) - Prepositional phrase
16. Period, statement, declarative sentence
17. Go back to the verb - divide the complete subject from the complete predicate.

```
                        SP  V     P   A   OP     P  PP  OP    P  PP  OP
Classified Sentence:   SN V    She / climbed (aboard the train) (with her ticket) (in her hand).  D
                        P1
```

TEACHING SCRIPT FOR A PRACTICE SENTENCE

> Put these labels on the board: **A Adj Adj SN V Adv P PP Adj OP**

Look at the new sentence labels on the board: **A Adj Adj SN V Adv P PP Adj OP**. I will guide you again through the process of writing a sentence to practice all the parts that you have learned.

Get out a sheet of notebook paper. On the top line of your notebook paper, write the title *Practice Sentence*. Copy the sentence labels from the board onto your notebook paper. Be sure to leave plenty of writing space between each label. Now, I will guide you through the process you will use whenever you write a Practice Sentence with a prepositional phrase.

1. Go to the **SN** label for the subject noun. Think of a noun that you want to use as your subject. Write the noun you have chosen on the line *under* the **SN** label.

2. Go to the **V** label for the verb. Think of a verb that tells what your subject does. Make sure that your verb makes sense with the subject noun. Write the verb you have chosen on the line *under* the **V** label.

CHAPTER 14 LESSON 3 CONTINUED

3. Go to the **Adv** label for the adverb. Immediately go to the verb in your sentence and ask an adverb question. What are the adverb questions? (*How, When, Where*) Choose one adverb question to ask and write your adverb answer *under* the **Adv** label.

4. Go to the **P** label for the preposition. Think of a preposition word that tells something about your verb. You must be careful to choose a preposition word that makes sense with the noun you will choose for the object of the preposition in your next step. Write the word you have chosen for a preposition *under* the **P** label.

5. Go to the **OP** label for the object of the preposition. If you like the noun you thought of while thinking of a preposition, write it down under the **OP** label. If you prefer, think of another noun by asking **what** or **whom** after your preposition. Check to make sure the preposition and object of the preposition make sense together and also make sense with the rest of the sentence. Remember, the object of the preposition will always answer the question **what** or **whom** after the preposition. Write the word you have chosen for the object of the preposition *under* the **OP** label.

6. Go to the **Adj** label for the adjective. Go to the object of the preposition that you just wrote and ask an adjective question to describe the object-of-the-preposition noun. What are the adjective questions? (*What kind, Which one, How many*) Choose one adjective question to ask and write your adjective answer *under* the **Adj** label next to the object of the preposition. Always check to make sure your answers are making sense in the sentence.

7. Go to the **PP** label for the possessive pronoun that is part of your prepositional phrase. Repeat the Possessive Pronoun Jingle to help you think of a pronoun that you want to use as your possessive pronoun. You will choose one of the possessive pronouns that makes the best sense in your sentence. Write the possessive pronoun you have chosen *under* the **PP** label.

8. Go to the **Adj** label for another adjective. Go to the subject noun of your sentence and ask an adjective question. What are the adjective questions again? (*What kind, Which one, How many*) Choose one adjective question to ask and write your adjective answer *under* the **Adj** label next to the subject noun.

9. Go to the **Adj** label for the third adjective. Go to the subject noun again and ask another adjective question. You can ask the same adjective question, or you can ask a different adjective question. Write another adjective *under* the third **Adj** label.

10. Go to the **A** label for the article adjective in the subject area. What are the three article adjectives again? (*a, an,* and *the*) Choose the article adjective that makes the best sense in your sentence. Write the article adjective you have chosen *under* the **A** label.

11. Finally, check your Practice Sentence to make sure it has the necessary parts to be a complete sentence. What are the five parts of a complete sentence? (*subject, verb, complete sense, capital letter, and an end mark*) Does your Practice Sentence have the five parts of a complete sentence? (*Allow time for students to read over their sentences and to make any corrections they need to make.*)

Level 2—Shurley English—Homeschool Edition

CHAPTER 14 LESSON 3 CONTINUED

TEACHING SCRIPT FOR THE IMPROVED SENTENCE

Under your Practice Sentence, write the title *Improved Sentence* on another line. To improve your Practice Sentence, you will make two synonym changes, one antonym change, and your choice of a complete word change or another synonym or antonym change.

I will give you time to write your Improved Sentence. *(Always encourage students to use a thesaurus, synonym-antonym book, or a dictionary to help them develop an interesting and improved writing vocabulary. After students have finished, check and discuss students' Practice and Improved Sentences.)*

 PRACTICE TIME

Have students turn to page 56 in the Practice Section of their book and find Chapter 14, Lesson 3, Practice *(1-2)*. Go over the directions to make sure they understand what to do. Check and discuss the Practices after students have finished. *(Chapter 14, Lesson 3, Practice keys are given below.)*

Chapter 14, Lesson 3, Practice 1: Underline the correct homonym in each sentence.

1. I couldn't (<u>hear</u>, here) the telephone ring.
2. We (<u>threw</u>, through) a surprise party for Joe.
3. The citizens prayed for (<u>peace</u>, piece).
4. The puppy searched for (it's, <u>its</u>) bone.

Chapter 14, Lesson 3, Practice 2: Correct the capitalization and punctuation mistakes. Write the rule numbers above the capitalization corrections and below the punctuation corrections. Use Reference 24 for the capitalization rules and Reference 26 for the punctuation rules. The references are located on pages 18 and 19 in your Reference Section.

```
  1                6                  (capitalization rule numbers)
  T                J
1. the  letter  was  dated  july  6,  2001.   (Editing Guide: 2 capitals & 2 punctuation)
                              4    5      (punctuation rule numbers)


 1 (or 3)   3                   5      5      (capitalization rule numbers)
   D        T                   R      V
2. dana and tiffany are my cousins from richmond, virginia.  (Editing Guide: 4 capitals & 2 punctuation)
                                          3        5     (punctuation rule numbers)
```

(End of lesson.)

Level 2—Shurley English—Homeschool Edition

CHAPTER 14   LESSON 4

Objectives: Jingles, Study, Test, Check, Writing (Journal), and State Activity.

 JINGLE TIME

Have students turn to the Jingle Section in their books and recite the previously-taught jingles.

 STUDY TIME

Have students study the vocabulary words in their vocabulary notebooks. Remind students that any vocabulary word in their notebooks could be on their test. Also, have students study any of the skills in the Practice Section that they need to review.

 TEST TIME

Have students turn to page 93 in the Test Section of their book and find Chapter 14 Test. Go over the directions to make sure they understand what to do. (*Chapter 14 Test key is on the next page.*)

 CHECK TIME

After students have finished, check and discuss their test papers. Make sure they understand why their answers are right or wrong. (*For total points, count each required answer as a point.*)

 STATE ACTIVITY TIME

Students will continue to draw or trace the states and to write the following questions and answers.

Maine	Maryland
1. What is the state on the front of this card? **Maine**	1. What is the state on the front of this card? **Maryland**
2. What is the capital of Maine? **Augusta**	2. What is the capital of Maryland? **Annapolis**
3. What is the postal abbreviation of Maine? **ME**	3. What is the postal abbreviation of Maryland? **MD**

Color these states. Use the cards to quiz family members, friends, and relatives. You may want to time the responses to your questions.

(End of lesson.)

Chapter 14 Test
(Student Page 93)

80 pts

Exercise 1: Classify each sentence.

1. SN V / P1 — SP V P A Adj OP Adv — I / climbed (up the big hill) yesterday. D

2. SN V / P1 — A Adj SN V Adv P PP OP — The three kittens / sat lazily (in their basket). D

Exercise 2: Use Sentence 2 to underline the complete subject once and the complete predicate twice and to complete the table below.

List the Noun Used	List the Noun Job	Singular or Plural	Common or Proper	Simple Subject	Simple Predicate
1. kittens	2. SN	3. P	4. C	5. kittens	6. sat
7. basket	8. OP	9. S	10. C		

Exercise 3: Name the six parts of speech that you have studied. (*You may use abbreviations.*)
(The order of answers may vary.)

1. Noun   2. Verb   3. Adjective   4. Adverb   5. Preposition   6. Pronoun

Exercise 4: Identify each pair of words as synonyms or antonyms by putting parentheses ( ) around **syn** or **ant**.

1. counsel, advice	(syn)	ant	4. collect, gather	(syn)	ant	7. cranky, grouchy	(syn)	ant
2. deep, shallow	syn	(ant)	5. unsteady, stable	syn	(ant)	8. burrow, tunnel	(syn)	ant
3. senior, junior	syn	(ant)	6. retire, begin	syn	(ant)	9. appear, emerge	(syn)	ant

Exercises 5: Correct the capitalization and punctuation mistakes. Write the rule numbers above the capitalization corrections and below the punctuation corrections. Use Reference 24 for the capitalization rules and Reference 26 for the punctuation rules. The references are located on pages 18 and 19 in your Reference Section.

1. 1(or 3) 3   5 5 5   (capitalization rule numbers)
   R   J   C C N
   ray and judy moved to carson city, nevada. (Editing Guide: 5 capitals & 2 punctuation)
                                   3   5   (punctuation rule numbers)

2. 1(or 4) 4 3   6   (capitalization rule numbers)
   M   M D   O
   mr. and mrs. davis were married on october 5, 2001. (Editing Guide: 4 capitals & 4 punctuation)
      2   2   4 5   (punctuation rule numbers)

Exercise 6: In your journal, write a paragraph summarizing what you have learned this week.

CHAPTER 14 LESSON 4 CONTINUED

TEACHER INSTRUCTIONS

Use the Question and Answer Flows below for the sentences on the Chapter 14 Test.

Question and Answer Flow for Sentence 1: I climbed up the big hill yesterday.

1. Who climbed up the big hill yesterday? I - SP
2. What is being said about I? I climbed - V
3. Up - P
4. Up what? hill - OP
5. What kind of hill? big - Adj
6. The - A
7. Climbed when? yesterday - Adv
8. SN V P1 Check
9. (Up the big hill) - Prepositional phrase
10. Period, statement, declarative sentence
11. Go back to the verb - divide the complete subject from the complete predicate.

```
                            SP    V     P  A  Adj OP    Adv
Classified Sentence:   SN V    I / climbed (up the big hill) yesterday.  D
                       P1
```

Question and Answer Flow for Sentence 2: The three kittens sat lazily in their basket.

1. What sat lazily in their basket? kittens - SN
2. What is being said about kittens? kittens sat - V
3. Sat how? lazily - Adv
4. In - P
5. In what? basket - OP
6. Whose basket? their - PP
7. How many kittens? three - Adj
8. The - A
9. SN V P1 Check
10. (In their basket) - Prepositional phrase
11. Period, statement, declarative sentence
12. Go back to the verb - divide the complete subject from the complete predicate.

```
                         A   Adj   SN    V   Adv  P  PP   OP
Classified Sentence:   SN V    The three kittens / sat lazily (in their basket).  D
                       P1
```

CHAPTER 14   LESSON 5

Objectives: Writing Assignment #8 and Sentence Time.

 WRITING TIME

TEACHER INSTRUCTIONS FOR WRITING ASSIGNMENT #8

Give Writing Assignment #8 from the box below. Remind students to use the Writing Checklist in Reference 17 to check their finished writing assignment.

Read, check, and discuss Writing Assignment #8 after students have finished their final papers. Use the Writing Checklist (*Reference 17 on teacher's page 112*) as you check and discuss students' papers. Make sure students are using the checklist correctly. In the beginning, you must also check students' papers carefully for <u>form</u> mistakes. This will ensure that students are learning the two-point format correctly.

Writing Assignment Box
Writing Assignment #8: Two-Point Expository Paragraph
Writing topic choices: Special Family Activities   or   My Chores   or   Things That Make Me Laugh

 SENTENCE TIME

Chapter 14, Lesson 5, Sentence: Use colored markers to match each label with the correct sentence part by drawing a line from one to the other. Then, use the labels to arrange the sentence parts into a sentence that you will write on the sentence line below. *(The order of the words in your sentence should be in the same sequence as the vertical list of sentence labels.)* Create other labels and scrambled sentence parts on notebook paper for family members to solve. You may color code the sentence parts. *(See page 113 in the student book.)*

Labels for Order of Sentence	Scrambled Sentence Parts
A	rain
Adj	the
SN	heavy
V	after
P	appeared
A	beautiful
OP	sky
P	the
A	rainbow
Adj	across
OP	a

Sentence: A beautiful rainbow appeared across the sky after the heavy rain.

(End of lesson.)

CHAPTER 15   LESSON 1
Objectives: Jingles, Grammar (Introductory Sentences, Possessive Noun, Noun Check with Possessive Nouns, Skill Builder Check), Practice Exercise, and Vocabulary #1.

 **JINGLE TIME**

Have students turn to the Jingle Section in their books and recite the previously-taught jingles.

 GRAMMAR TIME

Put the introductory sentences from the box below on the board. Use these sentences as you go through each new concept covered in your teaching script. For the greatest benefit, students must participate orally with the teacher. (*You might put the introductory sentences on notebook paper if you are doing one-on-one instruction with your students.*)

Chapter 15, Introductory Sentences for Lesson 1
1. _____ The puppy sat contentedly in Kim's lap.
2. _____ My sister's boyfriend left early for a dental appointment.
3. _____ Larry's soccer team practices after school today.

TEACHING SCRIPT FOR POSSESSIVE NOUN

Today, we will learn about a very special noun: the possessive noun. Since there is not a jingle for possessive nouns, information about the possessive noun is listed in the Reference Section on page 20. Look at Reference 27. Follow along as I explain the six things you should know about the possessive noun. (*Read and discuss the information about possessive nouns in the reference box below.*)

Reference 27: Possessive Nouns
1. A possessive noun is the name of a person, place, or thing that owns something.
2. A possessive noun will always have an apostrophe after it. It will be either an *apostrophe s* ('s) or an *s apostrophe* (s'). The apostrophe makes a noun show ownership. (*Tyler's camera*)
3. A possessive noun's main job is to show ownership or possession.
4. Use the abbreviation **PN** (possessive noun).
5. Include possessive nouns when you are asked to identify possessive nouns or adjectives. Do not include possessive nouns when you are asked to identify regular nouns because of their special job.
6. To find a possessive noun, begin with the question *whose*. (*Whose camera? Tyler's - PN*)

CHAPTER 15 LESSON 1 CONTINUED

Since you use the *whose* question to find a possessive noun and a possessive pronoun, you must remember one important fact about each one in order to tell them apart. Remember, all possessive nouns have an apostrophe, and the seven possessive pronouns do not. Possessive pronouns can be found in the Possessive Pronoun Jingle that you have already learned. *(You may want your students to recite the Possessive Pronoun Jingle again to reinforce what you have just said.)* You will use this information as you classify Sentences 1-3 with me. Begin.

Question and Answer Flow for Sentence 1: The puppy sat contentedly in Kim's lap.

1. What sat contentedly in Kim's lap? puppy - SN
2. What is being said about puppy? puppy sat - V
3. Sat how? contentedly - Adv
4. In - P
5. In what? lap - OP
6. Whose lap? Kim's - PN (possessive noun)
7. The - A
8. SN V P1 Check
9. (In Kim's lap) - Prepositional phrase
10. Period, statement, declarative sentence
11. Go back to the verb - divide the complete subject from the complete predicate.

```
                          A    SN  V     Adv      P  PN   OP
Classified Sentence:   SN V    The puppy / sat contentedly (in Kim's lap). D
                       ----
                       P1
```

Question and Answer Flow for Sentence 2: My sister's boyfriend left early for a dental appointment.

1. Who left early for a dental appointment? boyfriend - SN
2. What is being said about boyfriend? boyfriend left - V
3. Left when? early - Adv
4. For - P
5. For what? appointment - OP
6. What kind of appointment? dental - Adj
7. A - A
8. Whose boyfriend? sister's - PN (possessive noun)
9. Whose sister? my - PP
10. SN V P1 Check
11. (For a dental appointment) - Prepositional phrase
12. Period, statement, declarative sentence
13. Go back to the verb - divide the complete subject from the complete predicate.

```
                          PP    PN      SN      V   Adv  P A  Adj     OP
Classified Sentence:   SN V    My sister's boyfriend / left early (for a dental appointment). D
                       ----
                       P1
```

Question and Answer Flow for Sentence 3: Larry's soccer team practices after school today.

1. What practices after school today? team - SN
2. What is being said about team? team practices - V
3. After - P
4. After what? school - OP
5. Practices when? today - Adv
6. What kind of team? soccer - Adj
7. Whose team? Larry's - PN (possessive noun)
8. SN V P1 Check
9. (After school) - Prepositional phrase
10. Period, statement, declarative sentence
11. Go back to the verb - divide the complete subject from the complete predicate.

```
                          PN    Adj    SN     V      P   OP   Adv
Classified Sentence:   SN V    Larry's soccer team / practices (after school) today. D
                       ----
                       P1
```

Level 2—Shurley English—Homeschool Edition

CHAPTER 15 LESSON 1 CONTINUED

TEACHING SCRIPT FOR A NOUN CHECK WHEN POSSESSIVE NOUNS ARE IN THE SENTENCES

We will only do a Noun Check today to show you how to deal with possessive nouns when you are identifying nouns. A possessive noun's part of speech is an adjective. Remember, a Noun Check is a check for nouns. If there is a possessive noun, we will not classify it as a noun because we are looking only for noun jobs that give us regular nouns, not special nouns that function as possessives and adjectives. Let's start with number one and go through the Noun Check for Sentences 1-3, looking for nouns. (*Recite the information below with your students.*)

Sentence 1: Subject noun *puppy*, yes. (*Circle* **puppy** *because it is a noun.*) Object of the preposition *lap*, yes. (*Circle* **lap** *because it is a noun.*)
Sentence 2: Subject noun *boyfriend*, yes. (*Circle* **boyfriend** *because it is a noun.*) Object of the preposition *appointment*, yes. (*Circle* **appointment** *because it is a noun.*)
Sentence 3: Subject noun *team*, yes. (*Circle* **team** *because it is a noun.*) Object of the preposition *school*, yes. (*Circle* **school** *because it is a noun.*)

Use Sentences 1-3 that you just classified with your students to finish the Skill Builder Check. Use the guidelines below.

Skill Builder Check	
1. Noun check. (Say the job and then say the noun. Circle each noun.)	**5. Identify the complete subject and the complete predicate.** (Underline the complete subject once and the complete predicate twice.)
2. Identify the nouns as singular or plural. (Write **S** or **P** above each noun.)	**6. Identify the simple subject and simple predicate.** (Underline the simple subject once and the simple predicate twice. Bold, or highlight, the lines to distinguish them from the complete subject and complete predicate.)
3. Identify the nouns as common or proper. (Follow established procedure for oral identification.)	
4. Do a vocabulary check. (Follow established procedure for oral identification.)	

 PRACTICE TIME

Have students turn to page 57 in the Practice Section of their book and find Chapter 15, Lesson 1, Practice *(1-4)*. Go over the directions to make sure they understand what to do. Check and discuss the Practices after students have finished. (*Chapter 15, Lesson 1, Practice keys are given below and on the next page.*)

Chapter 15, Lesson 1, Practice 1: On notebook paper, write seven subject pronouns and seven possessive pronouns. **(Use the pronoun jingles to check students' papers.)**

CHAPTER 15 LESSON 1 CONTINUED

Chapter 15, Lesson 1, Practice 2: For each sentence, do these four things: (1) Write the subject. (2) Write **S** if the subject is singular or **P** if the subject is plural. (3) Write the rule number. (4) Underline the correct verb in the sentence.

Rule 1: A singular subject must use a singular verb form that ends in **s**: *is, was, has, does,* or verbs ending with **es**.

Rule 2: A plural subject, a compound subject, or the subject **YOU** must use a plural verb form that has **no s** ending: *are, were, do, have,* or verbs without **s** or **es** endings. (A plural verb form is also called the *plain form*.)

Subject	S or P	Rule	
raindrops	P	2	1. The **raindrops** (splashes, <u>splash</u>) in the puddle.
cat	S	1	2. The lazy **cat** (<u>yawns</u>, yawn) sleepily.
singers	P	2	3. The **singers** (smiles, <u>smile</u>) at the audience.
container	S	1	4. The **container** of salt (spill, <u>spills</u>) on the floor.
you	P	2	5. **You** (cuts, <u>cut</u>) the page in half.

Chapter 15, Lesson 1, Practice 3: Underline the correct homonym in each sentence.

1. The child ignored his mother's (<u>counsel</u>, council).
2. (There, <u>They're</u>) helping at the banquet.
3. They brought (<u>their</u>, they're) own lunch.
4. The deli is located over (their, <u>there</u>).

Chapter 15, Lesson 1, Practice 4: Correct the capitalization and punctuation mistakes. Write the rule numbers above the capitalization corrections and below the punctuation corrections. Use Reference 24 for the capitalization rules and Reference 26 for the punctuation rules. The references are located on pages 18 and 19 in your Reference Section.

```
    1   2           4   3        6            (capitalization rule numbers)
    M   I           D   L        T
1.  may i meet with dr. lewis on tuesday?     (Editing Guide: 5 capitals & 2 punctuation)
                    2            5            (punctuation rule numbers)
```

VOCABULARY TIME

Assign Chapter 15, Vocabulary Words #1 on page 7 in the Reference Section for students to define in their Vocabulary notebooks. Tell students they are to use a dictionary or thesaurus to look up the meanings of the vocabulary words.

Chapter 15, Vocabulary Words #1
(contented, dissatisfied, rehearse, practice)

(End of lesson.)

CHAPTER 15   LESSON 2

Objectives: Jingles, Grammar (Practice Sentences), Skill (Making Nouns Possessive), Practice Exercise, and Vocabulary #2.

 **JINGLE TIME**

Have students turn to the Jingle Section in their books and recite the previously-taught jingles.

 GRAMMAR TIME

Put the Practice Sentences from the box below on the board or on notebook paper. Use these sentences as you practice the concepts that have been taught.

Chapter 15, Practice Sentences for Lesson 2
1. _____ John went to Will's birthday party yesterday.
2. _____ We ate at Judy's house after the soccer game.
3. _____ Kelly's mother rode to the airport in a cab.

TEACHING SCRIPT FOR CLASSIFYING PRACTICE SENTENCES

We will classify three different sentences to practice the grammar skills in the Question and Answer Flows. We will classify the sentences together. Begin.

Question and Answer Flow for Sentence 1: John went to Will's birthday party yesterday.

1. Who went to Will's birthday party yesterday? John - SN
2. What is being said about John? John went - V
3. To - P
4. To what? party - OP
5. What kind of party? birthday - Adj
6. Whose party? Will's - PN
7. Went when? yesterday - Adv
8. SN V P1 Check
9. (To Will's birthday party) - Prepositional phrase
10. Period, statement, declarative sentence
11. Go back to the verb - divide the complete subject from the complete predicate.

```
                               SN  V  P  PN  Adj  OP   Adv
Classified Sentence:    SN V   John / went (to Will's birthday party) yesterday.  D
                        P1
```

Question and Answer Flow for Sentence 2: We ate at Judy's house after the soccer game.

1. Who ate at Judy's house after the soccer game? we - SP
2. What is being said about we? we ate - V
3. At - P
4. At what? house - OP
5. Whose house? Judy's - PN
6. After - P
7. After what? game - OP
8. What kind of game? soccer - Adj
9. The - A
10. SN V P1 Check
11. (At Judy's house) - Prepositional phrase
12. (After the soccer game) - Prepositional phrase
13. Period, statement, declarative sentence
14. Go back to the verb - divide the complete subject from the complete predicate.

```
                               SP  V  P  PN  OP   P  A  Adj  OP
Classified Sentence:    SN V   We / ate (at Judy's house) (after the soccer game).  D
                        P1
```

CHAPTER 15 LESSON 2 CONTINUED

Question and Answer Flow for Sentence 3: Kelly's mother rode to the airport in a cab.

1. Who rode to the airport in a cab? mother - SN
2. What is being said about mother? mother rode - V
3. To - P
4. To what? airport - OP
5. The - A
6. In - P
7. In what? cab - OP
8. A - A
9. Whose mother? Kelly's - PN
10. SN V P1 Check
11. (To the airport) - Prepositional phrase
12. (In a cab) - Prepositional phrase
13. Period, statement, declarative sentence
14. Go back to the verb - divide the complete subject from the complete predicate.

Classified Sentence:

SN V P1   PN   SN   V P A   OP   P A OP
           Kelly's mother / rode (to the airport) (in a cab). D

SKILL TIME

TEACHING SCRIPT FOR MAKING NOUNS POSSESSIVE

You have just learned how to recognize and classify a possessive noun. You know that a possessive noun shows ownership and has an apostrophe to help us identify it. Today, we will learn more about making nouns possessive. This skill is really simple, but, again, students and adults alike have a lot of trouble with it when they write if they do not know the rules. The more practice you have in making nouns possessive, the more likely you will use possessive nouns correctly in your writing.

You already know that a possessive noun has an apostrophe. In order to form possessive nouns correctly, you must first decide if the noun is singular or plural before you add the apostrophe. After you know whether a noun is singular or plural, you can then use three rules to tell you how to place the apostrophe to make the noun possessive.

Look at Reference 28 on page 20 in the Reference Section of your book and follow along as we go through the three rules and practice samples. (*The information and practice samples are reproduced for you below.*) Remember, we always read the directions first. Listen carefully because we have several things to do.

Reference 28: Making Nouns Possessive		
1. For a singular noun - add (**'s**) Rule 1: **girl's**	2. For a plural noun that ends in **s** - add (**'**) Rule 2: **girls'**	3. For a plural noun that does not end in **s** - add (**'s**) Rule 3: **women's**
Use the following guidelines to make each noun possessive. First, identify each noun as singular or plural by writing **S** or **P** in the first blank. Next, write the correct rule number from the list above in the second blank. Finally, write the possessive form of each noun as singular possessive or as plural possessive.		

Noun	S-P	Rule	Singular Possessive	Plural Possessive
1. pelican	S	1	**pelican's**	
2. students	P	2		**students'**
3. Ashley	S	1	**Ashley's**	
4. firemen	P	3		**firemen's**

CHAPTER 15 LESSON 2 CONTINUED

I will use the information in Reference 28 to explain what you will do as you learn to make nouns possessive. First, you identify each noun as singular or plural by writing **S** or **P** in the first blank. Is *pelican* singular or plural? (*Singular*) Since the word *pelican* is singular, the letter **S** is written in the blank under the column marked **S-P**.

Next, we will look at the three rules for making nouns possessive. (*Discuss the three rules and the example given for each one.*) Which rule do we use since *pelican* is singular? (*Rule 1*) A number 1 is written in the blank under the column marked *Rule*. What does Rule 1 tell us to do? (*For a singular noun, add an apostrophe and s.*)

Finally, we are asked to write the possessive form of each noun either as singular possessive or as plural possessive. This is easy since you have already determined whether the noun is singular or plural. The singular possessive noun *pelican's* is written under the column marked *Singular Possessive*. (*Work through the rest of the nouns in the same way to make sure your students understand how to use the rule box for making nouns possessive.*)

 PRACTICE TIME

Have students turn to page 58 in the Practice Section of their book and find Chapter 15, Lesson 2, Practice. Go over the directions to make sure they understand what to do. Check and discuss the Practice after students have finished. (*Chapter 15, Lesson 2, Practice key is given below.*)

Chapter 15, Lesson 2, Practice: First, identify each noun as singular or plural by writing **S** or **P** in the first blank. Next, write the correct rule number from the list below in the second blank. Finally, write the possessive form of each noun as singular possessive or as plural possessive.

1. For a singular noun - add (**'s**) Rule 1: girl's		2. For a plural noun that ends in **s** - add (**'**) Rule 2: girls'		3. For a plural noun that does not end in **s** - add (**'s**) Rule 3: women's	
Noun	S-P	Rule	Singular Possessive		Plural Possessive
1. tree	S	1	tree's		
2. candles	P	2			candles'
3. dress	S	1	dress's		
4. postmen	P	3			postmen's

 VOCABULARY TIME

Assign Chapter 15, Vocabulary Words **#2** on page 7 in the Reference Section for students to define in their Vocabulary notebooks.

Chapter 15, Vocabulary Words #2
(crisp, soggy, performance, recital)

(End of lesson.)

CHAPTER 15   LESSON 3

Objectives: Jingles, Grammar (Practice Sentences, Practice and Improved Sentence), and Practice Exercise.

 **JINGLE TIME**

Have students turn to the Jingle Section in their books and recite the previously-taught jingles.

 GRAMMAR TIME

Put the Practice Sentences from the box below on the board or on notebook paper. Use these sentences as you practice the concepts that have been taught. For the greatest benefit, students must participate orally with the teacher.

Chapter 15, Practice Sentences for Lesson 3
1. _____ John's retirement begins tomorrow.
2. _____ We traveled on dirt roads to my grandfather's house.
3. _____ My cousin's mother works during the day at the hospital.

TEACHING SCRIPT FOR CLASSIFYING PRACTICE SENTENCES

We will classify three different sentences to practice the grammar skills in the Question and Answer Flows. We will classify the sentences together. Begin. (*You might have students write the labels above the sentences at this time.*)

Question and Answer Flow for Sentence 1: John's retirement begins tomorrow.
1. What begins tomorrow? retirement - SN   5. SN V P1 Check
2. What is being said about retirement?   6. No prepositional phrases
retirement begins - V   7. Period, statement, declarative sentence
3. Begins when? tomorrow - Adv   8. Go back to the verb - divide the complete subject
4. Whose retirement? John's - PN   from the complete predicate.
PN   SN   V   Adv
Classified Sentence: SN V   John's retirement / begins tomorrow. D
P1

CHAPTER 15 LESSON 3 CONTINUED

Question and Answer Flow for Sentence 2: We traveled on dirt roads to my grandfather's house.

1. Who traveled on dirt roads to my grandfather's house? we - SP
2. What is being said about we? we traveled - V
3. On - P
4. On what? roads - OP
5. What kind of roads? dirt - Adj
6. To - P
7. To what? house - OP
8. Whose house? grandfather's - PN
9. Whose grandfather? my - PP
10. SN V P1 Check
11. (On dirt roads) - Prepositional phrase
12. (To my grandfather's house) - Prepositional phrase
13. Period, statement, declarative sentence
14. Go back to the verb - divide the complete subject from the complete predicate.

Classified Sentence:

SN V / P1   SP V   P Adj OP   P PP PN   OP
We / traveled (on dirt roads) (to my grandfather's house). D

Question and Answer Flow for Sentence 3: My cousin's mother works during the day at the hospital.

1. Who works during the day at the hospital? mother - SN
2. What is being said about mother? mother works - V
3. During - P
4. During what? day - OP
5. The - A
6. At - P
7. At what? hospital - OP
8. The - A
9. Whose mother? cousin's - PN
10. Whose cousin? my - PP
11. SN V P1 Check
12. (During the day) - Prepositional phrase
13. (At the hospital) - Prepositional phrase
14. Period, statement, declarative sentence
15. Go back to the verb - divide the complete subject from the complete predicate.

Classified Sentence:

SN V / P1   PP PN SN   V   P A OP   P A OP
My cousin's mother / works (during the day) (at the hospital). D

TEACHING SCRIPT FOR THE PRACTICE SENTENCE

Put these labels on the board: **SP V Adv P PP PN Adj OP**

Look at the new sentence labels on the board: **SP V Adv P PP PN Adj OP**. I will guide you again through the process of writing a sentence to practice the different parts that you have learned.

Get out a sheet of notebook paper. On the top line of your notebook paper, write the title *Practice Sentence*. Copy the sentence labels from the board onto your notebook paper. Be sure to leave plenty of writing space between each label. I will guide you through the process you will use whenever you write a Practice Sentence with possessive pronouns and possessive nouns.

CHAPTER 15 LESSON 3 CONTINUED

1. Go to the **SP** label for the subject pronoun. Repeat the Subject Pronoun Jingle to help you think of a pronoun that you want to use as your subject. Write the pronoun you have chosen on the line *under* the **SP** label.

2. Go to the **V** label for the verb. Think of a verb that tells what your subject does. Make sure that your verb makes sense with the subject pronoun. Write the verb you have chosen on the line *under* the **V** label.

3. Go to the **Adv** label for the adverb. Immediately go to the verb in your sentence and ask an adverb question. What are the adverb questions? (*How, When, Where*) Choose one adverb question to ask and write your adverb answer *under* the **Adv** label.

4. Go to the **P** label for the preposition. Think of a preposition word that tells something about your verb. You must be careful to choose a preposition word that makes sense with the noun you will choose for the object of the preposition in your next step. Write the word you have chosen for a preposition *under* the **P** label.

5. Go to the **OP** label for the object of the preposition. If you like the noun you thought of while thinking of a preposition, write it down under the **OP** label. If you prefer, think of another noun by asking **what** or **whom** after your preposition. Check to make sure the preposition and object of the preposition make sense together and also make sense with the rest of the sentence. Remember, the object of the preposition will always answer the question **what** or **whom** after the preposition. Write the word you have chosen for the object of the preposition *under* the **OP** label.

6. Go to the **Adj** label for the adjective. Go to the object of the preposition that you just wrote and ask an adjective question to describe the object-of-the-preposition noun. What are the adjective questions? (*What kind, Which one, How many*) Choose one adjective question to ask and write your adjective answer *under* the **Adj** label next to the object of the preposition. Always check to make sure your answers are making sense in the sentence.

7. Go to the **PN** label for the possessive noun that is part of your prepositional phrase. Think of a possessive noun that answers "whose" when you refer to the object-of-the-preposition noun. Make sure the possessive noun makes sense in your sentence. Also, make sure you write the apostrophe correctly as you write the possessive noun you have chosen *under* the **PN** label.

8. Go to the **PP** label for the possessive pronoun that is part of your prepositional phrase. Repeat the Possessive Pronoun Jingle to help you think of a pronoun that you want to use as your possessive pronoun. Now, you will choose one of the possessive pronouns that makes the best sense in your sentence. Write the possessive pronoun you have chosen *under* the **PP** label.

9. Finally, check your Practice Sentence to make sure it has the necessary parts to be a complete sentence. What are the five parts of a complete sentence? (*subject, verb, complete sense, capital letter, and an end mark*) Does your Practice Sentence have the five parts of a complete sentence? (*Allow time for students to read over their sentences and to make any corrections they need to make.*)

CHAPTER 15 LESSON 3 CONTINUED

TEACHING SCRIPT FOR THE IMPROVED SENTENCE

Under your Practice Sentence, write the title *Improved Sentence* on another line. To improve your Practice Sentence, you will make two synonym changes, one antonym change, and your choice of a complete word change or another synonym or antonym change.

Since it is harder to find words that can be changed to an antonym, it is usually wise to go through your sentence to find an antonym change first. Then, look through your sentence again to find words that can be improved with synonyms. Finally, make a decision about whether your last change will be a complete word change, another synonym change, or another antonym change. I will give you time to write your Improved Sentence. *(After students have finished, check and discuss students' Practice and Improved Sentences.)*

 PRACTICE TIME

Now, have students turn to page 58 in the Practice Section of their book and find Chapter 15, Lesson 3, Practice *(1-2)*. Go over the directions to make sure they understand what to do. Check and discuss the Practices after students have finished. Discuss strong areas as well as weak areas. *(Chapter 15, Lesson 3, Practice keys are given below.)*

Chapter 15, Lesson 3, Practice 1: Number 1-9 on a sheet of paper. Write the answers to the questions listed below.

1. What are the three article adjectives? **a, an, the**
2. What is an exclamatory sentence? **strong feeling**
3. What is a declarative sentence? **a statement**
4. What is an interrogative sentence? **a question**
5. What punctuation mark does a possessive noun always have? **an apostrophe (')**
6. What is the abbreviation used for a possessive noun? **PN**
7. What is the definition of a pronoun? **A pronoun takes the place of a noun**.
8. Name the seven subject pronouns. **I, we, he, she, it, they, you**
9. Name the seven possessive pronouns. **my, our, his, her, its, their, your**

Chapter 15, Lesson 3, Practice 2: First, identify each noun as singular or plural by writing **S** or **P** in the first blank. Next, write the correct rule number from the list below in the second blank. Finally, write the possessive form of each noun as singular possessive or as plural possessive.

1. For a singular noun - add ('s) Rule 1: girl's		2. For a plural noun that ends in *s* - add (') Rule 2: girls'	3. For a plural noun that does not end in *s* - add ('s) Rule 3: women's
Noun	**S-P**	**Rule**	**Singular Possessive**	**Plural Possessive**
1. man	S	1	man's	
2. nurses	P	2		nurses'
3. women	P	3		women's
4. shadow	S	1	shadow's	
5. Austin	S	1	Austin's	
6. pillows	P	2		pillows'

(End of lesson.)

CHAPTER 15   LESSON 4

Objectives: Jingles, Study, Test, Check, Writing (Journal), and State Activity.

 JINGLE TIME

Have students turn to the Jingle Section in their books and recite the previously-taught jingles.

 STUDY TIME

Have students study the vocabulary words in their vocabulary notebooks. Remind students that any vocabulary word in their notebooks could be on their test. Also, have students study any of the skills in the Practice Section that they need to review.

 TEST TIME

Have students turn to page 94 in the Test Section of their book and find Chapter 15 Test. Go over the directions to make sure they understand what to do. *(Chapter 15 Test key is on the next page.)*

 CHECK TIME

After students have finished, check and discuss their test papers. Make sure they understand why their answers are right or wrong. *(For total points, count each required answer as a point.)*

 STATE ACTIVITY TIME

Students will continue to draw or trace the states and to write the following questions and answers.

Massachusetts	Michigan
1. What is the state on the front of this card? **Massachusetts**	1. What is the state on the front of this card? **Michigan**
2. What is the capital of Massachusetts? **Boston**	2. What is the capital of Michigan? **Lansing**
3. What is the postal abbreviation of Massachusetts? **MA**	3. What is the postal abbreviation of Michigan? **MI**

Color these states. Use the cards to quiz family members, friends, and relatives. You may want to time the responses to your questions.

(End of lesson.)

Level 2—Shurley English—Homeschool Edition

Chapter 15 Test
(Student Page 94)

Exercise 1: Classify each sentence.

```
         SP  V    Adv    P   PN   Adj    OP
1. SN V   I / went willingly (to Susan's dance recital).   D
   P1

         PP  SN      V  P PP  PN   Adj   OP
2. SN V   My neighbor / ate (at my mom's new restaurant).   D
   P1
```

Exercise 2: Use Sentence 2 to underline the complete subject once and the complete predicate twice and to complete the table below.

List the Noun Used	List the Noun Job	Singular or Plural	Common or Proper	Simple Subject	Simple Predicate
1. **neighbor**	2. **SN**	3. **S**	4. **C**	5. **neighbor**	6. **ate**
7. **restaurant**	8. **OP**	9. **S**	10. **C**		

Exercise 3: Name the six parts of speech that you have studied. (*You may use abbreviations.*)
(The order of answers may vary.)

1. **noun**   2. **verb**   3. **adjective**   4. **adverb**   5. **preposition**   6. **pronoun**

Exercise 4: Identify each pair of words as synonyms or antonyms by putting parentheses ( ) around *syn* or *ant*.

1. burrow, tunnel	**(syn)** ant	4. senior, junior	syn **(ant)**	7. practice, rehearse	**(syn)** ant
2. crisp, soggy	syn **(ant)**	5. begin, retire	syn **(ant)**	8. contented, dissatisfied	syn **(ant)**
3. advice, counsel	**(syn)** ant	6. appear, emerge	**(syn)** ant	9. performance, recital	**(syn)** ant

Exercise 5: Use the following guidelines to make each noun possessive. First, identify each noun as singular or plural by writing **S** or **P** in the first blank. Next, write the correct rule number from the list below in the second blank. Finally, write the possessive form of each noun as singular possessive or as plural possessive.

1. For a singular noun - add (**'s**) Rule 1: girl's		2. For a plural noun that ends in *s* - add (**'**) Rule 2: girls'		3. For a plural noun that does not end in *s* - add (**'s**) Rule 3: women's	
Noun	**S-P**	**Rule**	**Singular Possessive**	**Plural Possessive**	
1. bulbs	P	2		bulbs'	
2. jelly	S	1	jelly's		
3. women	P	3		women's	
4. Ben	S	1	Ben's		
5. man	S	1	man's		
6. knives	P	2		knives'	

Exercise 6: On notebook paper, write seven subject pronouns and seven possessive pronouns.

Exercise 7: In your journal, write a paragraph summarizing what you have learned this week.

CHAPTER 15 LESSON 4 CONTINUED

TEACHER INSTRUCTIONS

Use the Question and Answer Flows below for the sentences on the Chapter 15 Test.

Question and Answer Flow for Sentence 1: I went willingly to Susan's dance recital.

1. Who went willingly to Susan's dance recital? I - SP
2. What is being said about I? I went - V
3. Went how? willingly - Adv
4. To - P
5. To what? recital - OP
6. What kind of recital? dance - Adj
7. Whose recital? Susan's - PN
8. SN V P1 Check
9. (To Susan's dance recital) - Prepositional phrase
10. Period, statement, declarative sentence
11. Go back to the verb - divide the complete subject from the complete predicate.

```
                         SP  V    Adv   P    PN     Adj   OP
Classified Sentence:  SN V    I / went willingly (to Susan's dance recital).  D
                      P1
```

Question and Answer Flow for Sentence 2: My neighbor ate at my mom's new restaurant.

1. Who ate at my mom's new restaurant? neighbor - SN
2. What is being said about neighbor? neighbor ate - V
3. At - P
4. At what? restaurant - OP
5. What kind of restaurant? new - Adj
6. Whose restaurant? mom's - PN
7. Whose mom? my - PP
8. Whose neighbor? my - PP
9. SN V P1 Check
10. (At my mom's new restaurant) - Prepositional phrase
11. Period, statement, declarative sentence
12. Go back to the verb - divide the complete subject from the complete predicate.

```
                         PP     SN    V   P  PP   PN    Adj   OP
Classified Sentence:  SN V    My neighbor / ate (at my mom's new restaurant).  D
                      P1
```

Level 2—Shurley English—Homeschool Edition

CHAPTER 15   LESSON 5
Objectives: Writing (Three-Point Expository Paragraph), Writing Assignment #9, and Sentence Time.

 **WRITING TIME**

TEACHING SCRIPT FOR INTRODUCING THE THREE-POINT EXPOSITORY PARAGRAPH

In this writing lesson, you will learn how to write a three-point expository paragraph. Remember, **expository paragraphs** give facts or directions, explain ideas, or define words. Any time you write an expository paragraph, you should focus on making your meaning clear and understandable. The three-point paragraph is basically like the two-point paragraph except that there are three points instead of two. This means that a three-point paragraph will have two more sentences: a third-point sentence and a supporting sentence for that point. These two new sentences will come right before the concluding sentence.

Now, we will make a comparison between the two-point expository paragraph and the three-point expository paragraph. Look at Reference 29 on page 20. (*Read and discuss the two guidelines, showing students the similarities and differences.*)

Reference 29: Two- and Three-Point Expository Paragraph Guidelines	
2-Point Expository Paragraph Guidelines	**3-Point Expository Paragraph Guidelines**
Paragraph (7 sentences) A. Topic sentence B. A two-point sentence C. A **first-point sentence** D. A **supporting** sentence for the first point E. A **second-point sentence** F. A **supporting** sentence for the second point G. A concluding sentence	Paragraph (9 sentences) A. Topic sentence B. A three-point sentence C. A **first-point sentence** D. A **supporting** sentence for the first point E. A **second-point sentence** F. A **supporting** sentence for the second point G. A **third-point sentence** H. A **supporting** sentence for the third point I. A concluding sentence

Now look at Reference 30 on page 21. Follow the three-point expository paragraph guideline and sample paragraph at the bottom of Reference 30 as I go over the steps in writing a three-point expository paragraph. (*Read the steps and examples provided on the next page as students follow the guidelines for a three-point expository paragraph in Reference 30.*)

CHAPTER 15 LESSON 5 CONTINUED

Reference 30: Three-Point Expository Paragraph Example

Topic: **My favorite animals**
Three main points: 1. **frogs**   2. **koalas**   3. **whales**

Sentence #1 – <u>Topic Sentence</u> (*Use words in the topic and tell how many points will be used.*)
I have three favorite animals.

Sentence #2 – <u>3-Point Sentence</u> (*List the 3 points in the order you will present them.*)
These animals are frogs, koalas, and whales.

Sentence #3 – <u>First Point</u>
My first favorite animal is a frog.

Sentence #4 – <u>Supporting Sentence</u> for the first point
I like frogs because they are so funny when they hop around.

Sentence #5 – <u>Second Point</u>
My second favorite animal is a koala.

Sentence #6 – <u>Supporting Sentence</u> for the second point
I like koalas because they are excellent tree climbers.

Sentence #7 – <u>Third Point</u>
My third favorite animal is a whale.

Sentence #8 – <u>Supporting Sentence</u> for the third point
I think whales are enormous ballerinas in the water.

Sentence #9 – <u>Concluding (final) Sentence</u> (*Restate the topic sentence and add an extra thought.*)
My three favorite animals are very fascinating creatures.

SAMPLE PARAGRAPH

My Favorite Animals

    I have three favorite animals. These animals are frogs, koalas, and whales. My first favorite animal is a frog. I like frogs because they are so funny when they hop around. My second favorite animal is a koala. I like koalas because they are excellent tree climbers. My third favorite animal is a whale. I think whales are enormous ballerinas in the water. My three favorite animals are very fascinating creatures.

General Checklist: Check the Finished Paragraph	The Three-Point Expository Paragraph Outline
(1) Have you followed the pattern for a 3-point paragraph? (*Indent, topic sentence, 3-point sentence, 3 main points, 3 supporting sentences, and a concluding sentence.*)	Topic 3 points about the topic Sentence #1: **Topic** sentence Sentence #2: A **three-point** sentence
(2) Do you have complete sentences?	Sentence #3: A **first-point sentence**
(3) Have you capitalized the first word and put an end mark at the end of every sentence?	Sentence #4: A **supporting** sentence for the 1st point
(4) Have you checked your sentences for capitalization and punctuation mistakes?	Sentence #5: A **second-point sentence** Sentence #6: A **supporting** sentence for the 2nd point
(5) Have you checked for misspelled words and incorrect homonym choices?	Sentence #7: A **third-point sentence** Sentence #8: A **supporting** sentence for the 3rd point
(6) Have you indented each paragraph?	Sentence #9: A **concluding** sentence

Level 2—Shurley English—Homeschool Edition

CHAPTER 15 LESSON 5 CONTINUED

<u>*TEACHER INSTRUCTIONS FOR WRITING ASSIGNMENT #9*</u>

Give Writing Assignment #9 from the box below. Remind students to follow the Writing Guidelines as they prepare their writings.

Writing Assignment Box

Writing Assignment #9: Three-Point Expository Paragraph

Writing topic choices: Things I Like About Myself   or   My Favorite Foods   or   My Favorite Movies

---

SENTENCE TIME

Chapter 15, Lesson 5, Sentence: Use colored markers to match each label with the correct sentence part by drawing a line from one to the other. Then, use the labels to arrange the sentence parts into a sentence that you will write on the sentence line below. *(The order of the words in your sentence should be in the same sequence as the vertical list of sentence labels.)* Create other labels and scrambled sentence parts on notebook paper for family members to solve. You may color code the sentence parts. *(See page 113 in the student book.)*

Labels for Order of Sentence	Scrambled Sentence Parts
SP	Grandmother's
V	for
Adv	arrival
P	we
PN	anxiously
OP	after
P	waited
A	snowstorm
OP	the

Sentence: We waited anxiously for Grandmother's arrival after the snowstorm.

(End of lesson.)

CHAPTER 16   LESSON 1

Objectives: Jingles, Grammar (Practice Sentences, Skill Builder Check), Practice Exercise, and Vocabulary #1.

 **JINGLE TIME**

Have students turn to the Jingle Section in their books and recite the previously-taught jingles.

 GRAMMAR TIME

Put the Practice Sentences from the box below on the board or on notebook paper. Use these sentences as you practice the concepts that have been taught. For the greatest benefit, students must participate orally with the teacher.

Chapter 16, Practice Sentences for Lesson 1
1. _____ The mechanic looked under the car's hood.
2. _____ Our mother drove along the coast in her new car.
3. _____ Her brother's thumb stuck in the spokes of his bicycle.

TEACHING SCRIPT FOR CLASSIFYING PRACTICE SENTENCES

We will classify three different sentences to practice the grammar skills in the Question and Answer Flows. We will classify the sentences together. Begin. (*You might have students write the labels above the sentences at this time.*)

Question and Answer Flow for Sentence 1: The mechanic looked under the car's hood.	
1. Who looked under the car's hood? mechanic - SN	7. The - A
2. What is being said about mechanic? mechanic looked - V	8. SN V P1 Check
	9. (Under the car's hood) - Prepositional phrase
3. Under - P	10. Period, statement, declarative sentence
4. Under what? hood - OP	11. Go back to the verb - divide the complete subject
5. Whose hood? car's - PN	from the complete predicate.
6. The - A	

```
                          A    SN    V      P   A   PN   OP
Classified Sentence:   SN V    The mechanic / looked (under the car's hood).  D
                       P1
```

Level 2 Homeschool Teacher's Manual

CHAPTER 16 LESSON 1 CONTINUED

Question and Answer Flow for Sentence 2: Our mother drove along the coast in her new car.

1. Who drove along the coast in her new car? mother - SN
2. What is being said about mother? mother drove - V
3. Along - P
4. Along what? coast - OP
5. The - A
6. In - P
7. In what? car - OP
8. What kind of car? new - Adj
9. Whose car? her - PP
10. Whose mother? our - PP
11. SN V P1 Check
12. (Along the coast) - Prepositional phrase
13. (In her new car) - Prepositional phrase
14. Period, statement, declarative sentence
15. Go back to the verb - divide the complete subject from the complete predicate.

Classified Sentence:

SN V / P1

PP SN V P A OP P PP Adj OP
Our mother / drove (along the coast) (in her new car). D

Question and Answer Flow for Sentence 3: Her brother's thumb stuck in the spokes of his bicycle.

1. What stuck in the spokes of his bicycle? thumb - SN
2. What is being said about thumb? thumb stuck - V
3. In - P
4. In what? spokes - OP
5. The - A
6. Of - P
7. Of what? bicycle - OP
8. Whose bicycle? his - PP
9. Whose thumb? brother's - PN
10. Whose brother? her - PP
11. SN V P1 Check
12. (In the spokes) - Prepositional phrase
13. (Of his bicycle) - Prepositional phrase
14. Period, statement, declarative sentence
15. Go back to the verb - divide the complete subject from the complete predicate.

Classified Sentence:

SN V / P1

PP PN SN V P A OP P PP OP
Her brother's thumb / stuck (in the spokes) (of his bicycle). D

Use Sentences 1-3 that you just classified with your students to do a Skill Builder Check. Use the guidelines below.

Skill Builder Check

1. **Noun check.**
   (Say the job and then say the noun. Circle each noun.)
2. **Identify the nouns as singular or plural.**
   (Write **S** or **P** above each noun.)
3. **Identify the nouns as common or proper.**
   (Follow established procedure for oral identification.)
4. **Do a vocabulary check.**
   (Follow established procedure for oral identification.)
5. **Identify the complete subject and the complete predicate.** (Underline the complete subject once and the complete predicate twice.)
6. **Identify the simple subject and simple predicate.**
   (Underline the simple subject once and the simple predicate twice. Bold, or highlight, the lines to distinguish them from the complete subject and complete predicate.)

CHAPTER 16 LESSON 1 CONTINUED

PRACTICE TIME

Have students turn to page 59 in the Practice Section of their book and find Chapter 16, Lesson 1, Practice (1-2). Go over the directions to make sure they understand what to do. Check and discuss the Practices after students have finished. *(Chapter 16, Lesson 1, Practice keys are given below.)*

Chapter 16, Lesson 1, Practice 1: First, identify each noun as singular or plural by writing **S** or **P** in the first blank. Next, write the correct rule number from the list below in the second blank. Finally, write the possessive form of each noun as singular possessive or as plural possessive.

1. For a singular noun - add (**'s**) Rule 1: girl's	2. For a plural noun that ends in **s** - add (**'**) Rule 2: girls'	3. For a plural noun that does not end in **s** - add (**'s**) Rule 3: women's

Noun	S-P	Rule	Singular Possessive	Plural Possessive
1. king	S	1	king's	
2. olives	P	2		olives'
3. Matthew	S	1	Matthew's	
4. costume	S	1	costume's	
5. children	P	3		children's
6. sleeves	P	2		sleeves'

Chapter 16, Lesson 1, Practice 2: Correct the capitalization and punctuation mistakes. Write the rule numbers above the capitalization corrections and below the punctuation corrections. Use Reference 24 for the capitalization rules and Reference 26 for the punctuation rules. The references are located on pages 18 and 19 in your Reference Section.

```
    1(or 2)            3              (capitalization rule numbers)
      I                P
1.  i  have  a  rabbit  named  peter.   (Editing Guide: 2 capitals & 1 punctuation)
                                 5      (punctuation rule numbers)
```

VOCABULARY TIME

Assign Chapter 16, Vocabulary Words **#1** on page 7 in the Reference Section for students to define in their Vocabulary notebooks. Tell students they are to use a dictionary or thesaurus to look up the meanings of the vocabulary words.

Chapter 16, Vocabulary Words #1
(coast, shore, edge, middle)

(End of lesson.)

Level 2—Shurley English—Homeschool Edition

CHAPTER 16   LESSON 2
Objectives: Jingles, Grammar (Practice Sentences), Skill (Introduce Contractions), Practice Exercise, and Vocabulary #2.

 **JINGLE TIME**

Have students turn to the Jingle Section in their books and recite the previously-taught jingles.

 GRAMMAR TIME

Put the Practice Sentences from the box below on the board or on notebook paper. Use these sentences as you practice the concepts that have been taught. For the greatest benefit, students must participate orally with the teacher.

Chapter 16, Practice Sentences for Lesson 2
1. _____ The exchange student stayed at my teacher's house.
2. _____ Dad's boss fell off a ladder at his house yesterday.
3. _____ Billy's purple crayon broke during art time.

TEACHING SCRIPT FOR CLASSIFYING PRACTICE SENTENCES

We will classify three different sentences to practice the grammar skills in the Question and Answer Flows. We will classify the sentences together. Begin. (*You might have students write the labels above the sentences at this time.*)

Question and Answer Flow for Sentence 1: The exchange student stayed at my teacher's house.
1. Who stayed at my teacher's house? student - SN
2. What is being said about student? student stayed - V
3. At - P
4. At what? house - OP
5. Whose house? teacher's - PN
6. Whose teacher? my - PP
7. What kind of student? exchange - Adj
8. The - A
9. SN V P1 Check
10. (At my teacher's house) - Prepositional phrase
11. Period, statement, declarative sentence
12. Go back to the verb - divide the complete subject from the complete predicate.
A   Adj   SN   V   P PP   PN   OP
Classified Sentence: SN V   The exchange student / stayed (at my teacher's house).   D
P1

CHAPTER 16 LESSON 2 CONTINUED

Question and Answer Flow for Sentence 2: Dad's boss fell off a ladder at his house yesterday.

1. Who fell off a ladder at his house yesterday? boss - SN
2. What is being said about boss? boss fell - V
3. Off - P
4. Off what? ladder - OP
5. A - A
6. At - P
7. At what? house - OP
8. Whose house? his - PP
9. Fell when? yesterday - Adv
10. Whose boss? Dad's - PN
11. SN V P1 Check
12. (Off a ladder) - Prepositional phrase
13. (At his house) - Prepositional phrase
14. Period, statement, declarative sentence
15. Go back to the verb - divide the complete subject from the complete predicate.

Classified Sentence:

```
                        PN   SN   V  P A  OP  P PP  OP    Adv
        SN V     Dad's boss / fell (off a ladder) (at his house) yesterday.  D
        P1
```

Question and Answer Flow for Sentence 3: Billy's purple crayon broke during art time.

1. What broke during art time? crayon - SN
2. What is being said about crayon? crayon broke - V
3. During - P
4. During what? time - OP
5. What kind of time? art - Adj
6. Which crayon? purple - Adj
7. Whose crayon? Billy's - PN
8. SN V P1 Check
9. (During art time) - Prepositional phrase
10. Period, statement, declarative sentence
11. Go back to the verb - divide the complete subject from the complete predicate.

Classified Sentence:

```
                        PN   Adj   SN    V    P  Adj  OP
        SN V     Billy's purple crayon / broke (during art time).  D
        P1
```

SKILL TIME

TEACHING SCRIPT FOR INTRODUCING CONTRACTIONS

The next skill you will learn is contractions. Contractions are not hard, but you need a lot of practice in writing and using them correctly. A contraction is two words shortened into one word, and the new word always has an apostrophe. The apostrophe takes the place of the letters that have been left out.

When we worked with homonyms, you learned how important it was to choose the correct word. You had to constantly be aware of the spelling of certain words and their meanings. This will still be important as you work with contractions. You must know how to spell contractions correctly and which contraction is correct. And, of course, some contractions can be confused with possessive pronouns, so you must always be aware of the right choices.

Look at Reference 31 on page 22. This is a list of contractions and their meanings according to their verb families. Notice that the contraction chart is also divided into three columns. We will work with one column at a time at the beginning so you will not have so many contractions at once.

We will work with Column 1 today. Using only Column 1, I want you to repeat with me the words from which the contraction is made and then repeat the contraction. (*Go over all the contractions in Column 1 in this manner. This will help your students see them, say them, and hear them correctly. Develop a singsong chant that has enough rhythm to sound good and to be fun at the same time. The contraction chart is reproduced for you on the next page.*)

CHAPTER 16 LESSON 2 CONTINUED

Reference 31: Contraction Chart					
Column 1		**Column 2**		**Column 3**	
Words Contracted	Contraction	Words Contracted	Contraction	Pronoun	Contraction
AM I am	– I'm	**HAS** has not he has she has	– hasn't – he's – she's	**its** (owns) *its coat*	**it's** (it is) *it's cute*
IS is not he is she is it is who is that is what is there is	– isn't – he's – she's – it's – who's – that's – what's – there's	**HAVE** have not I have you have we have they have	– haven't – I've – you've – we've – they've	**your** (owns) *your car*	**you're** (you are) *you're right*
ARE are not you are we are they are	– aren't – you're – we're – they're	**HAD** had not I had he had she had you had we had they had	– hadn't – I'd – he'd – she'd – you'd – we'd – they'd	**their** (owns) *their house*	**they're** (they are) *they're gone*
WAS, WERE was not were not	– wasn't – weren't	**WILL, SHALL** will not I will he will she will you will we will they will	– won't – I'll – he'll – she'll – you'll – we'll – they'll	**whose** (owns) *whose cat*	**who's** (who is) *who's going*
DO, DOES, DID do not does not did not	– don't – doesn't – didn't				
CAN cannot	– can't	**WOULD** would not I would he would she would you would we would they would	– wouldn't – I'd – he'd – she'd – you'd – we'd – they'd		
LET let us	– let's	**SHOULD, COULD** should not could not	– shouldn't – couldn't		

Sentence Samples:
1. (<u>Their</u>, They're) house is new.
2. We <u>have not</u> eaten today. **haven't**
3. He <u>doesn't</u> fish often. **does not**

CHAPTER 16 LESSON 2 CONTINUED

 PRACTICE TIME

Have students turn to pages 59 and 60 in the Practice Section of their book and find Chapter 16, Lesson 2, Practice (*1-3*). Tell students that they will have only the contractions from Column 1 on this practice set today. Make sure they know to use their contraction chart to help them find answers. Go over the directions to make sure they understand what to do. Check and discuss the Practice after students have finished. (*Chapter 16, Lesson 2, Practice keys are given below.*)

Chapter 16, Lesson 2, Practice 1: Copy the following words on notebook paper. Write the correct contraction beside each word. **Key: he's, who's, there's, we're, weren't, didn't, let's, I'm, she's, they're.**
<u>Words</u>: he is, who is, there is, we are, were not, did not, let us, I am, she is, they are.

Chapter 16, Lesson 2, Practice 2: Copy the following contractions on notebook paper. Write the correct word beside each contraction. **Key: is not, it is, who is, there is, you are, was not, do not, cannot, does not, she is.**
<u>Contractions</u>: isn't, it's, who's, there's, you're, wasn't, don't, can't, doesn't, she's.

Chapter 16, Lesson 2, Practice 3: Use the following guidelines to make each noun possessive. First, identify each noun as singular or plural by writing **S** or **P** in the first blank. Next, write the correct rule number from the list below in the second blank. Finally, write the possessive form of each noun as singular possessive or as plural possessive.					
1. For a singular noun - add (**'s**) Rule 1: girl's		2. For a plural noun that ends in **s** - add (**'**) Rule 2: girls'			3. For a plural noun that does not end in **s** - add (**'s**) Rule 3: women's
Noun	S-P	Rule	Singular Possessive		Plural Possessive
1. stems	P	2			stems'
2. visitors	P	2			visitors'
3. wagon	S	1	wagon's		
4. children	P	3			children's
5. waitress	S	1	waitress's		
6. Allen	S	1	Allen's		

 VOCABULARY TIME

Assign Chapter 16, Vocabulary Words **#2** on page 7 in the Reference Section for students to define in their Vocabulary notebooks. Tell students they are to use a dictionary or thesaurus to look up the meanings of the vocabulary words.

Chapter 16, Vocabulary Words #2
(awaited, unexpected, favorite, preferred)

(End of lesson.)

Level 2—Shurley English—Homeschool Edition

CHAPTER 16   LESSON 3
Objectives: Jingles, Grammar (Practice Sentences, Practice and Improved Sentence), Skill (More Contractions), and Practice Exercise.

 **JINGLE TIME**

Have students turn to the Jingle Section in their books and recite the previously-taught jingles.

 GRAMMAR TIME

Put the Practice Sentences from the box below on the board or on notebook paper. Use these sentences as you practice the concepts that have been taught. For the greatest benefit, students must participate orally with the teacher.

Chapter 16, Practice Sentences for Lesson 3
1. _____ Jim's bicycle tire rolled over a broken bottle in the street.
2. _____ Kevin's wife walks during lunch for her exercise.
3. _____ The wild duck ate from my dad's hand!

TEACHING SCRIPT FOR CLASSIFYING PRACTICE SENTENCES

We will classify three different sentences to practice the grammar skills in the Question and Answer Flows. We will classify the sentences together. Begin. (*You might have students write the labels above the sentences at this time.*)

Question and Answer Flow for Sentence 1: Jim's bicycle tire rolled over a broken bottle in the street.
1. What rolled over a broken bottle in the street? tire - SN   10. What kind of tire? bicycle - Adj
2. What is being said about tire? tire rolled - V   11. Whose tire? Jim's - PN
3. Over - P   12. SN V P1 Check
4. Over what? bottle - OP   13. (Over a broken bottle) - Prepositional phrase
5. What kind of bottle? broken - Adj   14. (In the street) - Prepositional phrase
6. A - A   15. Period, statement, declarative sentence
7. In - P   16. Go back to the verb - divide the complete
8. In what? street - OP   subject from the complete predicate.
9. The - A
PN   Adj   SN   V   P   A Adj   OP   P   A   OP
Classified Sentence: SN V   Jim's bicycle tire / rolled (over a broken bottle) (in the street).   D
P1

CHAPTER 16 LESSON 3 CONTINUED

Question and Answer Flow for Sentence 2: Kevin's wife walks during lunch for her exercise.

1. Who walks during lunch for her exercise? wife - SN
2. What is being said about wife? wife walks - V
3. During - P
4. During what? lunch - OP
5. For - P
6. For what? exercise - OP
7. Whose exercise? her - PP
8. Whose wife? Kevin's - PN
9. SN V P1 Check
10. (During lunch) - Prepositional phrase
11. (For her exercise) - Prepositional phrase
12. Period, statement, declarative sentence
13. Go back to the verb - divide the complete subject from the complete predicate.

                           PN   SN V   P   OP   P   PP   OP

Classified Sentence: SN V / P1   Kevin's wife / walks (during lunch) (for her exercise). D

Question and Answer Flow for Sentence 3: The wild duck ate from my dad's hand!

1. What ate from my dad's hand? duck - SN
2. What is being said about duck? duck ate - V
3. From - P
4. From what? hand - OP
5. Whose hand? dad's - PN
6. Whose dad? my - PP
7. What kind of duck? wild - Adj
8. The - A
9. SN V P1 Check
10. (From my dad's hand) - Prepositional phrase
11. Exclamation point, strong feeling, exclamatory sentence
12. Go back to the verb - divide the complete subject from the complete predicate.

                           A Adj SN   V   P   PP   PN   OP

Classified Sentence: SN V / P1   The wild duck / ate (from my dad's hand)! E

TEACHING SCRIPT FOR THE PRACTICE SENTENCE

                         Put these labels on the board: **SP V Adv P PP PN Adj OP**

Look at the new sentence labels on the board: **SP V Adv P PP PN Adj OP**. I will guide you again through the process of writing a sentence to practice the different parts that you have learned.

Get out a sheet of notebook paper. On the top line of your notebook paper, write the title *Practice Sentence*. Copy the sentence labels from the board onto your notebook paper. Be sure to leave plenty of writing space between each label. I will guide you through the process you will use whenever you write a Practice Sentence with pronouns and possessive nouns.

1. Go to the **SP** label for the subject pronoun. Repeat the Subject Pronoun Jingle to help you think of a pronoun that you want to use as your subject. Write the pronoun you have chosen on the line *under* the **SP** label.

2. Go to the **V** label for the verb. Think of a verb that tells what your subject does. Make sure that your verb makes sense with the subject pronoun. Write the verb you have chosen on the line *under* the **V** label.

3. Go to the **Adv** label for the adverb. Immediately go to the verb in your sentence and ask an adverb question. What are the adverb questions? (*How, When, Where*) Choose one adverb question to ask and write your adverb answer *under* the **Adv** label.

CHAPTER 16 LESSON 3 CONTINUED

4. Go to the **P** label for the preposition. Think of a preposition word that tells something about your verb. You must be careful to choose a preposition word that makes sense with the noun you will choose for the object of the preposition in your next step. Write the word you have chosen for a preposition *under* the **P** label.

5. Go to the **OP** label for the object of the preposition. If you like the noun you thought of while thinking of a preposition, write it down under the **OP** label. If you prefer, think of another noun by asking **what** or **whom** after your preposition. Check to make sure the preposition and object of the preposition make sense together and also make sense with the rest of the sentence. Remember, the object of the preposition will always answer the question **what** or **whom** after the preposition. Write the word you have chosen for the object of the preposition *under* the **OP** label.

6. Go to the **Adj** label for the adjective. Go to the object of the preposition that you just wrote and ask an adjective question to describe the object-of-the-preposition noun. What are the adjective questions? (*What kind, Which one, How many*) Choose one adjective question to ask and write your adjective answer *under* the **Adj** label next to the object of the preposition. Always check to make sure your answers are making sense in the sentence.

7. Go to the **PN** label for the possessive noun that is part of your prepositional phrase. Think of a possessive noun that answers "whose" when you refer to the object of the preposition noun. Make sure the possessive noun makes sense in your sentence. Also, make sure you write the apostrophe correctly as you write the possessive noun you have chosen *under* the **PN** label.

8. Go to the **PP** label for the possessive pronoun that is part of your prepositional phrase. Repeat the Possessive Pronoun Jingle to help you think of a pronoun that you want to use as your possessive pronoun. Now, you will choose one of the possessive pronouns that makes the best sense in your sentence. Write the possessive pronoun you have chosen *under* the **PP** label.

9. Finally, check your Practice Sentence to make sure it has the necessary parts to be a complete sentence. What are the five parts of a complete sentence? (*subject, verb, complete sense, capital letter, and an end mark*) Does your Practice Sentence have the five parts of a complete sentence? (*Allow time for students to read over their sentences and to make any corrections they need to make.*)

10. Under your Practice Sentence, write the title *Improved Sentence* on another line. To improve your Practice Sentence, you will make two synonym changes, one antonym change, and your choice of a complete word change or another synonym or antonym change. I will give you time to write your Improved Sentence. (*After students have finished, check and discuss students' Practice and Improved Sentences.*)

 SKILL TIME

<u>TEACHING SCRIPT FOR INTRODUCING MORE CONTRACTIONS</u>

We will work with another column of contractions today. Before we begin, I want to give you a short review. A contraction is two words shortened into one word, and the new word always contains an apostrophe. The apostrophe takes the place of the letter(s) that has(have) been left out.

CHAPTER 16 LESSON 3 CONTINUED

Look at Reference 31 on page 22 of your Reference Section. We will work with Column 2 today. Using only Column 2, I want you to repeat with me the words from which the contraction is made and then repeat the contraction. (*Go over all the contractions in Column 2 in this manner. Remember to use a sing-song chant for rhythm and fun. The contraction chart is reproduced for you on teacher's page 242.*)

You will have only the contractions from Column 2 on your practice exercises today. You must look up the answers from the contraction chart to use for your practice exercises. (*This will make sure students are learning contractions correctly.*)

 PRACTICE TIME

Have students turn to page 60 in the Practice Section of their book and find Chapter 16, Lesson 3, Practice (*1-3*). Tell students that they will have only the contractions from Column 2 on this practice set today. Make sure they know to use their contraction chart to help them find answers. Go over the directions to make sure they understand what to do. Check and discuss the Practices after students have finished. (*Chapter 16, Lesson 3, Practice keys are given below.*)

Chapter 16, Lesson 3, Practice 1: Copy the following words on notebook paper. Write the correct contraction beside each word. **Key: hasn't, she's, I've, we've, hadn't, you'd, they'd, I'll, he'll, you'll, they'll, wouldn't, she'd, shouldn't.**
Words: has not, she has, I have, we have, had not, you had, they had, I will, he will, you will, they will, would not, she would, should not.

Chapter 16, Lesson 3, Practice 2: Copy the following contractions on notebook paper. Write the correct word beside each contraction. **Key: he has, we have, he had or he would, will not, we will, you had or you would, they had or they would, could not, I will, they will, had not, have not, has not, should not.**
Contractions: he's, we've, he'd, won't, we'll, you'd, they'd, couldn't, I'll, they'll, hadn't, haven't, hasn't, shouldn't.

Chapter 16, Lesson 3, Practice 3: Use the following guidelines to make each noun possessive. First, identify each noun as singular or plural by writing **S** or **P** in the first blank. Next, write the correct rule number from the list below in the second blank. Finally, write the possessive form of each noun as singular possessive or as plural possessive.				
1. For a singular noun - add (**'s**) Rule 1: girl's		2. For a plural noun that ends in ***s*** - add (**'**) Rule 2: girls'	3. For a plural noun that does not end in ***s*** - add (**'s**) Rule 3: women's	
Noun	S-P	Rule	Singular Possessive	Plural Possessive
1. zebra	S	1	zebra's	
2. packages	P	2		packages'
3. Paul	S	1	Paul's	
4. men	P	3		men's
5. postman	S	1	postman's	

(End of lesson.)

Level 2—Shurley English—Homeschool Edition

CHAPTER 16   LESSON 4

Objectives: Jingles, Study, Test, Check, Writing (Journal), State Activity, and Oral Contraction Review.

 JINGLE TIME

Have students turn to the Jingle Section in their books and recite the previously-taught jingles.

 STUDY TIME

Have students study the vocabulary words in their vocabulary notebooks. Remind students that any vocabulary word in their notebooks could be on their test. Also, give students an Oral Contraction Review before the test. *(The review is located on page 250 of the teacher's manual.)*

 TEST TIME

Have students turn to page 95 in the Test Section of their book and find Chapter 16 Test. Remind students that the contractions are taken from columns 1 and 2 for their tests. Go over the directions to make sure they understand what to do. *(Chapter 16 Test key is on the next page.)*

 CHECK TIME

After students have finished, check and discuss their test papers. Make sure they understand why their answers are right or wrong. *(For total points, count each required answer as a point.)*

 STATE ACTIVITY TIME

Students will continue to draw or trace the states and to write the following questions and answers.

Minnesota	Mississippi
1. What is the state on the front of this card? **Minnesota**	1. What is the state on the front of this card? **Mississippi**
2. What is the capital of Minnesota? **St. Paul**	2. What is the capital of Mississippi? **Jackson**
3. What is the postal abbreviation of Minnesota? **MN**	3. What is the postal abbreviation of Mississippi? **MS**

Color these states. Use the cards to quiz family members, friends, and relatives. You may want to time the responses to your questions.

(End of lesson.)

Chapter 16 Test
(Student Page 95)

Exercise 1: Classify each sentence.

```
            SP    V     Adv   P  A    Adj       Adj    OP      P          PN        OP
1. SN V     She / looked sadly (at the broken tree limbs) (in Grandmother's backyard).  D
   P1
```

```
            A   Adj    SN          V   P  A    PN      Adj    OP
2. SN V     The kind babysitter / smiled (at the children's funny jokes).  D
   P1
```

Exercise 2: Use Sentence 1 to underline the complete subject once and the complete predicate twice and to complete the table below.

List the Noun Used	List the Noun Job	Singular or Plural	Common or Proper	Simple Subject	Simple Predicate
1. limbs	2. OP	3. P	4. C	5. she	6. looked
7. backyard	8. OP	9. S	10. C		

Exercise 3: Name the six parts of speech that you have studied. (*You may use abbreviations.*)
(The order of answers may vary.)

1. noun   2. verb   3. adjective   4. adverb   5. preposition   6. pronoun

Exercise 4: Identify each pair of words as synonyms or antonyms by putting parentheses ( ) around *syn* or *ant*.

1. practice, rehearse	(syn) ant	4. crisp, soggy	syn (ant)	7. unexpected, awaited	syn (ant)
2. unsteady, stable	syn (ant)	5. middle, edge	syn (ant)	8. dissatisfied, contented	syn (ant)
3. favorite, preferred	(syn) ant	6. coast, shore	(syn) ant	9. performance, recital	(syn) ant

Exercise 5: Copy the following words on notebook paper. Write the correct contraction beside each word.
Key: isn't, it's, aren't, we're, wasn't, don't, didn't, can't, let's, I'm, he's, who's, what's, weren't.
<u>Words:</u> is not, it is, are not, we are, was not, do not, did not, cannot, let us, I am, he is, who is, what is, were not.

Exercise 6: Copy the following contractions on notebook paper. Write the correct word beside each contraction.
Key: has not, could not, we had or we would, I had or I would, would not, you will, he will, they had or they would, you had or you would, had not, they have, I have, she is or she has.
<u>Contractions:</u> hasn't, couldn't, we'd, I'd, wouldn't, you'll, he'll, they'd, you'd, hadn't, they've, I've, she's.

Exercise 7: Use the following guidelines to make each noun possessive. First, identify each noun as singular or plural by writing **S** or **P** in the first blank. Next, write the correct rule number from the list below in the second blank. Finally, write the possessive form of each noun as singular possessive or as plural possessive.

1. For a singular noun - add ('s) Rule 1: girl's		2. For a plural noun that ends in *s* - add (') Rule 2: girls'		3. For a plural noun that does not end in *s* - add ('s) Rule 3: women's	
Noun	**S-P**	**Rule**	**Singular Possessive**	**Plural Possessive**	
1. donut	S	1	donut's		
2. posters	P	2		posters'	
3. children	P	3		children's	
4. Albert	S	1	Albert's		

Exercise 8: In your journal, write a paragraph summarizing what you have learned this week.

CHAPTER 16 LESSON 4 CONTINUED

TEACHER INSTRUCTIONS

Use the Question and Answer Flows below for the sentences on the Chapter 16 Test.

Question and Answer Flow for Sentence 1: She looked sadly at the broken tree limbs in Grandmother's backyard.

1. Who looked sadly at the broken tree limbs in Grandmother's backyard? she - SP
2. What is being said about she? she looked - V
3. Looked how? sadly - Adv
4. At - P
5. At what? limbs - OP
6. What kind of limbs? tree - Adj
7. What kind of limbs? broken - Adj
8. The - A
9. In - P
10. In what? backyard - OP
11. Whose backyard? Grandmother's - PN
12. SN V P1 Check
13. (At the broken tree limbs) - Prepositional phrase
14. (In Grandmother's backyard) - Prepositional phrase
15. Period, statement, declarative sentence
16. Go back to the verb - divide the complete subject from the complete predicate.

Classified Sentence:
    SN V / P1   SP   V   Adv   P   A   Adj   Adj   OP   P   PN   OP
    She / looked sadly (at the broken tree limbs) (in Grandmother's backyard). D

Question and Answer Flow for Sentence 2: The kind babysitter smiled at the children's funny jokes.

1. Who smiled at the children's funny jokes? babysitter - SN
2. What is being said about babysitter? babysitter smiled - V
3. At - P
4. At what? jokes - OP
5. What kind of jokes? funny - Adj
6. Whose jokes? children's - PN
7. The - A
8. What kind of babysitter? kind - Adj
9. The - A
10. SN V P1 Check
11. (At the children's funny jokes) - Prepositional phrase
12. Period, statement, declarative sentence
13. Go back to the verb - divide the complete subject from the complete predicate.

Classified Sentence:
    SN V / P1   A   Adj   SN   V   P   A   PN   Adj   OP
    The kind babysitter / smiled (at the children's funny jokes). D

Oral Contraction Review

Before the test, give students a review of contractions orally. In the first chart, repeat the contractions in bold and have students respond with the correct words that stand for each contraction. In the second chart, repeat the words and have students respond with the correct contractions.

Chart 1:

who's - who is	**it's** - it is	**they'll** - they will	**hasn't** - has not
hadn't - had not	**isn't** - is not	**aren't** - are not	**she's** - she is or she has
don't - do not	**you're** - you are	**we'll** - we will	**they've** - they have

Chart 2:

she has - she's	**you had** - you'd	**that is** - that's	**I will** - I'll
could not - couldn't	**did not** - didn't	**they are** - they're	**I would** - I'd
we had - we'd	**you would** - you'd	**she is** - she's	**we would** - we'd

Level 2—Shurley English—Homeschool Edition

CHAPTER 16   LESSON 5

Objectives: Writing Assignment #10 and Sentence Time.

 **WRITING TIME**

<u>TEACHER INSTRUCTIONS FOR WRITING ASSIGNMENT #10</u>

Give Writing Assignment #10 from the box below. Remind students to use the Writing Checklist in Reference 17 to check their finished writing assignment.

Read, check, and discuss Writing Assignment #10 after students have finished their final papers. Use the Writing Checklist (*Reference 17 on teacher's page 112*) as you check and discuss students' papers. Make sure students are using the checklist correctly. In the beginning, you must also check students' papers carefully for <u>form</u> mistakes. This will ensure that students are learning the three-point format correctly.

Writing Assignment Box
Writing Assignment #10: Three-Point Expository Paragraph
Writing topic choices: Things I Would Need to Be a Gardener/Carpenter   or   Different Kinds of Dinosaurs   or   My Favorite Months of the Year

 SENTENCE TIME

Chapter 16, Lesson 5, Sentence: Use colored markers to match each label with the correct sentence part by drawing a line from one to the other. Then, use the labels to arrange the sentence parts into a sentence that you will write on the sentence line below. *(The order of the words in your sentence should be in the same sequence as the vertical list of sentence labels.)* Create other labels and scrambled sentence parts on notebook paper for family members to solve. You may color code the sentence parts. *(See page 113 in the student book.)*

Labels for Order of Sentence	Scrambled Sentence Parts
PP	belonged
Adj	friend
SN	brother's
V	our
P	my
PP	to
PN	puppy
OP	new

Sentence: Our new puppy belonged to my brother's friend.

(End of lesson.)

Level 2 Homeschool Teacher's Manual

Level 2—Shurley English—Homeschool Edition

CHAPTER 17   LESSON 1
Objectives: Jingles, Grammar (Practice Sentences, Skill Builder), Skill (More Contractions), Practice Exercise, and Vocabulary #1.

 **JINGLE TIME**

Have students turn to the Jingle Section in their books and recite the previously-taught jingles.

 GRAMMAR TIME

Put the Practice Sentences from the box below on the board or on notebook paper. Use these sentences as you practice the concepts that have been taught. For the greatest benefit, students must participate orally with the teacher.

Chapter 17, Practice Sentences for Lesson 1
1. _____ My favorite teacher came to my house for my birthday party.
2. _____ The furry rabbits hopped quickly through my grandparents' yard.
3. _____ They ran to the house for a cool drink of lemonade.

TEACHING SCRIPT FOR CLASSIFYING PRACTICE SENTENCES

We will classify three different sentences to practice the grammar skills in the Question and Answer Flows. We will classify the sentences together. Begin. (*You might have students write the labels above the sentences at this time.*)

Question and Answer Flow for Sentence 1: My favorite teacher came to my house for my birthday party.
1. Who came to my house for my birthday party? teacher - SN
2. What is being said about teacher? teacher came - V
3. To - P
4. To what? house - OP
5. Whose house? my - PP
6. For - P
7. For what? party - OP
8. What kind of party? birthday - Adj
9. Whose party? my - PP
10. What kind of teacher? favorite - Adj
11. Whose teacher? my - PP
12. SN V P1 Check
13. (To my house) - Prepositional phrase
14. (For my birthday party) - Prepositional phrase
15. Period, statement, declarative sentence
16. Go back to the verb - divide the complete subject from the complete predicate.

```
                          PP   Adj    SN      V    P  PP    OP   P  PP   Adj   OP
Classified Sentence:      SN V  My favorite teacher / came (to my house) (for my birthday party).  D
                          P1
```

Page 252

CHAPTER 17 LESSON 1 CONTINUED

Question and Answer Flow for Sentence 2: The furry rabbits hopped quickly through my grandparents' yard.

1. What hopped quickly through my grandparents' yard? rabbits - SN
2. What is being said about rabbits? rabbits hopped - V
3. Hopped how? quickly - Adv
4. Through - P
5. Through what? yard - OP
6. Whose yard? grandparents' - PN
7. Whose grandparents? my - PP
8. What kind of rabbits? furry - Adj
9. The - A
10. SN V P1 Check
11. (Through my grandparents' yard) - Prepositional phrase
12. Period, statement, declarative sentence
13. Go back to the verb - divide the complete subject from the complete predicate.

```
                           A   Adj   SN        V      Adv     P    PP     PN    OP
Classified Sentence:    SN V   The furry rabbits / hopped quickly (through my grandparents' yard).  D
                        P1
```

Question and Answer Flow for Sentence 3: They ran to the house for a cool drink of lemonade.

1. Who ran to the house for a cool drink of lemonade? they - SP
2. What is being said about they? they ran - V
3. To - P
4. To what? house - OP
5. The - A
6. For - P
7. For what? drink - OP
8. What kind of drink? cool - Adj
9. A - A
10. Of - P
11. Of what? lemonade - OP
12. SN V P1 Check
13. (To the house) - Prepositional phrase
14. (For a cool drink) - Prepositional phrase
15. (Of lemonade) - Prepositional phrase
16. Period, statement, declarative sentence
17. Go back to the verb - divide the complete subject from the complete predicate.

```
                           SP    V    P  A   OP    P  A  Adj  OP    P    OP
Classified Sentence:    SN V   They / ran (to the house) (for a cool drink) (of lemonade).  D
                        P1
```

Use Sentences 1-3 that you just classified with your students to do a Skill Builder Check. Use the guidelines below.

Skill Builder Check	
1. **Noun check.** (Say the job and then say the noun. Circle each noun.)	5. **Identify the complete subject and the complete predicate.** (Underline the complete subject once and the complete predicate twice.)
2. **Identify the nouns as singular or plural.** (Write **S** or **P** above each noun.)	6. **Identify the simple subject and simple predicate.** (Underline the simple subject once and the simple predicate twice. Bold, or highlight, the lines to distinguish them from the complete subject and complete predicate.)
3. **Identify the nouns as common or proper.** (Follow established procedure for oral identification.)	
4. **Do a vocabulary check.** (Follow established procedure for oral identification.)	

Level 2—Shurley English—Homeschool Edition

CHAPTER 17 LESSON 1 CONTINUED

 SKILL TIME

TEACHING SCRIPT FOR INTRODUCING MORE CONTRACTIONS

We will work with another column of contractions today. Before we begin, I want to give you a short review again. A contraction is two words shortened into one word, and the new word always has an apostrophe. The apostrophe takes the place of the letter(s) that has/have been left out.

Look at Reference 31 on page 22 of your Reference Section. We will work with Column 3 today. Using only Column 3, I want you to repeat with me the possessive pronoun and then repeat the pronoun contraction. (*Discuss the difference between each possessive pronoun and contraction. The contraction chart is reproduced for you on teacher's page 242.*)

Since we have covered all the contractions, you must look up the answers from the contraction chart to use for your practice or test exercises. (*This will ensure that your students are learning contractions correctly.*)

 PRACTICE TIME

Have students turn to page 61 in the Practice Section of their book and find Chapter 17, Lesson 1, Practice (*1-2*). Go over the directions to make sure they understand what to do. Check and discuss the Practices after students have finished. (*Chapter 17, Lesson 1, Practice keys are given below.*)

Chapter 17, Lesson 1, Practice 1: Copy the following words on notebook paper. Write the correct contraction beside each word. **Key: let's, wasn't, there's, you've, hasn't, shouldn't, they're, you'll, I'd, won't, haven't, didn't, I'll.**
Words: let us, was not, there is, you have, has not, should not, they are, you will, I would, will not, have not, did not, I will.

Chapter 17, Lesson 1, Practice 2: Copy the following contractions on notebook paper. Write the correct word beside each contraction. **Key: it is, I am, they will, does not, did not, you are, cannot, could not, had not, who is, he is or he has, we had or we would, let us, they are, is not.**
Contractions: it's, I'm, they'll, doesn't, didn't, you're, can't, couldn't, hadn't, who's, he's, we'd, let's, they're, isn't.

 VOCABULARY TIME

Assign Chapter 17, Vocabulary Words #1 on page 7 in the Reference Section for students to define in their Vocabulary notebooks. Tell students they are to use a dictionary or thesaurus to look up the meanings of the vocabulary words.

Chapter 17, Vocabulary Words #1
(fresh, moldy, desolate, barren)

(End of lesson.)

Level 2—Shurley English—Homeschool Edition

CHAPTER 17   LESSON 2
Objectives: Jingles, Grammar (Practice Sentences), Skills (Contractions, Oral Contraction Review), Practice Exercise, Vocabulary #2, and Activity.

 **JINGLE TIME**

Have students turn to the Jingle Section in their books and recite the previously-taught jingles.

 GRAMMAR TIME

Put the Practice Sentences from the box below on the board or on notebook paper. Use these sentences as you practice the concepts that have been taught. For the greatest benefit, students must participate orally with the teacher.

Chapter 17, Practice Sentences for Lesson 2
1. _____ The twin sisters marched in the homecoming parade.
2. _____ The neighbor's dog chewed happily on my shoe.
3. _____ He lived on a high cliff above the river.

TEACHING SCRIPT FOR CLASSIFYING PRACTICE SENTENCES

We will classify three different sentences to practice the grammar skills in the Question and Answer Flows. We will classify the sentences together. Begin. (*You might have students write the labels above the sentences at this time.*)

Question and Answer Flow for Sentence 1: The twin sisters marched in the homecoming parade.
1. Who marched in the homecoming parade? sisters - SN   8. The - A
2. What is being said about sisters? sisters marched - V   9. SN V P1 Check
3. In - P   10. (In the homecoming parade) - Prepositional phrase
4. In what? parade - OP   11. Period, statement, declarative sentence
5. What kind of parade? homecoming - Adj   12. Go back to the verb - divide the complete subject from the complete predicate.
6. The - A
7. What kind of sisters? twin - Adj
A Adj SN   V   P A   Adj   OP
Classified Sentence: SN V   The twin sisters / marched (in the homecoming parade). D
P1

Level 2—Shurley English—Homeschool Edition

CHAPTER 17 LESSON 2 CONTINUED

Question and Answer Flow for Sentence 2: The neighbor's dog chewed happily on my shoe.

1. What chewed happily on my shoe? dog - SN
2. What is being said about dog? dog chewed - V
3. Chewed how? happily - Adv
4. On - P
5. On what? shoe - OP
6. Whose shoe? my - PP
7. Whose dog? neighbor's - PN
8. The - A
9. SN V P1 Check
10. (On my shoe) - Prepositional phrase
11. Period, statement, declarative sentence
12. Go back to the verb - divide the complete subject from the complete predicate.

```
                          A  PN   SN    V    Adv  P PP OP
Classified Sentence:  SN V   The neighbor's dog / chewed happily (on my shoe).  D
                      P1
```

Question and Answer Flow for Sentence 3: He lived on a high cliff above the river.

1. Who lived on a high cliff above the river? he - SP
2. What is being said about he? he lived - V
3. On - P
4. On what? cliff - OP
5. What kind of cliff? high - Adj
6. A - A
7. Above - P
8. Above what? river - OP
9. The - A
10. SN V P1 Check
11. (On a high cliff) - Prepositional phrase
12. (Above the river) - Prepositional phrase
13. Period, statement, declarative sentence
14. Go back to the verb - divide the complete subject from the complete predicate.

```
                          SP  V    P A Adj  OP     P  A  OP
Classified Sentence:  SN V   He / lived (on a high cliff) (above the river).  D
                      P1
```

 SKILL TIME

TEACHING SCRIPT FOR INTRODUCING CONTRACTIONS IN SENTENCES

Today, we will work with contractions in sentences. Turn to page 22 and look at the bottom of Reference 31 under Sentence Samples. In Column 3, we learned that you have to know the difference between possessive pronouns and contractions. This is demonstrated in sentence 1. You will have two choices in parentheses. You will underline the correct answer. *(Read and discuss sentence 1.)* The second sample shows the words from which a contraction is made. You will write the correct contraction in the blank at the end of the sentence. *(Read and discuss sentence 2).* The third sample shows a contraction in the sentence. You will write the correct words from which the contraction was made in the blank at the end of the sentence. *(Read and discuss sentence 3.)* Use the contraction chart every time you work with contractions until you know them.

Sentence Samples:
1. (**Their**, They're) house is new.
2. We have not eaten today. **haven't**
3. He doesn't fish often. **does not**

CHAPTER 17 LESSON 2 CONTINUED

Oral Contraction Review

To develop listening skills, give students a review of contractions orally. In the first chart, repeat the contractions in bold and have students respond with the correct words that stand for each contraction. In the second chart, repeat the words and have students respond with the correct contractions.

Chart 1:

haven't - have not	**I've** - I have	**we're** - we are	**shouldn't** - should not
let's - let us	**won't** - will not	**can't** - cannot	**wouldn't** - would not
you've - you have	**I'm** - I am	**doesn't** - does not	**wasn't** - was not

Chart 2:

she will - she'll	**they are** - they're	**they had** - they'd	**they would** - they'd
he would - he'd	**we have** - we've	**I will** - I'll	**he had** - he'd
were not - weren't	**what is** - what's	**you will** - you'll	**did not** - didn't

 PRACTICE TIME

Have students turn to page 61 in the Practice Section of their book and find Chapter 17, Lesson 2, Practice (*1-3*). Go over the directions to make sure they understand what to do. Check and discuss the Practices after students have finished. (*Chapter 17, Lesson 2, Practice keys are given below.*)

Chapter 17, Lesson 2, Practice 1: Copy the following words on notebook paper. Write the correct contraction beside each word. **Key: who's, what's, you're, wasn't, doesn't, let's, he's, we've, she'd, won't, you'll, I'd, couldn't.**
<u>Words:</u> who is, what is, you are, was not, does not, let us, he is, we have, she would, will not, you will, I had, could not.

Chapter 17, Lesson 2, Practice 2: Copy the following contractions on notebook paper. Write the correct word beside each contraction. **Key: I am, is not, it is, are not, was not, do not, cannot, he is or he has, have not, they have, I will, she had or she would, should not.**
<u>Contractions:</u> I'm, isn't, it's, aren't, wasn't, don't, can't, he's, haven't, they've, I'll, she'd, shouldn't.

Chapter 17, Lesson 2, Practice 3: Write the correct answer for each sentence.

1. <u>Who is</u> first in line? <u>Who's</u>
2. <u>You'll</u> need a jacket. <u>You will</u>
3. He <u>has not</u> worked today. <u>hasn't</u>
4. You <u>weren't</u> in class today. <u>were not</u>
5. <u>She will</u> visit her aunt. <u>She'll</u>
6. <u>I'm</u> taller than Jason is. <u>I am</u>
7. <u>It is</u> raining outside. <u>It's</u>
8. We thought <u>they'd</u> be gone. <u>they would</u>

CHAPTER 17 LESSON 2 CONTINUED

 VOCABULARY TIME

Assign Chapter 17, Vocabulary Words **#2** on page 7 in the Reference Section for students to define in their Vocabulary notebooks. Tell students they are to use a dictionary or thesaurus to look up the meanings of the vocabulary words.

Chapter 17, Vocabulary Words #2
(huge, enormous, ease, effort)

 ACTIVITY / ASSIGNMENT TIME

Have students number from 1-24 on a sheet of notebook paper. Without showing students the story below, have them give you an example of the part of speech that corresponds with each number. Fill in the story with their responses. Enjoy reading the silly story back to the students when it is completed.

Susan was in the **(1. noun - place)** baking a cake for **(2. possessive noun)** birthday party when **(3. pronoun)** opened the **(4. noun - thing)** and **(5. verb - past tense)** that she had no **(6. noun - thing)**. She **(7. verb - past tense)** her purse, jumped in her **(8. noun - thing)**, and dashed to the **(9. adjective)** store. **(10. preposition)** the store, she ran into **(11. noun - person)**, who was looking for the **(12. noun - place)**. She helped **(13. noun - person)** find his way and **(14. adverb)** grabbed a **(15. noun - thing)** of eggs. The **(16. adjective)** lines were long, but **(17. pronoun)** waited **(18. adverb)**.

(19. preposition) her way home, she got stuck behind a **(20. adjective)** bus, and barely beat **(21. noun - person)** in the door. She **(22. adverb)** finished the **(23. noun - thing)**, but it was still baking **(24. preposition)** the oven when the guests arrived!

(End of lesson.)

Level 2—Shurley English—Homeschool Edition

CHAPTER 17   LESSON 3
Objectives: Jingles, Grammar (Practice Sentences, Practice and Improved Sentence), and Practice Exercise.

 JINGLE TIME

Have students turn to the Jingle Section in their books and recite the previously-taught jingles.

 GRAMMAR TIME

Put the Practice Sentences from the box below on the board or on notebook paper. Use these sentences as you practice the concepts that have been taught. For the greatest benefit, students must participate orally with the teacher.

Chapter 17, Practice Sentences for Lesson 3
1. _____ The big truck honked loudly at the dogs in the road.
2. _____ My mom's car stopped in the middle of the driveway.
3. _____ The yellow school bus turned right at the stop sign.

TEACHING SCRIPT FOR CLASSIFYING PRACTICE SENTENCES

We will classify three different sentences to practice the grammar skills in the Question and Answer Flows. We will classify the sentences together. Begin. (*You might have students write the labels above the sentences at this time.*)

Question and Answer Flow for Sentence 1: The big truck honked loudly at the dogs in the road.

1. What honked loudly at the dogs in the road? truck - SN
2. What is being said about truck? truck honked - V
3. Honked how? loudly - Adv
4. At - P
5. At what? dogs - OP
6. The - A
7. In - P
8. In what? road - OP
9. The - A
10. What kind of truck? big - Adj
11. The - A
12. SN V P1 Check
13. (At the dogs) - Prepositional phrase
14. (In the road) - Prepositional phrase
15. Period, statement, declarative sentence
16. Go back to the verb - divide the complete subject from the complete predicate.

Classified Sentence:

```
                    A  Adj  SN      V      Adv   P A  OP   P A  OP
        SN V        The big truck / honked loudly (at the dogs) (in the road).  D
        P1
```

Page 259

Level 2—Shurley English—Homeschool Edition

CHAPTER 17 LESSON 3 CONTINUED

Question and Answer Flow for Sentence 2: My mom's car stopped in the middle of the driveway.

1. What stopped in the middle of the driveway?
   car - SN
2. What is being said about car? car stopped - V
3. In - P
4. In what? middle - OP
5. The - A
6. Of - P
7. Of what? driveway - OP
8. The - A
9. Whose car? mom's - PN
10. Whose mom? my - PP
11. SN V P1 Check
12. (In the middle) - Prepositional phrase
13. (Of the driveway) - Prepositional phrase
14. Period, statement, declarative sentence
15. Go back to the verb - divide the complete subject from the complete predicate.

```
                            PP  PN  SN    V    P A   OP    P A   OP
Classified Sentence:    SN V    My mom's car / stopped (in the middle) (of the driveway).  D
                        ──
                        P1
```

Question and Answer Flow for Sentence 3: The yellow school bus turned right at the stop sign.

1. What turned right at the stop sign? bus - SN
2. What is being said about bus? bus turned - V
3. Turned where? right - Adv
4. At - P
5. At what? sign - OP
6. What kind of sign? stop - Adj
7. The - A
8. What kind of bus? school - Adj
9. What kind of bus? yellow - Adj
10. The - A
11. SN V P1 Check
12. (At the stop sign) - Prepositional phrase
13. Period, statement, declarative sentence
14. Go back to the verb - divide the complete subject from the complete predicate.

```
                            A   Adj  Adj  SN    V     Adv  P A   Adj  OP
Classified Sentence:    SN V    The yellow school bus / turned right (at the stop sign).  D
                        ──
                        P1
```

TEACHING SCRIPT FOR THE PRACTICE SENTENCE

Put these labels on the board: **SP V Adv P PP PN Adj OP**

Look at the new sentence labels on the board: **SP V Adv P PP PN Adj OP**. I will guide you again through the process of writing a sentence to practice the different parts that you have learned.

Get out a sheet of notebook paper. On the top line of your notebook paper, write the title *Practice Sentence*. Copy the sentence labels from the board onto your notebook paper. Be sure to leave plenty of writing space between each label. I will guide you through the process you will use whenever you write a Practice Sentence with possessive pronouns and possessive nouns.

CHAPTER 17 LESSON 3 CONTINUED

1. Go to the **SP** label for the subject pronoun. Repeat the Subject Pronoun Jingle to help you think of a pronoun that you want to use as your subject. Write the pronoun you have chosen on the line *under* the **SP** label.

2. Go to the **V** label for the verb. Think of a verb that tells what your subject does. Make sure that your verb makes sense with the subject pronoun. Write the verb you have chosen on the line *under* the **V** label.

3. Go to the **Adv** label for the adverb. Immediately go to the verb in your sentence and ask an adverb question. What are the adverb questions? (*How, When, Where*) Choose one adverb question to ask and write your adverb answer *under* the **Adv** label.

4. Go to the **P** label for the preposition. Think of a preposition word that tells something about your verb. You must be careful to choose a preposition word that makes sense with the noun you will choose for the object of the preposition in your next step. Write the word you have chosen for a preposition *under* the **P** label.

5. Go to the **OP** label for the object of the preposition. If you like the noun you thought of while thinking of a preposition, write it down under the **OP** label. If you prefer, think of another noun by asking **what** or **whom** after your preposition. Check to make sure the preposition and object of the preposition make sense together and also make sense with the rest of the sentence. Remember, the object of the preposition will always answer the question **what** or **whom** after the preposition. Write the word you have chosen for the object of the preposition *under* the **OP** label.

6. Go to the **Adj** label for the adjective. Go to the object of the preposition that you just wrote and ask an adjective question to describe the object-of-the-preposition noun. What are the adjective questions? (*What kind, Which one, How many*) Choose one adjective question to ask and write your adjective answer *under* the **Adj** label next to the object of the preposition. Always check to make sure your answers are making sense in the sentence.

7. Go to the **PN** label for the possessive noun that is part of your prepositional phrase. Think of a possessive noun that answers "whose" when you refer to the object of the preposition noun. Make sure the possessive noun makes sense in your sentence. Also, make sure you write the apostrophe correctly as you write the possessive noun you have chosen *under* the **PN** label.

8. Go to the **PP** label for the possessive pronoun that is part of your prepositional phrase. Repeat the Possessive Pronoun Jingle to help you think of a pronoun that you want to use as your possessive pronoun. Now, you will choose one of the possessive pronouns that makes the best sense in your sentence. Write the possessive pronoun you have chosen *under* the **PP** label.

9. Finally, check your Practice Sentence to make sure it has the necessary parts to be a complete sentence. What are the five parts of a complete sentence? (*subject, verb, complete sense, capital letter, and an end mark*) Does your Practice Sentence have the five parts of a complete sentence? (*Allow time for students to read over their sentences and to make any corrections they need to make.*)

Level 2—Shurley English—Homeschool Edition

CHAPTER 17 LESSON 3 CONTINUED

TEACHING SCRIPT FOR THE IMPROVED SENTENCE

Under your Practice Sentence, write the title *Improved Sentence* on another line. To improve your Practice Sentence, you will make two synonym changes, one antonym change, and your choice of a complete word change or another synonym or antonym change. I will give you time to write your Improved Sentence. *(After students have finished, check and discuss students' Practice and Improved Sentences.)*

 PRACTICE TIME

Have students turn to pages 61 and 62 in the Practice Section of their book and find Chapter 17, Lesson 3, Practice *(1-4)*. Go over the directions to make sure they understand what to do. Check and discuss the Practices after students have finished. *(Chapter 17, Lesson 3, Practice keys are given below.)*

Chapter 17, Lesson 3, Practice 1: Copy the following words on notebook paper. Write the correct contraction beside each word. **Key: he's, who's, there's, we're, weren't, didn't, let's, she's, you've, hadn't, he'll, we'll.**
Words: he has, who is, there is, we are, were not, did not, let us, she is, you have, had not, he will, we will.

Chapter 17, Lesson 3, Practice 2: Copy the following contractions on notebook paper. Write the correct word beside each contraction. **Key: is not, it is, what is, we are, do not, cannot, I have, he had or he would, we had or we would, I will, would not, will not, should not.**
Contractions: isn't, it's, what's, we're, don't, can't, I've, he'd, we'd, I'll, wouldn't, won't, shouldn't.

Chapter 17, Lesson 3, Practice 3: Write the correct answer for each sentence.
1. I shouldn't swim alone. should not
2. They are on a ship. They're
3. You have two dollars left. You've
4. What is your name? What's
5. I didn't see you yesterday. did not
6. It is a great party! It's

Chapter 17, Lesson 3, Practice 4: First, identify each noun as singular or plural by writing S or P in the first blank. Next, write the correct rule number from the list below in the second blank. Finally, write the possessive form of each noun as singular possessive or as plural possessive.					
1. For a singular noun - add (**'s**) Rule 1: girl's		2. For a plural noun that ends in **s** - add (**'**) Rule 2: girls'		3. For a plural noun that does not end in **s** - add (**'s**) Rule 3: women's	
Noun	S-P	Rule	Singular Possessive	Plural Possessive	
1. castle	S	1	castle's		
2. cashiers	P	2		cashiers'	
3. James	S	1	James's		
4. men	P	3		men's	
5. maps	P	2		maps'	

(End of lesson.)

Level 2—Shurley English—Homeschool Edition

CHAPTER 17   LESSON 4

Objectives: Jingles, Study, Test, Check, Writing (Journal), State Activity, and Oral Contraction Review.

 JINGLE TIME

Have students turn to the Jingle Section in their books and recite the previously-taught jingles.

 STUDY TIME

Have students study the vocabulary words in their vocabulary notebooks. Remind students that any vocabulary word in their notebooks could be on their test. Also, give students an Oral Contraction Review before the test. The review is found on page 265 of the teacher's manual.

 TEST TIME

Have students turn to page 96 in the Test Section of their book and find Chapter 17 Test. Go over the directions to make sure they understand what to do. (*Chapter 17 Test key is on the next page.*)

 CHECK TIME

After students have finished, check and discuss their test papers. Make sure they understand why their answers are right or wrong. (*For total points, count each required answer as a point.*)

 STATE ACTIVITY TIME

Students will continue to draw or trace the states and to write the following questions and answers.

Missouri	Montana
1. What is the state on the front of this card? **Missouri**	1. What is the state on the front of this card? **Montana**
2. What is the capital of Missouri? **Jefferson City**	2. What is the capital of Montana? **Helena**
3. What is the postal abbreviation of Missouri? **MO**	3. What is the postal abbreviation of Montana? **MT**

Color these states. Use the cards to quiz family members, friends, and relatives. You may want to time the responses to your questions.

(End of lesson.)

Level 2—Shurley English—Homeschool Edition

Chapter 17 Test
(Student Page 96)

Exercise 1: Classify each sentence.

```
              SP     V     P   A   Adj    OP     Adv
1. SN V       We / sunned (on the barren beach) yesterday.  D
   P1

              PP  PN   Adj  SN    V    Adv   P   A   OP
2. SN V       My dad's new boat / sails easily (on the water).  D
   P1
```

Exercise 2: Use Sentence 2 to underline the complete subject once and the complete predicate twice and to complete the table below.

List the Noun Used	List the Noun Job	Singular or Plural	Common or Proper	Simple Subject	Simple Predicate
1. **boat**	2. **SN**	3. **S**	4. **C**	5. **boat**	6. **sails**
7. **water**	8. **OP**	9. **S**	10. **C**		

Exercise 3: Identify each pair of words as synonyms or antonyms by putting parentheses ( ) around *syn* or *ant*.

1. coast, shore	**(syn)** ant	4. barren, desolate	**(syn)** ant	7. awaited, unexpected	syn **(ant)**
2. fresh, moldy	syn **(ant)**	5. edge, middle	syn **(ant)**	8. contented, dissatisfied	syn **(ant)**
3. enormous, huge	**(syn)** ant	6. effort, ease	syn **(ant)**	9. favorite, preferred	**(syn)** ant

Exercise 4: Copy the following words on notebook paper. Write the correct contraction beside each word.
Key: couldn't, you'd, wouldn't, she'll, they'd, he'd, we've, she's, can't, weren't, you're, that's.
<u>Words</u>: could not, you had, would not, she will, they would, he had, we have, she has, cannot, were not, you are, that is.

Exercise 5: Copy the following contractions on notebook paper. Write the correct word beside each contraction.
Key: should not, she had or she would, they will, he will, we had or we would, had not, I have, let us, do not, you are, who is, is not.
<u>Contractions</u>: shouldn't, she'd, they'll, he'll, we'd, hadn't, I've, let's, don't, you're, who's, isn't.

Exercise 6: Write the correct answer for each sentence.
1. She <u>won't</u> share with me. <u>will not</u>
2. <u>They are</u> my neighbors. <u>They're</u>
3. <u>We'd</u> like to go with you. <u>We would</u>
4. <u>They have</u> bought a new car. <u>They've</u>

Exercise 7: Use the following guidelines to make each noun possessive. First, identify each noun as singular or plural by writing **S** or **P** in the first blank. Next, write the correct rule number from the list below in the second blank. Finally, write the possessive form of each noun as singular possessive or as plural possessive.

1. For a singular noun - add (**'s**)			2. For a plural noun that ends in *s* - add (**'**)	3. For a plural noun that does not end in *s* - add (**'s**)
Rule 1: girl's			Rule 2: girls'	Rule 3: women's
Noun	S-P	Rule	Singular Possessive	Plural Possessive
1. ants	P	2		ants'
2. Bob	S	1	Bob's	
3. policemen	P	3		policemen's
4. reporter	S	1	reporter's	

Exercise 8: In your journal, write a paragraph summarizing what you have learned this week.

CHAPTER 17 LESSON 4 CONTINUED

TEACHER INSTRUCTIONS

Use the Question and Answer Flows below for the sentences on the Chapter 17 Test.

Question and Answer Flow for Sentence 1: We sunned on the barren beach yesterday.

1. Who sunned on the barren beach yesterday? we - SP
2. What is being said about we? we sunned - V
3. On - P
4. On what? beach - OP
5. What kind of beach? barren - Adj
6. The - A
7. Sunned when? yesterday - Adv
8. SN V P1 Check
9. (On the barren beach) - Prepositional phrase
10. Period, statement, declarative sentence
11. Go back to the verb - divide the complete subject from the complete predicate.

```
                       SP   V    P  A  Adj   OP     Adv
Classified Sentence:   SN V     We / sunned (on the barren beach) yesterday.  D
                       P1
```

Question and Answer Flow for Sentence 2: My dad's new boat sails easily on the water.

1. What sails easily on the water? boat - SN
2. What is being said about boat? boat sails - V
3. Sails how? easily - Adv
4. On - P
5. On what? water - OP
6. The - A
7. What kind of boat? new - Adj
8. Whose boat? dad's - PN
9. Whose dad? my - PP
10. SN V P1 Check
11. (On the water) - Prepositional phrase
12. Period, statement, declarative sentence
13. Go back to the verb - divide the complete subject from the complete predicate.

```
                       PP  PN  Adj  SN    V    Adv   P  A  OP
Classified Sentence:   SN V     My dad's new boat / sails easily (on the water).  D
                       P1
```

Oral Contraction Review

Before the test, give students a review of contractions orally. In the first chart, repeat the contractions in bold and have students respond with the correct words that stand for each contraction. In the second chart, repeat the words and have students respond with the correct contractions.

Chart 1:

won't - will not	**I'm** - I am	**you've** - you have	**let's** - let us
wasn't - was not	**I've** - I have	**can't** - cannot	**we're** - we are
shouldn't - should not	**haven't** - have not	**wouldn't** - would not	**doesn't** - does not

Chart 2:

she will - she'll	**what is** - what's	**we have** - we've	**he had** - he'd
did not - didn't	**they would** - they'd	**they had** - they'd	**were not** - weren't
you will - you'll	**I will** - I'll	**they are** - they're	**he would** - he'd

Level 2—Shurley English—Homeschool Edition

CHAPTER 17   LESSON 5
Objectives: Writing Assignment #11 and Sentence Time.

 WRITING TIME

TEACHER INSTRUCTIONS FOR WRITING ASSIGNMENT #11

Give Writing Assignment #11 from the box below. Remind students to use the Writing Checklist in Reference 17 to check their finished writing assignment.

Read, check, and discuss Writing Assignment #11 after students have finished their final papers. Use the Writing Checklist (*Reference 17 on teacher's page 112*) as you check and discuss students' papers. Make sure students are using the checklist correctly. In the beginning, you must also check students' papers carefully for <u>form</u> mistakes. This will ensure that students are learning the three-point format correctly.

Writing Assignment Box

Writing Assignment #11: Three-Point Expository Paragraph

Writing topic choices: Things That Worry Me   or   My Favorite Adults   or   My Favorite Birds

---

 SENTENCE TIME

Chapter 17, Lesson 5, Sentence: Use colored markers to match each label with the correct sentence part by drawing a line from one to the other. Then, use the labels to arrange the sentence parts into a sentence that you will write on the sentence line below. *(The order of the words in your sentence should be in the same sequence as the vertical list of sentence labels.)* Create other labels and scrambled sentence parts on notebook paper for family members to solve. You may color code the sentence parts. *(See page 114 in the student book.)*

Labels for Order of Sentence	Scrambled Sentence Parts
A	wildly
SN	team
V	quarterback's
Adv	fans
P	touchdown
PP	the
OP	for
P	after
A	yelled
PN	their
Adj	the
OP	outstanding

Sentence: The fans yelled wildly for their team after the quarterback's outstanding touchdown.

(End of lesson.)

Level 2—Shurley English—Homeschool Edition

CHAPTER 18   LESSON 1
Objectives: Jingles, Grammar (Practice Sentences, Skill Builder Check, Review Six Parts of Speech), Skills (Complete Sentence, Sentence Fragments, Matching Subject Parts and Predicate Parts, Correcting Sentence Fragments), Practice Exercise, Vocabulary #1, and Activity.

 JINGLE TIME

Have students turn to the Jingle Section in their books and recite the previously-taught jingles.

 **GRAMMAR TIME**

Put the Practice Sentences from the box below on the board or on notebook paper. Use these sentences as you practice the concepts that have been taught. For the greatest benefit, students must participate orally with the teacher.

Chapter 18, Practice Sentences for Lesson 1
1. _____ The walnuts in their garage molded in the sack.
2. _____ The five big whales swam gracefully in the ocean.
3. _____ The baby snored loudly during the preacher's prayer meeting.

TEACHING SCRIPT FOR CLASSIFYING PRACTICE SENTENCES

We will classify three different sentences to practice the grammar skills in the Question and Answer Flows. We will classify the sentences together. Begin. (*You might have students write the labels above the sentences at this time.*)

Question and Answer Flow for Sentence 1: The walnuts in their garage molded in the sack.
1. What molded in the sack? walnuts - SN   9. The - A   2. What is being said about walnuts? walnuts molded - V   10. SN V P1 Check   3. In - P   11. (In their garage) - Prepositional phrase   4. In what? sack - OP   12. (In the sack) - Prepositional phrase   5. The - A   13. Period, statement, declarative sentence   6. In - P   14. Go back to the verb - divide the complete subject   7. In what? garage - OP   from the complete predicate.   8. Whose garage? their - PP
A   SN   P   PP   OP   V   P   A   OP   **Classified Sentence:**   SN V   The walnuts (in their garage) / molded (in the sack).   D   P1

CHAPTER 18 LESSON 1 CONTINUED

Question and Answer Flow for Sentence 2: The five big whales swam gracefully in the ocean.

1. What swam gracefully in the ocean? whales - SN
2. What is being said about whales? whales swam - V
3. Swam how? gracefully - Adv
4. In - P
5. In what? ocean - OP
6. The - A
7. What kind of whales? big - Adj
8. How many whales? five - Adj
9. The - A
10. SN V P1 Check
11. (In the ocean) - Prepositional phrase
12. Period, statement, declarative sentence
13. Go back to the verb - divide the complete subject from the complete predicate.

```
                            A   Adj  Adj   SN        V       Adv    P   A   OP
Classified Sentence:   SN V   The  five  big  whales / swam  gracefully (in the ocean).  D
                       P1
```

Question and Answer Flow for Sentence 3: The baby snored loudly during the preacher's prayer meeting.

1. Who snored loudly during the preacher's prayer meeting? baby - SN
2. What is being said about baby? baby snored - V
3. Snored how? loudly - Adv
4. During - P
5. During what? meeting - OP
6. What kind of meeting? prayer - Adj
7. Whose meeting? preacher's - PN
8. The - A
9. The - A
10. SN V P1 Check
11. (During the preacher's prayer meeting) - Prepositional phrase
12. Period, statement, declarative sentence
13. Go back to the verb - divide the complete subject from the complete predicate.

```
                            A   SN      V    Adv      P    A    PN     Adj    OP
Classified Sentence:   SN V   The baby / snored loudly (during the preacher's prayer meeting).  D
                       P1
```

Use Sentences 1-3 that you just classified with your students to do a Skill Builder Check. Use the guidelines below.

Skill Builder Check

1. **Noun check.**
   (Say the job and then say the noun. Circle each noun.)
2. **Identify the nouns as singular or plural.**
   (Write **S** or **P** above each noun.)
3. **Identify the nouns as common or proper.**
   (Follow established procedure for oral identification.)
4. **Do a vocabulary check.**
   (Follow established procedure for oral identification.)
5. **Identify the complete subject and the complete predicate.** (Underline the complete subject once and the complete predicate twice.)
6. **Identify the simple subject and simple predicate.** (Underline the simple subject once and the simple predicate twice. Bold, or highlight, the lines to distinguish them from the complete subject and complete predicate.)

TEACHING SCRIPT FOR REVIEWING THE SIX PARTS OF SPEECH

What are the six parts of speech that we have covered? *(noun, verb, adjective, adverb, preposition,* and *pronoun)* (Chant the six parts of speech that the students have learned several times for reinforcement and fun.)

Level 2—Shurley English—Homeschool Edition

CHAPTER 18 LESSON 1 CONTINUED

SKILL TIME

TEACHING SCRIPT FOR IDENTIFYING COMPLETE SENTENCES AND SENTENCE FRAGMENTS

Today, you will learn the difference between a complete sentence and a fragment. Most of the time, you will have no trouble writing a complete sentence because you know the five rules that make a sentence correct. Let's recite the sentence jingle again to make sure we are all focused on the same thing. (*Recite the sentence jingle.*)

When you are writing, sometimes you will put a thought down without checking the five parts. If you do not have a subject or a verb or a complete thought, you could have a sentence fragment. This lesson is to teach you how to recognize and prevent sentence fragments so all your sentences will be correct. Turn to page 23 in your Reference section. Look at Reference 32 as I go over it with you. (*Read and discuss the information in the reference box below.*)

Reference 32: Complete Sentences and Sentence Fragments
Identifying simple sentences and fragments: Write **S** for a complete sentence and **F** for a sentence fragment on the line beside each group of words below.
S   1. Two monkeys wrestled playfully.
F   2. Over the bridge.
S   3. Taxi waited.
S   4. Peter walks to the park.
F   5. Ran around the fence.
F   6. The tiny tadpoles.

TEACHING SCRIPT FOR MATCHING SUBJECT PARTS AND PREDICATE PARTS

Now, you will learn to match subject parts with predicate parts to make sentences that make sense. This exercise will help strengthen your ability to recognize a complete sentence. Look at Reference 33 as I go over it with you. (*Read and discuss the information in the reference box below.*)

Reference 33: Matching Subject Parts and Predicate Parts
Directions: Match each subject part with the correct predicate part by writing the correct sentence number in the blank.

Subject Parts		Predicate Parts
1. The tiny egg	3	stopped at the red light.
2. The hungry hawk	2	searched for food.
3. The yellow bus	5	melted on the bread.
4. The farmer	1	cracked slowly open.
5. The butter	4	harvested the wheat.

CHAPTER 18 LESSON 1 CONTINUED

TEACHING SCRIPT FOR CORRECTING SENTENCE FRAGMENTS

Once you recognize that you have a fragment, you must know how to add the missing parts to make a sentence complete. This exercise will help you learn how to correct fragments. Look at Reference 34 as I go over it with you. (*Read and discuss the information in the reference box below.*)

Reference 34: Correcting Sentence Fragments

Directions: Make each fragment below into a complete sentence. Underline the parts that are added.

1. Add a subject part to this fragment: **floated under the bridge**
   <u>The wooden raft</u> floated under the bridge.

2. Add a predicate part to this fragment: **The birds**
   The birds <u>flew around the cage</u>.

 PRACTICE TIME

Have students turn to pages 62 and 63 and find Chapter 18, Lesson 1, Practice (*1-3*). Go over the directions to make sure students understand what to do. Check and discuss the Practices after students have finished. (*Chapter 18, Lesson 1, Practice keys are given below.*)

Chapter 18, Lesson 1, Practice 1: On notebook paper, make each fragment below into a complete sentence. Underline the parts you add. **(Sentences will vary.)**

1. Add a subject part to this fragment: **rolled down the hill**
2. Add a predicate part to this fragment: **The brilliant scientist**

Chapter 18, Lesson 1, Practice 2: Identify each kind of sentence by writing the abbreviation in the blank. **(S, F)**

S	1.	The horses trotted.
F	2.	Around the corner of the building.
S	3.	The sweater shrank in the wash.
F	4.	Mowing my neighbor's yard.
F	5.	The poster on the wall in my room.

Chapter 18, Lesson 1, Practice 3: Match each subject part with the correct predicate part by writing the correct sentence number in the blank.

	Subject Parts		**Predicate Parts**
1.	Our pumpkin pie	**5**	performed many tricks.
2.	The dry leaves	**3**	has five bedrooms.
3.	Our new house	**4**	marched in the parade.
4.	The school band	**1**	baked in the oven.
5.	The talented magician	**2**	fluttered to the ground.

CHAPTER 18 LESSON 1 CONTINUED

VOCABULARY TIME

Assign Chapter 18, Vocabulary Words **#1** on page 7 in the Reference Section for students to define in their Vocabulary notebooks. Tell students they may use a dictionary or thesaurus. After they write each word and its meaning, students are to write a sentence using the vocabulary word.

Chapter 18, Vocabulary Words #1
(distant, remote, restless, patient)

ACTIVITY / ASSIGNMENT TIME

Have students use the directions below to create a **personality poem** that uses parts of speech. Have students create a **personality poem** for themselves and one for each family member and for a friend or other relative. (*Write the directions and the sample below on the board for your students.*)

Directions for each line of a personality poem:
1. Write your first name.
2. Write two adjectives that describe your personality.
3. Write four words that describe your appearance.
   (*adjective, noun, adjective, noun*)
4. Write five nouns naming things you enjoy.
5. Write any descriptive word you choose about yourself.

Sample:
Matthew
Bold, brave
Strong arms, long legs
Hiking, football, nature, food, friends
Daring

(End of lesson.)

Level 2—Shurley English—Homeschool Edition

CHAPTER 18   LESSON 2
Objectives: Jingles, Grammar (Practice Sentences), Practice Exercise, and Vocabulary #2.

 **JINGLE TIME**

Have students turn to the Jingle Section in their books and recite the previously-taught jingles.

 GRAMMAR TIME

Put the Practice Sentences from the box below on the board or on notebook paper. Use these sentences as you practice the concepts that have been taught. For the greatest benefit, students must participate orally with the teacher.

Chapter 18, Practice Sentences for Lesson 2
1. _____ She laughed uncontrollably during her sister's dress rehearsal.
2. _____ The huge deer ran quickly through the woods.
3. _____ A squirrel chattered loudly on our roof for several days.

TEACHING SCRIPT FOR CLASSIFYING PRACTICE SENTENCES

We will classify three different sentences to practice the grammar skills in the Question and Answer Flows. We will classify the sentences together. Begin. (*You might have students write the labels above the sentences at this time.*)

Question and Answer Flow for Sentence 1: She laughed uncontrollably during her sister's dress rehearsal.

1. Who laughed uncontrollably during her sister's dress rehearsal? she - SP
2. What is being said about she? she laughed - V
3. Laughed how? uncontrollably - Adv
4. During - P
5. During what? rehearsal - OP
6. What kind of rehearsal? dress - Adj
7. Whose rehearsal? sister's - PN
8. Whose sister? her - PP
9. SN V P1 Check
10. (During her sister's dress rehearsal) - Prepositional phrase
11. Period, statement, declarative sentence
12. Go back to the verb - divide the complete subject from the complete predicate.

```
                           SP    V     Adv            P   PP  PN   Adj    OP
Classified Sentence:      SN  V  She / laughed uncontrollably (during her sister's dress rehearsal).  D
                          P1
```

Page 272

CHAPTER 18 LESSON 2 CONTINUED

Question and Answer Flow for Sentence 2: The huge deer ran quickly through the woods.

1. What ran quickly through the woods? deer - SN
2. What is being said about deer? deer ran - V
3. Ran how? quickly - Adv
4. Through - P
5. Through what? woods - OP
6. The - A
7. What kind of deer? huge - Adj
8. The - A
9. SN V P1 Check
10. (Through the woods) - Prepositional phrase
11. Period, statement, declarative sentence
12. Go back to the verb - divide the complete subject from the complete predicate.

```
                              A   Adj  SN    V    Adv   P    A   OP
Classified Sentence:   SN V   The huge deer / ran quickly (through the woods).  D
                       P1
```

Question and Answer Flow for Sentence 3: A squirrel chattered loudly on our roof for several days.

1. What chattered loudly on our roof for several days? squirrel - SN
2. What is being said about squirrel? squirrel chattered - V
3. Chattered how? loudly - Adv
4. On - P
5. On what? roof - OP
6. Whose roof? our - PP
7. For - P
8. For what? days - OP
9. How many days? several - Adj
10. A - A
11. SN V P1 Check
12. (On our roof) - Prepositional phrase
13. (For several days) - Prepositional phrase
14. Period, statement, declarative sentence
15. Go back to the verb - divide the complete subject from the complete predicate.

```
                              A   SN       V    Adv  P  PP  OP    P   Adj    OP
Classified Sentence:   SN V   A squirrel / chattered loudly (on our roof) (for several days).  D
                       P1
```

PRACTICE TIME

Have students turn to pages 63 and 64 in the Practice Section of their book and find Chapter 18, Lesson 2, Practice *(1-5)*. Go over the directions to make sure they understand what to do. Check and discuss the Practices after students have finished. *(Chapter 18, Lesson 2, Practice keys are given below and on the next page.)*

Chapter 18, Lesson 2, Practice 1: Underline the correct homonym in each sentence.

1. We walked (<u>through</u>, threw) the museum.
2. John (<u>knew</u>, new) how to get there.
3. We have one more (weak, <u>week</u>) until vacation.
4. The class had (to, too, <u>two</u>) new students.
5. The king (<u>sent</u>, scent) his jester away.
6. She handed me a (<u>piece</u>, peace) of candy.

Chapter 18, Lesson 2, Practice 2: Copy the following words on notebook paper. Write the correct contraction beside each word. **Key:** they've, she's, didn't, they're, what's, he's, shouldn't, he'd, won't, I'd, haven't, can't.
<u>Words:</u> they have, she is, did not, they are, what is, he has, should not, he would, will not, I had, have not, cannot.

Level 2—Shurley English—Homeschool Edition

CHAPTER 18 LESSON 2 CONTINUED

Chapter 18, Lesson 2, Practice 3: On notebook paper, make each fragment below into a complete sentence. Underline the parts you add. **(Sentences will vary.)**

1. Add a subject part to this fragment: **turned into a beast**
2. Add a predicate part to this fragment: **The crowd of people**

Chapter 18, Lesson 2, Practice 4: Identify each kind of sentence by writing the abbreviation in the blank. **(S, F)**

S	1.	The tulips bloomed.
S	2.	The cool water rushed through the creek bed.
F	3.	The voice on the radio.
S	4.	The workers moved the heavy boxes.
F	5.	Through the winter storm.

Chapter 18, Lesson 2, Practice 5: Match each subject part with the correct predicate part by writing the correct sentence number in the blank.

	Subject Parts		Predicate Parts
1.	Mom's beautiful painting	2	drank the milk.
2.	The little kitten	4	were empty.
3.	The gentle nurse	5	took pictures at the wedding.
4.	Both cardboard boxes	1	hangs on the wall.
5.	The photographer	3	took my temperature.

 VOCABULARY TIME

Assign Chapter 18, Vocabulary Words **#2** on page 7 in the Reference Section for students to define in their Vocabulary notebooks. Tell students they are to use a dictionary or thesaurus to look up the meanings of the vocabulary words.

Chapter 18, Vocabulary Words #2
(arrogant, proud, wide, narrow)

(End of lesson.)

CHAPTER 18 LESSON 3

Objectives: Jingles, Grammar (Practice Sentences, Practice and Improved Sentence), and Practice Exercise.

 **JINGLE TIME**

Have students turn to the Jingle Section in their books and recite the previously-taught jingles.

 GRAMMAR TIME

Put the Practice Sentences from the box below on the board or on notebook paper. Use these sentences as you practice the concepts that have been taught. For the greatest benefit, students must participate orally with the teacher.

Chapter 18, Practice Sentences for Lesson 3
1. _____ Cathy's black cat walked arrogantly to her bowl of food on the kitchen floor.
2. _____ The pretty yellow flowers bloomed brilliantly during the summer.
3. _____ We went to their school play yesterday.

TEACHING SCRIPT FOR CLASSIFYING PRACTICE SENTENCES

We will classify three different sentences to practice the grammar skills in the Question and Answer Flows. We will classify the sentences together. Begin. (*You might have students write the labels above the sentences at this time.*)

Question and Answer Flow for Sentence 1: Cathy's black cat walked arrogantly to her bowl of food on the kitchen floor.

1. What walked arrogantly to her bowl of food on the kitchen floor? cat - SN
2. What is being said about cat? cat walked - V
3. Walked how? arrogantly - Adv
4. To - P
5. To what? bowl - OP
6. Whose bowl? her - PP
7. Of - P
8. Of what? food - OP
9. On - P
10. On what? floor - OP
11. What kind of floor? kitchen - Adj
12. The - A
13. What kind of cat? black - Adj
14. Whose cat? Cathy's - PN
15. SN V P1 Check
16. (To her bowl) - Prepositional phrase
17. (Of food) - Prepositional phrase
18. (On the kitchen floor) - Prepositional phrase
19. Period, statement, declarative sentence
20. Go back to the verb - divide the complete subject from the complete predicate.

```
                        PN   Adj  SN   V      Adv     P PP  OP    P  OP   P  A   Adj    OP
Classified Sentence:  SN V   Cathy's black cat / walked arrogantly (to her bowl) (of food) (on the kitchen floor).  D
                      P1
```

CHAPTER 18 LESSON 3 CONTINUED

Question and Answer Flow for Sentence 2: The pretty yellow flowers bloomed brilliantly during the summer.

1. What bloomed brilliantly during the summer?
   flowers - SN
2. What is being said about flowers?
   flowers bloomed - V
3. Bloomed how? brilliantly - Adv
4. During - P
5. During what? summer - OP
6. The - A
7. What kind of flowers? yellow - Adj
8. What kind of flowers? pretty - Adj
9. The - A
10. SN V P1 Check
11. (During the summer) - Prepositional phrase
12. Period, statement, declarative sentence
13. Go back to the verb - divide the complete subject from the complete predicate.

```
                          A   Adj   Adj   SN    V      Adv    P   A    OP
Classified Sentence:  SN V    The pretty yellow flowers / bloomed brilliantly (during the summer).   D
                      P1
```

Question and Answer Flow for Sentence 3: We went to their school play yesterday.

1. Who went to their school play yesterday? we - SP
2. What is being said about we? we went - V
3. To - P
4. To what? play - OP
5. What kind of play? school - Adj
6. Whose play? their - PP
7. Went when? yesterday - Adv
8. SN V P1 Check
9. (To their school play) - Prepositional phrase
10. Period, statement, declarative sentence
11. Go back to the verb - divide the complete subject from the complete predicate.

```
                          SP   V   P   PP   Adj   OP    Adv
Classified Sentence:  SN V    We / went (to their school play) yesterday.   D
                      P1
```

TEACHING SCRIPT FOR A PRACTICE SENTENCE

Put these labels on the board: **A Adj Adj SN V Adv P PP Adj OP**

Look at the new sentence labels on the board: **A Adj Adj SN V Adv P PP Adj OP**. I will guide you again through the process of writing a sentence to practice all the parts that you have learned.

Get out a sheet of notebook paper. On the top line of your notebook paper, write the title *Practice Sentence*. Copy the sentence labels from the board onto your notebook paper. Be sure to leave plenty of writing space between each label. Now, I will guide you through the process you will use whenever you write a Practice Sentence with a prepositional phrase.

1. Go to the **SN** label for the subject noun. Think of a noun that you want to use as your subject. Write the noun you have chosen on the line *under* the **SN** label.

2. Go to the **V** label for the verb. Think of a verb that tells what your subject does. Make sure that your verb makes sense with the subject noun. Write the verb you have chosen on the line *under* the **V** label.

CHAPTER 18 LESSON 3 CONTINUED

3. Go to the **Adv** label for the adverb. Immediately go to the verb in your sentence and ask an adverb question. What are the adverb questions? (*How, When, Where*) Choose one adverb question to ask and write your adverb answer *under* the **Adv** label.

4. Go to the **P** label for the preposition. Think of a preposition word that tells something about your verb. You must be careful to choose a preposition word that makes sense with the noun you will choose for the object of the preposition in your next step. Write the word you have chosen for a preposition *under* the **P** label.

5. Go to the **OP** label for the object of the preposition. If you like the noun you thought of while thinking of a preposition, write it down under the **OP** label. If you prefer, think of another noun by asking **what** or **whom** after your preposition. Check to make sure the preposition and object of the preposition make sense together and also make sense with the rest of the sentence. Remember, the object of the preposition will always answer the question **what** or **whom** after the preposition. Write the word you have chosen for the object of the preposition *under* the **OP** label.

6. Go to the **Adj** label for the adjective. Go to the object of the preposition that you just wrote and ask an adjective question to describe the object-of-the-preposition noun. What are the adjective questions? (*What kind, Which one, How many*) Choose one adjective question to ask and write your adjective answer *under* the **Adj** label next to the object of the preposition. Always check to make sure your answers are making sense in the sentence.

7. Go to the **PP** label for the possessive pronoun that is part of your prepositional phrase. Repeat the Possessive Pronoun Jingle to help you think of a pronoun that you want to use as your possessive pronoun. You will choose one of the possessive pronouns that makes the best sense in your sentence. Write the possessive pronoun you have chosen *under* the **PP** label.

8. Go to the **Adj** label for another adjective. Go to the subject noun of your sentence and ask an adjective question. What are the adjective questions again? (*What kind, Which one, How many*) Choose one adjective question to ask and write your adjective answer *under* the **Adj** label next to the subject noun.

9. Go to the **Adj** label for the third adjective. Go to the subject noun again and ask another adjective question. You can ask the same adjective question, or you can ask a different adjective question. Write another adjective *under* the third **Adj** label.

10. Go to the **A** label for the article adjective in the subject area. What are the three article adjectives again? (*a, an,* and *the*) Choose the article adjective that makes the best sense in your sentence. Write the article adjective you have chosen *under* the **A** label.

11. Finally, check your Practice Sentence to make sure it has the necessary parts to be a complete sentence. What are the five parts of a complete sentence? (*subject, verb, complete sense, capital letter, and an end mark*) Does your Practice Sentence have the five parts of a complete sentence? (*Allow time for students to read over their sentences and to make any corrections they need to make.*)

Level 2—Shurley English—Homeschool Edition

CHAPTER 18 LESSON 3 CONTINUED

TEACHING SCRIPT FOR THE IMPROVED SENTENCE

Under your Practice Sentence, write the title *Improved Sentence* on another line. To improve your Practice Sentence, you will make two synonym changes, one antonym change, and your choice of a complete word change or another synonym or antonym change. I will give you time to write your Improved Sentence. *(After students have finished, check and discuss students' Practice and Improved Sentences.)*

 PRACTICE TIME

Have students turn to page 64 in the Practice Section of their book and find Chapter 18, Lesson 3, Practice *(1-4)*. Go over the directions to make sure they understand what to do. Check and discuss the Practices after students have finished. *(Chapter 18, Lesson 3, Practice keys are given below.)*

Chapter 18, Lesson 3, Practice 1: On notebook paper, make each fragment below into a complete sentence. Underline the parts you add. **(Sentences will vary.)**

1. Add a subject part to this fragment: **worked in the garden**
2. Add a predicate part to this fragment: **The silver coin**

Chapter 18, Lesson 3, Practice 2: Identify each kind of sentence by writing the abbreviation in the blank. **(S, F)**

F	1.	By the new grocery store.
F	2.	Waiting patiently in the den.
S	3.	The ice melted in my glass.
F	4.	Ran around in circles.
S	5.	The tree swayed in the wind.

Chapter 18, Lesson 3, Practice 3: Match each subject part with the correct predicate part by writing the correct sentence number in the blank.

	Subject Parts		Predicate Parts
1.	The old chair	5	chewed on bamboo.
2.	My throat	1	collapsed under me.
3.	The postman	3	stamped the packages.
4.	The dance rehearsal	2	feels sore.
5.	The panda	4	lasted for hours.

Chapter 18, Lesson 3, Practice 4: Copy the following contractions on notebook paper. Write the correct word beside each contraction. **Key: has not, you have, he had or he would, will not, we will, she had or she would, could not, it is, are not, were not, let us, was not.**
Contractions: hasn't, you've, he'd, won't, we'll, she'd, couldn't, it's, aren't, weren't, let's, wasn't.

(End of lesson.)

CHAPTER 18   LESSON 4

Objectives: Jingles, Study, Test, Check, Writing (Journal), and State Activity.

JINGLE TIME

Have students turn to the Jingle Section in their books and recite the previously-taught jingles.

STUDY TIME

Have students study the vocabulary words in their vocabulary notebooks. Remind students that any vocabulary word in their notebooks could be on their test. Also, have students study any of the skills in the Practice Section that they need to review.

TEST TIME

Have students turn to page 97 in the Test Section of their book and find Chapter 18 Test. Go over the directions to make sure they understand what to do. (*Chapter 18 Test key is on the next page.*)

CHECK TIME

After students have finished, check and discuss their test papers. Make sure they understand why their answers are right or wrong. (*For total points, count each required answer as a point.*)

STATE ACTIVITY TIME

Students will continue to draw or trace the states and to write the following questions and answers.

Nebraska	Nevada
1. What is the state on the front of this card? **Nebraska**	1. What is the state on the front of this card? **Nevada**
2. What is the capital of Nebraska? **Lincoln**	2. What is the capital of Nevada? **Carson City**
3. What is the postal abbreviation of Nebraska? **NE**	3. What is the postal abbreviation of Nevada? **NV**

Color these states. Use the cards to quiz family members, friends, and relatives. You may want to time the responses to your questions.

(End of lesson.)

Chapter 18 Test
(Student Page 97)

Exercise 1: Classify each sentence.

```
              PP   Adj    SN    V    P      A     OP    P   OP     P  PP   OP
1. SN V       My baby brother / ran (toward the street) (in front) (of our house)!  E
   P1

              SP   V   P   PP    OP         P     A    OP
2. SN V       They / hid (in their basement) (during the storm).  D
   P1
```

Exercise 2: Use Sentence 1 to underline the complete subject once and the complete predicate twice and to complete the table below.

List the Noun Used	List the Noun Job	Singular or Plural	Common or Proper	Simple Subject	Simple Predicate
1. brother	2. SN	3. S	4. C	5. brother	6. ran
7. street	8. OP	9. S	10. C		
11. front	12. OP	13. S	14. C		
15. house	16. OP	17. S	18. C		

Exercise 3: Identify each pair of words as synonyms or antonyms by putting parentheses ( ) around *syn* or *ant*.

1. distant, remote	(syn) ant	4. effort, ease	syn (ant)	7. practice, rehearse	(syn) ant
2. barren, desolate	(syn) ant	5. restless, patient	syn (ant)	8. favorite, preferred	(syn) ant
3. narrow, wide	syn (ant)	6. enormous, huge	(syn) ant	9. arrogant, proud	(syn) ant

Exercise 4: On notebook paper, make each fragment below into a complete sentence. Underline the parts you add. **(Sentences will vary.)**

1. Add a subject part to this fragment: **tiptoed through the empty room**
2. Add a predicate part to this fragment: **The basketball team**

Exercise 5: Identify each kind of sentence by writing the abbreviation in the blank. (S, F)

```
   F    1. The pretty yellow kitten.
   S    2. The purple balloon floated in the breeze.
   S    3. The young boy played the trumpet loudly.
   F    4. Running quickly down the street.
   S    5. The volcano erupted.
```

Exercise 6: Match each subject part with the correct predicate part by writing the correct sentence number in the blank.

Subject Parts		Predicate Parts
1. The choir members	2	sizzled in the pan.
2. The pancake	3	gave orders to the crew.
3. The ship's captain	5	brought drinks to us.
4. My teacher	1	sang in the church service.
5. Our waiter	4	assigned math homework.

Exercise 7: In your journal, write a paragraph summarizing what you have learned this week.

CHAPTER 18 LESSON 4 CONTINUED

TEACHER INSTRUCTIONS

Use the Question and Answer Flows below for the sentences on the Chapter 18 Test.

Question and Answer Flow for Sentence 1: My baby brother ran toward the street in front of our house!

1. Who ran toward the street in front of our house? brother - SN
2. What is being said about brother? brother ran - V
3. Toward - P
4. Toward what? street - OP
5. The - A
6. In - P
7. In what? front - OP
8. Of - P
9. Of what? house - OP
10. Whose house? our - PP
11. What kind of brother? baby - Adj
12. Whose brother? my - PP
13. SN V P1 Check
14. (Toward the street) - Prepositional phrase
15. (In front) - Prepositional phrase
16. (Of our house) - Prepositional phrase
17. Exclamation point, strong feeling, exclamatory sentence
18. Go back to the verb - divide the complete subject from the complete predicate.

```
                        PP  Adj  SN    V   P   A   OP    P  OP   P  PP  OP
Classified Sentence:    SN V    My baby brother / ran (toward the street) (in front) (of our house)!  E
                        P1
```

Question and Answer Flow for Sentence 2: They hid in their basement during the storm.

1. Who hid in their basement during the storm? they - SP
2. What is being said about they? they hid - V
3. In - P
4. In what? basement - OP
5. Whose basement? their - PP
6. During - P
7. During what? storm - OP
8. The - A
9. SN V P1 Check
10. (In their basement) - Prepositional phrase
11. (During the storm) - Prepositional phrase
12. Period, statement, declarative sentence
13. Go back to the verb - divide the complete subject from the complete predicate.

```
                        SP   V  P  PP   OP      P  A  OP
Classified Sentence:    SN V    They / hid (in their basement) (during the storm).  D
                        P1
```

Level 2—Shurley English—Homeschool Edition

CHAPTER 18   LESSON 5

Objectives: Writing (Introduce Descriptive Writing), Writing assignment #12, and Sentence Time.

 WRITING TIME

TEACHING SCRIPT FOR INTRODUCING DESCRIPTIVE WRITING

An artist paints a picture on canvas with paint. A descriptive writer paints a picture on paper with words. Both the artist and writer must select what he will include in his picture. Descriptive writing **shows** the reader what is being described. It does not just **tell** him about it.

Even though you can use description in other kinds of writing, sometimes you are asked to write only a descriptive piece of writing. Then, you must know that a **descriptive paragraph** gives a detailed picture of a person, place, thing, or idea.

A descriptive paragraph will usually start by naming what you are describing. That will be your topic sentence. Then, you will add supporting sentences that give more description about the topic. To make a description clear, these detail sentences should include as much information as possible about how the topic looks, sounds, feels, or tastes. The details that you include will depend on what you are describing. Since all the senses are not needed in all situations, the following guidelines on descriptive writing will give you the types of details that you should consider when you are describing certain topics.

Look at Reference 35 on page 24 in your Reference section. Follow along as I read the guidelines for descriptive writing. This reference will give you ideas and help guide you as you write descriptive paragraphs. (*Read and discuss Reference 35 below with your students. You might even want to make a descriptive guidelines poster for the wall so students can have a visual guide as they write descriptive paragraphs.*)

Reference 35: Descriptive Writing Guidelines

1. **When describing people,** it is helpful to notice these types of details:
   How they look, how they walk, how they talk, their way of doing things, any special event that happened to the person being described, and any other details that will help make that person stand out in your mind.

2. **When describing places or things,** it is helpful to notice these types of details:
   What you can see, smell, or touch (*including color, shape, size, age*), any other unusual information about a place or thing, any special event that happened in the place or to the thing being described, and whether or not the place or the thing is special to you.

3. **When describing nature,** it is helpful to notice these types of details:
   The special part or quality of the season, the sights, smells, sounds, colors, animals, insects, birds, and any special happening related to the scene being described.

4. **When describing an incident or an event,** it is helpful to notice these types of details:
   The order in which the events take place, any specific facts that will keep the story moving from a beginning to an ending, the answers to any of the *who, what, when, where, why*, and *how* questions that the reader needs to know, and especially the details that will create a clear picture, such as how things look, sound, smell, feel, etc.

CHAPTER 18 LESSON 5 CONTINUED

Now look at Reference 36 on page 24 and follow the sample paragraph as I go over the steps in writing a descriptive paragraph. (*Read the steps and examples below as students follow the guidelines in the reference box.*)

♦ Writing Topic: **Thanksgiving Dinner**
♦ <u>The Title</u> - Since there are many possibilities for titles, decide if you want to leave the topic as your title or if you want to write a different phrase to tell what your paragraph is about. **(Thanksgiving Dinner)**

1. Sentence #1 - Write a topic sentence that introduces what is being described.
   (Every year, our family meets at Grandmother's house for a huge Thanksgiving feast.)

2. Sentences #2 - #6 -Write sentences that give a description of your topic. (Use the descriptive writing guidelines in Reference 35 to help you.)
   (When we arrive, Grandmother is baking a delicious turkey in the oven. Aunt Carol brings a pumpkin pie, and Aunt Judy makes the dinner rolls. The kitchen fills with wonderful smells as dinner is being prepared. I quickly help Mom set the dinner table, and everyone gathers for a prayer of thanks. We sit down and enjoy our dinner and the time that we spend together.)

3. Sentence #7 -Write a concluding (final) sentence that summarizes your paragraph or relates it back to the topic sentence. Read the topic sentence again and then restate it by using some of the same words to say the same thing in a different way. **(There is nothing like a Thanksgiving dinner at Grandmother's house.)**

Reference 36: Descriptive Paragraph Example

A. Sentence 1 is the topic sentence that introduces **what is being described.**
B. For Sentences 2-6, use **the descriptive details** in Reference 35.
C. Sentence 7 is a concluding sentence that **restates or relates back to the topic sentence.**

Thanksgiving Dinner

Every year, our family meets at Grandmother's house for a huge Thanksgiving feast. When we arrive, Grandmother is baking a delicious turkey in the oven. Aunt Carol brings a pumpkin pie, and Aunt Judy makes the dinner rolls. The kitchen fills with wonderful smells as dinner is being prepared. I quickly help Mom set the dinner table, and everyone gathers for a prayer of thanks. We sit down and enjoy our dinner and the time that we spend together. There is nothing like a Thanksgiving dinner at Grandmother's house.

Teacher's Notes: The descriptive writing guideline is a suggested guide to help students as they learn to write descriptive paragraphs. However, some students will be able to organize their ideas and stick to the topic without following the guideline exactly. The number of sentences may also vary.

Now, you will write a descriptive paragraph. Remember to read through the whole paragraph after you finish to make sure it sounds correct. Sometimes, we find mistakes if we really listen to what we have written.

Level 2—Shurley English—Homeschool Edition

CHAPTER 18 LESSON 5 CONTINUED

<u>TEACHING INSTRUCTIONS FOR WRITING ASSIGNMENT #12</u>

Give Writing Assignment #12 from the box below. Remind students to use the Writing Checklist in Reference 17 to check their finished writing assignment.

Read, check, and discuss Writing Assignment #12 after students have finished their final papers. Use the Writing Checklist (*Reference 17 on teacher's page 112*) as you check and discuss students' papers. Make sure students are using the checklist correctly.

Writing Assignment Box

Writing Assignment #12:   Descriptive Paragraph

Writing topic choices: My Grandmother's House   or   A Beautiful Sunset/Sunrise   or   My Best Friend

---

 SENTENCE TIME

Chapter 18, Lesson 5, Sentence: Use colored markers to match each label with the correct sentence part by drawing a line from one to the other. Then, use the labels to arrange the sentence parts into a sentence that you will write on the sentence line below. *(The order of the words in your sentence should be in the same sequence as the vertical list of sentence labels.)* Create other labels and scrambled sentence parts on notebook paper for family members to solve. You may color code the sentence parts. *(See page 114 in the student book.)*

Labels for Order of Sentence	Scrambled Sentence Parts
PP	mother
SN	children's
V	laughter
P	playtime
PP	my
PN	her
OP	their
P	at
PP	during
OP	smiled

Sentence: My mother smiled at her children's laughter during their playtime.

(End of lesson.)

CHAPTER 19   LESSON 1

Objectives: Jingles, Grammar (Practice Sentences, Skill Builder Check, Review the Six Parts of Speech), Practice Exercise, and Vocabulary #1.

JINGLE TIME

Have students turn to the Jingle Section in their books and recite the previously-taught jingles.

GRAMMAR TIME

Put the Practice Sentences from the box below on the board or on notebook paper. Use these sentences as you practice the concepts that have been taught. For the greatest benefit, students must participate orally with the teacher.

Chapter 19, Practice Sentences for Lesson 1
1. _____ The sheep grazed peacefully in the green pasture beside the road.
2. _____ A kind policeman talked to the students about home safety.
3. _____ We waited patiently for Jim's phone call.

TEACHING SCRIPT FOR CLASSIFYING PRACTICE SENTENCES

We will classify three different sentences to practice the grammar skills in the Question and Answer Flows. We will classify the sentences together. Begin. (*You might have students write the labels above the sentences at this time.*)

Question and Answer Flow for Sentence 1: The sheep grazed peacefully in the green pasture beside the road.

1. What grazed peacefully in the green pasture beside the road? sheep - SN
2. What is being said about sheep? sheep grazed - V
3. Grazed how? peacefully - Adv
4. In - P
5. In what? pasture - OP
6. What kind of pasture? green - Adj
7. The - A
8. Beside - P
9. Beside what? road - OP
10. The - A
11. The - A
12. SN V P1 Check
13. (In the green pasture) - Prepositional phrase
14. (Beside the road) - Prepositional phrase
15. Period, statement, declarative sentence
16. Go back to the verb - divide the complete subject from the complete predicate.

```
                          A   SN   V     Adv      P  A  Adj   OP      P   A   OP
Classified Sentence:     SN V   The sheep / grazed peacefully (in the green pasture) (beside the road).  D
                         P1
```

Level 2—Shurley English—Homeschool Edition

CHAPTER 19 LESSON 1 CONTINUED

Question and Answer Flow for Sentence 2: A kind policeman talked to the students about home safety.

1. Who talked to the students about home safety? policeman - SN
2. What is being said about policeman? policeman talked - V
3. To - P
4. To whom? students - OP
5. The - A
6. About - P
7. About what? safety - OP
8. What kind of safety? home - Adj
9. What kind of policeman? kind - Adj
10. A - A
11. SN V P1 Check
12. (To the students) - Prepositional phrase
13. (About home safety) - Prepositional phrase
14. Period, statement, declarative sentence
15. Go back to the verb - divide the complete subject from the complete predicate.

Classified Sentence:
<u>SN V</u> A Adj SN V P A OP P Adj OP
P1   A kind policeman / talked (to the students) (about home safety).   D

Question and Answer Flow for Sentence 3: We waited patiently for Jim's phone call.

1. Who waited patiently for Jim's phone call? we - SP
2. What is being said about we? we waited - V
3. Waited how? patiently - Adv
4. For - P
5. For what? call - OP
6. What kind of call? phone - Adj
7. Whose call? Jim's - PN
8. SN V P1 Check
9. (For Jim's phone call) - Prepositional phrase
10. Period, statement, declarative sentence
11. Go back to the verb - divide the complete subject from the complete predicate.

Classified Sentence:
<u>SN V</u> SP V Adv P PN Adj OP
P1   We / waited patiently (for Jim's phone call).   D

Use Sentences 1-3 that you just classified with your students to do a Skill Builder Check. Use the guidelines below.

Skill Builder Check

1. **Noun check.**
   (Say the job and then say the noun. Circle each noun.)
2. **Identify the nouns as singular or plural.**
   (Write **S** or **P** above each noun.)
3. **Identify the nouns as common or proper.**
   (Follow established procedure for oral identification.)
4. **Do a vocabulary check.**
   (Follow established procedure for oral identification.)
5. **Identify the complete subject and the complete predicate.** (Underline the complete subject once and the complete predicate twice.)
6. **Identify the simple subject and simple predicate.**
   (Underline the simple subject once and the simple predicate twice. Bold, or highlight, the lines to distinguish them from the complete subject and complete predicate.)

TEACHING SCRIPT FOR REVIEWING THE SIX PARTS OF SPEECH

What are the six parts of speech that we have covered? *(noun, verb, adjective, adverb, preposition,* and *pronoun)* *(Chant the six parts of speech that the students have learned several times for reinforcement and fun.)*

CHAPTER 19 LESSON 1 CONTINUED

 PRACTICE TIME

Have students turn to page 65 in the Practice Section of their book and find Chapter 19, Lesson 1, Practice *(1-4)*. Go over the directions to make sure they understand what to do. Check and discuss the Practices after students have finished. *(Chapter 19, Lesson 1, Practice keys are given below.)*

Chapter 19, Lesson 1, Practice 1: On notebook paper, make each fragment below into a complete sentence. Underline the parts you add. **(Sentences will vary.)**

1. Add a subject part to this fragment: **waded into the ocean**
2. Add a predicate part to this fragment: **The gold medal**

Chapter 19, Lesson 1, Practice 2: Identify each kind of sentence by writing the abbreviation in the blank. **(S, F)**

F	1.	Near the edge of the water.
S	2.	We played violins in the orchestra.
F	3.	A bag of chocolate candy.
F	4.	Fell down the stairs.
S	5.	The tiger jumped through the burning hoop.

Chapter 19, Lesson 1, Practice 3: Match each subject part with the correct predicate part by writing the correct sentence number in the blank.

	Subject Parts		**Predicate Parts**
1.	The onions	4	fits well.
2.	The gray rat	5	melted in my lap.
3.	Several dark clouds	2	nibbled on a piece of cheese.
4.	My new suit	1	made my eyes burn.
5.	The ice cream sundae	3	covered the sky.

Chapter 19, Lesson 1, Practice 4: Copy the following words on notebook paper. Write the correct contraction beside each word. **Key: didn't, we're, who's, I'm, she'd, you'll, we'd, they've, she's, let's, can't, it's.**
Words: did not, we are, who is, I am, she had, you will, we would, they have, she has, let us, cannot, it is.

 VOCABULARY TIME

Assign Chapter 19, Vocabulary Words #1 on page 7 in the Reference Section for students to define in their Vocabulary notebooks. Tell students they are to use a dictionary or thesaurus to look up the meanings of the vocabulary words.

Chapter 19, Vocabulary Words #1
(shout, murmur, shelf, ledge)

(End of lesson.)

Level 2—Shurley English—Homeschool Edition

CHAPTER 19   LESSON 2

Objectives: Jingles, Grammar (Practice Sentences), Practice Exercise, and Vocabulary #2.

 **JINGLE TIME**

Have students turn to the Jingle Section in their books and recite the previously-taught jingles.

 GRAMMAR TIME

Put the Practice Sentences from the box below on the board or on notebook paper. Use these sentences as you practice the concepts that have been taught. For the greatest benefit, students must participate orally with the teacher.

Chapter 19, Practice Sentences for Lesson 2
1. _____ The large family picture fell off the wall today.
2. _____ The chocolate candy melted on the table in the hallway.
3. _____ We stood on the rocky ledge behind our house.

TEACHING SCRIPT FOR CLASSIFYING PRACTICE SENTENCES

We will classify three different sentences to practice the grammar skills in the Question and Answer Flows. We will classify the sentences together. Begin. (*You might have students write the labels above the sentences at this time.*)

Question and Answer Flow for Sentence 1: The large family picture fell off the wall today.

1. What fell off the wall today? picture - SN
2. What is being said about picture? picture fell - V
3. Off - P
4. Off what? wall - OP
5. The - A
6. Fell when? today - Adv
7. What kind of picture? family - Adj
8. What kind of picture? large - Adj
9. The - A
10. SN V P1 Check
11. (Off the wall) - Prepositional phrase
12. Period, statement, declarative sentence
13. Go back to the verb - divide the complete subject from the complete predicate.

```
                              A  Adj  Adj  SN   V  P  A  OP  Adv
Classified Sentence:    SN V    The large family picture / fell (off the wall) today.   D
                        P1
```

CHAPTER 19 LESSON 2 CONTINUED

Question and Answer Flow for Sentence 2: The chocolate candy melted on the table in the hallway.

1. What melted on the table in the hallway? candy - SN
2. What is being said about candy? candy melted - V
3. On - P
4. On what? table - OP
5. The - A
6. In - P
7. In what? hallway - OP
8. The - A
9. What kind of candy? chocolate - Adj
10. The - A
11. SN V P1 Check
12. (On the table) - Prepositional phrase
13. (In the hallway) - Prepositional phrase
14. Period, statement, declarative sentence
15. Go back to the verb - divide the complete subject from the complete predicate.

```
                           A    Adj   SN   V    P  A  OP   P  A   OP
Classified Sentence:   SN V     The chocolate candy / melted (on the table) (in the hallway).  D
                       P1
```

Question and Answer Flow for Sentence 3: We stood on the rocky ledge behind our house.

1. Who stood on the rocky ledge behind our house? we - SP
2. What is being said about we? we stood - V
3. On - P
4. On what? ledge - OP
5. What kind of ledge? rocky - Adj
6. The - A
7. Behind - P
8. Behind what? house - OP
9. Whose house? our - PP
10. SN V P1 Check
11. (On the rocky ledge) - Prepositional phrase
12. (Behind our house) - Prepositional phrase
13. Period, statement, declarative sentence
14. Go back to the verb - divide the complete subject from the complete predicate.

```
                           SP   V   P  A  Adj  OP    P   PP  OP
Classified Sentence:   SN V     We / stood (on the rocky ledge) (behind our house).  D
                       P1
```

PRACTICE TIME

Have students turn to pages 65 and 66 in the Practice Section of their book and find Chapter 19, Lesson 2, Practice *(1-4)*. Go over the directions to make sure they understand what to do. Check and discuss the Practices after students have finished. *(Chapter 19, Lesson 2, Practice keys are given below and on the next page.)*

Chapter 19, Lesson 2, Practice 1: On notebook paper, make each fragment below into a complete sentence. Underline the parts you add. **(Sentences will vary.)**

1. Add a subject part to this fragment: **painted a picture**
2. Add a predicate part to this fragment: **The colorful rainbow**

Chapter 19, Lesson 2, Practice 2: Identify each kind of sentence by writing the abbreviation in the blank. **(S, F)**

__S__ 1. The children built a snowman.
__S__ 2. Joey and Matt hiked up the trail.
__F__ 3. Delivered the papers daily.
__F__ 4. The thick mane on the lion's head.
__S__ 5. Our yard was filled with yellow dandelions.

Level 2—Shurley English—Homeschool Edition

CHAPTER 19 LESSON 2 CONTINUED

Chapter 19, Lesson 2, Practice 3: Match each subject part with the correct predicate part by writing the correct sentence number in the blank.

	Subject Parts		Predicate Parts
1.	The little girl's blue dress	__2__	shattered into pieces.
2.	My dresser mirror	__1__	had ruffles.
3.	The boy's shoelaces	__4__	served hamburgers for lunch.
4.	Our school cafeteria	__5__	had long horns.
5.	John's goat	__3__	were tied in knots.

Chapter 19, Lesson 2, Practice 4: For each sentence, do these four things: (1) Write the subject. (2) Write **S** if the subject is singular or **P** if the subject is plural. (3) Write the rule number. (4) Underline the correct verb in the sentence.

Rule 1: A singular subject must use a singular verb form that ends in **s**: *is, was, has, does,* or verbs ending with **es**.

Rule 2: A plural subject, a compound subject, or the subject **YOU** must use a plural verb form that has **no s** ending: *are, were, do, have,* or verbs without **s** or **es** endings. (A plural verb form is also called the *plain form.*)

Subject	S or P	Rule	
lizard	S	1	1. The green **lizard** (chase, <u>chases</u>) the grasshopper.
crab	S	1	2. A **crab** (pinch, <u>pinches</u>) my toe.
girls	P	2	3. The **girls** (<u>wear</u>, wears) ribbons in their hair.
ship	S	1	4. The **ship** (sail, <u>sails</u>) across the ocean.
Robin and Lisa	P	2	5. **Robin** and **Lisa** (<u>shiver</u>, shivers) in the cold.
you	P	2	6. **You** (<u>tie</u>, ties) your shoes.

 VOCABULARY TIME

Assign Chapter 19, Vocabulary Words **#2** on page 7 in the Reference Section for students to define in their Vocabulary notebooks. Tell students they are to use a dictionary or thesaurus to look up the meanings of the vocabulary words.

Chapter 19, Vocabulary Words #2
(shine, sparkle, victory, defeat)

(End of lesson.)

Level 2—Shurley English—Homeschool Edition

CHAPTER 19   LESSON 3
Objectives: Jingles, Grammar (Practice Sentences, Practice and Improved Sentence), Practice Exercise, and Activity.

 JINGLE TIME

Have students turn to the Jingle Section in their books and recite the previously-taught jingles.

 GRAMMAR TIME

Put the Practice Sentences from the box below on the board or on notebook paper. Use these sentences as you practice the concepts that have been taught. For the greatest benefit, students must participate orally with the teacher.

Chapter 19, Practice Sentences for Lesson 3
1. _____ Spaghetti sauce simmers on Grandma's stove.
2. _____ His sisters sat proudly on their new ponies.
3. _____ The long country road turned suddenly to the left.

<u>*TEACHING SCRIPT FOR CLASSIFYING PRACTICE SENTENCES*</u>

We will classify three different sentences to practice the grammar skills in the Question and Answer Flows. We will classify the sentences together. Begin. (*You might have students write the labels above the sentences at this time.*)

Question and Answer Flow for Sentence 1: **Spaghetti sauce simmers on Grandma's stove.**

1. What simmers on Grandma's stove?   6. What kind of sauce? spaghetti - Adj
   sauce - SN   7. SN V P1 Check
2. What is being said about sauce? sauce simmers - V   8. (On Grandma's stove) - Prepositional phrase
3. On - P   9. Period, statement, declarative sentence
4. On what? stove - OP   10. Go back to the verb - divide the complete subject
5. Whose stove? Grandma's - PN   from the complete predicate.
 	
                               Adj   SN   V   P   PN   OP
Classified Sentence: <u>SN V</u>   Spaghetti sauce / simmers (on Grandma's stove). D
                                  P1

Level 2 Homeschool Teacher's Manual

Level 2—Shurley English—Homeschool Edition

CHAPTER 19 LESSON 3 CONTINUED

Question and Answer Flow for Sentence 2: His sisters sat proudly on their new ponies.

1. Who sat proudly on their new ponies? sisters - SN
2. What is being said about sisters? sisters sat - V
3. Sat how? proudly - Adv
4. On - P
5. On what? ponies - OP
6. What kind of ponies? new - Adj
7. Whose ponies? their - PP
8. Whose sisters? his - PP
9. SN V P1 Check
10. (On their new ponies) - Prepositional phrase
11. Period, statement, declarative sentence
12. Go back to the verb - divide the complete subject from the complete predicate.

```
                          PP   SN   V    Adv    P   PP  Adj  OP
Classified Sentence:     SN V   His sisters / sat proudly (on their new ponies).  D
                          P1
```

Question and Answer Flow for Sentence 3: The long country road turned suddenly to the left.

1. What turned suddenly to the left? road - SN
2. What is being said about road? road turned - V
3. Turned how? suddenly - Adv
4. To - P
5. To what? left - OP
6. The - A
7. What kind of road? country - Adj
8. What kind of road? long - Adj
9. The - A
10. SN V P1 Check
11. (To the left) - Prepositional phrase
12. Period, statement, declarative sentence
13. Go back to the verb - divide the complete subject from the complete predicate.

```
                          A   Adj   Adj   SN    V    Adv    P  A  OP
Classified Sentence:     SN V   The long country road / turned suddenly (to the left).  D
                          P1
```

TEACHING SCRIPT FOR A PRACTICE SENTENCE

Put these labels on the board: **A Adj Adj SN V Adv P PP Adj OP**

Look at the new sentence labels on the board: **A Adj Adj SN V Adv P PP Adj OP**. I will guide you again through the process of writing a sentence to practice all the parts that you have learned.

Get out a sheet of notebook paper. On the top line of your notebook paper, write the title *Practice Sentence*. Copy the sentence labels from the board onto your notebook paper. Be sure to leave plenty of writing space between each label. Now, I will guide you through the process you will use whenever you write a Practice Sentence with a prepositional phrase.

1. Go to the **SN** label for the subject noun. Think of a noun that you want to use as your subject. Write the noun you have chosen on the line *under* the **SN** label.

2. Go to the **V** label for the verb. Think of a verb that tells what your subject does. Make sure that your verb makes sense with the subject noun. Write the verb you have chosen on the line *under* the **V** label.

CHAPTER 19 LESSON 3 CONTINUED

3. Go to the **Adv** label for the adverb. Immediately go to the verb in your sentence and ask an adverb question. What are the adverb questions? (*How, When, Where*) Choose one adverb question to ask and write your adverb answer *under* the **Adv** label.

4. Go to the **P** label for the preposition. Think of a preposition word that tells something about your verb. You must be careful to choose a preposition word that makes sense with the noun you will choose for the object of the preposition in your next step. Write the word you have chosen for a preposition *under* the **P** label.

5. Go to the **OP** label for the object of the preposition. If you like the noun you thought of while thinking of a preposition, write it down under the **OP** label. If you prefer, think of another noun by asking **what** or **whom** after your preposition. Check to make sure the preposition and object of the preposition make sense together and also make sense with the rest of the sentence. Remember, the object of the preposition will always answer the question **what** or **whom** after the preposition. Write the word you have chosen for the object of the preposition *under* the **OP** label.

6. Go to the **Adj** label for the adjective. Go to the object of the preposition that you just wrote and ask an adjective question to describe the object-of-the-preposition noun. What are the adjective questions? (*What kind, Which one, How many*) Choose one adjective question to ask and write your adjective answer *under* the **Adj** label next to the object of the preposition. Always check to make sure your answers are making sense in the sentence.

7. Go to the **PP** label for the possessive pronoun that is part of your prepositional phrase. Repeat the Possessive Pronoun Jingle to help you think of a pronoun that you want to use as your possessive pronoun. You will choose one of the possessive pronouns that makes the best sense in your sentence. Write the possessive pronoun you have chosen *under* the **PP** label.

8. Go to the **Adj** label for another adjective. Go to the subject noun of your sentence and ask an adjective question. What are the adjective questions again? (*What kind, Which one, How many*) Choose one adjective question to ask and write your adjective answer *under* the **Adj** label next to the subject noun.

9. Go to the **Adj** label for the third adjective. Go to the subject noun again and ask another adjective question. You can ask the same adjective question, or you can ask a different adjective question. Write another adjective *under* the third **Adj** label.

10. Go to the **A** label for the article adjective in the subject area. What are the three article adjectives again? (*a, an,* and *the*) Choose the article adjective that makes the best sense in your sentence. Write the article adjective you have chosen *under* the **A** label.

11. Finally, check your Practice Sentence to make sure it has the necessary parts to be a complete sentence. What are the five parts of a complete sentence? (*subject, verb, complete sense, capital letter, and an end mark*) Does your Practice Sentence have the five parts of a complete sentence? (*Allow time for students to read over their sentences and to make any corrections they need to make.*)

CHAPTER 19 LESSON 3 CONTINUED

TEACHING SCRIPT FOR THE IMPROVED SENTENCE

Under your Practice Sentence, write the title *Improved Sentence* on another line. To improve your Practice Sentence, you will make two synonym changes, one antonym change, and your choice of a complete word change or another synonym or antonym change. I will give you time to write your Improved Sentence. *(After students have finished, check and discuss students' Practice and Improved Sentences.)*

 PRACTICE TIME

Have students turn to pages 67 and 68 in the Practice Section of their book and find Chapter 19, Lesson 3, Practice *(1-5)*. Go over the directions to make sure they understand what to do. Check and discuss the Practices after students have finished. *(Chapter 19, Lesson 3, Practice keys are given below and on the next page.)*

Chapter 19, Lesson 3, Practice 1: Use the following guidelines to make each noun possessive. First, identify each noun as singular or plural by writing **S** or **P** in the first blank. Next, write the correct rule number from the list below in the second blank. Finally, write the possessive form of each noun as singular possessive or as plural possessive.

1. For a singular noun - add (**'s**) Rule 1: girl's		2. For a plural noun that ends in *s* - add (**'**) Rule 2: girls'		3. For a plural noun that does not end in *s* - add (**'s**) Rule 3: women's
Noun	**S-P**	**Rule**	**Singular Possessive**	**Plural Possessive**
1. towers	P	2		towers'
2. worm	S	1	worm's	
3. children	P	3		children's
4. melons	P	2		melons'
5. Kelly	S	1	Kelly's	

Chapter 19, Lesson 3, Practice 2: Match each subject part with the correct predicate part by writing the correct sentence number in the blank.

Subject Parts
1. My wrinkled shirt
2. Two lifeguards
3. A handsome prince
4. The jelly jar
5. A wasp

Predicate Parts
_4_ was made of glass.
_2_ watched the children swim.
_5_ stung my arm.
_3_ rescued the princess.
_1_ needs to be ironed.

Chapter 19, Lesson 3, Practice 3: Identify each kind of sentence by writing the abbreviation in the blank. (**S, F**)

_F_ 1. Through the hole in the door.
_S_ 2. I made a strawberry milkshake.
_F_ 3. Ticking loudly on the wall.
_S_ 4. The stranger asked for a dollar.
_F_ 5. Up the rocky hill.

CHAPTER 19 LESSON 3 CONTINUED

Chapter 19, Lesson 3, Practice 4: On notebook paper, make each fragment below into a complete sentence. Underline the parts you add. **(Sentences will vary.)**

1. Add a subject part to this fragment: **skated across the pond**
2. Add a predicate part to this fragment: **The shaggy dog**

Chapter 19, Lesson 3, Practice 5: Correct the capitalization and punctuation mistakes. Write the rule numbers above the capitalization corrections and below the punctuation corrections. Use Reference 24 for the capitalization rules and Reference 26 for the punctuation rules. The references are located on pages 18 and 19 in your Reference Section.

```
   1 (or 2)                  5     5        5         (Capitalization Rule numbers)
      I                      F     C        C
1. i  went  to  a  conference  in  ft.  collins,  colorado.   (Editing Guide: 4 capitals & 3 punctuation)
                                    2        3         5    (Punctuation Rule numbers)
```

 ACTIVITY / ASSIGNMENT TIME

Read the first paragraph below to your students. After you read the paragraph, ask students if the meaning was very clear. Tell students the story was so confusing because it didn't contain any pronouns, possessive nouns, or possessive pronouns, therefore forcing the noun **Tina** to be repeated. Discuss the importance of pronouns, possessive nouns, and possessive pronouns with your students. Then, help them improve the story with subject pronouns, possessive nouns, and possessive pronouns.

This is the book of Tina. Tina left the book of Tina at the house of Tina. Tina must use the book of Julie while Tina is at school. Tina wrote on the calendar of Tina to remember the book of Tina today because the class of Tina is doing an important project and Tina needs the book of Tina to finish it. Tina promised the teacher of Tina that Tina would remember the book of Tina tomorrow.

Sample improved paragraph:

This is Tina's book. She left her book at her house. Tina must use Julie's book while she is at school. Tina wrote on her calendar to remember her book today because her class is doing an important project and she needs her book to finish it. She promised her teacher that she would remember her book tomorrow.

(End of lesson.)

Level 2—Shurley English—Homeschool Edition

CHAPTER 19   LESSON 4

Objectives: Jingles, Study, Test, Check, Writing (Journal), and State Activity.

 JINGLE TIME

Have students turn to the Jingle Section in their books and recite the previously-taught jingles.

 STUDY TIME

Have students study the vocabulary words in their vocabulary notebooks. Remind students that any vocabulary word in their notebooks could be on their test. Also, have students study any of the skills in the Practice Section that they need to review.

 TEST TIME

Have students turn to page 98 in the Test Section of their book and find Chapter 19 Test. Go over the directions to make sure they understand what to do. (*Chapter 19 Test key is on the next page.*)

 CHECK TIME

After students have finished, check and discuss their test papers. Make sure they understand why their answers are right or wrong. (*For total points, count each required answer as a point.*)

 STATE ACTIVITY TIME

Students will continue to draw or trace the states and to write the following questions and answers.

New Hampshire	New Jersey
1. What is the state on the front of this card? **New Hampshire**	1. What is the state on the front of this card? **New Jersey**
2. What is the capital of New Hampshire? **Concord**	2. What is the capital of New Jersey? **Trenton**
3. What is the postal abbreviation of New Hampshire? **NH**	3. What is the postal abbreviation of New Jersey? **NJ**

Color these states. Use the cards to quiz family members, friends, and relatives. You may want to time the responses to your questions.

(End of lesson.)

Chapter 19 Test
(Student Page 98)

Exercise 1: Classify each sentence.

```
            PN      SN        V      P  A    Adj    OP
1. SN V    Arthur's brother / lives (on a deserted island).  D
   P1

            A    SN       V      Adv   P  A   OP
2. SN V    The stars / sparkled brightly (in the night).  D
   P1
```

Exercise 2: Use Sentence 2 to underline the complete subject once and the complete predicate twice and to complete the table below.

List the Noun Used	List the Noun Job	Singular or Plural	Common or Proper	Simple Subject	Simple Predicate
1. stars	2. SN	3. P	4. C	5. stars	6. sparkled
7. night	8. OP	9. S	10. C		

Exercise 3: Identify each pair of words as synonyms or antonyms by putting parentheses ( ) around **syn** or **ant**.

1. remote, distant	**(syn)** ant	4. victory, defeat	syn **(ant)**	7. sparkle, shine	**(syn)** ant
2. shout, murmur	syn **(ant)**	5. narrow, wide	syn **(ant)**	8. arrogant, proud	**(syn)** ant
3. shelf, ledge	**(syn)** ant	6. moldy, fresh	syn **(ant)**	9. restless, patient	syn **(ant)**

Exercise 4: Use the following guidelines to make each noun possessive. First, identify each noun as singular or plural by writing **S** or **P** in the first blank. Next, write the correct rule number from the list below in the second blank. Finally, write the possessive form of each noun as singular possessive or as plural possessive.

1. For a singular noun - add (**'s**) Rule 1: girl's	2. For a plural noun that ends in **s** - add (**'**) Rule 2: girls'	3. For a plural noun that does not end in **s** - add (**'s**) Rule 3: women's

Noun	S-P	Rule	Singular Possessive	Plural Possessive
1. horse	S	1	horse's	
2. men	P	3		men's
3. tractors	P	2		tractors'

Exercise 5: Match each subject part with the correct predicate part by writing the correct sentence number in the blank.

Subject Parts
1. The tea kettle
2. The juicy tomatoes
3. The crispy toast
4. Several candles
5. The willow branches

Predicate Parts
- 3   burned in the toaster.
- 4   flickered in the dark.
- 1   whistled loudly.
- 5   swayed in the wind.
- 2   ripened on the vine.

Exercise 6: Copy the following words on notebook paper. Write the correct contraction beside each word.
Key: he'd, you've, hasn't, don't, you're, who's, you'd, they'll, I'll, won't, hadn't.
Words: he would, you have, has not, do not, you are, who is, you had, they will, I will, will not, had not.

Exercise 7: In your journal, write a paragraph summarizing what you have learned this week.

Level 2—Shurley English—Homeschool Edition

CHAPTER 19 LESSON 4 CONTINUED

<u>TEACHER INSTRUCTIONS</u>

Use the Question and Answer Flows below for the sentences on the Chapter 19 Test.

Question and Answer Flow for Sentence 1: Arthur's brother lives on a deserted island.

1. Who lives on a deserted island? brother - SN
2. What is being said about brother? brother lives - V
3. On - P
4. On what? island - OP
5. What kind of island? deserted - Adj
6. A - A
7. Whose brother? Arthur's - PN
8. SN V P1 Check
9. (On a deserted island) - Prepositional phrase
10. Period, statement, declarative sentence
11. Go back to the verb - divide the complete subject from the complete predicate.

Classified Sentence:
```
                       PN      SN    V   P A  Adj    OP
         SN V    Arthur's brother / lives (on a deserted island).  D
         P1
```

Question and Answer Flow for Sentence 2: The stars sparkled brightly in the night.

1. What sparkled brightly in the night? stars - SN
2. What is being said about stars? stars sparkled - V
3. Sparkled how? brightly - Adv
4. In - P
5. In what? night - OP
6. The - A
7. The - A
8. SN V P1 Check
9. (In the night) - Prepositional phrase
10. Period, statement, declarative sentence
11. Go back to the verb - divide the complete subject from the complete predicate.

Classified Sentence:
```
                  A  SN     V      Adv    P  A  OP
         SN V   The stars / sparkled brightly (in the night).  D
         P1
```

CHAPTER 19   LESSON 5

Objectives: Writing Assignment #13 and Sentence Time.

 WRITING TIME

TEACHING INSTRUCTIONS FOR WRITING ASSIGNMENT #13

Give Writing Assignment #13 from the box below. Remind students to use the Writing Checklist in Reference 17 to check their finished writing assignment.

Read, check, and discuss Writing Assignment #13 after students have finished their final papers. Use the Writing Checklist (*Reference 17 on teacher's page 112*) as you check and discuss students' papers. Make sure students are using the checklist correctly.

Writing Assignment Box

Writing Assignment #13:   Descriptive Paragraph

Writing topic choices: My Day at the Beach   or   My Funniest Relative   or   The Big Cookout

---

 SENTENCE TIME

Chapter 19, Lesson 5, Sentence: Use colored markers to match each label with the correct sentence part by drawing a line from one to the other. Then, use the labels to arrange the sentence parts into a sentence that you will write on the sentence line below. *(The order of the words in your sentence should be in the same sequence as the vertical list of sentence labels.)* Create other labels and scrambled sentence parts on notebook paper for family members to solve. You may color code the sentence parts. *(See page 115 in the student book.)*

Labels for Order of Sentence	Scrambled Sentence Parts
PP	frantically
PN	today
SN	my
V	her
Adv	sister's
P	for
PP	looked
Adj	ring
OP	friend
Adv	diamond

Sentence: My sister's friend looked frantically for her diamond ring today.

(End of lesson.)

CHAPTER 20   LESSON 1

Objectives: Jingles, Grammar (Practice Sentences, Skill Builder Check, Review Six Parts of Speech), Skill (Identify Verb Tenses), Practice Exercise, Vocabulary #1, and Activity.

 **JINGLE TIME**

Have students turn to the Jingle Section in their books and recite the previously-taught jingles.

 GRAMMAR TIME

Put the Practice Sentences from the box below on the board or on notebook paper. Use these sentences as you practice the concepts that have been taught. For the greatest benefit, students must participate orally with the teacher.

Chapter 20, Practice Sentences for Lesson 1
1. _____ Our family cat crawls between my feet before breakfast.
2. _____ A bucket of paint fell on the floor!
3. _____ The snow fell gently on the trees in the garden.

TEACHING SCRIPT FOR CLASSIFYING PRACTICE SENTENCES

We will classify three different sentences to practice the grammar skills in the Question and Answer Flows. We will classify the sentences together. Begin. (*You might have students write the labels above the sentences at this time.*)

Question and Answer Flow for Sentence 1: Our family cat crawls between my feet before breakfast.

1. What crawls between my feet before breakfast? cat - SN
2. What is being said about cat? cat crawls - V
3. Between - P
4. Between what? feet - OP
5. Whose feet? my - PP
6. Before - P
7. Before what? breakfast - OP
8. What kind of cat? family - Adj
9. Whose cat? our - PP
10. SN V P1 Check
11. (Between my feet) - Prepositional phrase
12. (Before breakfast) - Prepositional phrase
13. Period, statement, declarative sentence
14. Go back to the verb - divide the complete subject from the complete predicate.

```
                           PP  Adj  SN   V        P  PP OP   P    OP
Classified Sentence:       SN  V    Our family / crawls (between my feet) (before breakfast). D
                           P1
```

CHAPTER 20 LESSON 1 CONTINUED

Question and Answer Flow for Sentence 2: A bucket of paint fell on the floor!

1. What fell on the floor? bucket - SN
2. What is being said about bucket? bucket fell - V
3. On - P
4. On what? floor - OP
5. The - A
6. Of - P
7. Of what? paint - OP
8. A - A
9. SN V P1 Check
10. (Of paint) - Prepositional phrase
11. (On the floor) - Prepositional phrase
12. Exclamation point, strong feeling, exclamatory sentence
13. Go back to the verb - divide the complete subject from the complete predicate.

```
                                   A  SN     P   OP    V    P  A   OP
Classified Sentence:     SN V      A bucket (of paint) / fell (on the floor)!  E
                         P1
```

Question and Answer Flow for Sentence 3: The snow fell gently on the trees in the garden.

1. What fell gently on the trees in the garden? snow - SN
2. What is being said about snow? snow fell - V
3. Fell how? gently - Adv
4. On - P
5. On what? trees - OP
6. The - A
7. In - P
8. In what? garden - OP
9. The - A
10. The - A
11. SN V P1 Check
12. (On the trees) - Prepositional phrase
13. (In the garden) - Prepositional phrase
14. Period, statement, declarative sentence
15. Go back to the verb - divide the complete subject from the complete predicate.

```
                                  A  SN    V   Adv    P  A   OP    P  A    OP
Classified Sentence:    SN V      The snow / fell gently (on the trees) (in the garden).  D
                        P1
```

Use Sentences 1-3 that you just classified with your students to do a Skill Builder Check. Use the guidelines below.

Skill Builder Check

1. **Noun check.**
   (Say the job and then say the noun. Circle each noun.)
2. **Identify the nouns as singular or plural.**
   (Write **S** or **P** above each noun.)
3. **Identify the nouns as common or proper.**
   (Follow established procedure for oral identification.)
4. **Do a vocabulary check.**
   (Follow established procedure for oral identification.)
5. **Identify the complete subject and the complete predicate.** (Underline the complete subject once and the complete predicate twice.)
6. **Identify the simple subject and simple predicate.**
   (Underline the simple subject once and the simple predicate twice. Bold, or highlight, the lines to distinguish them from the complete subject and complete predicate.)

TEACHING SCRIPT FOR REVIEWING THE SIX PARTS OF SPEECH

What are the six parts of speech that we have covered? *(noun, verb, adjective, adverb, preposition,* and *pronoun)* (Chant several times the six parts of speech that the students have learned for reinforcement and fun.)

CHAPTER 20 LESSON 1 CONTINUED

SKILL TIME

TEACHING SCRIPT FOR IDENTIFYING VERB TENSES

You are going to learn about verb tenses to help you understand verbs better. As you learn more about verbs, it will help improve your writing. Look at Reference 37 on page 25 while I go over this important information with you. *(Read the information to your students and work through the guided examples provided.)*

Reference 37: Present, Past, and Future Verb Tenses
When you are writing paragraphs, you must use verbs that are in the same tense. Tense means time. The tense of a verb shows the time of the action. There are three basic tenses that show when an action takes place. They are **present tense, past tense,** and **future tense.** Now you will learn to recognize each kind of tense.
1. The **present tense** shows that something is happening now, in the present. Present tense verbs that are singular end in "s." Present tense verbs that are plural do not end in "s." (Singular present tense verb: walks) (Plural present tense verb: walk) (**Examples:** The girl <u>walks</u> to school. The girls <u>walk</u> to school.)
2. The **past tense** shows that something has happened sometime in the past. Most past tense verbs end in -ed, -d, or -t for both the singular and plural forms. (Singular past tense verb: walked) (Plural past tense verb: walked) (**Examples:** The girl <u>walked</u> to school. The girls <u>walked</u> to school.)
3. The **future tense** shows that something will happen sometime in the future. The future tense form has the helping verb *will* or *shall* before the main verb for both the singular and plural forms. (Singular future tense verb: will walk) (Plural future tense verb: will walk) (**Examples:** The girl <u>will walk</u> to school. The girls <u>will walk</u> to school.)

Present Tense	Past Tense	Future Tense
What to look for: **one verb** with s, es, or plain ending.	What to look for: **one verb** with -ed, -d, or -t.	What to look for: **will** or **shall** with a main verb.
The pirates <u>search</u> for the treasure.	The pirates <u>searched</u> for the treasure.	The pirates <u>will search</u> for the treasure.

Directions: Identify the tense of each underlined verb by writing a number **1** for present tense, a number **2** for past tense, and a number **3** for future tense.

Verb Tense	Verbs	Verb Tense	Verbs
2	1. They <u>worked</u> on the science project.	3	4. The snowflakes <u>will drift</u> to the ground.
3	2. They <u>will work</u> on the science project.	1	5. The snowflakes <u>drift</u> to the ground.
1	3. They <u>work</u> on the science project.	2	6. The snowflakes <u>drifted</u> to the ground.

Level 2—Shurley English—Homeschool Edition

CHAPTER 20 LESSON 1 CONTINUED

 PRACTICE TIME

Have students turn to page 69 in the Practice Section of their book and find Chapter 20, Lesson 1, Practice. Go over the directions to make sure they understand what to do. Check and discuss the Practice after students have finished. (*Chapter 20, Lesson 1, Practice key is given below.*)

Chapter 20, Lesson 1, Practice: Identify the tense of each underlined verb by writing a number **1** for present tense, a number **2** for past tense, and a number **3** for future tense.

Verb Tense	Verbs	Verb Tense	Verbs
2	1. He <u>played</u> the trombone.	1	4. The teams <u>rest</u> after the long game.
1	2. He <u>plays</u> the trombone.	3	5. The teams <u>will rest</u> after the long game.
3	3. He <u>will play</u> the trombone.	2	6. The teams <u>rested</u> after the long game.

 VOCABULARY TIME

Assign Chapter 20, Vocabulary Words **#1** on page 7 in the Reference Section for students to define in their Vocabulary notebooks. Tell students they are to use a dictionary or thesaurus to look up the meanings of the vocabulary words.

Chapter 20, Vocabulary Words #1
(rely, depend, clear, murky)

 ACTIVITY / ASSIGNMENT TIME

This activity will expose students to a variety of describing words and increase their vocabulary. First, you should pick a familiar object in a designated room to describe. Ask students to close their eyes or use a blindfold for more fun. Without using the name of the object, give hints about the object. Use one descriptive word at a time. The students must keep their eyes closed the entire time the object is being described. Keep score by adding up the number of hints you must give before students guess the object. Then, give the students a turn to pick out an object and give descriptive hints to you. Again, keep up with the number of hints given before the object is guessed. Play this guessing game for several rounds. The player with the lowest score at the end of the game wins. This game can be played with other family members.

(End of lesson.)

Level 2 Homeschool Teacher's Manual

Level 2—Shurley English—Homeschool Edition

CHAPTER 20   LESSON 2

Objectives: Jingles, Grammar (Practice Sentences), Skill (Identify Regular and Irregular Verbs), and Vocabulary #2.

 **JINGLE TIME**

Have students turn to the Jingle Section in their books and recite the previously-taught jingles.

 GRAMMAR TIME

Put the Practice Sentences from the box below on the board or on notebook paper. Use these sentences as you practice the concepts that have been taught. For the greatest benefit, students must participate orally with the teacher.

Chapter 20, Practice Sentences for Lesson 2
1. _____ They played in the city park for several hours.
2. _____ Mother's trip depended on the weather conditions.
3. _____ My friends camped in the woods overnight.

TEACHING SCRIPT FOR CLASSIFYING PRACTICE SENTENCES

We will classify three different sentences to practice the grammar skills in the Question and Answer Flows. We will classify the sentences together. Begin. (*You might have students write the labels above the sentences at this time.*)

Question and Answer Flow for Sentence 1: They played in the city park for several hours.
1. Who played in the city park for several hours? they - SP
2. What is being said about they? they played - V
3. In - P
4. In what? park - OP
5. What kind of park? city - Adj
6. The - A
7. For - P
8. For what? hours - OP
9. How many hours? several - Adj
10. SN V P1 Check
11. (In the city park) - Prepositional phrase
12. (For several hours) - Prepositional phrase
13. Period, statement, declarative sentence
14. Go back to the verb - divide the complete subject from the complete predicate.
Classified Sentence: SP   V   P A Adj OP   P   Adj   OP
SN V   They / played (in the city park) (for several hours). D
P1

CHAPTER 20 LESSON 2 CONTINUED

Question and Answer Flow for Sentence 2: Mother's trip depended on the weather conditions.

1. What depended on the weather conditions? trip - SN
2. What is being said about trip? trip depended - V
3. On - P
4. On what? conditions - OP
5. What kind of conditions? weather - Adj
6. The - A
7. Whose trip? Mother's - PN
8. SN V P1 Check
9. (On the weather conditions) - Prepositional phrase
10. Period, statement, declarative sentence
11. Go back to the verb - divide the complete subject from the complete predicate.

Classified Sentence:
               PN SN V P A Adj   OP
    SN V   Mother's trip / depended (on the weather conditions). D
     P1

Question and Answer Flow for Sentence 3: My friends camped in the woods overnight.

1. Who camped in the woods overnight? friends - SN
2. What is being said about friends? friends camped - V
3. In - P
4. In what? woods - OP
5. The - A
6. Camped when? overnight - Adv
7. Whose friends? my - PP
8. SN V P1 Check
9. (In the woods) - Prepositional phrase
10. Period, statement, declarative sentence
11. Go back to the verb - divide the complete subject from the complete predicate.

Classified Sentence:
              PP SN   V   P A OP   Adv
    SN V   My friends / camped (in the woods) overnight. D
     P1

SKILL TIME

TEACHING SCRIPT FOR IDENTIFYING REGULAR AND IRREGULAR VERBS

In order to work effectively with verbs, there are two terms you must know and use. These words are *regular* and *irregular*. Let's say these two words together several times. (*Say the words regular and irregular several times together.*) Look at Reference 38 while I go over information about regular and irregular verbs with you. (*Discuss the information below and on the next page with your students.*)

Reference 38: Regular and Irregular Verbs
All verbs can be changed to past tense. The way you change a verb to past tense will make it a regular or irregular verb.
Regular Verbs: As you have just learned, you add -ed, -d, or -t to most verbs to form the past tense. Verbs that are made past tense by adding -ed, -d, or -t are called **regular verbs**. Most verbs are regular verbs because they form their past tense by adding -ed,-d, or -t.
Irregular Verbs: However, a few verbs, like the verbs on the irregular verb chart, are made past tense by a spelling change. The verbs from the verb chart are called **irregular verbs**. The only way to learn how to write and speak using irregular verbs is to memorize them.

CHAPTER 20 LESSON 2 CONTINUED

Reference 38: Regular and Irregular Verbs (continued)
1. **Regular and irregular present tense verbs:**   (Regular present tense verbs: walk, walks) (Irregular present tense verbs: fall, falls)   (**Examples:** The girls <u>walk</u> to school. The leaves <u>fall</u> from the tree.)
2. **Regular and irregular past tense verbs:**   (Regular past tense verb: walked) (Irregular past tense verb: fell)   (**Examples:** The girls <u>walked</u> to school. The leaves <u>fell</u> from the tree.)
3. **Regular and irregular future tense verbs:**   (Regular future tense verb: will walk) (Irregular future tense verb: will fall)   (**Examples:** The girls <u>will walk</u> to school. The leaves <u>will fall</u> from the tree.)

Present Tense	Past Tense	Future Tense
What to look for: **one verb** with s, es, or plain ending.	What to look for: **one verb** with -ed, -d, or -t or an irregular spelling word.	What to look for: **will** or **shall** with a main verb.
1. We <u>climb</u> up the tree. 2. The ducks <u>fly</u> over the pond.	3. We <u>climbed</u> up the tree. 4. The ducks <u>flew</u> over the pond.	5. We <u>will climb</u> up the tree. 6. The ducks <u>will fly</u> over the pond.

Directions: Identify the tense of each underlined verb by writing a number **1** for present tense, a number **2** for past tense, and a number **3** for future tense. Use the verb chart for the irregular verbs.

Verb Tense	Regular Verbs	Verb Tense	Irregular Verbs
1	1. Grandmother <u>bakes</u> cookies.	1	4. We <u>drink</u> milk for breakfast.
2	2. Grandmother <u>baked</u> cookies.	2	5. We <u>drank</u> milk for breakfast.
3	3. Grandmother <u>will bake</u> cookies.	3	6. We <u>will drink</u> milk for breakfast.

TEACHING SCRIPT FOR ADDING IRREGULAR VERBS TO THE SKILL BUILDER CHECK

We will now add an Irregular Verb Chart to the Skill Builder Check. Look at the Irregular Verb Chart that is located in Reference 39 on page 27 in your book. (*The irregular verb chart is reproduced for you on the next page.*) We will recite the Irregular Verb Chart during the Skill Builder Checks to help you learn the different parts of some irregular verbs.

Even though this is only a partial listing of irregular verbs, it will expose you to the correct forms on a consistent basis. We can add more irregular verbs as we think of them. (*You do not need to chant all of the verb chart for every Skill Builder Check. Pick only a few verbs to chant if your child does not have a problem with irregular verb usage.*)

If you use an irregular verb incorrectly, either spoken or written, I will say, "I need a correction for the verb ____," and you will be expected to recite the two corrections several times in short sentences. If you cannot remember how to use the two corrections in short sentences, you could use the chart to help you. (*Explain the example below.*)

        Example: He **seen** the movie.   Verb used incorrectly: **seen**

1. Correction with the past tense form: He **saw** the movie; He **saw** the movie; He **saw** the movie.
2. Correction with a helping verb: He **had seen** the movie; He **had seen** the movie; He **had seen** the movie.

CHAPTER 20 LESSON 2 CONTINUED

Reference 39: Irregular Verb Chart			
PRESENT	PAST	PAST PARTICIPLE	PRESENT PARTICIPLE
become	became	(has) become	(is) becoming
blow	blew	(has) blown	(is) blowing
break	broke	(has) broken	(is) breaking
bring	brought	(has) brought	(is) bringing
burst	burst	(has) burst	(is) bursting
buy	bought	(has) bought	(is) buying
choose	chose	(has) chosen	(is) choosing
come	came	(has) come	(is) coming
drink	drank	(has) drunk	(is) drinking
drive	drove	(has) driven	(is) driving
eat	ate	(has) eaten	(is) eating
fall	fell	(has) fallen	(is) falling
fly	flew	(has) flown	(is) flying
freeze	froze	(has) frozen	(is) freezing
get	got	(has) gotten	(is) getting
give	gave	(has) given	(is) giving
grow	grew	(has) grown	(is) growing
know	knew	(has) known	(is) knowing
lie	lay	(has) lain	(is) lying
lay	laid	(has) laid	(is) laying
make	made	(has) made	(is) making
ride	rode	(has) ridden	(is) riding
ring	rang	(has) rung	(is) ringing
rise	rose	(has) risen	(is) rising
sell	sold	(has) sold	(is) selling
sing	sang	(has) sung	(is) singing
sink	sank	(has) sunk	(is) sinking
set	set	(has) set	(is) setting
sit	sat	(has) sat	(is) sitting
shoot	shot	(has) shot	(is) shooting
swim	swam	(has) swum	(is) swimming
take	took	(has) taken	(is) taking
tell	told	(has) told	(is) telling
throw	threw	(has) thrown	(is) throwing
wear	wore	(has) worn	(is) wearing
write	wrote	(has) written	(is) writing

VOCABULARY TIME

Assign Chapter 20, Vocabulary Words **#2** on page 7 in the Reference Section for students to define in their Vocabulary notebooks. Students should use a dictionary or thesaurus to look up vocabulary words.

Chapter 20, Vocabulary Words #2
(relaxed, anxious, damage, injure)

(End of lesson.)

CHAPTER 20   LESSON 3

Objectives: Jingles, Grammar (Practice Sentences, Practice and Improved Sentence), and Practice Exercise.

JINGLE TIME

Have students turn to the Jingle Section in their books and recite the previously-taught jingles.

GRAMMAR TIME

Put the Practice Sentences from the box below on the board or on notebook paper. Use these sentences as you practice the concepts that have been taught. For the greatest benefit, students must participate orally with the teacher.

Chapter 20, Practice Sentences for Lesson 3
1. _____ The circus clowns painted on our faces yesterday.
2. _____ We went to church on Sunday.
3. _____ Jan's family camped in the mountains on their vacation.

TEACHING SCRIPT FOR CLASSIFYING PRACTICE SENTENCES

We will classify three different sentences to practice the grammar skills in the Question and Answer Flows. We will classify the sentences together. Begin. (*You might have students write the labels above the sentences at this time.*)

Question and Answer Flow for Sentence 1: The circus clowns painted on our faces yesterday.
1. Who painted on our faces yesterday? clowns - SN
2. What is being said about clowns? clowns painted - V
3. On - P
4. On what? faces - OP
5. Whose faces? our - PP
6. Painted when? yesterday - Adv
7. What kind of clowns? circus - Adj
8. The - A
9. SN V P1 Check
10. (On our faces) - Prepositional phrase
11. Period, statement, declarative sentence
12. Go back to the verb - divide the complete subject from the complete predicate.

Classified Sentence:

```
                        A   Adj    SN        V     P  PP   OP      Adv
         SN V           The circus clowns / painted (on our faces) yesterday.  D
         ----
         P1
```

CHAPTER 20 LESSON 3 CONTINUED

Question and Answer Flow for Sentence 2: We went to church on Sunday.

1. Who went to church on Sunday? we - SP
2. What is being said about we? we went - V
3. To - P
4. To what? church - OP
5. On - P
6. On what? Sunday - OP
7. SN V P1 Check
8. (To church) - Prepositional phrase
9. (On Sunday) - Prepositional phrase
10. Period, statement, declarative sentence
11. Go back to the verb - divide the complete subject from the complete predicate.

Classified Sentence:
```
                     SP   V   P   OP   P   OP
          SN V       We / went (to church) (on Sunday).  D
          P1
```

Question and Answer Flow for Sentence 3: Jan's family camped in the mountains on their vacation.

1. Who camped in the mountains on their vacation? family - SN
2. What is being said about family? family camped - V
3. In - P
4. In what? mountains - OP
5. The - A
6. On - P
7. On what? vacation - OP
8. Whose vacation? their - PP
9. Whose family? Jan's - PN
10. SN V P1 Check
11. (In the mountains) - Prepositional phrase
12. (On their vacation) - Prepositional phrase
13. Period, statement, declarative sentence
14. Go back to the verb - divide the complete subject from the complete predicate.

Classified Sentence:
```
                     PN     SN    V     P  A   OP       P   PP    OP
          SN V       Jan's family / camped (in the mountains) (on their vacation).  D
          P1
```

TEACHING SCRIPT FOR A PRACTICE SENTENCE

> Put these labels on the board: **A Adj Adj SN V Adv P PP Adj OP**

Look at the new sentence labels on the board: **A Adj Adj SN V Adv P PP Adj OP**. I will guide you again through the process of writing a sentence to practice all the parts that you have learned.

Get out a sheet of notebook paper. On the top line of your notebook paper, write the title *Practice Sentence*. Copy the sentence labels from the board onto your notebook paper. Be sure to leave plenty of writing space between each label. Now, I will guide you through the process you will use whenever you write a Practice Sentence with a prepositional phrase.

1. Go to the **SN** label for the subject noun. Think of a noun that you want to use as your subject. Write the noun you have chosen on the line *under* the **SN** label.

2. Go to the **V** label for the verb. Think of a verb that tells what your subject does. Make sure that your verb makes sense with the subject noun. Write the verb you have chosen on the line *under* the **V** label.

CHAPTER 20 LESSON 3 CONTINUED

3. Go to the **Adv** label for the adverb. Immediately go to the verb in your sentence and ask an adverb question. What are the adverb questions? (*How, When, Where*) Choose one adverb question to ask and write your adverb answer *under* the **Adv** label.

4. Go to the **P** label for the preposition. Think of a preposition word that tells something about your verb. You must be careful to choose a preposition word that makes sense with the noun you will choose for the object of the preposition in your next step. Write the word you have chosen for a preposition *under* the **P** label.

5. Go to the **OP** label for the object of the preposition. If you like the noun you thought of while thinking of a preposition, write it down under the **OP** label. If you prefer, think of another noun by asking **what** or **whom** after your preposition. Check to make sure the preposition and object of the preposition make sense together and also make sense with the rest of the sentence. Remember, the object of the preposition will always answer the question **what** or **whom** after the preposition. Write the word you have chosen for the object of the preposition *under* the **OP** label.

6. Go to the **Adj** label for the adjective. Go to the object of the preposition that you just wrote and ask an adjective question to describe the object-of-the-preposition noun. What are the adjective questions? (*What kind, Which one, How many*) Choose one adjective question to ask and write your adjective answer *under* the **Adj** label next to the object of the preposition. Always check to make sure your answers are making sense in the sentence.

7. Go to the **PP** label for the possessive pronoun that is part of your prepositional phrase. Repeat the Possessive Pronoun Jingle to help you think of a pronoun that you want to use as your possessive pronoun. You will choose one of the possessive pronouns that makes the best sense in your sentence. Write the possessive pronoun you have chosen *under* the **PP** label.

8. Go to the **Adj** label for another adjective. Go to the subject noun of your sentence and ask an adjective question. What are the adjective questions again? (*What kind, Which one, How many*) Choose one adjective question to ask and write your adjective answer *under* the **Adj** label next to the subject noun.

9. Go to the **Adj** label for the third adjective. Go to the subject noun again and ask another adjective question. You can ask the same adjective question, or you can ask a different adjective question. Write another adjective *under* the third **Adj** label.

10. Go to the **A** label for the article adjective in the subject area. What are the three article adjectives again? (*a, an,* and *the*) Choose the article adjective that makes the best sense in your sentence. Write the article adjective you have chosen *under* the **A** label.

11. Finally, check your Practice Sentence to make sure it has the necessary parts to be a complete sentence. What are the five parts of a complete sentence? (*subject, verb, complete sense, capital letter, and an end mark*) Does your Practice Sentence have the five parts of a complete sentence? (*Allow time for students to read over their sentences and to make any corrections they need to make.*)

CHAPTER 20 LESSON 3 CONTINUED

TEACHING SCRIPT FOR THE IMPROVED SENTENCE

Under your Practice Sentence, write the title *Improved Sentence* on another line. To improve your Practice Sentence, you will make two synonym changes, one antonym change, and your choice of a complete word change or another synonym or antonym change. I will give you time to write your Improved Sentence. *(After students have finished, check and discuss students' Practice and Improved Sentences.)*

 PRACTICE TIME

Have students turn to page 69 in the Practice Section of their book and find Chapter 20, Lesson 3, Practice. Go over the directions to make sure they understand what to do. Check and discuss the Practice after students have finished. *(Chapter 20, Lesson 3, Practice key is given below.)*

Chapter 20, Lesson 3, Practice: Identify the tense of each underlined verb by writing a number **1** for present tense, a number **2** for past tense, and a number **3** for future tense. Use the verb chart for the irregular verbs.

Verb Tense	Regular Verbs	Verb Tense	Irregular Verbs
3	1. The crowd <u>will bow</u> to the king.	2	9. Steven <u>drove</u> a truck.
2	2. The crowd <u>bowed</u> to the king.	1	10. Steven <u>drives</u> a truck.
1	3. The crowd <u>bows</u> to the king.	3	11. Steven <u>will drive</u> a truck.
1	4. The ice <u>melts</u> in her glass.	2	12. I <u>ate</u> a piece of her cake.
3	5. The ice <u>will melt</u> in her glass.	3	13. I <u>will eat</u> a piece of her cake.
1	6. I <u>lock</u> the bolt on the door.	1	14. The dog <u>digs</u> a hole to hide his bone.
3	7. I <u>will lock</u> the bolt on the door.	3	15. The dog <u>will dig</u> a hole to hide his bone.
2	8. I <u>locked</u> the bolt on the door.	2	16. The dog <u>dug</u> a hole to hide his bone.

(End of lesson.)

Level 2—Shurley English—Homeschool Edition

CHAPTER 20   LESSON 4

Objectives: Jingles, Study, Test, Check, Writing (Journal), and State Activity.

 JINGLE TIME

Have students turn to the Jingle Section in their books and recite the previously-taught jingles.

 STUDY TIME

Have students study the vocabulary words in their vocabulary notebooks. Remind students that any vocabulary word in their notebooks could be on their test. Also, have students study any of the skills in the Practice Section that they need to review.

 TEST TIME

Have students turn to page 99 in the Test Section of their book and find Chapter 20 Test. Go over the directions to make sure they understand what to do. (*Chapter 20 Test key is on the next page.*)

 CHECK TIME

After students have finished, check and discuss their test papers. Make sure they understand why their answers are right or wrong. (*For total points, count each required answer as a point.*)

 STATE ACTIVITY TIME

Students will continue to draw or trace the states and to write the following questions and answers.

New Mexico	New York
1. What is the state on the front of this card? **New Mexico**	1. What is the state on the front of this card? **New York**
2. What is the capital of New Mexico? **Santa Fe**	2. What is the capital of New York? **Albany**
3. What is the postal abbreviation of New Mexico? **NM**	3. What is the postal abbreviation of New York? **NY**

Color these states. Use the cards to quiz family members, friends, and relatives. You may want to time the responses to your questions.

(End of lesson.)

Level 2—Shurley English—Homeschool Edition

Chapter 20 Test
(Student Page 99)

81 pts.

Exercise 1: Classify each sentence.

1. **SN V**   PN   SN   V   P   A   Adj   OP   P   A   OP
    P1   Andy's guitar / fell (into the murky waters) (of the pond). **D**

2. **SN V**   A   Adj   SN   V   P   A   OP
    P1   An injured whale / swam (beside the ship)! **E**

Exercise 2: Use Sentence 2 to underline the complete subject once and the complete predicate twice and to complete the table below.

List the Noun Used	List the Noun Job	Singular or Plural	Common or Proper	Simple Subject	Simple Predicate
1. whale	2. SN	3. S	4. C	5. whale	6. swam
7. ship	8. OP	9. S	10. C		

Exercise 3: Name the six parts of speech that you have studied. (*You may use abbreviations.*)
(The order of answers may vary.)

1. __Noun__   2. __Verb__   3. __Adjective__   4. __Adverb__   5. __Preposition__   6. __Pronoun__

Exercise 4: Identify each pair of words as synonyms or antonyms by putting parentheses ( ) around **syn** or **ant**.

1. ledge, shelf	(syn) ant	4. injure, damage	(syn) ant	7. shout, murmur	syn (ant)
2. depend, rely	(syn) ant	5. victory, defeat	syn (ant)	8. patient, restless	syn (ant)
3. anxious, relaxed	syn (ant)	6. sparkle, shine	(syn) ant	9. murky, clear	syn (ant)

Exercise 5: Identify the tense of each underlined verb by writing a number **1** for present tense, a number **2** for past tense, and a number **3** for future tense. Use the verb chart for the irregular verbs.

Verb Tense	Regular Verbs	Verb Tense	Irregular Verbs
2	1. The pilot landed the plane.	3	9. The wind will blow against my window.
1	2. The pilot lands the plane.	1	10. The wind blows against my window.
3	3. The pilot will land the plane.	2	11. The wind blew against my window.
3	4. Our pizza will cook in the oven.	2	12. The author wrote her second novel.
1	5. Our pizza cooks in the oven.	3	13. The author will write her second novel.
2	6. Our pizza cooked in the oven.	1	14. The author writes her second novel.
2	7. My team scored a point.	1	15. My father wears his new suit.
3	8. My team will score a point.	3	16. My father will wear his new suit.

Exercise 6: Copy the following words on notebook paper. Write the correct contraction beside each word.
Key: shouldn't, I'd, we'll, won't, you'd, hadn't, they've, hasn't, can't, didn't, we're, aren't.
Words: should not, I had, we will, will not, you would, had not, they have, has not, cannot, did not, we are, are not.

Exercise 7: In your journal, write a paragraph summarizing what you have learned this week.

Level 2—Shurley English—Homeschool Edition

CHAPTER 20 LESSON 4 CONTINUED

TEACHER INSTRUCTIONS

Use the Question and Answer Flows below for the sentences on the Chapter 20 Test.

Question and Answer Flow for Sentence 1: Andy's guitar fell into the murky waters of the pond.

1. What fell into the murky waters of the pond? guitar - SN
2. What is being said about guitar? guitar fell - V
3. Into - P
4. Into what? waters - OP
5. What kind of waters? murky - Adj
6. The - A
7. Of - P
8. Of what? pond - OP
9. The - A
10. Whose guitar? Andy's - PN
11. SN V P1 Check
12. (Into the murky waters) - Prepositional phrase
13. (Of the pond) - Prepositional phrase
14. Period, statement, declarative sentence
15. Go back to the verb - divide the complete subject from the complete predicate.

```
                          PN    SN   V   P  A  Adj   OP    P  A  OP
Classified Sentence:   SN V    Andy's guitar / fell (into the murky waters) (of the pond).  D
                       P1
```

Question and Answer Flow for Sentence 2: An injured whale swam beside the ship!

1. What swam beside the ship? whale - SN
2. What is being said about whale? whale swam - V
3. Beside - P
4. Beside what? ship - OP
5. The - A
6. What kind of whale? injured - Adj
7. An - A
8. SN V P1 Check
9. (Beside the ship) - Prepositional phrase
10. Exclamation point, strong feeling, exclamatory sentence
11. Go back to the verb - divide the complete subject from the complete predicate.

```
                             A  Adj    SN    V    P  A  OP
Classified Sentence:   SN V   An injured whale / swam (beside the ship)!  E
                       P1
```

Level 2—Shurley English—Homeschool Edition

CHAPTER 20   LESSON 5
Objectives: Writing Assignment #14 and Sentence Time.

 WRITING TIME

TEACHER INSTRUCTIONS FOR WRITING ASSIGNMENT #14

Give Writing Assignment #14 from the box below. Remind students to use the Writing Checklist in Reference 17 to check their finished writing assignment.

Read, check, and discuss Writing Assignment #14 after students have finished their final papers. Use the Writing Checklist (*Reference 17 on teacher's page 112*) as you check and discuss students' papers. Make sure students are using the checklist correctly.

Writing Assignment Box

Writing Assignment #14: Descriptive Paragraph

Writing topic choices: My Hero   or   A Day at the Lake   or   My Favorite Memory

---

 SENTENCE TIME

Chapter 20, Lesson 5, Sentence: Use colored markers to match each label with the correct sentence part by drawing a line from one to the other. Then, use the labels to arrange the sentence parts into a sentence that you will write on the sentence line below. *(The order of the words in your sentence should be in the same sequence as the vertical list of sentence labels.)* Create other labels and scrambled sentence parts on notebook paper for family members to solve. You may color code the sentence parts. *(See page 115 in the student book.)*

Labels for Order of Sentence	Scrambled Sentence Parts
A	in
SN	during
P	the
A	the
OP	the
V	wood
Adv	fireplace
P	day
A	brightly
Adj	cold
Adj	burned
OP	winter

Sentence: The wood in the fireplace burned brightly during the cold winter day.

(End of lesson.)

Level 2—Shurley English—Homeschool Edition

CHAPTER 21   LESSON 1
Objectives: Jingles, Grammar (Practice Sentences, Skill Builder Check, Review the Six Parts of Speech), Practice Exercise, and Vocabulary #1.

 **JINGLE TIME**

Have students turn to the Jingle Section in their books and recite the previously-taught jingles.

 GRAMMAR TIME

Put the Practice Sentences from the box below on the board or on notebook paper. Use these sentences as you practice the concepts that have been taught. For the greatest benefit, students must participate orally with the teacher.

Chapter 21, Practice Sentences for Lesson 1
1. _____ The baby chick slept in the barn with the puppy.
2. _____ Our science class talked about precipitation.
3. _____ The two children climbed quickly into their beds.

TEACHING SCRIPT FOR CLASSIFYING PRACTICE SENTENCES

We will classify three different sentences to practice the grammar skills in the Question and Answer Flows. We will classify the sentences together. Begin. (*You might have students write the labels above the sentences at this time.*)

Question and Answer Flow for Sentence 1: The baby chick slept in the barn with the puppy.

1. What slept in the barn with the puppy? chick - SN
2. What is being said about chick? chick slept - V
3. In - P
4. In what? barn - OP
5. The - A
6. With - P
7. With what? puppy - OP
8. The - A
9. What kind of chick? baby - Adj
10. The - A
11. SN V P1 Check
12. (In the barn) - Prepositional phrase
13. (With the puppy) - Prepositional phrase
14. Period, statement, declarative sentence
15. Go back to the verb - divide the complete subject from the complete predicate.

```
                     A  Adj  SN    V  P A  OP   P  A  OP
Classified Sentence:  SN V   The baby chick / slept (in the barn) (with the puppy).  D
                      P1
```

Page 316   Level 2 Homeschool Teacher's Manual

© SHURLEY INSTRUCTIONAL MATERIALS, INC.

CHAPTER 21 LESSON 1 CONTINUED

Question and Answer Flow for Sentence 2: Our science class talked about precipitation.

1. Who talked about precipitation? class - SN
2. What is being said about class? class talked - V
3. About - P
4. About what? precipitation - OP
5. What kind of class? science - Adj
6. Whose class? our - PP
7. SN V P1 Check
8. (About precipitation) - Prepositional phrase
9. Period, statement, declarative sentence
10. Go back to the verb - divide the complete subject from the complete predicate.

                             PP   Adj   SN   V   P   OP

Classified Sentence: SN V   Our science class / talked (about precipitation). D
                               P1

Question and Answer Flow for Sentence 3: The two children climbed quickly into their beds.

1. Who climbed quickly into their beds? children - SN
2. What is being said about children? children climbed - V
3. Climbed how? quickly - Adv
4. Into - P
5. Into what? beds - OP
6. Whose beds? their - PP
7. How many children? two - Adj
8. The - A
9. SN V P1 Check
10. (Into their beds) - Prepositional phrase
11. Period, statement, declarative sentence
12. Go back to the verb - divide the complete subject from the complete predicate.

                             A Adj   SN   V   Adv   P   PP   OP

Classified Sentence: SN V   The two children / climbed quickly (into their beds). D
                               P1

Use Sentences 1-3 that you just classified with your students to do a Skill Builder Check. Use the guidelines below.

Skill Builder Check	
1. **Noun check.** (Say the job and then say the noun. Circle each noun.)	5. **Identify the complete subject and the complete predicate.** (Underline the complete subject once and the complete predicate twice.)
2. **Identify the nouns as singular or plural.** (Write **S** or **P** above each noun.)	6. **Identify the simple subject and simple predicate.** (Underline the simple subject once and the simple predicate twice. Bold, or highlight, the lines.)
3. **Identify the nouns as common or proper.** (Follow established procedure for oral identification.)	7. **Recite the irregular verb chart.** (Located on student page 27 and teacher page 307.)
4. **Do a vocabulary check.** (Follow established procedure for oral identification.)	

TEACHING SCRIPT FOR REVIEWING THE SIX PARTS OF SPEECH

What are the six parts of speech that we have covered? *(noun, verb, adjective, adverb, preposition,* and *pronoun)* *(Chant the six parts of speech that the students have learned several times for reinforcement and fun.)*

Level 2—Shurley English—Homeschool Edition

CHAPTER 21 LESSON 1 CONTINUED

 PRACTICE TIME

Have students turn to pages 69 and 70 in the Practice Section of their book and find Chapter 21, Lesson 1, Practice *(1-3)*. Go over the directions to make sure they understand what to do. Check and discuss the Practices after students have finished. *(Chapter 21, Lesson 1, Practice keys are given below.)*

Chapter 21, Lesson 1, Practice 1: Identify the tense of each underlined verb by writing a number **1** for present tense, a number **2** for past tense, and a number **3** for future tense. Use the verb chart for the irregular verbs.

Verb Tense	Regular Verbs	Verb Tense	Irregular Verbs
2	1. The dogs <u>chased</u> the rabbits.	1	9. Jacob <u>shakes</u> his wrapped present.
1	2. The dogs <u>chase</u> the rabbits.	3	10. Jacob <u>will shake</u> his wrapped present.
3	3. The dogs <u>will chase</u> the rabbits.	2	11. Jacob <u>shook</u> his wrapped present.
2	4. My dad <u>shaved</u> his beard.	3	12. The bell <u>will ring</u> at the end of class.
3	5. My dad <u>will shave</u> his beard.	2	13. The bell <u>rang</u> at the end of class.
1	6. My dad <u>shaves</u> his beard.	1	14. The bell <u>rings</u> at the end of class.
2	7. Jim <u>showed</u> me his new bike.	3	15. Marshall <u>will come</u> to the party.
3	8. Jim <u>will show</u> me his new bike.	2	16. Marshall <u>came</u> to the party.

Chapter 21, Lesson 1, Practice 2: Copy the following words on notebook paper. Write the correct contraction beside each word. **Key: isn't, it's, that's, there's, you're, they're, don't, didn't, let's, I've.**
<u>Words</u>: is not, it is, that is, there is, you are, they are, do not, did not, let us, I have.

Chapter 21, Lesson 1, Practice 3: Copy the following contractions on notebook paper. Write the correct word beside each contraction. **Key: could not, they had or they would, we will, you had or you would, I have, she is or she has, cannot, does not, he is or he has, I am.**
<u>Contractions</u>: couldn't, they'd, we'll, you'd, I've, she's, can't, doesn't, he's, I'm.

 VOCABULARY TIME

Assign Chapter 21, Vocabulary Words **#1** on page 7 in the Reference Section for students to define in their Vocabulary notebooks. Tell students they are to use a dictionary or thesaurus to look up the meanings of the vocabulary words.

Chapter 21, Vocabulary Words #1
(frisky, lively, whisper, howl)

(End of lesson.)

Level 2—Shurley English—Homeschool Edition

CHAPTER 21   LESSON 2
Objectives: Jingles, Grammar (Practice Sentences), Practice Exercise, Vocabulary #2.

 **JINGLE TIME**

Have students turn to the Jingle Section in their books and recite the previously-taught jingles.

 GRAMMAR TIME

Put the Practice Sentences from the box below on the board or on notebook paper. Use these sentences as you practice the concepts that have been taught.

Chapter 21, Practice Sentences for Lesson 2
1. _____ Alabama's governor returned to the state capital.
2. _____ The farmer's strawberry plants grow in rows.
3. _____ That big black dog jumped over the fence!

TEACHING SCRIPT FOR CLASSIFYING PRACTICE SENTENCES

We will classify three different sentences to practice the grammar skills in the Question and Answer Flows. We will classify the sentences together. Begin.

Question and Answer Flow for Sentence 1: Alabama's governor returned to the state capital.	
1. Who returned to the state capital? governor - SN	7. Whose governor? Alabama's - PN
2. What is being said about governor? governor returned - V	8. SN V P1 Check
3. To - P	9. (To the state capital) - Prepositional phrase
4. To what? capital - OP	10. Period, statement, declarative sentence
5. Which capital? state - Adj	11. Go back to the verb - divide the complete subject from the complete predicate.
6. The - A	

                                  PN   SN   V   P A Adj   OP
Classified Sentence: SN V   Alabama's governor / returned (to the state capital). D
                          P1

Question and Answer Flow for Sentence 2: The farmer's strawberry plants grow in rows.	
1. What grow in rows? plants - SN	7. The - A
2. What is being said about plants? plants grow - V	8. SN V P1 Check
3. In - P	9. (In rows) - Prepositional phrase
4. In what? rows - OP	10. Period, statement, declarative sentence
5. What kind of plants? strawberry - Adj	11. Go back to the verb - divide the complete subject from the complete predicate.
6. Whose plants? farmer's - PN	

                           A   PN   Adj   SN   V   P OP
Classified Sentence: SN V   The farmer's strawberry plants / grow (in rows). D
                          P1

CHAPTER 21 LESSON 2 CONTINUED

> **Question and Answer Flow for Sentence 3:** That big black dog jumped over the fence!
>
> 1. What jumped over the fence? dog - SN
> 2. What is being said about dog? dog jumped - V
> 3. Over - P
> 4. Over what? fence - OP
> 5. The - A
> 6. What kind of dog? black - Adj
> 7. What kind of dog? big - Adj
> 8. Which dog? that - Adj
> 9. SN V P1 Check
> 10. (Over the fence) - Prepositional phrase
> 11. Exclamation point, strong feeling, exclamatory sentence
> 12. Go back to the verb - divide the complete subject from the complete predicate.
>
> ```
>                         Adj Adj Adj  SN    V    P   A   OP
> Classified Sentence:   SN V   That big black dog / jumped (over the fence)!  E
>                         P1
> ```

 PRACTICE TIME

Have students turn to page 70 in the Practice Section of their book and find Chapter 21, Lesson 2, Practice. Go over the directions to make sure they understand what to do. Check and discuss the Practice after students have finished. (*Chapter 21, Lesson 2, Practice key is given below.*)

Chapter 21, Lesson 2, Practice: Identify the tense of each underlined verb by writing a number **1** for present tense, a number **2** for past tense, and a number **3** for future tense. Use the verb chart for the irregular verbs.

Verb Tense	Regular Verbs	Verb Tense	Irregular Verbs
2	1. We <u>skated</u> down the hill.	3	9. The class <u>will take</u> the exam.
1	2. We <u>skate</u> down the hill.	1	10. The class <u>takes</u> the exam.
3	3. We <u>will skate</u> down the hill.	2	11. The class <u>took</u> the exam.
2	4. I <u>stepped</u> over the mud puddle.	1	12. The sun <u>rises</u> in the east.
3	5. I <u>will step</u> over the mud puddle.	2	13. The sun <u>rose</u> in the east.
1	6. I <u>step</u> over the mud puddle.	3	14. The sun <u>will rise</u> in the east.
3	7. The zookeeper <u>will touch</u> the snake.	2	15. The Smiths <u>sold</u> their house.
1	8. The zookeeper <u>touches</u> the snake.	3	16. The Smiths <u>will sell</u> their house.

 VOCABULARY TIME

Assign Chapter 21, Vocabulary Words **#2** on page 7 in the Reference Section for students to define in their Vocabulary notebooks. Tell students they are to use a dictionary or thesaurus to look up the meanings of the vocabulary words.

Chapter 21, Vocabulary Words #2
(pale, colorful, thrive, flourish)

(End of lesson.)

Level 2—Shurley English—Homeschool Edition

CHAPTER 21   LESSON 3

Objectives: Jingles, Grammar (Practice Sentences), and Practice Exercise.

 **JINGLE TIME**

Have students turn to the Jingle Section in their books and recite the previously-taught jingles.

 GRAMMAR TIME

Put the Practice Sentences from the box below on the board or on notebook paper. Use these sentences as you practice the concepts that have been taught. For the greatest benefit, students must participate orally with the teacher.

Chapter 21, Practice Sentences for Lesson 3
1. _____ My brother plays in a baseball game tomorrow.
2. _____ We went to the movies over the weekend.
3. _____ The encyclopedia salesman traveled to many homes in our community.

TEACHING SCRIPT FOR CLASSIFYING PRACTICE SENTENCES

We will classify three different sentences to practice the grammar skills in the Question and Answer Flows. We will classify the sentences together. Begin. (*You might have students write the labels above the sentences at this time.*)

Question and Answer Flow for Sentence 1: My brother plays in a baseball game tomorrow.
1. Who plays in a baseball game tomorrow? brother - SN
2. What is being said about brother? brother plays - V
3. In - P
4. In what? game - OP
5. What kind of game? baseball - Adj
6. A - A
7. Plays when? tomorrow - Adv
8. Whose brother? my - PP
9. SN V P1 Check
10. (In a baseball game) - Prepositional phrase
11. Period, statement, declarative sentence
12. Go back to the verb - divide the complete subject from the complete predicate.

```
                        PP   SN    V    P  A  Adj    OP    Adv
Classified Sentence:  SN V   My brother / plays (in a baseball game) tomorrow. D
                      P1
```

Level 2 Homeschool Teacher's Manual

CHAPTER 21 LESSON 3 CONTINUED

Question and Answer Flow for Sentence 2: We went to the movies over the weekend.

1. Who went to the movies over the weekend? we - SP
2. What is being said about we? we went - V
3. To - P
4. To what? movies - OP
5. The - A
6. Over - P
7. Over what? weekend - OP
8. The - A
9. SN V P1 Check
10. (To the movies) - Prepositional phrase
11. (Over the weekend) - Prepositional phrase
12. Period, statement, declarative sentence
13. Go back to the verb - divide the complete subject from the complete predicate.

```
                                  SP  V   P  A   OP    P   A   OP
Classified Sentence:    SN V      We / went (to the movies) (over the weekend).  D
                        P1
```

Question and Answer Flow for Sentence 3: The encyclopedia salesman traveled to many homes in our community.

1. Who traveled to many homes in our community? salesman - SN
2. What is being said about salesman? salesman traveled - V
3. To - P
4. To what? homes - OP
5. How many homes? many - Adj
6. In - P
7. In what? community - OP
8. Whose community? our - PP
9. What kind of salesman? encyclopedia - Adj
10. The - A
11. SN V P1 Check
12. (To many homes) - Prepositional phrase
13. (In our community) - Prepositional phrase
14. Period, statement, declarative sentence
15. Go back to the verb - divide the complete subject from the complete predicate.

```
                           A    Adj         SN       V    P  Adj   OP     P  PP      OP
Classified Sentence:  SN V The encyclopedia salesman / traveled (to many homes) (in our community).  D
                      P1
```

 PRACTICE TIME

Have students turn to page 70 in the Practice Section of their book and find Chapter 21, Lesson 3, Practice. Go over the directions to make sure they understand what to do. Check and discuss the Practice after students have finished. (*Chapter 21, Lesson 3, Practice key is given below.*)

Chapter 21, Lesson 3, Practice: Identify the tense of each underlined verb by writing a number **1** for present tense, a number **2** for past tense, and a number **3** for future tense. Use the verb chart for the irregular verbs.

Verb Tense	Regular Verbs	Verb Tense	Irregular Verbs
2	1. The actors <u>danced</u> across the stage.	3	6. We <u>will swim</u> in the hotel's pool.
1	2. The actors <u>dance</u> across the stage.	2	7. We <u>swam</u> in the hotel's pool.
3	3. The actors <u>will dance</u> across the stage.	1	8. We <u>swim</u> in the hotel's pool.
2	4. My costume <u>scared</u> Rita.	2	9. Angela <u>made</u> a quilt.
3	5. My costume <u>will scare</u> Rita.	1	10. Angela <u>makes</u> a quilt.

(End of lesson.)

CHAPTER 21   LESSON 4

Objectives: Jingles, Study, Test, Check, Writing (Journal), and State Activity.

 JINGLE TIME

Have students turn to the Jingle Section in their books and recite the previously-taught jingles.

 STUDY TIME

Have students study the vocabulary words in their vocabulary notebooks. Remind students that any vocabulary word in their notebooks could be on their test. Also, have students study any of the skills in the Practice Section that they need to review.

 TEST TIME

Have students turn to page 100 in the Test Section of their book and find Chapter 21 Test. Go over the directions to make sure they understand what to do. (*Chapter 21 Test key is on the next page.*)

 CHECK TIME

After students have finished, check and discuss their test papers. Make sure they understand why their answers are right or wrong. (*For total points, count each required answer as a point.*)

 STATE ACTIVITY TIME

Students will continue to draw or trace the states and to write the following questions and answers.

North Carolina	North Dakota
1. What is the state on the front of this card? **North Carolina**	1. What is the state on the front of this card? **North Dakota**
2. What is the capital of North Carolina? **Raleigh**	2. What is the capital of North Dakota? **Bismarck**
3. What is the postal abbreviation of North Carolina? **NC**	3. What is the postal abbreviation of North Dakota? **ND**

Color these states. Use the cards to quiz family members, friends, and relatives. You may want to time the responses to your questions.

(End of lesson.)

Level 2—Shurley English—Homeschool Edition

71 pts

Chapter 21 Test
(Student Page 100)

Exercise 1: Classify each sentence.

```
              SN   V   Adv   P   PP   OP    P    OP
1.  SN  V     Bill / ran swiftly (to his house) (after school).   D
    P1
```

```
              A   Adj   SN   V    Adv   P    PP  Adj   OP
2.  SN  V     The mother duck / swam proudly (around her ten ducklings).   D
    P1
```

Exercise 2: Use Sentence 1 to underline the complete subject once and the complete predicate twice and to complete the table below.

List the Noun Used	List the Noun Job	Singular or Plural	Common or Proper	Simple Subject	Simple Predicate
1. **Bill**	2. **SN**	3. **S**	4. **P**	5. **Bill**	6. **ran**
7. **house**	8. **OP**	9. **S**	10. **C**		
11. **school**	12. **OP**	13. **S**	14. **C**		

Exercise 3: Name the six parts of speech that you have studied. (*You may use abbreviations.*)
(The order of answers may vary.)

1. **Noun**   2. **Verb**   3. **Adjective**   4. **Adverb**   5. **Preposition**   6. **Pronoun**

Exercise 4: Identify each pair of words as synonyms or antonyms by putting parentheses ( ) around **syn** or **ant**.

1. depend, rely	**(syn)** ant	4. howl, whisper	syn **(ant)**	7. injure, damage	**(syn)** ant
2. frisky, lively	**(syn)** ant	5. clear, murky	syn **(ant)**	8. victory, defeat	syn **(ant)**
3. colorful, pale	syn **(ant)**	6. relaxed, anxious	syn **(ant)**	9. thrive, flourish	**(syn)** ant

Exercise 5: Identify the tense of each underlined verb by writing a number **1** for present tense, a number **2** for past tense, and a number **3** for future tense. Use the verb chart for the irregular verbs.

Verb Tense	Regular Verbs	Verb Tense	Irregular Verbs
1	1. He grumbles about his chores.	3	8. Justin will bring the punch.
3	2. He will grumble about his chores.	1	9. Justin brings the punch.
2	3. He grumbled about his chores.	2	10. Justin brought the punch.
2	4. I wrapped her gift.	3	11. The grass will grow in the spring.
1	5. The candle glows in the darkness.	2	12. The grass grew in the spring.
3	6. I will wrap her gift.	1	13. The snow falls softly to the ground.
2	7. The candle glowed in the darkness.	3	14. The snow will fall softly to the ground.

Exercise 6: In your journal, write a paragraph summarizing what you have learned this week.

CHAPTER 21 LESSON 4 CONTINUED

TEACHER INSTRUCTIONS

Use the Question and Answer Flows below for the sentences on the Chapter 21 Test.

Question and Answer Flow for Sentence 1: Bill ran swiftly to his house after school.

1. Who ran swiftly to his house after school? Bill - SN
2. What is being said about Bill? Bill ran - V
3. Ran how? swiftly - Adv
4. To - P
5. To what? house - OP
6. Whose house? his - PP
7. After - P
8. After what? school - OP
9. SN V P1 Check
10. (To his house) - Prepositional phrase
11. (After school) - Prepositional phrase
12. Period, statement, declarative sentence
13. Go back to the verb - divide the complete subject from the complete predicate.

```
                           SN  V   Adv  P  PP  OP    P   OP
Classified Sentence:   SN V    Bill / ran swiftly (to his house) (after school).  D
                       ‾‾‾‾
                        P1
```

Question and Answer Flow for Sentence 2: The mother duck swam proudly around her ten ducklings.

1. What swam proudly around her ten ducklings? duck - SN
2. What is being said about duck? duck swam - V
3. Swam how? proudly - Adv
4. Around - P
5. Around what? ducklings - OP
6. How many ducklings? ten - Adj
7. Whose ducklings? her - PP
8. What kind of duck? mother - Adj
9. The - A
10. SN V P1 Check
11. (Around her ten ducklings) - Prepositional phrase
12. Period, statement, declarative sentence
13. Go back to the verb - divide the complete subject from the complete predicate.

```
                        A   Adj   SN    V     Adv      P   PP  Adj  OP
Classified Sentence:  SN V    The mother duck / swam proudly (around her ten ducklings).  D
                      ‾‾‾‾
                       P1
```

CHAPTER 21   LESSON 5

Objectives: Writing (Introduce Narrative Writing), Writing Assignment #15, and Sentence Time.

 **WRITING TIME**

TEACHING SCRIPT FOR INTRODUCING NARRATIVE WRITING

Narrative writing is simply the telling of a story. When you write stories, they are called narratives, or short stories. Short stories have certain characteristics that make them different from other types of writing. You will study five characteristics known as story elements. These story elements are main idea, setting, characters, plot, and ending. Your narrative writing skills will be developed through the use of the story elements. Narrative writing will have a beginning, a middle, and an end.

You will now learn how to use the five story elements: main idea, setting, characters, plot, and ending to make a Story Elements Outline. This outline will help keep your writing focused and help you choose details and events that support the main idea of your story. Before you begin every story writing assignment, you will make a Story Elements Outline like the one in Reference 40 on page 28. (*Have students go to Reference 40 on student page 28. Read and discuss the story elements and sample story with them.*)

Reference 40: Story Elements Outline

1. **Main Idea (Tell the problem or situation that needs a solution.)**
   Tracy is having a bad day.
2. **Setting (Tell when and where the story takes place, either clearly stated or implied.)**
   When – The story takes place on a rainy Friday afternoon.
   Where – The story takes place on Tracy's way home from school.
3. **Character (Tell who or what the story is about.)**
   The main characters are Tracy and her mom.
4. **Plot (Tell what the characters in the story do and what happens to them.)**
   The story is about Tracy's bad day.
5. **Ending (Use a strong ending that will bring the story to a close.)**
   The story ends with Tracy's mom leaving work early and surprising Tracy with homemade chocolate chip cookies.

Tracy's Gloomy Day

Tracy left school Friday with a sad look on her face. She pulled on her raincoat and sighed as she made her way home. The dark sky seemed to match her gloomy mood. As she walked a few blocks toward her house, she thought about all the horrible things that had happened that day. First of all, she was late to class. Then, she had to play by herself during recess because Laura, her best friend, was absent. Next, she forgot her lunch, and the cafeteria was serving chicken livers and Brussels sprouts. Suddenly, her stomach growled loudly.

When she was a block away from her house, it began to rain. She pulled the hood of her raincoat over her head and quickened her pace. She got to her house only to realize she had forgotten her key! She sat on the steps and began to cry. Just then, her mom opened the door. Tracy's mom had left work early and had prepared homemade chocolate chip cookies for Tracy. Tracy smiled as her mom helped her dry off. Now, Tracy's gloomy day had a wonderful ending as she followed her mother into the kitchen to eat warm, gooey cookies.

CHAPTER 21 LESSON 5 CONTINUED

Teacher's Notes: The narrative story elements guideline is a suggested guide to help students as they learn to write narrative paragraphs. However, some students will be able to organize their ideas and stick to the topic without following the guideline exactly. The number of sentences may also vary.

Now, you will write a narrative paragraph. Remember to make a Story Elements Outline before you begin. After you have finished writing your narrative paragraph, make sure you read through the whole paragraph to make sure it sounds correct. Sometimes, we find mistakes if we really listen to what we have written.

TEACHER INSTRUCTIONS FOR WRITING ASSIGNMENT #15

Give Writing Assignment #15 from the box below. Remind students to use the Writing Checklist in Reference 17 to check their finished writing assignment.

Read, check, and discuss Writing Assignment #15 after students have finished their final papers. Use the Writing Checklist (*Reference 17 on teacher's page 112*) as you check and discuss students' papers. Make sure students are using the checklist correctly.

Writing Assignment Box
Writing Assignment #15: Narrative Paragraph
Writing topic choices: The Day I Was President   or   The Wild Ride   or   Summer Camp/Church Camp

SENTENCE TIME

Chapter 21, Lesson 5, Sentence: For this assignment, make your own labels and scrambled sentence parts on notebook paper. You may still use colored markers to match each label with the correct sentence part by drawing a line from one to the other. Then, use the labels to arrange the sentence parts into a sentence that you will use for an answer key on your paper. Have family members unscramble your sentences according to the grammar labels. You may color code the sentence parts. (*See page 116 in the student book.*)

Labels for Order of Sentence	Scrambled Sentence Parts
Independent sentence assignment.	

(End of lesson.)

Level 2—Shurley English—Homeschool Edition

CHAPTER 22   LESSON 1

Objectives: Jingles, Grammar (Practice Sentences), Skill (Writing a Friendly Letter), Vocabulary #1, and Activity.

 **JINGLE TIME**

Have students turn to the Jingle Section in their books and recite the previously-taught jingles.

 GRAMMAR TIME

Put the Practice Sentences from the box below on the board or on notebook paper. Use these sentences as you practice the concepts that have been taught. For the greatest benefit, students must participate orally with the teacher.

Chapter 22, Practice Sentences for Lesson 1
1. _____ She joked with the lively comedian during the show.
2. _____ The damaged ship drifted slowly toward the rocky shore!
3. _____ My sister jogged with her best friend in the afternoon.

TEACHING SCRIPT FOR CLASSIFYING PRACTICE SENTENCES

We will classify three different sentences to practice the grammar skills in the Question and Answer Flows. We will classify the sentences together. Begin. (*You might have students write the labels above the sentences at this time.*)

Question and Answer Flow for Sentence 1: She joked with the lively comedian during the show.

1. Who joked with the lively comedian during the show?
   she - SP
2. What is being said about she? she joked - V
3. With - P
4. With whom? comedian - OP
5. What kind of comedian? lively - Adj
6. The - A
7. During - P
8. During what? show - OP
9. The - A
10. SN V P1 Check
11. (With the lively comedian) - Prepositional phrase
12. (During the show) - Prepositional phrase
13. Period, statement, declarative sentence
14. Go back to the verb - divide the complete subject from the complete predicate.

```
                              SP   V   P  A  Adj    OP     P   A   OP
Classified Sentence:    SN V  She / joked (with the lively comedian) (during the show).  D
                        P1
```

Page 328   Level 2 Homeschool Teacher's Manual

© SHURLEY INSTRUCTIONAL MATERIALS, INC.

CHAPTER 22 LESSON 1 CONTINUED

Question and Answer Flow for Sentence 2: The damaged ship drifted slowly toward the rocky shore!

1. What drifted slowly toward the rocky shore? ship - SN
2. What is being said about ship? ship drifted - V
3. Drifted how? slowly - Adv
4. Toward - P
5. Toward what? shore - OP
6. What kind of shore? rocky - Adj
7. The - A
8. What kind of ship? damaged - Adj
9. The - A
10. SN V P1 Check
11. (Toward the rocky shore) - Prepositional phrase
12. Exclamation point, strong feeling, exclamatory sentence
13. Go back to the verb - divide the complete subject from the complete predicate.

```
                       A   Adj   SN   V   Adv   P   A   Adj   OP
Classified Sentence:   SN V    The damaged ship / drifted slowly (toward the rocky shore)!  E
                       P1
```

Question and Answer Flow for Sentence 3: My sister jogged with her best friend in the afternoon.

1. Who jogged with her best friend in the afternoon? sister - SN
2. What is being said about sister? sister jogged - V
3. With - P
4. With whom? friend - OP
5. What kind of friend? best - Adj
6. Whose friend? her - PP
7. In - P
8. In what? afternoon - OP
9. The - A
10. Whose sister? my - PP
11. SN V P1 Check
12. (With her best friend) - Prepositional phrase
13. (In the afternoon) - Prepositional phrase
14. Period, statement, declarative sentence
15. Go back to the verb - divide the complete subject from the complete predicate.

```
                       PP   SN    V    P   PP  Adj   OP    P   A    OP
Classified Sentence:   SN V   My sister / jogged (with her best friend) (in the afternoon).  D
                       P1
```

SKILL TIME

TEACHING SCRIPT FOR WRITING A FRIENDLY LETTER

Close your eyes. Now, picture a good friend or favorite relative that you really like but don't get to see very often. Open your eyes. The memory of that favorite person in your life brought a smile to your face, didn't it? Remember, keeping in touch with favorite people brings smiles to their faces, too. Writing a letter is a great way to stay in touch with people you care about and who care about you.

A letter written to or received from friends or relatives is called a **friendly letter**. Turn to page 28 and look at Reference 41. Follow along as I read some tips that will make your friendly letter interesting and enjoyable to read. (*Read the tips below to your students.*)

Reference 41: Tips for Writing Friendly Letters
Tip #1: Write as if you were talking to the person face-to-face. Share information about yourself and mutual friends. Tell stories, conversations, or jokes. Share photographs, articles, drawings, poems, etc. Avoid saying something about someone else that you'll be sorry for later.
Tip #2: If you are writing a return letter, be sure to answer any questions that were asked. Repeat the question so that your reader will know what you are writing about. (You asked about . . .)
Tip #3: End your letter in a positive way so that your reader will want to write a return letter.

Level 2—Shurley English—Homeschool Edition

CHAPTER 22 LESSON 1 CONTINUED

TEACHING SCRIPT FOR THE FIVE PARTS OF A FRIENDLY LETTER

Now that you know what things to write about, you must learn to put your friendly letter in correct friendly letter format. The friendly letter has five parts: the heading; the friendly greeting, which is also called the salutation; the body; the closing; and the signature.

Each of the parts of a friendly letter has a specific place it should be written in order for your letter to have correct friendly letter form. Look at the friendly letter sample in Reference 42 on page 29 in your book. We will now go over each of the five parts as we discuss the type of information in each part. You will also see where each part is placed in a friendly letter form as we study it. (*Go over the sample below.*)

Reference 42: Friendly Letter Sample

1. Heading
Write your address.
Write the date.

   19 Colt Drive
   Rapid City, SD 29033
   April 12, 20___

2. Friendly Greeting, (or Salutation)
Name the person receiving the letter.
Use a comma.

   Dear Wesley,

3. Body (Indent Paragraphs)
Write what you want to say. Indent.

   Mom and Dad have decided to take our family vacation in Florida this year. Disney World will be so much fun! I hope you have a great summer break, too!

4. Closing,
Capitalize the first word.
Use a comma.

   Your cousin,

5. Signature
Sign your name.

   Sally

Now that we have gone over an actual sample, we will now go over each of the five parts again. This time we will look at Reference 43. It will show us the five parts of a friendly letter and explain each part that you studied in the friendly letter sample. (*Go over the sample reproduced on the next page with your students.*)

CHAPTER 22 LESSON 1 CONTINUED

Reference 43: The Five Parts of a Friendly Letter

1. Heading	2. Friendly Greeting or Salutation
1. Box or street address of writer 2. City, state, zip code of writer 3. Date letter was written 4. Placement: upper right-hand corner	1. Begins with *Dear* 2. Names person receiving the letter 3. Has comma after person's name 4. Placement: at left margin, two lines below heading

3. Body	4. Closing	5. Signature
1. Tells reason the letter was written 2. Can have one or more paragraphs 3. Has indented paragraphs 4. Is placed one line after the greeting 5. Skips one line between each paragraph	1. Closes letter with a personal phrase-(Your friend, With love,) 2. Capitalizes only first word 3. Is followed by a comma 4. Is placed two lines below the body 5. Begins just to the right of the middle of the letter	1. Tells who wrote the letter 2. Is usually signed in cursive 3. Uses first name only unless there is a question as to which friend or relative you are 4. Is placed beneath the closing

VOCABULARY TIME

Assign Chapter 22, Vocabulary Words **#1** on page 7 in the Reference Section for students to define in their Vocabulary notebooks. Tell students they are to use a dictionary or thesaurus to look up the meanings of the vocabulary words.

Chapter 22, Vocabulary Words #1
(smooth, rough, meticulous, thorough)

ACTIVITY / ASSIGNMENT TIME

(*Have butcher paper, poster board, or large pieces of construction paper ready for this activity.*) Students can work together or individually on this project. They are to make a colorful wall poster identifying the five parts of a friendly letter. Students are to write the title of each letter part. Then, they will write the description that fits its title. They can use Reference 43 as their model. (*Make sure students have the supplies they might need for this project: rulers, colors, markers, pencils, paint, etc.*)

Students are to make the five parts of a friendly letter colorful and large enough for a wall display. After they have finished, they can display their artwork. Students should also make an oral presentation of the wall display that illustrates the five parts of a friendly letter. (*Students can use any creative method or material to develop and present their creation. This project may take several days. Students can work on it for short periods of time so they will not get too tired.*)

(End of lesson.)

CHAPTER 22 LESSON 2

Objectives: Jingles, Grammar (Practice Sentences), Skill (Friendly Letter), Practice Exercise, and Vocabulary #2.

 **JINGLE TIME**

Have students turn to the Jingle Section in their books and recite the previously-taught jingles.

 GRAMMAR TIME

Put the Practice Sentences from the box below on the board or on notebook paper. Use these sentences as you practice the concepts that have been taught. For the greatest benefit, students must participate orally with the teacher.

Chapter 22, Practice Sentences for Lesson 2
1. _____ I vacationed with my cousin on an island for ten days.
2. _____ Wild geese thrive in Canada's wilderness.
3. _____ An experienced plumber looked thoroughly for the water leak.

TEACHING SCRIPT FOR CLASSIFYING PRACTICE SENTENCES

We will classify three different sentences to practice the grammar skills in the Question and Answer Flows. We will classify the sentences together. Begin. (*You might have students write the labels above the sentences at this time.*)

Question and Answer Flow for Sentence 1: I vacationed with my cousin on an island for ten days.

1. Who vacationed with my cousin on an island for ten days? I - SP
2. What is being said about I? I vacationed - V
3. With - P
4. With whom? cousin - OP
5. Whose cousin? my - PP
6. On - P
7. On what? island - OP
8. An - A
9. For - P
10. For what? days - OP
11. How many days? ten - Adj
12. SN V P1 Check
13. (With my cousin) - Prepositional phrase
14. (On an island) - Prepositional phrase
15. (For ten days) - Prepositional phrase
16. Period, statement, declarative sentence
17. Go back to the verb - divide the complete subject from the complete predicate.

```
                          SP    V       P  PP  OP    P  A   OP    P  Adj  OP
Classified Sentence:     SN  V    I / vacationed (with my cousin) (on an island) (for ten days). D
                         P1
```

CHAPTER 22 LESSON 2 CONTINUED

Question and Answer Flow for Sentence 2: Wild geese thrive in Canada's wilderness.

1. What thrive in Canada's wilderness? geese - SN
2. What is being said about geese? geese thrive - V
3. In - P
4. In what? wilderness - OP
5. Whose wilderness? Canada's - PN
6. What kind of geese? wild - Adj
7. SN V P1 Check
8. (In Canada's wilderness) - Prepositional phrase
9. Period, statement, declarative sentence
10. Go back to the verb - divide the complete subject from the complete predicate.

```
                         Adj   SN      V    P    PN        OP
Classified Sentence:    SN V       Wild geese / thrive (in Canada's wilderness).  D
                         P1
```

Question and Answer Flow for Sentence 3: An experienced plumber looked thoroughly for the water leak.

1. Who looked thoroughly for the water leak? plumber - SN
2. What is being said about plumber? plumber looked - V
3. Looked how? thoroughly - Adv
4. For - P
5. For what? leak - OP
6. What kind of leak? water - Adj
7. The - A
8. What kind of plumber? experienced - Adj
9. An - A
10. SN V P1 Check
11. (For the water leak) - Prepositional phrase
12. Period, statement, declarative sentence
13. Go back to the verb - divide the complete subject from the complete predicate.

```
                         A   Adj          SN       V      Adv     P  A  Adj   OP
Classified Sentence:    SN V       An experienced plumber / looked thoroughly (for the water leak).  D
                         P1
```

SKILL TIME

TEACHING SCRIPT FOR UNSCRAMBLING THE PARTS OF A FRIENDLY LETTER

We have gone over the five parts of a friendly letter in an earlier lesson. We have also gone over samples of the five parts of a friendly letter. Now, we are going to unscramble all the parts of a friendly letter and put them in their proper places. The parts will be scrambled, so you must think about where to place them on the friendly letter outline you will be given. Then, you will answer a set of questions about the letter. Read all directions very carefully. (*Students may use the Reference section in their books for definitions and samples if needed.*)

PRACTICE TIME

Have students turn to pages 71 and 72 in the Practice Section of their book and find Chapter 22, Lesson 2, Practice *(1-3)*. Go over the directions to make sure they understand what to do. Check and discuss the Practices after students have finished. (*Chapter 22, Lesson 2, Practice keys are given on the next two pages.*)

Level 2—Shurley English—Homeschool Edition

CHAPTER 22 LESSON 2 CONTINUED

Chapter 22, Lesson 2, Practice 1: Write the parts of a friendly letter in the correct places in the friendly letter below.

1. **Heading**   2. **Greeting**   3. **Closing**   4. **Signature**

   23 Diamond Drive   Dear Teresa,   Your friend,   Emily
   Somerset, KY 26400
   July 9, 20___

5. **Body**

   My dog had five puppies today. Two of them have spots. They are all so cute!

<u>**Friendly Letter**</u>

Heading
23 Diamond Drive
Somerset, KY 26400
July 9, 20___

Greeting
Dear Teresa,

Body
My dog had five puppies today. Two of them have spots. They are all so cute!

Closing
Your friend,

Signature
Emily

CHAPTER 22 LESSON 2 CONTINUED

Chapter 22, Lesson 2, Practice 2: Use the information in Chapter 22, Lesson 2, Practice 1 to match the definitions. Write the correct letter of the word beside each definition.

F	1. person who wrote the letter	A.	Your friend,
C	2. person who will receive the letter	B.	Emily's new puppies
D	3. when the letter was written	C.	Teresa
G	4. where the writer lives	D.	July 9, 20___
A	5. the closing	E.	Dear Teresa,
E	6. the greeting	F.	Emily
B	7. what this letter is about	G.	23 Diamond Drive, Somerset, KY 26400

Chapter 22, Lesson 2, Practice 3: Write a friendly letter to a neighbor, nursing home resident, or relative. Before you start, review the references and tips for writing friendly letters. After your letter has been checked for mistakes, fold the letter and put it in an envelope. (*Students will learn how to address the envelope properly in Chapter 23.*)

 VOCABULARY TIME

Assign Chapter 22, Vocabulary Words **#2** on page 7 in the Reference Section for students to define in their Vocabulary notebooks. Tell students they are to use a dictionary or thesaurus to look up the meanings of the vocabulary words.

Chapter 22, Vocabulary Words #2
(stretch, shrink, question, inquire)

(End of lesson.)

Level 2—Shurley English—Homeschool Edition

CHAPTER 22   LESSON 3
Objectives: Jingles, Grammar (Practice Sentences), Skill (Friendly Letter), and Practice Exercise.

 JINGLE TIME

Have students turn to the Jingle Section in their books and recite the previously-taught jingles.

 GRAMMAR TIME

Put the Practice Sentences from the box below on the board or on notebook paper. Use these sentences as you practice the concepts that have been taught. For the greatest benefit, students must participate orally with the teacher.

Chapter 22, Practice Sentences for Lesson 3
1. _____ They inquired often about John's family in Ohio.
2. _____ The two coyotes howl loudly at night.
3. _____ His straw hat blew off his head during the storm.

TEACHING SCRIPT FOR CLASSIFYING PRACTICE SENTENCES

We will classify three different sentences to practice the grammar skills in the Question and Answer Flows. We will classify the sentences together. Begin. (*You might have students write the labels above the sentences at this time.*)

Question and Answer Flow for Sentence 1: They inquired often about John's family in Ohio.

1. Who inquired often about John's family in Ohio?
   they - SP
2. What is being said about they?
   they inquired - V
3. Inquired when? often - Adv
4. About - P
5. About what? family - OP
6. Whose family? John's - PN
7. In - P
8. In what? Ohio - OP
9. SN V P1 Check
10. (About John's family) - Prepositional phrase
11. (In Ohio) - Prepositional phrase
12. Period, statement, declarative sentence
13. Go back to the verb - divide the complete subject from the complete predicate.

```
                       SP     V     Adv    P    PN   OP   P  OP
Classified Sentence:   SN  V     They / inquired often (about John's family) (in Ohio).  D
                       P1
```

CHAPTER 22 LESSON 3 CONTINUED

Question and Answer Flow for Sentence 2: The two coyotes howl loudly at night.

1. What howl loudly at night? coyotes - SN
2. What is being said about coyotes? coyotes howl - V
3. Howl how? loudly - Adv
4. At - P
5. At what? night - OP
6. How many coyotes? two - Adj
7. The - A
8. SN V P1 Check
9. (At night) - Prepositional phrase
10. Period, statement, declarative sentence
11. Go back to the verb - divide the complete subject from the complete predicate.

```
                    A  Adj  SN      V    Adv  P   OP
Classified Sentence:  SN V    The two coyotes / howl loudly (at night).  D
                      P1
```

Question and Answer Flow for Sentence 3: His straw hat blew off his head during the storm.

1. What blew off his head during the storm? hat - SN
2. What is being said about hat? hat blew - V
3. Off - P
4. Off what? head - OP
5. Whose head? his - PP
6. During - P
7. During what? storm - OP
8. The - A
9. What kind of hat? straw - Adj
10. Whose hat? his - PP
11. SN V P1 Check
12. (Off his head) - Prepositional phrase
13. (During the storm) - Prepositional phrase
14. Period, statement, declarative sentence
15. Go back to the verb - divide the complete subject from the complete predicate.

```
                    PP  Adj  SN     V    P  PP  OP      P   A   OP
Classified Sentence:  SN V    His straw hat / blew (off his head) (during the storm).  D
                      P1
```

SKILL TIME

TEACHING SCRIPT FOR UNSCRAMBLING THE PARTS OF A FRIENDLY LETTER

We have gone over the five parts of a friendly letter in an earlier lesson. We have also gone over examples of the five parts of a friendly letter. Now, we are going to unscramble all the parts of a friendly letter and put them in their proper places.

The parts will be scrambled, so you must think about where to place them on the friendly letter outline you will be given. Read all directions very carefully. (*Students may use the Reference section in their books for definitions and examples if needed.*)

Level 2—Shurley English—Homeschool Edition

CHAPTER 22 LESSON 3 CONTINUED

 **PRACTICE TIME**

Have students turn to page 73 in the Practice Section of their book and find Chapter 22, Lesson 3, Practice *(1-2)*. Go over the directions to make sure they understand what to do. Check and discuss the Practices after students have finished. *(Chapter 22, Lesson 3, Practice keys are given below.)*

Chapter 22, Lesson 3, Practice 1: Write the parts of a friendly letter in the correct places in the friendly letter below.

1. **Heading**   2. **Greeting**   3. **Closing**   4. **Signature**

   13 West Plains Drive   Dear Aunt Kathy,   Your niece,   Gloria
   Casper, WY 56400
   May 22, 20___

5. **Body**

   Mom's birthday is next month, and I am having trouble finding the perfect gift. Do you have any ideas?

<u>**Friendly Letter**</u>

Heading
13 West Plains Drive
Casper, WY 56400
May 22, 20___

Greeting
Dear Aunt Kathy,

Body
Mom's birthday is next month, and I am having trouble finding the perfect gift. Do you have any ideas?

Closing
Your niece,

Signature
Gloria

Chapter 22, Lesson 3, Practice 2: Write a friendly letter to a special friend or relative. Before you start, review the references and tips for writing friendly letters. After your letter has been edited, fold the letter and put it in an envelope. *(Students will learn how to address the envelope properly in Chapter 23.)*

(End of lesson.)

CHAPTER 22   LESSON 4

Objectives: Jingles, Study, Test, Check, Writing (Journal), and State Activity.

JINGLE TIME

Have students turn to the Jingle Section in their books and recite the previously-taught jingles.

STUDY TIME

Have students study the vocabulary words in their vocabulary notebooks. Remind students that any vocabulary word in their notebooks could be on their test. Also, have students study any of the skills in the Practice Section that they need to review.

TEST TIME

Have students turn to page 101 in the Test Section of their book and find Chapter 22 Test. Go over the directions to make sure they understand what to do. (*Chapter 22 Test key is on the next page.*)

CHECK TIME

After students have finished, check and discuss their test papers. Make sure they understand why their answers are right or wrong. (*For total points, count each required answer as a point.*)

STATE ACTIVITY TIME

Students will continue to draw or trace the states and to write the following questions and answers.

Ohio	Oklahoma
1. What is the state on the front of this card? **Ohio**	1. What is the state on the front of this card? **Oklahoma**
2. What is the capital of Ohio? **Columbus**	2. What is the capital of Oklahoma? **Oklahoma City**
3. What is the postal abbreviation of Ohio? **OH**	3. What is the postal abbreviation of Oklahoma? **OK**

Color these states. Use the cards to quiz family members, friends, and relatives. You may want to time the responses to your questions.

(End of lesson.)

Level 2—Shurley English—Homeschool Edition

Chapter 22 Test
(Student Page 101)

Exercise 1: Classify each sentence.

```
              SN   V    P PP Adj    PN    Adj   OP
1. SN V       Robert / helped (at his little brother's soccer game).  D
   P1

              A  Adj  SN     V    Adv   P  PN   OP
2. SN V       The little bug / landed lightly (on Tim's nose).  D
   P1
```

Exercise 2: Use Sentence 2 to underline the complete subject once and the complete predicate twice and to complete the table below.

List the Noun Used	List the Noun Job	Singular or Plural	Common or Proper	Simple Subject	Simple Predicate
1. **bug**	2. **SN**	3. **S**	4. **C**	5. **bug**	6. **landed**
7. **nose**	8. **OP**	9. **S**	10. **C**		

Exercise 3: Identify each pair of words as synonyms or antonyms by putting parentheses ( ) around *syn* or *ant*.

1. inquire, question	**(syn)** ant	4. depend, rely	**(syn)** ant	7. thrive, flourish	**(syn)** ant
2. whisper, howl	syn **(ant)**	5. shrink, stretch	syn **(ant)**	8. thorough, meticulous	**(syn)** ant
3. lively, frisky	**(syn)** ant	6. rough, smooth	syn **(ant)**	9. colorful, pale	syn **(ant)**

Exercise 4: Write the parts of a friendly letter in the correct places in the friendly letter below.

1. **Heading**
   36 Ridge Road
   Buffalo, NY 81800
   March 16, 20___

2. **Greeting**
   Dear Henry,

3. **Closing**
   Your friend,

4. **Signature**
   Wayne

5. **Body**
   I got your letter yesterday. I can't wait for you to visit next month! Write soon.

Friendly Letter

Heading
36 Ridge Road
Buffalo, NY 81800
March 16, 20___

Greeting
Dear Henry,

Body
I got your letter yesterday. I can't wait for you to visit next month! Write soon.

Closing
Your friend,

Signature
Wayne

Exercise 5: In your journal, write a paragraph summarizing what you have learned this week.

CHAPTER 22 LESSON 4 CONTINUED

TEACHER INSTRUCTIONS

Use the Question and Answer Flows below for the sentences on the Chapter 22 Test.

Question and Answer Flow for Sentence 1: Robert helped at his little brother's soccer game.

1. Who helped at his little brother's soccer game?
   Robert - SN
2. What is being said about Robert? Robert helped - V
3. At - P
4. At what? game - OP
5. What kind of game? soccer - Adj
6. Whose game? brother's - PN
7. What kind of brother? little - Adj
8. Whose brother? his - PP
9. SN V P1 Check
10. (At his little brother's soccer game) - Prepositional phrase
11. Period, statement, declarative sentence
12. Go back to the verb - divide the complete subject from the complete predicate.

```
                        SN    V    P  PP  Adj    PN     Adj    OP
Classified Sentence:    SN  V    Robert / helped (at his little brother's soccer game).  D
                        P1
```

Question and Answer Flow for Sentence 2: The little bug landed lightly on Tim's nose.

1. What landed lightly on Tim's nose? bug - SN
2. What is being said about bug? bug landed - V
3. Landed how? lightly - Adv
4. On - P
5. On what? nose - OP
6. Whose nose? Tim's - PN
7. What kind of bug? little - Adj
8. The - A
9. SN V P1 Check
10. (On Tim's nose) - Prepositional phrase
11. Period, statement, declarative sentence
12. Go back to the verb - divide the complete subject from the complete predicate.

```
                        A  Adj  SN      V      Adv   P  PN   OP
Classified Sentence:    SN  V   The little bug / landed lightly (on Tim's nose).  D
                        P1
```

Level 2—Shurley English—Homeschool Edition

CHAPTER 22   LESSON 5

Objectives: Writing assignment #16 and Sentence Time.

 WRITING TIME

<u>TEACHER INSTRUCTIONS FOR WRITING ASSIGNMENT #16</u>

Give Writing Assignment #16 from the box below. Remind students to use the Writing Checklist in Reference 17 to check their finished writing assignments.

Read, check, and discuss Writing Assignment #16 after students have finished their final letter. Use the Writing Checklist (*Reference 17 on teacher's page 112*) as you check and discuss students' letters. Make sure students are using the checklist correctly.

Writing Assignment Box

Writing Assignment #16: Write a friendly letter to a person of your choice. Before you start, review the tips for writing friendly letters and any references about friendly letters. After your letter has been checked for mistakes, fold the letter and put it in an envelope. *(Students will learn how to properly address the envelope in Chapter 23.)*

 SENTENCE TIME

Chapter 22, Lesson 5, Sentence: Use colored markers to match each label with the correct sentence part by drawing a line from one to the other. Then, use the labels to arrange the sentence parts into a sentence that you will write on the sentence line below. *(The order of the words in your sentence should be in the same sequence as the vertical list of sentence labels.)* Create other labels and scrambled sentence parts on notebook paper for family members to solve. You may color code the sentence parts. *(See page 116 in the student book.)*

Labels for Order of Sentence	Scrambled Sentence Parts
PP	to
PN	new
SN	cousin's
V	the
P	his
A	elementary
Adj	yesterday
Adj	neighbor
OP	school
Adv	walked

Sentence: His cousin's neighbor walked to the new elementary school yesterday

(End of lesson.)

CHAPTER 23   LESSON 1

Objectives: Jingles, Grammar (Practice Sentences), Skill (Parts of an Envelope), Vocabulary #1, and Activity.

 **JINGLE TIME**

Have students turn to the Jingle Section in their books and recite the previously-taught jingles.

 GRAMMAR TIME

Put the Practice Sentences from the box below on the board or on notebook paper. Use these sentences as you practice the concepts that have been taught. For the greatest benefit, students must participate orally with the teacher.

Chapter 23, Practice Sentences for Lesson 1
1. _____ The golf ball bounced high over the fence.
2. _____ They crawled cautiously inside the dark cave with a flashlight.
3. _____ Paul's brother fell into a muddy ditch.

TEACHING SCRIPT FOR CLASSIFYING PRACTICE SENTENCES

We will classify three different sentences to practice the grammar skills in the Question and Answer Flows. We will classify the sentences together. Begin. (*You might have students write the labels above the sentences at this time.*)

Question and Answer Flow for Sentence 1:   The golf ball bounced high over the fence.
1. What bounced high over the fence? ball - SN
2. What is being said about ball? ball bounced - V
3. Bounced how? high - Adv
4. Over - P
5. Over what? fence - OP
6. The - A
7. What kind of ball? golf - Adj
8. The - A
9. SN V P1 Check
10. (Over the fence) - Prepositional phrase
11. Period, statement, declarative sentence
12. Go back to the verb - divide the complete subject from the complete predicate.

Classified Sentence:

```
                       A  Adj SN      V    Adv  P   A   OP
       SN V            The golf ball / bounced high (over the fence).  D
       P1
```

CHAPTER 23 LESSON 1 CONTINUED

Question and Answer Flow for Sentence 2: They crawled cautiously inside the dark cave with a flashlight.

1. Who crawled cautiously inside the dark cave with a flashlight? they - SP
2. What is being said about they? they crawled - V
3. Crawled how? cautiously - Adv
4. Inside - P
5. Inside what? cave - OP
6. What kind of cave? dark - Adj
7. The - A
8. With - P
9. With what? flashlight - OP
10. A - A
11. SN V P1 Check
12. (Inside the dark cave) - Prepositional phrase
13. (With a flashlight) - Prepositional phrase
14. Period, statement, declarative sentence
15. Go back to the verb - divide the complete subject from the complete predicate.

                                SP   V   Adv   P A Adj OP   P A   OP

Classified Sentence: SN V / P1   They / crawled cautiously (inside the dark cave) (with a flashlight). D

Question and Answer Flow for Sentence 3: Paul's brother fell into a muddy ditch.

1. Who fell into a muddy ditch? brother - SN
2. What is being said about brother? brother fell - V
3. Into - P
4. Into what? ditch - OP
5. What kind of ditch? muddy - Adj
6. A - A
7. Whose brother? Paul's - PN
8. SN V P1 Check
9. (Into a muddy ditch) - Prepositional phrase
10. Period, statement, declarative sentence
11. Go back to the verb - divide the complete subject from the complete predicate.

                             PN   SN   V   P A Adj   OP

Classified Sentence: SN V / P1   Paul's brother / fell (into a muddy ditch). D

SKILL TIME

TEACHING SCRIPT FOR THE PARTS OF AN ENVELOPE

In order to address the envelope of your friendly letter correctly, you must know the parts that go on the envelope and where to write them. Look at Reference 44 on page 30 and follow along as I read the information about the parts of an envelope. Notice what information is contained in the two parts and where each part is placed on the envelope. (*Go over the information and sample reproduced on the next page with your students.*)

CHAPTER 23 LESSON 1 CONTINUED

Reference 44: Envelope Parts	Friendly Envelope Sample
The return address: 1. Name of the person writing the letter 2. Box or street address of the writer 3. City, state, zip code of the writer **The mailing address:** 1. Name of the person receiving the letter 2. Street address of the person receiving the letter 3. City, state, zip code of the person receiving the letter	**Return Address** — Write your name and address. 　　　　Stamp Wesley Adams 19 Colt Drive Rapid City, SD 29033 **Mailing Address** — Write the name & address of the person receiving the letter. Sally Adams 89 West Brook Lane Blue Lake, NV 92800

VOCABULARY TIME

Assign Chapter 23, Vocabulary Words #1 on page 7 in the Reference Section for students to define in their Vocabulary notebooks. Tell students they are to use a dictionary or thesaurus to look up the meanings of the vocabulary words.

Chapter 23, Vocabulary Words #1
(lazy, industrious, assistant, helper)

ACTIVITY / ASSIGNMENT TIME

(Have butcher paper, poster board, or large pieces of construction paper ready for this activity.) Students can work together or individually on this project. They are to make a colorful wall poster identifying the parts of an envelope. Students are to write the title of each envelope part. Then, they will write the description that fits its title. They can use Reference 44 as their model. *(Make sure students have the supplies they might need for this project: rulers, colors, markers, pencils, paint, etc.)*

Students are to make the parts of an envelope colorful and large enough for a wall display. After they have finished, they can display their artwork. Students should also make an oral presentation of the wall display that illustrates the parts of an envelope. *(Students can use any creative method or material to develop and present their creation. This project may take several days. Students can work on it for short periods of time so they will not get too tired.)*

(End of lesson.)

Level 2—Shurley English—Homeschool Edition

CHAPTER 23   LESSON 2

Objectives: Jingles, Grammar (Practice Sentences), Skill (Parts of an Envelope), Practice Exercise, and Vocabulary #2.

 **JINGLE TIME**

Have students turn to the Jingle Section in their books and recite the previously-taught jingles.

 GRAMMAR TIME

Put the Practice Sentences from the box below on the board or on notebook paper. Use these sentences as you practice the concepts that have been taught. For the greatest benefit, students must participate orally with the teacher.

Chapter 23, Practice Sentences for Lesson 2

1. _____ We cooked over a campfire during the camping trip with our neighbors.
2. _____ David turned left at the green light.
3. _____ The office secretary worked frantically!

TEACHING SCRIPT FOR CLASSIFYING PRACTICE SENTENCES

We will classify three different sentences to practice the grammar skills in the Question and Answer Flows. We will classify the sentences together. Begin. (*You might have students write the labels above the sentences at this time.*)

Question and Answer Flow for Sentence 1: We cooked over a campfire during the camping trip with our neighbors.

1. Who cooked over a campfire during the camping trip with our neighbors? we - SP
2. What is being said about we? we cooked - V
3. Over - P
4. Over what? campfire - OP
5. A - A
6. During - P
7. During what? trip - OP
8. What kind of trip? camping - Adj
9. The - A
10. With - P
11. With whom? neighbors - OP
12. Whose neighbors? our - PP
13. SN V P1 Check
14. (Over a campfire) - Prepositional phrase
15. (During the camping trip) - Prepositional phrase
16. (With our neighbors) - Prepositional phrase
17. Period, statement, declarative sentence
18. Go back to the verb - divide the complete subject from the complete predicate.

```
                       SP   V    P  A   OP    P   A   Adj   OP   P  PP  OP
Classified Sentence:   SN V  We / cooked (over a campfire) (during the camping trip) (with our neighbors). D
                       P1
```

CHAPTER 23 LESSON 2 CONTINUED

Question and Answer Flow for Sentence 2: David turned left at the green light.

1. Who turned left at the green light? David - SN
2. What is being said about David? David turned - V
3. Turned where? left - Adv
4. At - P
5. At what? light - OP
6. What kind of light? green - Adj
7. The - A
8. SN V P1 Check
9. (At the green light) - Prepositional phrase
10. Period, statement, declarative sentence
11. Go back to the verb - divide the complete subject from the complete predicate.

```
                            SN   V     Adv P A    Adj  OP
Classified Sentence:       SN V      David / turned left (at the green light).  D
                            P1
```

Question and Answer Flow for Sentence 3: The office secretary worked frantically!

1. Who worked frantically? secretary - SN
2. What is being said about secretary? secretary worked - V
3. Worked how? frantically - Adv
4. What kind of secretary? office - Adj
5. The - A
6. SN V P1 Check
7. No prepositional phrases.
8. Exclamation point, strong feeling, exclamatory sentence
9. Go back to the verb - divide the complete subject from the complete predicate.

```
                            A   Adj     SN       V     Adv
Classified Sentence:       SN V      The office secretary / worked frantically!  E
                            P1
```

SKILL TIME

TEACHING SCRIPT FOR ADDRESSING AN ENVELOPE

We have gone over the parts of an envelope. Now, you will address an envelope correctly with the information given to you. Then, you will answer a set of questions about the envelope. Read all directions very carefully. (*Students may use the Reference section in their books for definitions and samples if needed.*)

PRACTICE TIME

Have students turn to page 74 in the Practice Section of their book and find Chapter 23, Lesson 2, Practice (*1-2*). Go over the directions to make sure they understand what to do. Check and discuss the Practices after students have finished. (*Chapter 23, Lesson 2, Practice keys are given on the next page.*)

CHAPTER 23 LESSON 2 CONTINUED

Chapter 23, Lesson 2, Practice 1: Fill in the blanks on the envelope with the sample parts below. Draw a stamp in the proper place on the envelope.

Sample Parts of an Envelope:

1. Emily Thompson (writer)
   23 Diamond Drive
   Somerset, KY 26400

2. Teresa Lewis (receiver)
   160 Lemon Street
   Macon, GA 53100

Envelope

Return address		Stamp
Emily Thompson		
23 Diamond Drive		
Somerset, KY 26400		
	Mailing address	
	Teresa Lewis	
	160 Lemon Street	
	Macon, GA 53100	

Chapter 23, Lesson 2, Practice 2: Use the information in Chapter 23, Lesson 2, Practice 1 to match the definitions. Write the correct letter of the word beside each definition.

C   1. person who wrote the letter   A. 160 Lemon Street, Macon, GA 53100
B   2. person who will receive the letter   B. Teresa Lewis
D   3. where the writer lives   C. Emily Thompson
A   4. where the person receiving the letter lives   D. 23 Diamond Drive, Somerset, KY 26400

 VOCABULARY TIME

Assign Chapter 23, Vocabulary Words #2 on page 7 in the Reference Section for students to define in their Vocabulary notebooks. Tell students they are to use a dictionary or thesaurus to look up the meanings of the vocabulary words.

Chapter 23, Vocabulary Words #2
(gentle, rowdy, annual, yearly)

(End of lesson.)

CHAPTER 23   LESSON 3

Objectives: Jingles, Grammar (Practice Sentences), and Practice Exercise.

 **JINGLE TIME**

Have students turn to the Jingle Section in their books and recite the previously-taught jingles.

 GRAMMAR TIME

Put the Practice Sentences from the box below on the board or on notebook paper. Use these sentences as you practice the concepts that have been taught. For the greatest benefit, students must participate orally with the teacher.

Chapter 23, Practice Sentences for Lesson 3
1. _____ Dad's office computer crashed yesterday.
2. _____ The industrious teacher practiced with us before our test.
3. _____ The big black spider crawled quickly under the leaf.

TEACHING SCRIPT FOR CLASSIFYING PRACTICE SENTENCES

We will classify three different sentences to practice the grammar skills in the Question and Answer Flows. We will classify the sentences together. Begin. (*You might have students write the labels above the sentences at this time.*)

Question and Answer Flow for Sentence 1: Dad's office computer crashed yesterday.	
1. What crashed yesterday? computer - SN	6. SN V P1 Check
2. What is being said about computer? computer crashed - V	7. No prepositional phrases.
3. Crashed when? yesterday - Adv	8. Period, statement, declarative sentence
4. What kind of computer? office - Adj	9. Go back to the verb - divide the complete
5. Whose computer? Dad's - PN	subject from the complete predicate.

```
                           PN    Adj   SN    V     Adv
Classified Sentence:   SN V   Dad's office computer / crashed yesterday.  D
                       P1
```

CHAPTER 23 LESSON 3 CONTINUED

Question and Answer Flow for Sentence 2: The industrious teacher practiced with us before our test.

1. Who practiced with us before our test? teacher - SN
2. What is being said about teacher? teacher practiced - V
3. With - P
4. With whom? us - OP
5. Before - P
6. Before what? test - OP
7. Whose test? our - PP
8. What kind of teacher? industrious - Adj
9. The - A
10. SN V P1 Check
11. (With us) - Prepositional phrase
12. (Before our test) - Prepositional phrase
13. Period, statement, declarative sentence
14. Go back to the verb - divide the complete subject from the complete predicate.

Classified Sentence:

```
                        A    Adj      SN      V     P   OP   P   PP  OP
           SN V     The industrious teacher / practiced (with us) (before our test).  D
           P1
```

Question and Answer Flow for Sentence 3: The big black spider crawled quickly under the leaf.

1. What crawled quickly under the leaf? spider - SN
2. What is being said about spider? spider crawled - V
3. Crawled how? quickly - Adv
4. Under - P
5. Under what? leaf - OP
6. The - A
7. What kind of spider? black - Adj
8. What kind of spider? big - Adj
9. The - A
10. SN V P1 Check
11. (Under the leaf) - Prepositional phrase
12. Period, statement, declarative sentence
13. Go back to the verb - divide the complete subject from the complete predicate.

Classified Sentence:

```
                    A  Adj  Adj   SN      V      Adv    P   A   OP
         SN V     The big black spider / crawled quickly (under the leaf).  D
         P1
```

 PRACTICE TIME

Have students turn to pages 75 and 76 in the Practice Section of their book and find Chapter 23, Lesson 3, Practice *(1-3)*. Go over the directions to make sure they understand what to do. Check and discuss the Practices after students have finished. (*Chapter 23, Lesson 3, Practice keys are given on the next page.*)

CHAPTER 23 LESSON 3 CONTINUED

Chapter 23, Lesson 3, Practice 1: Fill in the blanks on the envelope with the sample parts below. Draw a stamp in the proper place on the envelope.

Sample Parts of an Envelope:

1. Gloria Peterson (writer)
   13 West Plains Drive
   Casper, WY 56400

2. Kathy Peterson (receiver)
   244 Georgia Street
   Fresno, CA 67800

Envelope

Return address		Stamp
Gloria Peterson		
13 West Plains Drive		
Casper, WY 56400		
	Mailing address	
	Kathy Peterson	
	244 Georgia Street	
	Fresno, CA 67800	

Chapter 23, Lesson 3, Practice 2: Use the information in Chapter 23, Lesson 3, Practice 1 to match the definitions. Write the correct letter of the word beside each definition.

B 1. person who wrote the letter   A. Kathy Peterson
A 2. person who will receive the letter   B. Gloria Peterson
D 3. where the writer lives   C. 244 Georgia Street, Fresno, CA 67800
C 4. where the person receiving the letter lives   D. 13 West Plains Drive, Casper, WY 56400

Chapter 23, Lesson 3, Practice 3: Write a friendly letter to a special friend or relative. Before you start, review the references and tips for writing friendly letters. After your letter has been edited, fold the letter and put it in an envelope. Address the envelope properly and mail it. Don't forget the stamp. (E-mail does not take the place of this assignment.)

(End of lesson.)

CHAPTER 23   LESSON 4

Objectives: Jingles, Study, Test, Check, Writing (Journal), and State Activity.

 JINGLE TIME

Have students turn to the Jingle Section in their books and recite the previously-taught jingles.

 STUDY TIME

Have students study the vocabulary words in their vocabulary notebooks. Remind students that any vocabulary word in their notebooks could be on their test. Also, have students study any of the skills in the Practice Section that they need to review.

 TEST TIME

Have students turn to page 102 in the Test Section of their book and find Chapter 23 Test. Go over the directions to make sure they understand what to do. (*Chapter 23 Test key is on the next page.*)

 CHECK TIME

After students have finished, check and discuss their test papers. Make sure they understand why their answers are right or wrong. (*For total points, count each required answer as a point.*)

 STATE ACTIVITY TIME

Students will continue to draw or trace the states and to write the following questions and answers.

Oregon	Pennsylvania
1. What is the state on the front of this card? **Oregon**	1. What is the state on the front of this card? **Pennsylvania**
2. What is the capital of Oregon? **Salem**	2. What is the capital of Pennsylvania? **Harrisburg**
3. What is the postal abbreviation of Oregon? **OR**	3. What is the postal abbreviation of Pennsylvania? **PA**

Color these states. Use the cards to quiz family members, friends, and relatives. You may want to time the responses to your questions.

(End of lesson.)

Level 2—Shurley English—Homeschool Edition

Chapter 23 Test
(Student Page 102)

63 pts

Exercise 1: Classify each sentence.

```
                A   Adj   SN      V    P   A      OP       P  PP     OP
1. SN V         The lost tourist / waved (to the policeman) (for his assistance).  D
   P1

                SP   V    P  PP      OP         P      OP
2. SN V         We / stay (with our grandmother) (after school).  D
   P1
```

Exercise 2: Use Sentence 2 to underline the complete subject once and the complete predicate twice and to complete the table below.

List the Noun Used	List the Noun Job	Singular or Plural	Common or Proper	Simple Subject	Simple Predicate
1. grandmother	2. OP	3. S	4. C	5. we	6. stay
7. school	8. OP	9. S	10. C		

Exercise 3: Name the six parts of speech that you have studied. (*You may use abbreviations.*)
(The order of answers may vary.)

1. Noun   2. Verb   3. Adjective   4. Adverb   5. Preposition   6. Pronoun

Exercise 4: Identify each pair of words as synonyms or antonyms by putting parentheses ( ) around **syn** or **ant**.

1. yearly, annual	(syn) ant	4. rough, smooth	syn (ant)	7. meticulous, thorough	(syn) ant
2. rowdy, gentle	syn (ant)	5. assistant, helper	(syn) ant	8. question, inquire	(syn) ant
3. thrive, flourish	(syn) ant	6. industrious, lazy	syn (ant)	9. stretch, shrink	syn (ant)

Exercise 5: Fill in the envelope with the parts provided. Draw a stamp in the proper place on the envelope.

x✓

Sample Parts of an envelope:

1. Wayne Jones (writer)
   36 Ridge Road
   Buffalo, NY 81800

2. Henry Jackson (receiver)
   3445 Taylor Circle
   Fargo, ND 87200

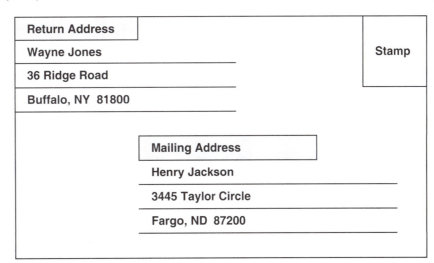

Exercise 6: In your journal, write a paragraph summarizing what you have learned this week.

Level 2—Shurley English—Homeschool Edition

CHAPTER 23 LESSON 4 CONTINUED

TEACHER INSTRUCTIONS

Use the Question and Answer Flows below for the sentences on the Chapter 23 Test.

Question and Answer Flow for Sentence 1: The lost tourist waved to the policeman for his assistance.

1. Who waved to the policeman for his assistance? tourist - SN
2. What is being said about tourist? tourist waved - V
3. To - P
4. To whom? policeman - OP
5. The - A
6. For - P
7. For what? assistance - OP
8. Whose assistance? his - PP
9. What kind of tourist? lost - Adj
10. The - A
11. SN V P1 Check
12. (To the policeman) - Prepositional phrase
13. (For his assistance) - Prepositional phrase
14. Period, statement, declarative sentence
15. Go back to the verb - divide the complete subject from the complete predicate.

```
                              A   Adj   SN        V    P  A    OP        P   PP       OP
Classified Sentence:    SN V   The lost tourist / waved (to the policeman) (for his assistance).   D
                         P1
```

Question and Answer Flow for Sentence 2: We stay with our grandmother after school.

1. Who stay with our grandmother after school? we - SP
2. What is being said about we? we stay - V
3. With - P
4. With whom? grandmother - OP
5. Whose grandmother? our - PP
6. After - P
7. After what? school - OP
8. SN V P1 Check
9. (With our grandmother) - Prepositional phrase
10. (After school) - Prepositional phrase
11. Period, statement, declarative sentence
12. Go back to the verb - divide the complete subject from the complete predicate.

```
                              SP   V    P   PP      OP        P    OP
Classified Sentence:    SN V   We / stay (with our grandmother) (after school).   D
                         P1
```

CHAPTER 23   LESSON 5

Objectives: Writing Assignment #17 and Sentence Time.

 WRITING TIME

TEACHER INSTRUCTIONS FOR WRITING ASSIGNMENT #17

Give Writing Assignment #17 from the box below. Remind students to use the Writing Checklist in Reference 17 to check their finished writing assignment.

Read, check, and discuss Writing Assignment #17 after students have finished their final letter. Use the Writing Checklist (*Reference 17 on teacher's page 112*) as you check and discuss students' letter. Make sure students are using the checklist correctly.

Writing Assignment Box

Writing Assignment #17: Write a friendly letter to a person of your choice. Before you start, review the tips for writing friendly letters and any references about friendly letters. After your letter has been checked for mistakes, fold the letter and put it in an envelope. Address the envelope properly and mail it. Don't forget the stamp.

 SENTENCE TIME

Chapter 23, Lesson 5, Sentence: Use colored markers to match each label with the correct sentence part by drawing a line from one to the other. Then, use the labels to arrange the sentence parts into a sentence that you will write on the sentence line below. *(The order of the words in your sentence should be in the same sequence as the vertical list of sentence labels.)* Create other labels and scrambled sentence parts on notebook paper for family members to solve. You may color code the sentence parts. *(See page 116 in the student book.)*

Labels for Order of Sentence	Scrambled Sentence Parts
A	snow
Adj	in
Adj	their
SN	yellow
V	the
P	for
A	pecked
OP	food
P	the
PP	pretty
OP	birds

Sentence: The pretty yellow birds pecked in the snow for their food.

(End of lesson.)

CHAPTER 24   LESSON 1

Objectives: Jingles, Grammar (Practice Sentences, Skill Builder Check, Review the Six Parts of Speech), Skill (Thank-You Notes), Practice Exercise, and Vocabulary #1.

 **JINGLE TIME**

Have students turn to the Jingle Section in their books and recite the previously-taught jingles.

 GRAMMAR TIME

Put the Practice Sentences from the box below on the board or on notebook paper. Use these sentences as you practice the concepts that have been taught. For the greatest benefit, students must participate orally with the teacher.

Chapter 24, Practice Sentences for Lesson 1
1. _____ We drove to my friend's house for a surprise birthday party.
2. _____ The huge bubbles floated effortlessly across the yard.
3. _____ The famous circus came yearly to our small town.

TEACHING SCRIPT FOR CLASSIFYING PRACTICE SENTENCES

We will classify three different sentences to practice the grammar skills in the Question and Answer Flows. We will classify the sentences together. Begin. (*You might have students write the labels above the sentences at this time.*)

Question and Answer Flow for Sentence 1: We drove to my friend's house for a surprise birthday party.	
1. Who drove to my friend's house for a surprise birthday party? we - SP	9. What kind of party? birthday - Adj
2. What is being said about we? we drove - V	10. What kind of party? surprise - Adj
3. To - P	11. A - A
4. To what? house - OP	12. SN V P1 Check
5. Whose house? friend's - PN	13. (To my friend's house) - Prepositional phrase
6. Whose friend? my - PP	14. (For a surprise birthday party) - Prepositional phrase
7. For - P	15. Period, statement, declarative sentence
8. For what? party - OP	16. Go back to the verb - divide the complete subject from the complete predicate.

```
                          SP    V    P  PP   PN      OP      P  A  Adj   Adj    OP
Classified Sentence:   SN  V    We / drove (to my friend's house) (for a surprise birthday party).  D
                       P1
```

CHAPTER 24 LESSON 1 CONTINUED

Question and Answer Flow for Sentence 2: The huge bubbles floated effortlessly across the yard.

1. What floated effortlessly across the yard? bubbles - SN
2. What is being said about bubbles? bubbles floated - V
3. Floated how? effortlessly - Adv
4. Across - P
5. Across what? yard - OP
6. The - A
7. What kind of bubbles? huge - Adj
8. The - A
9. SN V P1 Check
10. (Across the yard) - Prepositional phrase
11. Period, statement, declarative sentence
12. Go back to the verb - divide the complete subject from the complete predicate.

```
                            A   Adj   SN     V      Adv       P   A   OP
Classified Sentence:   SN  V    The huge bubbles / floated effortlessly (across the yard).  D
                        P1
```

Question and Answer Flow for Sentence 3: The famous circus came yearly to our small town.

1. What came yearly to our small town? circus - SN
2. What is being said about circus? circus came - V
3. Came when? yearly - Adv
4. To - P
5. To what? town - OP
6. What kind of town? small - Adj
7. Whose town? our - PP
8. What kind of circus? famous - Adj
9. The - A
10. SN V P1 Check
11. (To our small town) - Prepositional phrase
12. Period, statement, declarative sentence
13. Go back to the verb - divide the complete subject from the complete predicate.

```
                            A   Adj    SN      V     Adv   P  PP   Adj  OP
Classified Sentence:   SN  V    The famous circus / came yearly (to our small town).  D
                        P1
```

Use Sentences 1-3 that you just classified with your students to do a Skill Builder Check. Use the guidelines below.

Skill Builder Check

1. **Noun check.**
   (Say the job and then say the noun. Circle each noun.)
2. **Identify the nouns as singular or plural.**
   (Write **S** or **P** above each noun.)
3. **Identify the nouns as common or proper.**
   (Follow established procedure for oral identification.)
4. **Do a vocabulary check.**
   (Follow established procedure for oral identification.)
5. **Identify the complete subject and the complete predicate.** (Underline the complete subject once and the complete predicate twice.)
6. **Identify the simple subject and simple predicate.** (Underline the simple subject once and the simple predicate twice. Bold, or highlight, the lines.)
7. **Recite the irregular verb chart.**
   (Located on student page 27 and teacher page 307.)

TEACHING SCRIPT FOR REVIEWING THE SIX PARTS OF SPEECH

What are the six parts of speech that we have covered? *(noun, verb, adjective, adverb, preposition,* and *pronoun) (Chant the six parts of speech that the students have learned several times for reinforcement and fun.)*

CHAPTER 24 LESSON 1 CONTINUED

 **SKILL TIME**

TEACHING SCRIPT FOR THANK-YOU NOTES

Close your eyes. Relax and clear your mind of clutter. Now, think of a person who has done something nice for you or has given you a gift. Sometimes, a person even gives a gift of time, so a gift does not always mean a "physical" gift. After you have thought of someone, open your eyes. That person deserves a thank-you note from you after such a nice gesture. Therefore, it is time we learn about thank-you notes.

You usually write thank-you notes to thank someone for a gift or for doing something nice. In either case, a thank-you note should include at least three statements.

1. You should tell the person <u>what</u> you are thanking him/her for.
2. You should tell the person <u>how the gift was used</u> or <u>how it helped</u>.
3. You should tell the person <u>how much you appreciated the gift or action</u>.

A thank-you note should follow the same form as a friendly letter: heading, greeting, body, closing, and signature. Look at References 45 and 46 on pages 30 and 31. Follow along as I read the information about thank-you notes. (*Go over the information and examples reproduced below and on the next page.*)

Reference 45: Thank-You Note for a Gift
For a Gift
What -   Thank you for... (tell color, kind, and item)
Use -   Tell how the gift is used.
Thanks -   I appreciate your thinking of me at this time.
Example 1: Gift
Heading 87 West Brook Street / Billings, MT 11600 / April 3, 20___
Greeting Dear Matthew,
Body   Thank you for the golden locket that you gave me for my birthday. It is very beautiful, and I wear it every day. Again, I thank you for the birthday gift.
Closing Your friend,
Signature Mary

CHAPTER 24 LESSON 1 CONTINUED

Reference 46: Thank-You Note for an Action
For an Action
What -   Thank you for... (tell action)
Use -   Tell how the action helped.
Thanks -   I appreciate your remembering me.

Example 2: Action

`Heading`
251 Rose Court
Hempstead, NY 34800
September 16, 20____

`Greeting`
Dear Uncle John,

`Body`
　　Thank you for taking me fishing on Saturday. Although we didn't catch much, I still had fun. I appreciate your spending time with me.

`Closing`
Your nephew,

`Signature`
David

 PRACTICE TIME

Have students turn to page 76 in the Practice Section of their book and find Chapter 24, Lesson 1, Practice. Go over the directions to make sure they understand what to do. Check and discuss the Practice after students have finished. (*Chapter 24, Lesson 1, Practice instructions are given below.*)

Chapter 24, Lesson 1, Practice: Write your own thank-you note. First, think of a person who has done something nice for you or has given you a gift (even the gift of time). Next, write that person a thank-you note, using the information in the Reference Section as a guide. (*Check and discuss students' thank-you notes after they are finished.*)

 VOCABULARY TIME

Assign Chapter 24, Vocabulary Words #1 on page 7 in the Reference Section for students to define in their Vocabulary notebooks. Tell students they are to use a dictionary or thesaurus to look up the meanings of the vocabulary words.

Chapter 24, Vocabulary Words #1
(sweet, bitter, continuous, ceaseless)

(End of lesson.)

Level 2—Shurley English—Homeschool Edition

CHAPTER 24   LESSON 2

Objectives: Jingles, Grammar (Practice Sentences), Practice Exercise, and Vocabulary #2.

 **JINGLE TIME**

Have students turn to the Jingle Section in their books and recite the previously-taught jingles.

 GRAMMAR TIME

Put the Practice Sentences from the box below on the board or on notebook paper. Use these sentences as you practice the concepts that have been taught. For the greatest benefit, students must participate orally with the teacher.

Chapter 24, Practice Sentences for Lesson 2
1. _____ The seven rowdy puppies bounced everywhere today.
2. _____ A brilliant star shone above our heads after dark.
3. _____ Her youngest child coughed continuously through the night.

TEACHING SCRIPT FOR CLASSIFYING PRACTICE SENTENCES

We will classify three different sentences to practice the grammar skills in the Question and Answer Flows. We will classify the sentences together. Begin. (*You might have students write the labels above the sentences at this time.*)

Question and Answer Flow for Sentence 1: The seven rowdy puppies bounced everywhere today.

1. What bounced everywhere today? puppies - SN
2. What is being said about puppies?
   puppies bounced - V
3. Bounced where? everywhere - Adv
4. Bounced when? today - Adv
5. What kind of puppies? rowdy - Adj
6. How many puppies? seven - Adj
7. The - A
8. SN V P1 Check
9. No prepositional phrases.
10. Period, statement, declarative sentence
11. Go back to the verb - divide the complete subject from the complete predicate.

```
                       A   Adj   Adj    SN      V      Adv      Adv
Classified Sentence:   SN V     The seven rowdy puppies / bounced everywhere today.   D
                       P1
```

CHAPTER 24 LESSON 2 CONTINUED

Question and Answer Flow for Sentence 2: A brilliant star shone above our heads after dark.

1. What shone above our heads after dark? star - SN
2. What is being said about star? star shone - V
3. Above - P
4. Above what? heads - OP
5. Whose heads? our - PP
6. After - P
7. After what? dark - OP
8. What kind of star? brilliant - Adj
9. A - A
10. SN V P1 Check
11. (Above our heads) - Prepositional phrase
12. (After dark) - Prepositional phrase
13. Period, statement, declarative sentence
14. Go back to the verb - divide the complete subject from the complete predicate.

```
                        A  Adj   SN    V       P   PP   OP     P    OP
Classified Sentence:    SN  V    A brilliant star / shone (above our heads) (after dark).  D
                        P1
```

Question and Answer Flow for Sentence 3: Her youngest child coughed continuously through the night.

1. Who coughed continuously through the night? child - SN
2. What is being said about child? child coughed - V
3. Coughed how? continuously - Adv
4. Through - P
5. Through what? night - OP
6. The - A
7. Which child? youngest - Adj
8. Whose child? her - PP
9. SN V P1 Check
10. (Through the night) - Prepositional phrase
11. Period, statement, declarative sentence
12. Go back to the verb - divide the complete subject from the complete predicate.

```
                        PP   Adj    SN      V       Adv         P   A   OP
Classified Sentence:    SN V  Her youngest child / coughed continuously (through the night).  D
                        P1
```

PRACTICE TIME

Have students turn to page 76 in the Practice Section of their book and find Chapter 24, Lesson 2, Practice. Go over the directions to make sure they understand what to do. Check and discuss the Practice after students have finished. (*Chapter 24, Lesson 2, Practice instructions are given below.*)

Chapter 24, Lesson 2, Practice: Write another thank-you note. First, think of a person who has done something nice for you or has given you a gift (even the gift of time). Next, write that person a thank-you note, using the information in the Reference Section as a guide.

VOCABULARY TIME

Assign Chapter 24, Vocabulary Words #2 on page 7 in the Reference Section for students to define in their Vocabulary notebooks. Have students use a dictionary or thesaurus for the vocabulary words.

Chapter 24, Vocabulary Words #2
(polite, rude, limp, hobble)

(End of lesson.)

CHAPTER 24   LESSON 3

Objectives: Jingles, Grammar (Practice Sentences), and Activity.

 **JINGLE TIME**

Have students turn to the Jingle Section in their books and recite the previously-taught jingles.

 GRAMMAR TIME

Put the Practice Sentences from the box below on the board or on notebook paper. Use these sentences as you practice the concepts that have been taught. For the greatest benefit, students must participate orally with the teacher.

Chapter 24, Practice Sentences for Lesson 3
1. _____ The weak cat limped slowly to the house.
2. _____ Mary's colorful umbrella opened unexpectedly inside the flower shop.
3. _____ His beautiful painting appeared in the museum during the holidays.

TEACHING SCRIPT FOR CLASSIFYING PRACTICE SENTENCES

We will classify three different sentences to practice the grammar skills in the Question and Answer Flows. We will classify the sentences together. Begin. (*You might have students classify these sentences independently so they can participate in the activity on the next page.*)

Question and Answer Flow for Sentence 1: The weak cat limped slowly to the house.

1. What limped slowly to the house? cat - SN
2. What is being said about cat? cat limped - V
3. Limped how? slowly - Adv
4. To - P
5. To what? house - OP
6. The - A
7. What kind of cat? weak - Adj
8. The - A
9. SN V P1 Check
10. (To the house) - Prepositional phrase
11. Period, statement, declarative sentence
12. Go back to the verb - divide the complete subject from the complete predicate.

```
                         A   Adj  SN    V    Adv  P  A   OP
Classified Sentence:   SN V    The weak cat / limped slowly (to the house).  D
                       P1
```

CHAPTER 24 LESSON 3 CONTINUED

Question and Answer Flow for Sentence 2: Mary's colorful umbrella opened unexpectedly inside the flower shop.

1. What opened unexpectedly inside the flower shop? umbrella - SN
2. What is being said about umbrella? umbrella opened - V
3. Opened how? unexpectedly - Adv
4. Inside - P
5. Inside what? shop - OP
6. What kind of shop? flower - Adj
7. The - A
8. What kind of umbrella? colorful - Adj
9. Whose umbrella? Mary's - PN
10. SN V P1 Check
11. (Inside the flower shop) - Prepositional phrase
12. Period, statement, declarative sentence
13. Go back to the verb - divide the complete subject from the complete predicate.

```
                        PN    Adj    SN       V         Adv      P  A  Adj   OP
Classified Sentence:    SN V  Mary's colorful umbrella / opened unexpectedly (inside the flower shop).  D
                        P1
```

Question and Answer Flow for Sentence 3: His beautiful painting appeared in the museum during the holidays.

1. What appeared in the museum during the holidays? painting - SN
2. What is being said about painting? painting appeared - V
3. In - P
4. In what? museum - OP
5. The - A
6. During - P
7. During what? holidays - OP
8. The - A
9. What kind of painting? beautiful - Adj
10. Whose painting? his - PP
11. SN V P1 Check
12. (In the museum) - Prepositional phrase
13. (During the holidays) - Prepositional phrase
14. Period, statement, declarative sentence
15. Go back to the verb - divide the complete subject from the complete predicate.

```
                        PP   Adj       SN         V     P  A   OP      P   A    OP
Classified Sentence:    SN V His beautiful painting / appeared (in the museum) (during the holidays).  D
                        P1
```

ACTIVITY / ASSIGNMENT TIME

This activity will be a fun reminder of careless mistakes you may make while classifying sentences. This can be used with test or practice sentences. If you miss the classification of a word in a Question and Answer Flow, you must wear the following items for a designated time as a reminder of where you went wrong today.

Classification Error	Girls' Attire	Boys' Attire
1. Subject Noun	a lady's hat	a necktie
2. Verb (includes helping verbs)	unmatched shoes	unmatched shoes
3. Adjective (includes articles)	a neck scarf	one glove
4. Adverb	one earring	shirt on backwards
5. Preposition	curlers in your hair	a pair of overshoes
6. Object of a Preposition	an apron	a ballcap on backwards
7. Pronoun (includes SP and PP)	a pair of overshoes	4 garbage bags tied on your belt

(End of lesson.)

Level 2—Shurley English—Homeschool Edition

CHAPTER 24   LESSON 4

Objectives: Jingles, Study, Test, Check, Writing (Journal), and State Activity.

 JINGLE TIME

Have students turn to the Jingle Section in their books and recite the previously-taught jingles.

 STUDY TIME

Have students study the vocabulary words in their vocabulary notebooks. Remind students that any vocabulary word in their notebooks could be on their test. Also, have students study any of the skills in the Practice Section that they need to review.

 TEST TIME

Have students turn to page 103 in the Test Section of their book and find Chapter 24 Test. Go over the directions to make sure they understand what to do. (*Chapter 24 Test key is on the next page.*)

 CHECK TIME

After students have finished, check and discuss their test papers. Make sure they understand why their answers are right or wrong. (*For total points, count each required answer as a point.*)

 STATE ACTIVITY TIME

Students will continue to draw or trace the states and to write the following questions and answers.

Rhode Island	South Carolina
1. What is the state on the front of this card? **Rhode Island**	1. What is the state on the front of this card? **South Carolina**
2. What is the capital of Rhode Island? **Providence**	2. What is the capital of South Carolina? **Columbia**
3. What is the postal abbreviation of Rhode Island? **RI**	3. What is the postal abbreviation of South Carolina? **SC**

Color these states. Use the cards to quiz family members, friends, and relatives. You may want to time the responses to your questions.

(End of lesson.)

Level 2—Shurley English—Homeschool Edition

Chapter 24 Test
(Student Page 103)

Exercise 1: Classify each sentence.

              A   SN   V   Adv P PP OP   Adv
1. <u>SN V</u>   The pig / broke out **(**of its pen**)** yesterday. **D**
   <u>P1</u>

              SP   V   P PP   PN   OP   P   A   OP
2. <u>SN V</u>   We / stayed **(**at our grandparents' house**) (**during the holidays**)**. **D**
   <u>P1</u>

Exercise 2: Use Sentence 2 to underline the complete subject once and the complete predicate twice and to complete the table below.

List the Noun Used	List the Noun Job	Singular or Plural	Common or Proper	Simple Subject	Simple Predicate
1. **house**	2. **OP**	3. **S**	4. **C**	5. **we**	6. **stayed**
7. **holidays**	8. **OP**	9. **P**	10. **C**		

Exercise 3: Name the six parts of speech that you have studied. (*You may use abbreviations.*)
(The order of answers may vary.)

1. **Noun**   2. **Verb**   3. **Adjective**   4. **Adverb**   5. **Preposition**   6. **Pronoun**

Exercise 4: Identify each pair of words as synonyms or antonyms by putting parentheses ( ) around *syn* or *ant*.

1. annual, yearly	**(syn)** ant	4. rowdy, gentle	syn **(ant)**	7. thorough, meticulous	**(syn)** ant
2. limp, hobble	**(syn)** ant	5. sweet, bitter	syn **(ant)**	8. lazy, industrious	syn **(ant)**
3. rude, polite	syn **(ant)**	6. assistant, helper	**(syn)** ant	9. continuous, ceaseless	**(syn)** ant

Exercises 5: Correct the capitalization and punctuation mistakes. Write the rule numbers above the capitalization corrections and below the punctuation corrections. Use Reference 24 for the capitalization rules and Reference 26 for the punctuation rules. The references are located on pages 18 and 19 in your Reference Section.

    1 (or 2)   3   5   5   (capitalization rule numbers)
    I   M   M   O
   i visited margaret in medford, oregon.   (Editing Guide: 4 capitals & 2 punctuation)
                                        3   5   (punctuation rule numbers)

Exercise 6: Write your own thank-you note. First, think of a person who has done something nice for you or has given you a gift (even the gift of time). Next, write that person a thank-you note, using the information in the Reference Section as a guide. (*Check and discuss students' thank-you notes after they are finished.*)

Exercise 7: In your journal, write a paragraph summarizing what you have learned this week.

CHAPTER 24 LESSON 4 CONTINUED

TEACHER INSTRUCTIONS

Use the Question and Answer Flows below for the sentences on the Chapter 24 Test.

Question and Answer Flow for Sentence 1: The pig broke out of its pen yesterday.

1. What broke out of its pen yesterday? pig - SN
2. What is being said about pig? pig broke - V
3. Broke where? out - Adv
4. Of - P
5. Of what? pen - OP
6. Whose pen? its - PP
7. Broke when? yesterday - Adv
8. The - A
9. SN V P1 Check
10. (Of its pen) - Prepositional phrase
11. Period, statement, declarative sentence
12. Go back to the verb - divide the complete subject from the complete predicate.

```
                              A   SN    V    Adv  P  PP  OP    Adv
Classified Sentence:     SN V     The pig / broke out (of its pen) yesterday.  D
                         P1
```

Question and Answer Flow for Sentence 2: We stayed at our grandparents' house during the holidays.

1. Who stayed at our grandparents' house during the holidays? we - SP
2. What is being said about we? we stayed - V
3. At - P
4. At what? house - OP
5. Whose house? grandparents' - PN
6. Whose grandparents? our - PP
7. During - P
8. During what? holidays - OP
9. The - A
10. SN V P1 Check
11. (At our grandparents' house) - Prepositional phrase
12. (During the holidays) - Prepositional phrase
13. Period, statement, declarative sentence
14. Go back to the verb - divide the complete subject from the complete predicate.

```
                              SP   V   P  PP    PN     OP     P   A    OP
Classified Sentence:     SN V     We / stayed (at our grandparents' house) (during the holidays).  D
                         P1
```

Level 2—Shurley English—Homeschool Edition

CHAPTER 24   LESSON 5

Objectives: Writing Assignment #18 and Sentence Time.

 WRITING TIME

<u>*TEACHER INSTRUCTIONS FOR WRITING ASSIGNMENT #18*</u>

Give Writing Assignment #18 from the box below. Remind students to use the Writing Checklist in Reference 17 to check their finished writing assignment.

Read, check, and discuss Writing Assignment #18 after students have finished their final drafts. Use the Writing Checklist (*Reference 17 on teacher's page 112*) as you check and discuss students' papers. Make sure students are using the checklist correctly.

Writing Assignment Box

Writing Assignment #18: Narrative Paragraph

Writing topic choices: The Mysterious House/Stranger   or   The Fastest Car in Town   or   Lost in the Woods

---

 SENTENCE TIME

Chapter 24, Lesson 5, Sentence: Use colored markers to match each label with the correct sentence part by drawing a line from one to the other. Then, use the labels to arrange the sentence parts into a sentence that you will write on the sentence line below. *(The order of the words in your sentence should be in the same sequence as the vertical list of sentence labels.)* Create other labels and scrambled sentence parts on notebook paper for family members to solve. You may color code the sentence parts. *(See page 117 in the student book.)*

Labels for Order of Sentence	Scrambled Sentence Parts
SP	at
V	during
P	joke
PP	time
Adj	family
PN	funny
Adj	brother's
OP	I
P	my
Adj	laughed
OP	big

Sentence: I laughed at my big brother's funny joke during family time.

(End of lesson.)

Level 2—Shurley English—Homeschool Edition

CHAPTER 25   LESSON 1

Objectives: Jingles, Grammar (Practice Sentences, Skill Builder Check), Skill (The Three Main Parts of the Library), and Activity.

JINGLE TIME

Have students turn to the Jingle Section in their books and recite the previously-taught jingles.

GRAMMAR TIME

Put the Practice Sentences from the box below on the board or on notebook paper. Use these sentences as you practice the concepts that have been taught. For the greatest benefit, students must participate orally with the teacher.

Chapter 25, Practice Sentences for Lesson 1
1. _____ The mechanic worked on the flat tire during the night.
2. _____ My cousin's mother works during the day at the hospital.
3. _____ He walks daily to the neighborhood grocery store.

TEACHING SCRIPT FOR CLASSIFYING PRACTICE SENTENCES

We will classify three different sentences to practice the grammar skills in the Question and Answer Flows. We will classify the sentences together. Begin. (*You might have students write the labels above the sentences at this time.*)

Question and Answer Flow for Sentence 1: The mechanic worked on the flat tire during the night.

1. Who worked on the flat tire during the night?
   mechanic - SN
2. What is being said about mechanic?
   mechanic worked - V
3. On - P
4. On what? tire - OP
5. What kind of tire? flat - Adj
6. The - A
7. During - P
8. During what? night - OP
9. The - A
10. The - A
11. SN V P1 Check
12. (On the flat tire) - Prepositional phrase
13. (During the night) - Prepositional phrase
14. Period, statement, declarative sentence
15. Go back to the verb - divide the complete subject from the complete predicate.

```
                          A    SN     V      P  A Adj OP    P   A  OP
Classified Sentence:    SN V   The mechanic / worked (on the flat tire) (during the night).  D
                        P1
```

CHAPTER 25 LESSON 1 CONTINUED

Question and Answer Flow for Sentence 2: My cousin's mother works during the day at the hospital.

1. Who works during the day at the hospital? mother - SN
2. What is being said about mother? mother works - V
3. During - P
4. During what? day - OP
5. The - A
6. At - P
7. At what? hospital - OP
8. The - A
9. Whose mother? cousin's - PN
10. Whose cousin? my - PP
11. SN V P1 Check
12. (During the day) - Prepositional phrase
13. (At the hospital) - Prepositional phrase
14. Period, statement, declarative sentence
15. Go back to the verb - divide the complete subject from the complete predicate.

```
                         PP   PN    SN      V    P   A   OP   P   A   OP
Classified Sentence:     SN V   My cousin's mother / works (during the day) (at the hospital).   D
                         P1
```

Question and Answer Flow for Sentence 3: He walks daily to the neighborhood grocery store.

1. Who walks daily to the neighborhood grocery store? he - SP
2. What is being said about he? he walks - V
3. Walks when? daily - Adv
4. To - P
5. To what? store - OP
6. What kind of store? grocery - Adj
7. What kind of store? neighborhood - Adj
8. The - A
9. SN V P1 Check
10. (To the neighborhood grocery store) - Prepositional phrase
11. Period, statement, declarative sentence
12. Go back to the verb - divide the complete subject from the complete predicate.

```
                         SP    V    Adv   P  A     Adj       Adj      OP
Classified Sentence:     SN V   He / walks daily (to the neighborhood grocery store).   D
                         P1
```

Use Sentences 1-3 that you just classified with your students to do a Skill Builder Check. Use the guidelines below.

Skill Builder Check	
1. **Noun check.** (Say the job and then say the noun. Circle each noun.)	5. **Identify the complete subject and the complete predicate.** (Underline the complete subject once and the complete predicate twice.)
2. **Identify the nouns as singular or plural.** (Write **S** or **P** above each noun.)	6. **Identify the simple subject and simple predicate.** (Underline the simple subject once and the simple predicate twice. Bold, or highlight, the lines.)
3. **Identify the nouns as common or proper.** (Follow established procedure for oral identification.)	7. **Recite the irregular verb chart.** (Located on student page 27 and teacher page 307.)
4. **Do a vocabulary check.** (Follow established procedure for oral identification.)	

VOCABULARY TIME

Students will no longer have assigned Vocabulary Words. As they find new or interesting words, have students add them to their list in their Vocabulary notebook.

Level 2—Shurley English—Homeschool Edition

CHAPTER 25 LESSON 1 CONTINUED

SKILL TIME

TEACHING SCRIPT FOR INTRODUCING THE THREE MAIN PARTS OF THE LIBRARY

Whenever you go to the library to look up information, it should be a fun and easy experience. In order for you to enjoy the library and to utilize its full potential, you will need to know about some of the major sections in the library and the most common materials found in the library. We are going to discuss three of the major sections in the library. Look at Reference 47 on page 31 (*Discuss the three main parts of the library listed below with your students.*)

Reference 47: Three Main Parts of the Library

Fiction Section
Fiction books contain stories about people, places, or things that are not true.

Nonfiction Section
Nonfiction books contain information and stories that are true.

Reference Section
The Reference Section is designed to help you find information on many topics. The most common reference books are the dictionary and the encyclopedia.

ACTIVITY / ASSIGNMENT TIME

Make cards from large sheets of different-colored construction paper with these names on them: *Fiction Section, Nonfiction Section, and Reference Section.* Have students print the correct information from Reference 47 on the back of each card.

Spread the cards out with only the sections showing. Call out the name of each section, one at a time. As you name each section, have a student select the correct card and read the information printed there. Have students repeat this activity with several members of the family.

Extension: Have someone read the definitions, and different family members name the section.

(End of lesson.)

Level 2—Shurley English—Homeschool Edition

CHAPTER 25   LESSON 2

Objectives: Jingles, Grammar (Practice Sentences), and Activity.

 **JINGLE TIME**

Have students turn to the Jingle Section in their books and recite the previously-taught jingles.

 GRAMMAR TIME

Put the Practice Sentences from the box below on the board or on notebook paper. Use these sentences as you practice the concepts that have been taught. For the greatest benefit, students must participate orally with the teacher.

Chapter 25, Practice Sentences for Lesson 2
1. _____ The poor little bird flew around frantically.
2. _____ Clay looked excitedly at the snow from Bobby's bedroom window.
3. _____ The honking geese flew gracefully over our house.

TEACHING SCRIPT FOR CLASSIFYING PRACTICE SENTENCES

We will classify three different sentences to practice the grammar skills in the Question and Answer Flows. We will classify the sentences together. Begin. (*You might have students write the labels above the sentences at this time.*)

Question and Answer Flow for Sentence 1: The poor little bird flew around frantically.

1. What flew around frantically? bird - SN
2. What is being said about bird? bird flew - V
3. Flew where? around - Adv
4. Flew how? frantically - Adv
5. What kind of bird? little - Adj
6. What kind of bird? poor - Adj
7. The - A
8. SN V P1 Check
9. No prepositional phrases.
10. Period, statement, declarative sentence
11. Go back to the verb - divide the complete subject from the complete predicate.

```
                        A   Adj  Adj  SN    V    Adv     Adv
Classified Sentence:   SN V    The poor little bird / flew around frantically.  D
                        P1
```

Level 2 Homeschool Teacher's Manual

CHAPTER 25 LESSON 2 CONTINUED

Question and Answer Flow for Sentence 2: Clay looked excitedly at the snow from Bobby's bedroom window.

1. Who looked excitedly at the snow from Bobby's bedroom window? Clay - SN
2. What is being said about Clay? Clay looked - V
3. Looked how? excitedly - Adv
4. At - P
5. At what? snow - OP
6. The - A
7. From - P
8. From what? window - OP
9. What kind of window? bedroom - Adj
10. Whose window? Bobby's - PN
11. SN V P1 Check
12. (At the snow) - Prepositional phrase
13. (From Bobby's bedroom window) - Prepositional phrase
14. Period, statement, declarative sentence
15. Go back to the verb - divide the complete subject from the complete predicate.

Classified Sentence:

<u>SN V</u>   SN V   Adv   P A OP   P   PN   Adj   OP
P1   Clay / looked excitedly (at the snow) (from Bobby's bedroom window). D

Question and Answer Flow for Sentence 3: The honking geese flew gracefully over our house.

1. What flew gracefully over our house? geese - SN
2. What is being said about geese? geese flew - V
3. Flew how? gracefully - Adv
4. Over - P
5. Over what? house - OP
6. Whose house? our - PP
7. What kind of geese? honking - Adj
8. The - A
9. SN V P1 Check
10. (Over our house) - Prepositional phrase
11. Period, statement, declarative sentence
12. Go back to the verb - divide the complete subject from the complete predicate.

Classified Sentence:

<u>SN V</u>   A   Adj   SN   V   Adv   P   PP   OP
P1   The honking geese / flew gracefully (over our house).   D

ACTIVITY / ASSIGNMENT TIME

Take students on a field trip to visit their local library. Have them take pencils and notebooks to take notes and draw a diagram of the library. After they return home, have students design their own library and put it on poster board. They are to label and illustrate as many areas in the library as possible. Finally, have students write a report about their study of the library. After students have finished their library illustrations and reports, have students read and discuss them with family members and/or friends. (*This project may take several days.*)

(End of lesson.)

Level 2—Shurley English—Homeschool Edition

CHAPTER 25 LESSON 3
Objectives: Jingles, Grammar (Practice Sentences), and Practice Exercise.

 **JINGLE TIME**

Have students turn to the Jingle Section in their books and recite the previously-taught jingles.

 GRAMMAR TIME

Put the Practice Sentences from the box below on the board or on notebook paper. Use these sentences as you practice the concepts that have been taught. For the greatest benefit, students must participate orally with the teacher.

Chapter 25, Practice Sentences for Lesson 3
1. _____ A mysterious stranger looked cautiously through our store window.
2. _____ She hurried anxiously to the school.
3. _____ A bat flew quickly around Grandfather's barn.

TEACHING SCRIPT FOR CLASSIFYING PRACTICE SENTENCES

We will classify three different sentences to practice the grammar skills in the Question and Answer Flows. We will classify the sentences together. Begin. (*You might have students write the labels above the sentences at this time.*)

Question and Answer Flow for Sentence 1: A mysterious stranger looked cautiously through our store window.

1. Who looked cautiously through our store window? stranger - SN
2. What is being said about stranger? stranger looked - V
3. Looked how? cautiously - Adv
4. Through - P
5. Through what? window - OP
6. What kind of window? store - Adj
7. Whose window? our - PP
8. What kind of stranger? mysterious - Adj
9. A - A
10. SN V P1 Check
11. (Through our store window) - Prepositional phrase
12. Period, statement, declarative sentence
13. Go back to the verb - divide the complete subject from the complete predicate.

```
                              A   Adj       SN        V       Adv      P    PP  Adj  OP
Classified Sentence:   SN V   A mysterious stranger / looked cautiously (through our store window).  D
                       P1
```

Level 2 Homeschool Teacher's Manual

Level 2—Shurley English—Homeschool Edition

CHAPTER 25 LESSON 3 CONTINUED

Question and Answer Flow for Sentence 2: She hurried anxiously to the school.

1. Who hurried anxiously to the school? she - SP
2. What is being said about she? she hurried - V
3. Hurried how? anxiously - Adv
4. To - P
5. To what? school - OP
6. The - A
7. SN V P1 Check
8. (To the school) - Prepositional phrase
9. Period, statement, declarative sentence
10. Go back to the verb - divide the complete subject from the complete predicate.

Classified Sentence: SN V / P1   SP   V   Adv   P   A   OP
She / hurried anxiously (to the school).   D

Question and Answer Flow for Sentence 3: A bat flew quickly around Grandfather's barn.

1. What flew quickly around Grandfather's barn? bat - SN
2. What is being said about bat? bat flew - V
3. Flew how? quickly - Adv
4. Around - P
5. Around what? barn - OP
6. Whose barn? Grandfather's - PN
7. A - A
8. SN V P1 Check
9. (Around Grandfather's barn) - Prepositional phrase
10. Period, statement, declarative sentence
11. Go back to the verb - divide the complete subject from the complete predicate.

Classified Sentence: SN V / P1   A   SN   V   Adv   P   PN   OP
A bat / flew quickly (around Grandfather's barn).   D

TEACHER INSTRUCTIONS

Discuss students' favorite fiction books and nonfiction books. Discuss how they use the two main reference books in the Reference section (dictionary and encyclopedia). Discuss the parts of the library that they like best. Discuss why libraries are important.

 PRACTICE TIME

Have students turn to page 76 in the Practice Section of their book and find Chapter 25, Lesson 3, Practice. Go over the directions to make sure they understand what to do. Check and discuss the Practice after students have finished. (*Chapter 25, Lesson 3, Practice key is given below.*)

Chapter 25, Lesson 3, Practice: Underline the correct answer in each sentence.
1. Nonfiction books contain information and stories that are (**true**, not true).
2. Fiction books contain information and stories that are (true, **not true**).
3. The most common reference books are the dictionary and the encyclopedia. (**true**, not true)

(End of lesson.)

CHAPTER 25 LESSON 4

Objectives: Jingles, Study, Test, Check, Writing (Journal), and State Activity.

JINGLE TIME

Have students turn to the Jingle Section in their books and recite the previously-taught jingles.

STUDY TIME

Have students study the vocabulary words in their vocabulary notebooks. Remind students that any vocabulary word in their notebooks could be on their test. Also, have students study any of the skills in the Practice Section that they need to review.

TEST TIME

Have students turn to page 104 in the Test Section of their book and find Chapter 25 Test. Go over the directions to make sure they understand what to do. (*Chapter 25 Test key is on the next page.*)

CHECK TIME

After students have finished, check and discuss their test papers. Make sure they understand why their answers are right or wrong. (*For total points, count each required answer as a point.*)

STATE ACTIVITY TIME

Students will continue to draw or trace the states and to write the following questions and answers.

South Dakota	Tennessee
1. What is the state on the front of this card? **South Dakota**	1. What is the state on the front of this card? **Tennessee**
2. What is the capital of South Dakota? **Pierre**	2. What is the capital of Tennessee? **Nashville**
3. What is the postal abbreviation of South Dakota? **SD**	3. What is the postal abbreviation of Tennessee? **TN**

Color these states. Use the cards to quiz family members, friends, and relatives. You may want to time the responses to your questions.

(End of lesson.)

Level 2—Shurley English—Homeschool Edition

Chapter 25 Test
(Student Page 104)

75 pts

Exercise 1: Classify each sentence.

```
            A   Adj        SN    V     Adv    P  A   OP
1. SN V     The exhausted eagle / dropped slowly (from the sky).  D
   P1

            Adj Adj  SN       V      Adv    P  A    PN       OP
2. SN V     Two small dogs / barked loudly (at the mailman's truck).  D
   P1
```

Exercise 2: Use Sentence 2 to underline the complete subject once and the complete predicate twice and to complete the table below.

List the Noun Used	List the Noun Job	Singular or Plural	Common or Proper	Simple Subject	Simple Predicate
1. dogs	2. SN	3. P	4. C	5. dogs	6. barked
7. truck	8. OP	9. S	10. C		

Exercise 3: Name the six parts of speech that you have studied. (*You may use abbreviations.*) **(The order of answers may vary.)**

1. Noun   2. Verb   3. Adjective   4. Adverb   5. Preposition   6. Pronoun

Exercise 4: Identify each pair of words as synonyms or antonyms by putting parentheses ( ) around **syn** or **ant**.

1. hobble, limp	**(syn)** ant	4. thorough, meticulous	**(syn)** ant	7. shrink, stretch	syn **(ant)**
2. yearly, annual	**(syn)** ant	5. bitter, sweet	syn **(ant)**	8. whisper, howl	syn **(ant)**
3. polite, rude	syn **(ant)**	6. continuous, ceaseless	**(syn)** ant	9. industrious, lazy	syn **(ant)**

Exercise 5: Copy the following words on notebook paper. Write the correct contraction beside each word.
Key: we'd, they'll, won't, I'd, haven't, didn't, we're, who's, I'm, couldn't.
Words: we had, they will, will not, I would, have not, did not, we are, who is, I am, could not.

Exercise 6: Copy the following contractions on notebook paper. Write the correct word beside each contraction.
Key: should not, I had or I would, he will, she had or she would, we have, has not, do not, you are, that is, is not.
Contractions: shouldn't, I'd, he'll, she'd, we've, hasn't, don't, you're, that's, isn't.

Exercise 7: Underline the correct answer in each sentence.

1. Fiction books contain information and stories that are (**true, not true**).
2. Nonfiction books contain information and stories that are (**true, not true**).
3. The most common reference books are the dictionary and the encyclopedia. (**true, false**)

Exercise 8: In your journal, write a paragraph summarizing what you have learned this week.

CHAPTER 25 LESSON 4 CONTINUED

TEACHER INSTRUCTIONS

Use the Question and Answer Flows below for the sentences on the Chapter 25 Test.

Question and Answer Flow for Sentence 1: The exhausted eagle dropped slowly from the sky.

1. What dropped slowly from the sky? eagle - SN
2. What is being said about eagle? eagle dropped - V
3. Dropped how? slowly - Adv
4. From - P
5. From what? sky - OP
6. The - A
7. What kind of eagle? exhausted - Adj
8. The - A
9. SN V P1 Check
10. (From the sky) - Prepositional phrase
11. Period, statement, declarative sentence
12. Go back to the verb - divide the complete subject from the complete predicate.

```
                              A    Adj    SN     V     Adv    P  A  OP
Classified Sentence:   SN V   The exhausted eagle / dropped slowly (from the sky).  D
                       P1
```

Question and Answer Flow for Sentence 2: Two small dogs barked loudly at the mailman's truck.

1. What barked loudly at the mailman's truck? dogs - SN
2. What is being said about dogs? dogs barked - V
3. Barked how? loudly - Adv
4. At - P
5. At what? truck - OP
6. Whose truck? mailman's - PN
7. The - A
8. What kind of dogs? small - Adj
9. How many dogs? two - Adj
10. SN V P1 Check
11. (At the mailman's truck) - Prepositional phrase
12. Period, statement, declarative sentence
13. Go back to the verb - divide the complete subject from the complete predicate.

```
                              Adj  Adj   SN      V     Adv    P  A   PN        OP
Classified Sentence:   SN V   Two small dogs / barked loudly (at the mailman's truck).  D
                       P1
```

CHAPTER 25   LESSON 5

Objectives: Writing Assignment #19 and Sentence Time.

 WRITING TIME

TEACHER INSTRUCTIONS FOR WRITING ASSIGNMENT #19

Give Writing Assignment #19 from the box below. Remind students to use the Writing Checklist in Reference 17 to check their finished writing assignment.

Read, check, and discuss Writing Assignment #19 after students have finished their final papers. Use the Writing Checklist (*Reference 17 on teacher's page 112*) as you check and discuss students' papers. Make sure students are using the checklist correctly.

Writing Assignment Box

Writing Assignment #19: Narrative Paragraph

Writing topics: The Day Everyone Couldn't Stop Laughing   or   The Year of the Great Flood/Great Storm   or Space Cat (or Dog, Monkey, Boy, Girl, Family, etc.)

 SENTENCE TIME

Chapter 25, Lesson 5, Sentence: Use colored markers to match each label with the correct sentence part by drawing a line from one to the other. Then, use the labels to arrange the sentence parts into a sentence that you will write on the sentence line below. *(The order of the words in your sentence should be in the same sequence as the vertical list of sentence labels.)* Create other labels and scrambled sentence parts on notebook paper for family members to solve. You may color code the sentence parts. *(See page 117 in the student book.)*

Labels for Order of Sentence	Scrambled Sentence Parts
PP	my
Adj	my
SN	garden
V	new
P	prize-winning
PP	dug
PN	neighbor's
Adj	in
Adj	puppy
OP	flower

Sentence: My new puppy dug in my neighbor's prize-winning flower garden!

(End of lesson.)

CHAPTER 26   LESSON 1

Objectives: Jingles, Grammar (Practice Sentences), Skill (Introduce the Front Parts of a Book), and Practice Exercise.

 **JINGLE TIME**

Have students turn to the Jingle Section in their books and recite the previously-taught jingles.

 GRAMMAR TIME

Put the Practice Sentences from the box below on the board or on notebook paper. Use these sentences as you practice the concepts that have been taught. For the greatest benefit, students must participate orally with the teacher.

Chapter 26, Practice Sentences for Lesson 1
1. _____ He yelled excitedly to his friends from the window.
2. _____ His crazy dog jumped over the fence in the middle of the night.
3. _____ The actor's stunt car went over the edge of the cliff!

TEACHING SCRIPT FOR CLASSIFYING PRACTICE SENTENCES

We will classify three different sentences to practice the grammar skills in the Question and Answer Flows. We will classify the sentences together. Begin. (*You might have students write the labels above the sentences at this time.*)

Question and Answer Flow for Sentence 1: He yelled excitedly to his friends from the window.

1. Who yelled excitedly to his friends from the window? he - SP
2. What is being said about he? he yelled - V
3. Yelled how? excitedly - Adv
4. To - P
5. To whom? friends - OP
6. Whose friends? his - PP
7. From - P
8. From what? window - OP
9. The - A
10. SN V P1 Check
11. (To his friends) - Prepositional phrase
12. (From the window) - Prepositional phrase
13. Period, statement, declarative sentence
14. Go back to the verb - divide the complete subject from the complete predicate.

```
                          SP    V    Adv   P  PP  OP    P   A   OP
Classified Sentence:    SN V   He / yelled excitedly (to his friends) (from the window). D
                         P1
```

CHAPTER 26 LESSON 1 CONTINUED

Question and Answer Flow for Sentence 2: His crazy dog jumped over the fence in the middle of the night.

1. What jumped over the fence in the middle of the night? dog - SN
2. What is being said about dog? dog jumped - V
3. Over - P
4. Over what? fence - OP
5. The - A
6. In - P
7. In what? middle - OP
8. The - A
9. Of - P
10. Of what? night - OP
11. The - A
12. What kind of dog? crazy - Adj
13. Whose dog? his - PP
14. SN V P1 Check
15. (Over the fence) - Prepositional phrase
16. (In the middle) - Prepositional phrase
17. (Of the night) - Prepositional phrase
18. Period, statement, declarative sentence
19. Go back to the verb - divide the complete subject from the complete predicate.

```
                               PP  Adj SN    V    P  A  OP      P  A  OP    P  A  OP
Classified Sentence:    SN V   His crazy dog / jumped (over the fence) (in the middle) (of the night). D
                        P1
```

Question and Answer Flow for Sentence 3: The actor's stunt car went over the edge of the cliff!

1. What went over the edge of the cliff? car - SN
2. What is being said about car? car went - V
3. Over - P
4. Over what? edge - OP
5. The - A
6. Of - P
7. Of what? cliff - OP
8. The - A
9. What kind of car? stunt - Adj
10. Whose car? actor's - PN
11. The - A
12. SN V P1 Check
13. (Over the edge) - Prepositional phrase
14. (Of the cliff) - Prepositional phrase
15. Exclamation point, strong feeling, exclamatory sentence
16. Go back to the verb - divide the complete subject from the complete predicate.

```
                            A   PN  Adj SN    V   P  A  OP    P  A  OP
Classified Sentence:  SN V  The actor's stunt car / went (over the edge) (of the cliff)! E
                      P1
```

SKILL TIME

TEACHING SCRIPT FOR INTRODUCING THE FRONT PARTS OF A BOOK

Do you know the parts of a book? Let's see how many we can name. (*Ask students to name the parts they know. See the parts listed on the next page and page 384.*) Actually, the parts of a book can be divided into the front parts and back parts. We will learn the front parts of a book, and then we will learn the back parts. Any time you use a nonfiction book to help you with an assignment, it is necessary to understand how to use that book efficiently.

CHAPTER 26 LESSON 1 CONTINUED

Knowing the parts of a book will help you make full use of the special features that are sometimes found in nonfiction books. I will now give you a brief description of each of the features that could appear in a book. We will start with the front parts of a book. Look at Reference 48 on page 32 in the Reference Section of your book. (*Read and discuss the parts of a book in Reference 48 below with your students.*)

Reference 48: The Front Parts of a Book

AT THE FRONT:
1. **Title Page.** This page has the full title of the book, the author's name, the illustrator's name, the name of the publishing company, and the city where the book was published.
2. **Copyright Page.** This page is right after the title page and tells the year in which the book was published and who owns the copyright. If the book has an ISBN number (International Standard Book Number), it is listed here.
3. **Preface** (also called **introduction**). If a book has this page, it will come before the table of contents and will usually tell briefly why the book was written and what it is about.
4. **Table of Contents.** This section lists the major divisions of the book by units or chapters and tells their page numbers.
5. **Body.** This is the main section, or text, of the book.

 PRACTICE TIME

Have students turn to page 76 in the Practice Section of their book and find Chapter 26, Lesson 1, Practice. Go over the directions to make sure they understand what to do. Check and discuss the Practice after students have finished. (*Chapter 26, Lesson 1, Practice keys are given below.*)

Chapter 26, Lesson 1, Practice: Underline the correct homonym in each sentence.

1. The package was (<u>sent</u>, scent) yesterday.
2. It is (to, <u>too</u>, two) cold outside.
3. I (new, <u>knew</u>) that I was wrong.
4. (Right, <u>Write</u>) your birthday on my calendar.
5. Mark (through, <u>threw</u>) his jacket on the couch.
6. The drivers quickly finished the (<u>course</u>, coarse).

(End of lesson.)

Level 2—Shurley English—Homeschool Edition

CHAPTER 26   LESSON 2

Objectives: Jingles, Grammar (Practice Sentences), Skill (Introduce the Back Parts of a Book), and Practice Exercise,.

 **JINGLE TIME**

Have students turn to the Jingle Section in their books and recite the previously-taught jingles.

 GRAMMAR TIME

Put the Practice Sentences from the box below on the board or on notebook paper. Use these sentences as you practice the concepts that have been taught. For the greatest benefit, students must participate orally with the teacher.

Chapter 26, Practice Sentences for Lesson 2
1. _____ That green truck ran into a telephone pole!
2. _____ We flew in a big airplane on our trip.
3. _____ That boy's favorite rock sank to the bottom of the pool.

TEACHING SCRIPT FOR CLASSIFYING PRACTICE SENTENCES

We will classify three different sentences to practice the grammar skills in the Question and Answer Flows. We will classify the sentences together. Begin. (*You might have students write the labels above the sentences at this time.*)

Question and Answer Flow for Sentence 1: That green truck ran into a telephone pole!
1. What ran into a telephone pole? truck - SN
2. What is being said about truck? truck ran - V
3. Into - P
4. Into what? pole - OP
5. What kind of pole? telephone - Adj
6. A - A
7. What kind of truck? green - Adj
8. Which truck? that - Adj
9. SN V P1 Check
10. (Into a telephone pole) - Prepositional phrase
11. Exclamation point, strong feeling, exclamatory sentence
12. Go back to the verb - divide the complete subject from the complete predicate.

```
                        Adj  Adj  SN    V   P  A  Adj   OP
Classified Sentence:   SN V  That green truck / ran (into a telephone pole)!  E
                       P1
```

CHAPTER 26 LESSON 2 CONTINUED

Question and Answer Flow for Sentence 2: We flew in a big airplane on our trip.

1. Who flew in a big airplane on our trip? we - SP
2. What is being said about we? we flew - V
3. In - P
4. In what? airplane - OP
5. What kind of airplane? big - Adj
6. A - A
7. On - P
8. On what? trip - OP
9. Whose trip? our - PP
10. SN V P1 Check
11. (In a big airplane) - Prepositional phrase
12. (On our trip) - Prepositional phrase
13. Period, statement, declarative sentence
14. Go back to the verb - divide the complete subject from the complete predicate.

```
                           SP    V   P A  Adj   OP      P  PP  OP
Classified Sentence:   SN V   We / flew (in a big airplane) (on our trip).  D
                       P1
```

Question and Answer Flow for Sentence 3: That boy's favorite rock sank to the bottom of the pool.

1. What sank to the bottom of the pool? rock - SN
2. What is being said about rock? rock sank - V
3. To - P
4. To what? bottom - OP
5. The - A
6. Of - P
7. Of what? pool - OP
8. The - A
9. What kind of rock? favorite - Adj
10. Whose rock? boy's - PN
11. Which boy? that - Adj
12. SN V P1 Check
13. (To the bottom) - Prepositional phrase
14. (Of the pool) - Prepositional phrase
15. Period, statement, declarative sentence
16. Go back to the verb - divide the complete subject from the complete predicate.

```
                          Adj   PN    Adj    SN    V    P  A   OP    P  A  OP
Classified Sentence:   SN V   That boy's favorite rock / sank (to the bottom) (of the pool).  D
                       P1
```

SKILL TIME

TEACHING SCRIPT FOR INTRODUCING THE BACK PARTS OF A BOOK

Let's review the front parts of a book before we learn the back parts. (*Ask students to name and explain the front parts of a book. Allow them to use Reference 48 if they need help.*) I will now give you a brief description of each of the features that could appear in the back part of a book. Look at Reference 49 on page 32 in the Reference Section of your book. (*Read and discuss the parts of a book in Reference 49 on the next page with your students.*)

CHAPTER 26 LESSON 2 CONTINUED

> **Reference 49: The Back Parts of a Book**
>
> AT THE BACK:
> 1. **Appendix.** This section includes extra informative material such as maps, charts, tables, diagrams, letters, etc. It is always wise to find out what is in the appendix, since it may contain supplementary material that you could otherwise find only by going to the library.
> 2. **Glossary.** This section is like a dictionary and gives the meanings of some of the important words in the book.
> 3. **Bibliography.** This section includes a list of books used by the author. It could serve as a guide for further reading on a topic.
> 4. **Index.** This will probably be your most useful section. The purpose of the index is to help you quickly locate information about the topics in the book. It has an alphabetical list of specific topics and tells on which page that information can be found. It is similar to the table of contents, but it is much more detailed.

 PRACTICE TIME

Have students turn to page 77 in the Practice Section of their book and find Chapter 26, Lesson 2, Practice *(1-3)*. Go over the directions to make sure they understand what to do. Check and discuss the Practices after students have finished. *(Chapter 26, Lesson 2, Practice keys are given below.)*

Chapter 26, Lesson 2, Practice 1: Match each part of a book listed below with the type of information it may give you. Write the appropriate letter in the blank. You may use each letter only once.

| A. Index | B. Appendix | C. Bibliography | D. Preface | E. Body | F. Copyright page |

1. **D** Reason the book was written

2. **E** Text of the book

3. **F** ISBN number

4. **A** Exact page numbers for a particular topic and used to locate topics quickly

5. **B** Extra maps in a book

6. **C** Books listed for finding more information

Chapter 26, Lesson 2, Practice 2: On notebook paper, write the five parts found at the front of a book. **(Title Page, Copyright Page, Preface, Table of Contents, Body)** (The order of the answers may vary.)

Chapter 26, Lesson 2, Practice 3: On notebook paper, write the four parts found at the back of a book. **(Appendix, Glossary, Bibliography, Index)** (The order of the answers may vary.)

(End of lesson.)

CHAPTER 26   LESSON 3

Objectives: Jingles, Grammar (Practice Sentences), and Practice Exercise.

 **JINGLE TIME**

Have students turn to the Jingle Section in their books and recite the previously-taught jingles.

 GRAMMAR TIME

Put the Practice Sentences from the box below on the board or on notebook paper. Use these sentences as you practice the concepts that have been taught. For the greatest benefit, students must participate orally with the teacher.

Chapter 26, Practice Sentences for Lesson 3
1. _____ The four tired kittens slept peacefully in the barn yesterday.
2. _____ The three circus lions roared loudly today.
3. _____ The chipped vase sold for five dollars at the garage sale.

<u>TEACHING SCRIPT FOR CLASSIFYING PRACTICE SENTENCES</u>

We will classify three different sentences to practice the grammar skills in the Question and Answer Flows. We will classify the sentences together. Begin. (*You might have students write the labels above the sentences at this time.*)

Question and Answer Flow for Sentence 1: The four tired kittens slept peacefully in the barn yesterday.

1. What slept peacefully in the barn yesterday? kittens - SN
2. What is being said about kittens? kittens slept - V
3. Slept how? peacefully - Adv
4. In - P
5. In what? barn - OP
6. The - A
7. Slept when? yesterday - Adv
8. What kind of kittens? tired - Adj
9. How many kittens? four - Adj
10. The - A
11. SN V P1 Check
12. (In the barn) - Prepositional phrase
13. Period, statement, declarative sentence
14. Go back to the verb - divide the complete subject from the complete predicate.

```
                    A  Adj Adj SN    V     Adv    P  A  OP  Adv
Classified Sentence:    SN V   The four tired kittens / slept peacefully (in the barn) yesterday.  D
                        P1
```

Level 2—Shurley English—Homeschool Edition

CHAPTER 26 LESSON 3 CONTINUED

Question and Answer Flow for Sentence 2: The three circus lions roared loudly today.

1. What roared loudly today? lions - SN
2. What is being said about lions? lions roared - V
3. Roared how? loudly - Adv
4. Roared when? today - Adv
5. What kind of lions? circus - Adj
6. How many lions? three - Adj
7. The - A
8. SN V P1 Check
9. No prepositional phrases.
10. Period, statement, declarative sentence
11. Go back to the verb - divide the complete subject from the complete predicate.

```
                          A   Adj  Adj  SN    V   Adv  Adv
Classified Sentence:   SN V    The three circus lions / roared loudly today.  D
                       P1
```

Question and Answer Flow for Sentence 3: The chipped vase sold for five dollars at the garage sale.

1. What sold for five dollars at the garage sale? vase - SN
2. What is being said about vase? vase sold - V
3. For - P
4. For what? dollars - OP
5. How many dollars? five - Adj
6. At - P
7. At what? sale - OP
8. What kind of sale? garage - Adj
9. The - A
10. What kind of vase? chipped - Adj
11. The - A
12. SN V P1 Check
13. (For five dollars) - Prepositional phrase
14. (At the garage sale) - Prepositional phrase
15. Period, statement, declarative sentence
16. Go back to the verb - divide the complete subject from the complete predicate.

```
                          A    Adj   SN   V   P  Adj  OP    P  A  Adj   OP
Classified Sentence:   SN V    The chipped vase / sold (for five dollars) (at the garage sale).  D
                       P1
```

 PRACTICE TIME

Have students turn to page 77 in the Practice Section of their book and find Chapter 26, Lesson 3, Practice. Go over the directions to make sure they understand what to do. Check and discuss the Practice after students have finished. (*Chapter 26, Lesson 3, Practice instructions are given below.*)

Chapter 26, Lesson 3, Practice: Write the nine parts of a book on a poster and write a description beside each part. Illustrate and color the nine parts. **(Title Page, Copyright Page, Preface, Table of Contents, Body, Appendix, Glossary, Bibliography, Index)** (*Check and discuss students' definitions and illustrations after they have finished. Note: Students may use their reference pages to help them.*)

(End of lesson.)

CHAPTER 26   LESSON 4
Objectives: Jingles, Study, Test, Check, Writing (Journal), and State Activity.

 JINGLE TIME

Have students turn to the Jingle Section in their books and recite the previously-taught jingles.

 STUDY TIME

Have students study any of the skills in the Practice Section that they need to review.

 TEST TIME

Have students turn to page 105 in the Test Section of their book and find Chapter 26 Test. Go over the directions to make sure they understand what to do. *(Chapter 26 Test key is on the next page.)*

 CHECK TIME

After students have finished, check and discuss their test papers. Make sure they understand why their answers are right or wrong. *(For total points, count each required answer as a point.)*

 STATE ACTIVITY TIME

Students will continue to draw or trace the states and to write the following questions and answers.

Texas	Utah
1. What is the state on the front of this card? **Texas**	1. What is the state on the front of this card? **Utah**
2. What is the capital of Texas? **Austin**	2. What is the capital of Utah? **Salt Lake City**
3. What is the postal abbreviation of Texas? **TX**	3. What is the postal abbreviation of Utah? **UT**

Color these states. Use the cards to quiz family members, friends, and relatives. You may want to time the responses to your questions.

(End of lesson.)

Level 2—Shurley English—Homeschool Edition

Chapter 26 Test
(Student Page 105)

71 pts

Exercise 1: Classify each sentence.

```
         A    Adj       SN              V         Adv      P  PP  Adj    OP         P   A   OP
1. SN V       The science students / experimented frequently (in their new laboratory) (during the holidays).  D
   P1

              PN    Adj      SN          V       Adv     P  A  Adj OP
2. SN V       Jamie's computer mouse / moved smoothly (over the new pad).  D
   P1
```

Exercise 2: Use Sentence 1 to underline the complete subject once and the complete predicate twice and to complete the table below.

List the Noun Used	List the Noun Job	Singular or Plural	Common or Proper	Simple Subject	Simple Predicate
1. students	2. SN	3. P	4. C	5. students	6. experimented
7. laboratory	8. OP	9. S	10. C		
11. holidays	12. OP	13. P	14. C		

Exercise 3: Identify each pair of words as synonyms or antonyms by putting parentheses ( ) around **syn** or **ant**.

1. rude, polite	syn	(ant)	4. assistant, helper	(syn)	ant	7. continuous, ceaseless	(syn)	ant
2. rowdy, gentle	syn	(ant)	5. bitter, sweet	syn	(ant)	8. yearly, annual	(syn)	ant
3. limp, hobble	(syn)	ant	6. whisper, howl	syn	(ant)	9. lazy, industrious	syn	(ant)

Exercise 4: Match each part of a book listed below with the type of information it may give you. Write the appropriate letter in the blank. You may use each letter only once.

A. Title Page   B. Index   C. Appendix   D. Bibliography   E. Body   F. Preface   G. Copyright page

1. **B** Exact page numbers for a particular topic and used to locate topics quickly

2. **E** Text of the book

3. **F** Reason the book was written

4. **D** Books listed for finding more information

5. **G** ISBN number

6. **A** Publisher's name and city where the book was published

7. **C** Extra maps in a book

Exercise 5: On notebook paper, write the five parts found at the front of a book. **(Title Page, Copyright Page, Preface, Table of Contents, Body) (The order of the answers may vary.)**

Exercise 6: On notebook paper, write the four parts found at the back of a book. **(Appendix, Glossary, Bibliography, Index) (The order of the answers may vary.)**

Exercise 7: In your journal, write a paragraph summarizing what you have learned this week.

CHAPTER 26 LESSON 4 CONTINUED

TEACHER INSTRUCTIONS

Use the Question and Answer Flows below for the sentences on the Chapter 26 Test.

Question and Answer Flow for Sentence 1: The science students experimented frequently in their new laboratory during the holidays.

1. Who experimented frequently in their new laboratory during the holidays? students - SN
2. What is being said about students? students experimented - V
3. Experimented when? frequently - Adv
4. In - P
5. In what? laboratory - OP
6. What kind of laboratory? new - Adj
7. Whose laboratory? their - PP
8. During - P
9. During what? holidays - OP
10. The - A
11. What kind of students? science - Adj
12. The - A
13. SN V P1 Check
14. (In their new laboratory) - Prepositional phrase
15. (During the holidays) - Prepositional phrase
16. Period, statement, declarative sentence
17. Go back to the verb - divide the complete subject from the complete predicate.

```
                        A    Adj   SN        V        Adv   P  PP  Adj    OP
Classified Sentence:   SN V   The science students / experimented frequently (in their new laboratory)
                       P1      P    A    OP
                              (during the holidays).  D
```

Question and Answer Flow for Sentence 2: Jamie's computer mouse moved smoothly over the new pad.

1. What moved smoothly over the new pad? mouse - SN
2. What is being said about mouse? mouse moved - V
3. Moved how? smoothly - Adv
4. Over - P
5. Over what? pad - OP
6. What kind of pad? new - Adj
7. The - A
8. What kind of mouse? computer - Adj
9. Whose mouse? Jamie's - PN
10. SN V P1 Check
11. (Over the new pad) - Prepositional phrase
12. Period, statement, declarative sentence
13. Go back to the verb - divide the complete subject from the complete predicate.

```
                        PN      Adj     SN       V       Adv    P  A  Adj OP
Classified Sentence:   SN V   Jamie's computer mouse / moved smoothly (over the new pad).  D
                       P1
```

Level 2—Shurley English—Homeschool Edition

CHAPTER 26 LESSON 5

Objectives: Writing Assignment #20 and Sentence Time.

 WRITING TIME

TEACHER INSTRUCTIONS FOR WRITING ASSIGNMENT #20

Give Writing Assignment #20 from the box below. Remind students to use the Writing Checklist in Reference 17 to check their finished writing assignment.

Read, check, and discuss Writing Assignment #20 after students have finished their final papers. Use the Writing Checklist (*Reference 17 on teacher's page 112*) as you check and discuss students' papers. Make sure students are using the checklist correctly.

Writing Assignment Box

Writing Assignment #20: Narrative Paragraph

Writing topics: The Hidden Treasure   or   The Secret in the Jungle   or   Millionaire for a Day

---

 SENTENCE TIME

Chapter 26, Lesson 5, Sentence: Use colored markers to match each label with the correct sentence part by drawing a line from one to the other. Then, use the labels to arrange the sentence parts into a sentence that you will write on the sentence line below. *(The order of the words in your sentence should be in the same sequence as the vertical list of sentence labels.)* Create other labels and scrambled sentence parts on notebook paper for family members to solve. You may color code the sentence parts. *(See page 118 in the student book.)*

Labels for Order of Sentence	Scrambled Sentence Parts
SP	swiftly
V	recess
Adv	swings
P	we
A	to
OP	ran
P	the
OP	during

Sentence: We ran swiftly to the swings during recess.

(End of lesson.)

CHAPTER 27   LESSON 1

Objectives: Jingles, Grammar (Practice Sentences), and State Activity.

 **JINGLE TIME**

Have students turn to the Jingle Section in their books and recite the previously-taught jingles.

 GRAMMAR TIME

Put the Practice Sentences from the box below on the board or on notebook paper. Use these sentences as you practice the concepts that have been taught. For the greatest benefit, students must participate orally with the teacher.

Chapter 27, Practice Sentences for Lesson 1
1. _____ The polite young man sat nervously.
2. _____ We leave for the wildlife resort tomorrow.
3. _____ The tree's leaves fell after the heavy frost.

TEACHING SCRIPT FOR CLASSIFYING PRACTICE SENTENCES

We will classify three different sentences to practice the grammar skills in the Question and Answer Flows. We will classify the sentences together. Begin. (*You might have students write the labels above the sentences at this time.*)

Question and Answer Flow for Sentence 1: The polite young man sat nervously.

1. Who sat nervously? man - SN
2. What is being said about man? man sat - V
3. Sat how? nervously - Adv
4. What kind of man? young - Adj
5. What kind of man? polite - Adj
6. The - A
7. SN V P1 Check
8. No prepositional phrases.
9. Period, statement, declarative sentence
10. Go back to the verb - divide the complete subject from the complete predicate.

```
                          A   Adj   Adj   SN   V    Adv
Classified Sentence:  SN V  The polite young man / sat nervously. D
                      P1
```

CHAPTER 27 LESSON 1 CONTINUED

> **Question and Answer Flow for Sentence 2: We leave for the wildlife resort tomorrow.**
>
> 1. Who leave for the wildlife resort tomorrow?
>   we - SP
> 2. What is being said about we? we leave - V
> 3. For - P
> 4. For what? resort - OP
> 5. What kind of resort? wildlife - Adj
> 6. The - A
> 7. Leave when? tomorrow - Adv
> 8. SN V P1 Check
> 9. (For the wildlife resort) - Prepositional phrase
> 10. Period, statement, declarative sentence
> 11. Go back to the verb - divide the complete subject from the complete predicate.
>
> ```
>                           SP  V   P  A   Adj   OP   Adv
> Classified Sentence:    SN V   We / leave (for the wildlife resort) tomorrow.  D
>                         P1
> ```

> **Question and Answer Flow for Sentence 3: The tree's leaves fell after the heavy frost.**
>
> 1. What fell after the heavy frost? leaves - SN
> 2. What is being said about leaves? leaves fell - V
> 3. After - P
> 4. After what? frost - OP
> 5. What kind of frost? heavy - Adj
> 6. The - A
> 7. Whose leaves? tree's - PN
> 8. The - A
> 9. SN V P1 Check
> 10. (After the heavy frost) - Prepositional phrase
> 11. Period, statement, declarative sentence
> 12. Go back to the verb - divide the complete subject from the complete predicate.
>
> ```
>                          A  PN   SN    V   P  A   Adj   OP
> Classified Sentence:   SN V   The tree's leaves / fell (after the heavy frost).  D
>                        P1
> ```

STATE ACTIVITY TIME

Students will continue to draw or trace the states and to write the following questions and answers.

Vermont	Virginia
1. What is the state on the front of this card? **Vermont**	1. What is the state on the front of this card? **Virginia**
2. What is the capital of Vermont? **Montpelier**	2. What is the capital of Virginia? **Richmond**
3. What is the postal abbreviation of Vermont? **VT**	3. What is the postal abbreviation of Virginia? **VA**

Color these states. Use the cards to quiz family members, friends, and relatives. You may want to time the responses to your questions.

(End of lesson.)

CHAPTER 27   LESSON 2

Objectives: Jingles, Grammar (Practice Sentences), and State Activity.

 **JINGLE TIME**

Have students turn to the Jingle Section in their books and recite the previously-taught jingles.

 GRAMMAR TIME

Put the Practice Sentences from the box below on the board or on notebook paper. Use these sentences as you practice the concepts that have been taught. For the greatest benefit, students must participate orally with the teacher.

Chapter 27, Practice Sentences for Lesson 2
1. _____ She sat in the front seat of the bus during our field trip yesterday.
2. _____ The carpenter's tools scattered across the floor of the new house.
3. _____ An elephant at our zoo disappeared during the night!

<u>TEACHING SCRIPT FOR CLASSIFYING PRACTICE SENTENCES</u>

We will classify three different sentences to practice the grammar skills in the Question and Answer Flows. We will classify the sentences together. Begin. (*You might have students write the labels above the sentences at this time.*)

Question and Answer Flow for Sentence 1: She sat in the front seat of the bus during our field trip yesterday.

1. Who sat in the front seat of the bus during our field trip yesterday? she - SP
2. What is being said about she? she sat - V
3. In - P
4. In what? seat - OP
5. What kind of seat? front - Adj
6. The - A
7. Of - P
8. Of what? bus - OP
9. The - A
10. During - P
11. During what? trip - OP
12. What kind of trip? field - Adj
13. Whose trip? our - PP
14. Sat when? yesterday - Adv
15. SN V P1 Check
16. (In the front seat) - Prepositional phrase
17. (Of the bus) - Prepositional phrase
18. (During our field trip) - Prepositional phrase
19. Period, statement, declarative sentence
20. Go back to the verb - divide the complete subject from the complete predicate.

Classified Sentence:
```
                        SP   V  P A  Adj  OP   P A  OP    P   PP Adj OP   Adv
         SN V           She / sat (in the front seat) (of the bus) (during our field trip) yesterday.  D
         P1
```

CHAPTER 27 LESSON 2 CONTINUED

Question and Answer Flow for Sentence 2: The carpenter's tools scattered across the floor of the new house.

1. What scattered across the floor of the new house? tools - SN
2. What is being said about tools? tools scattered - V
3. Across - P
4. Across what? floor - OP
5. The - A
6. Of - P
7. Of what? house - OP
8. What kind of house? new - Adj
9. The - A
10. Whose tools? carpenter's - PN
11. The - A
12. SN V P1 Check
13. (Across the floor) - Prepositional phrase
14. (Of the new house) - Prepositional phrase
15. Period, statement, declarative sentence
16. Go back to the verb - divide the complete subject from the complete predicate.

```
                      A   PN       SN      V      P   A   OP    P  A   Adj   OP
Classified Sentence:  SN V   The carpenter's tools / scattered (across the floor) (of the new house).  D
                      P1
```

Question and Answer Flow for Sentence 3: An elephant at our zoo disappeared during the night!

1. What disappeared during the night? elephant - SN
2. What is being said about elephant? elephant disappeared - V
3. During - P
4. During what? night - OP
5. The - A
6. At - P
7. At what? zoo - OP
8. Whose zoo? our - PP
9. An - A
10. SN V P1 Check
11. (At our zoo) - Prepositional phrase
12. (During the night) - Prepositional phrase
13. Exclamation point, strong feeling, exclamatory sentence
14. Go back to the verb - divide the complete subject from the complete predicate.

```
                      A    SN     P  PP  OP     V        P    A   OP
Classified Sentence:  SN V   An elephant (at our zoo) / disappeared (during the night)!  E
                      P1
```

 STATE ACTIVITY TIME

Students will continue to draw or trace the states and to write the following questions and answers.

Washington	West Virginia
1. What is the state on the front of this card? **Washington**	1. What is the state on the front of this card? **West Virginia**
2. What is the capital of Washington? **Olympia**	2. What is the capital of West Virginia? **Charleston**
3. What is the postal abbreviation of Washington? **WA**	3. What is the postal abbreviation of West Virginia? **WV**

Color these states. Use the cards to quiz family members, friends, and relatives. You may want to time the responses to your questions.

(End of lesson.)

CHAPTER 27   LESSON 3

Objectives: Jingles, Grammar (Practice Sentences), and State Activity.

 **JINGLE TIME**

Have students turn to the Jingle Section in their books and recite the previously-taught jingles.

 GRAMMAR TIME

Put the Practice Sentences from the box below on the board or on notebook paper. Use these sentences as you practice the concepts that have been taught. For the greatest benefit, students must participate orally with the teacher.

Chapter 27, Practice Sentences for Lesson 3
1. _____ My big, gentle dog sleeps soundly on a mat beside my bed at night.
2. _____ He asked for another slice of birthday cake.
3. _____ The church bell rang loudly in my ears.

TEACHING SCRIPT FOR CLASSIFYING PRACTICE SENTENCES

We will classify three different sentences to practice the grammar skills in the Question and Answer Flows. We will classify the sentences together. Begin. (*You might have students write the labels above the sentences at this time.*)

Question and Answer Flow for Sentence 1: My big, gentle dog sleeps soundly on a mat beside my bed at night.

1. What sleeps soundly on a mat beside my bed at night? dog - SN
2. What is being said about dog? dog sleeps - V
3. Sleeps how? soundly - Adv
4. On - P
5. On what? mat - OP
6. A - A
7. Beside - P
8. Beside what? bed - OP
9. Whose bed? my - PP
10. At - P
11. At what? night - OP
12. What kind of dog? gentle - Adj
13. What kind of dog? big - Adj
14. Whose dog? my - PP
15. SN V P1 Check
16. (On a mat) - Prepositional phrase
17. (Beside my bed) - Prepositional phrase
18. (At night) - Prepositional phrase
19. Period, statement, declarative sentence
20. Go back to the verb - divide the complete subject from the complete predicate.

```
                         PP  Adj  Adj   SN     V      Adv    P A OP    P   PP  OP    P  OP
Classified Sentence:     SN  V    My big, gentle dog / sleeps soundly (on a mat) (beside my bed) (at night). D
                         P1
```

CHAPTER 27 LESSON 3 CONTINUED

Question and Answer Flow for Sentence 2: He asked for another slice of birthday cake.

1. Who asked for another slice of birthday cake? he - SP
2. What is being said about he? he asked - V
3. For - P
4. For what? slice - OP
5. Which slice? another - Adj
6. Of - P
7. Of what? cake - OP
8. What kind of cake? birthday - Adj
9. SN V P1 Check
10. (For another slice) - Prepositional phrase
11. (Of birthday cake) - Prepositional phrase
12. Period, statement, declarative sentence
13. Go back to the verb - divide the complete subject from the complete predicate.

```
                              SP   V    P   Adj   OP   P   Adj   OP
Classified Sentence:    SN V     He / asked (for another slice) (of birthday cake).  D
                         P1
```

Question and Answer Flow for Sentence 3: The church bell rang loudly in my ears.

1. What rang loudly in my ears? bell - SN
2. What is being said about bell? bell rang - V
3. Rang how? loudly - Adv
4. In - P
5. In what? ears - OP
6. Whose ears? my - PP
7. What kind of bell? church - Adj
8. The - A
9. SN V P1 Check
10. (In my ears) - Prepositional phrase
11. Period, statement, declarative sentence
12. Go back to the verb - divide the complete subject from the complete predicate.

```
                              A   Adj  SN      V    Adv   P  PP  OP
Classified Sentence:    SN V     The church bell / rang loudly (in my ears).  D
                         P1
```

 STATE ACTIVITY TIME

Students will continue to draw or trace the states and to write the following questions and answers.

Wisconsin	Wyoming
1. What is the state on the front of this card? **Wisconsin**	1. What is the state on the front of this card? **Wyoming**
2. What is the capital of Wisconsin? **Madison**	2. What is the capital of Wyoming? **Cheyenne**
3. What is the postal abbreviation of Wisconsin? **WI**	3. What is the postal abbreviation of Wyoming? **WY**

Color these states. Use the cards to quiz family members, friends, and relatives. You may want to time the responses to your questions.

(End of lesson.)

CHAPTER 27   LESSON 4

Objectives: Jingles, Study, Test, Check, and Writing (Journal).

 JINGLE TIME

Have students turn to the Jingle Section in their books and recite the previously-taught jingles.

 STUDY TIME

Have students study any of the skills in the Practice Section that they need to review.

 TEST TIME

Have students turn to page 106 in the Test Section of their book and find Chapter 27 Test. Go over the directions to make sure they understand what to do. (*Chapter 27 Test key is on the next page.*)

 CHECK TIME

After students have finished, check and discuss their test papers. Make sure they understand why their answers are right or wrong. (*For total points, count each required answer as a point.*)

(End of lesson.)

Level 2—Shurley English—Homeschool Edition

Chapter 27 Test
(Student Page 106)

85 pts

Exercise 1: Classify each sentence.

```
                    PN    SN    V   P  A  Adj      OP      P     A      OP
1. SN V    Paul's brother / fell (into a muddy ditch) (behind the playground).  D
   P1

                 A   SN    V    Adv     P    PP   Adj     OP
2. SN V    The sun / shines brightly (through my bedroom window).  D
   P1
```

Exercise 2: Use Sentence 1 to underline the complete subject once and the complete predicate twice and to complete the table below.

List the Noun Used	List the Noun Job	Singular or Plural	Common or Proper	Simple Subject	Simple Predicate
1. brother	2. SN	3. S	4. C	5. brother	6. fell
7. ditch	8. OP	9. S	10. C		
11. playground	12. OP	13. S	14. C		

Exercise 3: Underline the correct homonym in each sentence.

1. (Their, <u>There</u>) are five players on the court.
2. (<u>It's</u>, Its) time for dinner.
3. Does (<u>your</u>, you're) toy need batteries?
4. (<u>Here</u>, Hear) is my watch!
5. Can we go (<u>to</u>, too, two) the store?
6. (Right, <u>Write</u>) your name on your paper.

Exercise 4: For each sentence, do these four things: (1) Write the subject. (2) Write **S** if the subject is singular or **P** if the subject is plural. (3) Write the rule number. (4) Underline the correct verb in the sentence.

Rule 1 and Rule 2 are located in Reference 21 on page 17 in your student book.

Subject	S or P	Rule
violets	P	2
Tommy	S	1
cheese	S	1
soldiers	P	2
fog	S	1
you	P	2
members	P	2
book	S	1
Joseph	S	1

1. **Violets** (blooms, <u>bloom</u>) in the flowerbed.
2. **Tommy** (work, <u>works</u>) during the summer.
3. The mozzarella **cheese** (<u>melts</u>, melt) on the pizza.
4. The **soldiers** (stands, <u>stand</u>) in straight lines.
5. The **fog** (float, <u>floats</u>) across the lake.
6. **You** (combs, <u>comb</u>) your hair.
7. The city counsel **members** (<u>meet</u>, meets) next door.
8. Her math **book** (weigh, <u>weighs</u>) five pounds.
9. **Joseph** (stand, <u>stands</u>) next to Jennifer.

Exercise 5: In your journal, write a paragraph summarizing what you have learned this week.

Level 2—Shurley English—Homeschool Edition

CHAPTER 27 LESSON 4 CONTINUED

TEACHER INSTRUCTIONS

Use the Question and Answer Flows below for the sentences on the Chapter 27 Test.

Question and Answer Flow for Sentence 1: Paul's brother fell into a muddy ditch behind the playground.

1. Who fell into a muddy ditch behind the playground? brother - SN
2. What is being said about brother? brother fell - V
3. Into - P
4. Into what? ditch - OP
5. What kind of ditch? muddy - Adj
6. A - A
7. Behind - P
8. Behind what? playground - OP
9. The - A
10. Whose brother? Paul's - PN
11. SN V P1 Check
12. (Into a muddy ditch) - Prepositional phrase
13. (Behind the playground) - Prepositional phrase
14. Period, statement, declarative sentence
15. Go back to the verb - divide the complete subject from the complete predicate.

Classified Sentence:
```
            PN   SN  V  P  A  Adj  OP  P   A    OP
            SN V
             P1
Paul's brother / fell (into a muddy ditch) (behind the playground). D
```

Question and Answer Flow for Sentence 2: The sun shines brightly through my bedroom window.

1. What shines brightly through my bedroom window? sun - SN
2. What is being said about sun? sun shines - V
3. Shines how? brightly - Adv
4. Through - P
5. Through what? window - OP
6. What kind of window? bedroom - Adj
7. Whose window? my - PP
8. The - A
9. SN V P1 Check
10. (Through my bedroom window) - Prepositional phrase
11. Period, statement, declarative sentence
12. Go back to the verb - divide the complete subject from the complete predicate.

Classified Sentence:
```
         A  SN  V   Adv    P   PP   Adj    OP
         SN V
          P1
         The sun / shines brightly (through my bedroom window). D
```

Level 2—Shurley English—Homeschool Edition

CHAPTER 27   LESSON 5

Objectives: Writing Assignment #21 and Sentence Time.

WRITING TIME

TEACHER INSTRUCTIONS FOR WRITING ASSIGNMENT #21

Give Writing Assignment #21 from the box below. Remind students to use the Writing Checklist in Reference 17 to check their finished writing assignment.

Read, check, and discuss Writing Assignment #21 after students have finished their final papers. Use the Writing Checklist (*Reference 17 on teacher's page 112*) as you check and discuss students' papers. Make sure students are using the checklist correctly.

Writing Assignment Box

Writing Assignment #21: Descriptive Paragraph

Writing topic choices: The Most Annoying Insect   or   The Ultimate Toy   or   Thanksgiving Dinner

SENTENCE TIME

Chapter 27, Lesson 5, Sentence: Use colored markers to match each label with the correct sentence part by drawing a line from one to the other. Then, use the labels to arrange the sentence parts into a sentence that you will write on the sentence line below. (*The order of the words in your sentence should be in the same sequence as the vertical list of sentence labels.*) Create other labels and scrambled sentence parts on notebook paper for family members to solve. You may color code the sentence parts. (*See page 118 in the student book.*)

Labels for Order of Sentence	Scrambled Sentence Parts
A	the
Adj	the
SN	the
V	at
Adv	on
P	hungry
A	chocolate
Adj	longingly
OP	counter
P	boys
A	cake
OP	stared

Sentence: The hungry boys stared longingly at the chocolate cake on the counter.

(End of lesson.)

CHAPTER 28   LESSON 1

Objective: Writing Assignment #22.

WRITING TIME

TEACHER INSTRUCTIONS FOR WRITING ASSIGNMENT #22

Give Writing Assignment #22 from the box below. Remind students to use the Writing Checklist in Reference 17 to check their finished writing assignment. Read, check, and discuss Writing Assignment #22 after students have finished their final papers.

Writing Assignment Box

Writing Assignment #22: Three-Point Paragraph

Writing topic choices: Reflections of My Second Grade Year

Points to consider: 1. My favorite subject of the year
2. My most memorable learning experience
3. The most important event during my second grade year
4. Why second grade was an important year to me

(End of lesson.)

CHAPTER 28   LESSON 2

Objective: State Activity.

ACTIVITY TIME

State Card Game: Divide players into groups of four. Select someone to shuffle the state cards. Place the deck, picture side up, in the center of the table. The player to the left of the shuffler draws a card and tries to name the state, capital, and abbreviation. If they get it right, they keep the card. If not, it is put in a discard pile, picture side up. Then, the next player repeats these steps. This continues until all the cards have been drawn. Shuffle the discard pile and use it to continue the game. When all cards have been played, the player with the most cards wins the game. *(Players may include students, family members, friends, or relatives.)*

(End of lesson.)

CHAPTER 28   LESSON 3

Objective: State Activity.

ACTIVITY TIME

A-B-C Order Game: Shuffle the deck of state cards and place the deck in the center of the table with the picture side up. Have each player draw ten cards from the deck. Using pictures only, have players arrange their ten cards in alphabetical order. The player who arranges all ten cards in correct alphabetical order in the shortest amount of time wins the game. For a greater challenge, increase the number of cards to be alphabetized. *(Players may include students, family members, friends, or relatives.)*

(End of lesson.)

CHAPTER 28   LESSON 4

Objective: Activity.

ACTIVITY / ASSIGNMENT TIME

Booklet activity: This activity produces a booklet for any member of the family who would like to participate. It is a great keepsake. Follow the directions given below. (You will start the activity in this lesson and finish it in the next lesson unless you add more pages. For extra pages, you should allow more days to complete the project.)

1. Have two sheets of construction paper. Use one sheet for the title page of your booklet and one sheet for the back cover. *(You could also use a folder with brads so more pages could be added each year.)*
2. Make a title page and illustrate it or put a picture of yourself on it.
3. Make a separate page for each topic. Make each page special by doing some artwork for each topic.

Title Page: (A Booklet About a Very Special Person: Me) (Written by: put your name.) (Illustrated by: put your name.) (Leave the back of the title page blank.)

Page 1: Things I Like to Do
...with a friend.
...with my mom.
...with my dad.
...with other family members.
...by myself.
...that are different.
...that are special.

(End of lesson.)

CHAPTER 28 LESSON 5

Objectives: Activity (continued).

ACTIVITY / ASSIGNMENT TIME

Booklet activity (continued): Follow the directions given below for new pages. (Remember, if you add more pages, you should allow extra days to complete the project.)

Page 2: My Strengths
Page 3: My Weaknesses
Page 4: Why My Family is Important to Me
Page 5: Family Pictures
Page 6: Things That Make Me Laugh
Page 7: My Special Poem
Page 8: My Special Feelings

I am happy when...
I am angry when...
I hope that...
I am good at...
I admire...
I want to be...
I need...
I feel safe when...
I am thankful for...
I am afraid of...
I feel sorry for...
I am proud of...
I like the invention of...
I am surprised when...
I am brave when...
I am shy about...
I am helpful when...

(End of lesson.)

TEACHER INDEX

Due to the tremendous amount of review of concepts provided, this index lists only the page numbers on which the topic is introduced.

A
A/An choices, 29
Adjectives
 articles, 41
 definition of, 31
Adverbs
 definition of, 25
Agreement
 subject-verb, 145
Alphabetizing, 6
Antonyms, 12

B
Books
 appendix, 384
 bibliography, 384
 body, 381
 copyright page, 381
 glossary, 384
 index, 384
 preface, 381
 table of contents, 381
 title page, 381

C
Capitalization
 rules of, 181
Classifying Sentences
 definition of, 16
Contractions, 241

E
Editing
 checklist, 112

H
Homonyms, 131

J
Jingles
 adjective, 31
 adverb, 25
 article adjective, 41
 guidelines for, 11
 noun, 14
 object of the preposition, 114
 possessive pronoun, 191
 preposition, 114
 pronoun, 176
 sentence, 11
 subject pronoun, 176
 verb, 14

Q
Question and Answer Flow, 16

L
Letters
 friendly, 329
 friendly envelope, 345
 thank-you note, 358
Library
 fiction, 370
 non-fiction, 370
 reference, 370

N
Nouns
 common, 63
 definition of, 14
 object of the preposition, 118
 plural, 58
 possessive nouns, 220
 proper, 63
 singular, 58
 subject noun, 16

O
Oral Skill Builder
 definition of, 48, 59
 irregular verb chart, 307
 noun check, 58
 vocabulary check, 96

P
Patterns of sentences
 pattern 1 (SN V P1), 90
Poetry
 personality, 271
Predicate
 complete predicate, 77, 94, 269
 simple predicate, 76
Prepositions
 definition of, 118
 object of the preposition, 118
 prepositional phrase, 118
Pronouns
 definition of, 176
 possessive, 191
Punctuation
 rules of, 90

S
Sentences
 complete, 20, 269
 declarative, 45
 exclamatory, 45
 five parts of a sentence, 20
 fragment, 269
 improved, 55
 interrogative, 45
 practice, 53
Story elements
 character, 326
 ending, 326
 main idea, 326
 plot, 326
 setting, 326
Study Skills, 1
Subjects
 complete, 77, 94, 269
 simple subject, 76
Synonyms, 12

V
Verbs
 definition of, 14
 irregular verbs, 305
 regular verbs, 305
 irregular verb chart, 307
 simple tenses, 302

W
Writing
 changing plural categories to singular points, 174
 conclusions, 109
 descriptive, 282
 expository, 104
 journal, 4
 narrative, 326
 Non-supporting sentences, 71, 88
 paragraph, 71, 104
 supporting sentences, 71, 88
 three-point expository paragraph, 234
 topic, 71, 104
 topic sentence, 106
 two-point paragraph, 105
 two-point sentence, 107